THE WORLD OF INFORMATIVE-PERSUASIVE PROSE

Edited by
Keith F. McKean *and* Charles Wheeler
University of Northern Iowa

HOLT, RINEHART AND WINSTON, INC.
New York   Chicago   San Francisco   Atlanta   Dallas

Credits for Advertisements Reproduced in Chapter 12

What-is-a Truck, p. 193. *Saturday Review of Literature,* August 23, 1969. Reprinted by permission of the American Trucking Association, Inc.
Volkswagen, p. 194. *The New Yorker,* June 7, 1969. Reprinted by permission of Volkswagen of America, Inc.
Cadillac, p. 195. *Holiday Magazine,* November, 1968. Reprinted by permission of Cadillac Motor Car Division, General Motors Corporation.
Franklin Delano Roosevelt, p. 196. Reprinted by permission of the Magazine Publishers Association, Inc.
Kings Men Toiletries, p. 197. *Playboy,* May, 1967. Reprinted by permission of Helene Curtis Industries, Inc.
Berlitz, p. 198. *The Saturday Review of Literature,* May 10, 1969. Reprinted by permission of the Berlitz Schools of Languages of America, Inc.
Chiquita Banana, p. 199. *McCall's,* July, 1967. Reprinted by permission of United Fruit Sales Corporation.

Copyright © 1971 by Holt, Rinehart and Winston, Inc.

All Rights Reserved
Library of Congress Catalog Card Number: 70-138403
SBN: 03-083281-0
Printed in the United States of America
1 2 3 4   074 9 8 7 6 5 4 3 2 1

Preface

Many collections of readings for composition contain essays which are difficult in subject matter and elevated in style. Indeed, they are so literary that they are far removed from the student's life and his writing. The only thing that a freshman may learn about composition from such men as Mill, Stevenson, Lippman, or Russell is that these giants are great essayists and he is not. Such a rich literary diet may awe a freshman or even confuse and depress him. Rather than learning how to form a thesis of his own or how to develop it, he may simply conclude that such writing is not for him.

In contrast, we have tried to choose selections for *The World of Informative-Persuasive Prose* which provide a realistic cross-section of everyday prose of the kind most students are likely to read and to write. The collection is made up of illustrations from four areas: 1) features, news stories, personality sketches, interviews, editorials, and columns from newspapers and magazines; 2) articles, analyses, reviews, and how-to pieces from professional, business, and trade writing; 3) business letters, directives, proposals, memorandums, and reports from on-the-job writing; and 4) school newspaper articles, essay-type tests, and term papers from college writing. Each of these four areas is prefaced by a description of the forms, and followed by discussion questions and writing assignments.

But *The World of Informative-Persuasive Prose* is more than a collection; it is also a rhetoric in which two important points are stressed. The first is that many common writing problems can be solved in the prewriting phase of composition. Students are urged to imitate the professionals who explore and test their material *before* they write. A second point is that there is no essential difference in form and motive between an elegant literary essay, a magazine article, a business letter, or a freshman term paper. Each of these compositions consists of an introduction, body, and an appropriate close. And each boils down to some sort of thesis, which is set forth and developed in order to inform and persuade. Once the novice sees this similarity in structure, we think he will be better prepared for the writing he must do in school and later on.

The book opens with a concise "Overview" of the basic elements of composition and a look at "The Writing Process." Then come the selections themselves—history-making news stories, popular how-to pieces, current reviews, syndicated columns, and argumentative articles on such topics as black literature courses, women's rights, and a volunteer army. At the end of the book you will find some useful chapters on "Prevising" and "Revising," and a short glossary of grammar and diction.

In general, our view is that when students are asked to study illustrations drawn from the everyday world of informative-persuasive prose and are provided with the rhetoric which lies behind that prose, they will see the true relevance of improving their writing skills.

January 1971 Keith F. McKean
Cedar Falls, Iowa Charles Wheeler

Contents

PREFACE *v*

The Preliminaries

CHAPTER 1   AN OVERVIEW
   FORM AND MOTIVE   *1*
   VARIETY   *4*
   LANGUAGE   *6*
   AUTHORS AND AUDIENCE   *13*

CHAPTER 2   THE WRITING PROCESS
   TOPIC   *16*
   PREWRITING   *19*
   OUTLINES AND ROUGH DRAFTS   *28*

The Readings

CHAPTER 3   NEWS STORIES
   Introduction   *37*
   Examples   *39*
      Kennedy Is Killed by Sniper, *Tom Wicker*   *39*
      Man Walks on Moon!   *44*
      Queens Woman Is Stabbed to Death in Front of Home   *49*
      38 Who Saw Murder Didn't Call Police, *Martin Gansberg*   *50*
      2 Accept Medals Wearing Black Gloves   *53*

Negroes in Detroit Defy Curfew 54
Accused of Rape in "Mistaken Identity" Case 56
Students—Signs of Suicide 58
Things That Go Bump in the Night, *Tom Tiede* 59
Strippers "Busty"—That's News? 61
Hero: What Does He Look Like, *Gavin Scott* 61
Gardener Rolls Out Barrow 63
Sailor: Sea Turtle Saved Me 64
Suggested Writing Assignments 65

CHAPTER 4 HOW-TO ARTICLES
Introduction 66
Examples 68
Five Common Frauds, *Don Wharton* 68
There's More to the Dinner Party Than Dinner, *Bokara Legendre* 71
How To Make Housework Easier, *Joseph H. Quick* 74
The Volks/Roadster/Street Rod/Dune Buggy, *Ed Orr* 75
Fighting the Bank Robbery Boom, *Bill Surface* 78
How To Write Effectively to Congress, *Willard Clopton, Jr.* 81
How to Pick Ripe Melons, *Gene Logsdon* 83
Suggested Writing Assignments 84

CHAPTER 5 EDITORIALS
Introduction 85
Examples 86
Reflections on Moon Trip 86
College Co-operation With FBI 87
Leadership Needed 88
We Are Concerned 90
Summer in Blossom 91
The Chance To Invest in Survival? 92
Suggested Writing Assignments 93

CHAPTER 6 LETTERS TO THE EDITOR
Introduction 94
Examples 95
"Realistic Policy" 95
Children Riding 96
President's Critics 97
Does Cardinal Cuddle Bluejay? 98
Finds Miscegenation Philosophy "Interesting" 99
Communist Influence Everywhere 100
Protests Nude Paintings 101
Recalls Life in a Sod House 101
Suggested Writing Assignments 103

CHAPTER 7   THE INTERVIEW
Introduction   *104*
Examples   *106*
   Interview with Rod McKuen, *Harvey Aronson*   *106*
   Dope Addict Tells It Like It Was   *109*
   Broadway Producer Makes Baseball Suggestion, *Murray Chass*   *111*
   Moon Trip Means Little to Derelicts   *113*
   Interview with Julian Bond, *Tom Tiede*   *114*
   Why He Flunked, *Carole Martin*   *117*
   Interview with Roosevelt Grier, *Arthur Daley*   *119*
Suggested Writing Assignments   *120*

CHAPTER 8   THE PERSONALITY SKETCH
Introduction   *121*
Examples   *122*
   Bertrand Russell   *122*
   Traveling Tony Seeks Solutions   *125*
   W. Somerset Maugham   *127*
   Good-by to Shamrock, *Frederic A. Birmingham*   *130*
   Closeup of a Hippie   *132*
   Finds Joy in Hauling Kids   *134*
Suggested Writing Assignments   *135*

CHAPTER 9   THE REVIEW
Introduction   *136*
Examples   *138*
   Dr. Spock of the Emotions   *138*
   Pianists: Rescued from Limbo   *140*
   Angry Young Hamlet, *Raymond A. Sokolov*   *142*
   New Musicals: A Guide to Modcom   *143*
   The Bill Cosby Show, *Cleveland Amory*   *145*
   Movies, *Michael V. Korda*   *146*
Suggested Writing Assignments   *148*

CHAPTER 10   THE COLUMN
Introduction   *149*
Examples   *150*
   James Reston
     What's the Real Mr. Nixon Like?   *150*
     Senator Kennedy's Impossible Question   *152*
   Dr. Joyce Brothers
     Public Nudity   *154*
     Father-Daughter Relationship   *155*
   Sydney J. Harris
     A Good Reason To Use Slang   *157*
     America, Britain Divided by Language   *158*

Abigail Van Buren
    Apartment Living for Graduate *160*
    41-Year-Old Virgin *160*
    Lousy Housekeeper Wakes Up *162*
    Tango With 'Pill' Beats 'Rockabye Baby' *163*
Roy Wilkins
    Self-Defeating Black Violence *164*
    Dangerous Propaganda *165*
Mary Bryson
    Remember the Traditional Look *166*
    Mirror, Mirror on the Wall—Wow! *168*
Suggested Writing Assignments *169*

CHAPTER 11 THE ARGUMENTATIVE ARTICLE
Introduction *170*
Examples *172*
    The Case for a Volunteer Army *172*
    Women Demand Right To Create Own Life *176*
    The Case for Black Literature, *James C. Kilgore* *177*
    A Letter to Chris, *Mrs. Richard Plumer* *182*
    Still Playing It Dumb? *Laura Cunningham* *185*
    He Can't Purchase Fireworks, *Tom Tiede* *187*
Suggested Writing Assignments *188*

CHAPTER 12 ADVERTISING PROSE
Introduction *191*
Examples *193*
    What-is-a Truck? *193*
    After a few years, it starts to look beautiful *194*
    Cadillac *195*
    Franklin D. Roosevelt *196*
    Kings Men *197*
    Berlitz *198*
    A funny thing happened on the way to a better banana *199*
Questions *200*
Suggested Writing Assignments *201*

CHAPTER 13 THE PERSONAL ESSAY
Introduction *202*
Examples *203*
    Night of the Wolf Race, *David Snell* *203*
    A Shade of Difference, *Pat Alford* *206*
    Confessions of a Kite Hustler, *Barry Farrell* *208*
    His Record Was Perfect, *Parke Cummings* *210*
    The Simple Joys of Life, *Mrs. Minnie M. Bauer* *212*
    Up on the Upholstered Frontier, *Horace Sutton* *213*
Suggested Writing Assignments *216*

CHAPTER 14   BUSINESS, PROFESSIONAL, AND TRADE
  Introduction   *217*
  Examples   *218*
    Runaways, Hippies, and Marihuana, *Kaufman, Allen, and West*   *218*
    A First Step to Professional Identity, *M. R. Lohman, P.E.*   *222*
    The Poet in the Classroom, *Robert Russell*   *225*
    Is There a Nurse-Clinician Job in Your Future?
      Donna M. Ledney, R.N.   *231*
    New Trends in Fund Raising   *234*
    Power Powder, *Dolores Davis Miller*   *236*
  Suggested Writing Assignments   *238*

CHAPTER 15   ON-THE-JOB WRITING
  Introduction   *240*
  Examples   *241*
    Business Letter   *241*
    Inter-Company Directive   *243*
    Business Letters   *244*
    Memoranda   *247*
    Business Letters   *249*
    Progress Report   *251*
    Letters of Recommendation   *254*
    Committee Report   *257*
    Memorandum   *260*
  Suggested Writing Assignments   *263*

CHAPTER 16   SCHOOL AND COLLEGE WRITING
  Introduction   *264*
  Examples   *266*
    Student Article: A Freshman Speaks, *Jenny Matthews*   *266*
    The Campus Newspaper: "A Handful of Dust," *Gary Britson*   *269*
    Campus Letter to the Editor: "Experienced Vet Backs Moratorium,"
      Michael J. Knievel   *271*
    Campus Newspaper Article: "Barriers Tumble if You Are Willing To
      Learn," *Robert P. Hogan*   *272*
    Underground Newspaper: "Law (and Order But Justice?) in America,"
      Terry Cannon   *274*
    Midterm Exam: The American Novel   *276*
    Term Paper: "Stonehenge—An Unfolding Mystery," *Mary Jo Girsch*   *281*

Common Problems in Writing

CHAPTER 17   PREVISING THE THEME FOR COMMON
  PROBLEMS
  Thesis
    Vague or Missing   *298*

Contents

      Unrestricted *299*
      Lack of Specific Purpose *301*
      Wrong Focus *302*
      Trite *302*
   Background
      Failure To Create Interest *304*
      Missing Who, What, Where, When, and Why Information *308*
   Topic Sentences
      Unclear and Irrelevant *308*
   Detail
      Missing Examples, Explanations, Facts and Arguments *310*
   Closing *316*
      Lacks Punch and Sense of Completeness *316*
   Checklist of Errors for Prevision *320*

CHAPTER 18 REVISING THE THEME *321*
   Checklist of Errors for Revision *323*

GLOSSARY *324*

REFERENCE CHART *Inside front and back covers*

1

Informative-Persuasive Prose— An Overview

Form and Motive

When the student learns that he will be asked to try his hand at writing the various types of prose found in the popular and professional media, his first reaction is usually, "But there are so many different kinds of writing in magazines and newspapers!" Yes, there are many different kinds, but they all have a common form and motive. Once you grasp the underlying form and motive, what first appeared as a multitude of complex types turns out to be a rather simple mode of expression.

Consider motive. Why does a newspaper critic write reviews of books, motion pictures, and art exhibits? Obviously, he wants to inform us or persuade us or both. When a reviewer examines a recent novel and decides that it merits an evaluation, he will inform us of the plot, the chief characters, the theme, and so on. If he dislikes the story he will try to persuade us that it is not worth reading. If he has mixed feelings, he will explain what he likes and does not like. Clearly, reviewers write to inform and persuade.

As a second example, take news stories. Are they not written to inform the reading public of matters pertaining to foreign policy, taxes, space exploration, and breakthroughs in medical research? When we speak of reading the latest news, are we not talking about getting the latest information? The same thing is true of letters to the editor, columns, profiles, feature articles, and advertisements. All of these types are designed to inform and persuade.

So much for motive. But what about form? How are these communications set up? Again, the answer is surprisingly simple; they all consist of a flexible framework in which the main point or thesis is stated in the opening paragraphs, developed in the body, and brought to a close in the final paragraphs.

Consider the critic once again. If he enjoys a television series and wishes to convey this fact to his readers he will state his viewpoint at the beginning of his review, produce supporting evidence in the body based on his observations of the show, and bring the piece to a logical close by means of a summary or an exhortation to the viewer to tune it in.

This same introduction, body, closing pattern is common to news reporting. In writing up an account of, say, a local flood condition, the journalist begins with a lead paragraph of the main background facts, sets forth the bulk of the details in the body, and winds it up with a weather forecast, a warning to motorists, or perhaps an observation concerning flood control legislation.

This three-part pattern applies not merely to reviews and news stories but to practically all of the writing in the national media—columns, features, interviews, and advertisements. When a sports writer composes his column on the Super Bowl football game for the Sunday supplement, he may settle for a description of the stand-out players, focus on the dramatic moments in the action, or speculate as to where the strategy of the losing team went wrong. He may, in fact, do a number of these things. But whatever his topic, he will utilize the basic form of beginning, middle, and end. He will tell us in so many words what he is going to do, he will do it, and he will close.

A fashion columnist will proceed in a similar manner, whether her subject involves a new fad in hats, jewelry for formal occasions, or tips on using perfume.

Feature articles on topics ranging from civil rights and religion to travel and home gardening will be structured in the same manner: first the author's point or purpose; then the descriptive, illustrating, or factual support; then the resolving or closing of the piece. As for advertisements, it is common knowledge that they are written to persuade, which means that a product or service is identified and "sold" to the reader by arguments designed to persuade him to buy.

The question is, why do the various types of magazine and newspaper writing—not to mention the prose in business exchanges, professional journals, and college writing—follow this simple sequence of introduction, body, and closing? Because it is a logical and natural way of informing and persuading the reader. To date, no better means of communicating by means of non-fiction prose has been devised than that which requires the writer to state his thesis, carry it through, and close it.

There is, of course, more to the art of putting words on paper than appears in this pattern, but before noting the many refinements and variations which are involved it might be wise to take a closer look at the particular elements which make up the three main divisions of the sequence.

In the *introduction*, the writer states his thesis and provides preliminary information aimed at clarifying and creating reader interest in that thesis. For example, if he is writing an interview of a motion picture celebrity, he will give us his thesis—"Jim Jones is one of the busiest young stars in Hollywood"—together with clarifying material, perhaps the who, what, where, when, and why which occasioned the interview. To pique our curiosity, he may throw in a statement which runs contrary to the public view—"Jim Jones is in great demand by producers and directors these days, but he keeps saying no."

Preliminary information has many names—background, orienting material, build up, and lead—but its importance should never be underestimated. The reader who is bored or confused in the opening paragraph is not likely to be impressed.

Suppose a business executive composes a directive concerning the new policy in regard to hiring office personnel. If he neglects to indicate by whose authority the change was made, the rationale behind it, the date it is to become effective, and other pertinent information, the order may not be understood and enforced. Here a badly written introduction could result not merely in boredom or confusion, but in reprimand, demotion, or dismissal.

The *body* constitutes the largest division of the composition since in this section the writer must fully develop his thesis by means of examples, illustrations, comparisons, definitions, facts, and other evidence. He usually states and discusses one point at a time, although he may cover a number of sub-points in a single paragraph and a single point in a number of paragraphs. In order to guide the reader through the body of the text, the writer identifies each point with a key or topic sentence.

Consider the staff writer who does a profile on Kenny Kaufman, T.V. comic, with the slant that Kaufman's early ups and downs helped make him the durable performer that he is today. In supporting his thesis in the body, the writer may advance and elaborate upon a number of topics—Kaufman's boyhood, his first performance, his financial problems, his attempt to find his own style—but each paragraph will be placed there by deliberate design, in that it constitutes a link in the chain. The body, then, consists of the individual bits and blocks of information which make up the total thesis message.

As for the *closing*, the third and final division of basic form, the writer may repeat or paraphrase his original thesis, summarize the chief ideas in the body, or draw a conclusion. Although the appropriate means of closing is determined by the subject matter, perhaps the most common element found in the final paragraphs of workaday prose is a conclusion, which may take the form of a recommendation, solution, endorsement, prediction, warning, exhortation, or lament. The possibilities are endless because any number of implications, deductions, and applications can be drawn from the thousand and one subjects on which we write.

To illustrate the naturalness of conclusion-drawing, let us suppose that the writer who did the interview on Kenny Kaufman established in the body of his story the fact that the comedian's early ups and downs do help explain his durability as a television personality. How might the writer close? He could draw the conclusion that it is just because Kaufman graduated from the school of hard knocks that he is always ready to give a deserving young newcomer a push up the ladder. Or he might round off the interview with a quote from the star, such as: "Yeah, I had it rough in those days. I thought my permanent theme song was going to be, 'I'll Walk Alone.' But when I look back, I wouldn't change a thing. Rough is just the name of the game."

The graph which follows will help you visualize the divisions of informative-persuasive prose and the elements which comprise them.

Introductory Paragraphs

> The writer's thesis or purpose is established together with the preliminary information which

> clarifies and arouses interest in the thesis.

Paragraphs in the Body

> A topic sentence is provided which identifies

> the main point of each paragraph. The examples,

> illustrations, facts, and other details

> are given which are needed to discuss the topic.

Closing Paragraphs

> The writer may repeat or paraphrase his thesis,

> summarize the main ideas, or draw a conclusion.

Variety

Now that you have some understanding of the three-part sequence of informative-persuasive writing, one point must be made perfectly clear: as an unalterable blueprint this sequence is no good at all. Anyone who supposes that the basic pattern of introduction, body, and closing can be laid over any piece of popular, professional, or college prose and fit, element by element, is in for a rude awakening. The writing pattern presented here is *a guideline, not a gimmick*. There can never be a "method" of writing which, when applied, will resolve all of the variations and fine points found in informative-persuasive prose or in any other kind of prose.

As an example of variety, take the thesis or purpose idea. Will it always be stated in a single sentence at the end of a one-paragraph introduction? No, the thesis may be implied rather than stated, it may appear anywhere in a one-paragraph, a two-paragraph, a five-paragraph opening, or it may be omitted altogether if the writer chooses to begin at once with a supporting idea and build toward his thesis formulation.

Variety also applies to the preliminary information, which may be anecdotal, definitive, statistical; lengthy or brief. The sample introductions which follow illustrate some of the many possibilities.

The Florida Keys: Hunting Ground for Treasure, Sports, Romance

HAROLD M. FARHAS

> Are you interested in the finest in water sports? Or diving for sunken treasure? Or perhaps an offbeat honeymoon spot? Well, a vacation in the Florida Keys fits the bill on all counts.
>
> Family Weekly, *January 12, 1969*

The Ugly American Goes to Hawaii

NEA

> American tourists, it always seemed to me, were much maligned—undeserving of the criticism so often directed at them.
>
> In my travels through countries in Europe, only once did I encounter the "unsophisticated, noisy boorish" American I had been led to believe was legion. The one time was in a restaurant in Florence where a wife complained loudly that the place was full of Italians while her husband asked a speechless waiter for catsup for his scallopini. To me, people like this were the exception, not the rule. But now I know why I only once came across this breed in Europe. They all go to Hawaii.
>
> The Record, *September 23, 1968*

What's Wrong With the Railroads?

PERRY M. SHOEMAKER

> The remedy for the present railroad situation can be summed up in railroad language: get government the hell out of clumsy interference with transportation.
>
> Fortune, *January, 1960*

The introduction on the Florida Keys consists of four sentences and the thesis is stated. The introduction on American tourists is a two-paragraph presentation which contains a great deal of preliminary information and the thesis is implied. In the final example on railroads, a single sentence conveys both background and thesis intention.

In a moment the variations which characterize the body and the closing will be illustrated, but first one should note that there are two excellent reasons why variety is a constant factor in all prose. First, writers would bore themselves and their readers by adhering to an unchanging pattern in which each part was made to march across the page in unbroken regularity: introduction, preliminary material, thesis; first point stated and discussed; second point stated and discussed; and so on. No one would want to read, or write, such prose.

An even more important justification for flexibility involves clarity. Remember that to write is to communicate and if a writer is hamstrung by a fixed form he simply cannot express himself fully, clearly, and truthfully.

As part of a flexible framework, the body and closing are also subject to countless modifications. For instance, the supporting paragraphs in the body may vary greatly in length and the topic sentences may appear first, last, or in the middle. Sometimes the writer combines two or three topics in one paragraph and sometimes it suits his purpose to divide his treatment of one point into several paragraphs.

The same variety is found in closings. The final paragraphs may be long or short, contain a summary and a conclusion, several conclusions, or a single conclusion drawn at some length. In many instances the writer will not include a formal closing, particularly when the final supporting paragraphs in the body serve to bring the piece to a logical end.

It should be obvious from this discussion of form and variety that the three-part sequence is a simplification of the actual structure of popular, professional, and scholastic writing. But by experimenting with the basic parts and confirming for yourself the flexibility of the pattern, you will begin to see the shape and movement of written discourse. As mentioned earlier, the basic pattern taken as a rigid rule is of no value in writing, but utilized as a guideline, it is invaluable.

Language

If it has now become apparent that you have perhaps never fully appreciated the uses and value of modern prose, it should come as no surprise that you have probably not examined, in any close fashion, the language of everyday writing. To be sure, you have studied literary masterpieces by Thoreau and Twain, but you probably have not been asked to examine current prose as it is written in magazines, newspapers, journals, and job reports.

The simplest way to distinguish workaday prose from the scholarly writing anthologized in many textbooks is to examine selections of both kinds. First, however, it might be wise to review certain terms and definitions which are commonly applied.

Identifying the levels of language is a useful way to begin. There are two styles or levels of standard English, the formal and the informal. Workaday prose is generally informal; scholarly prose is generally formal. In noting the characteristics of the two styles, remember that neither constitutes a pure category. There is a great deal of overlapping, so that we often find traits of both styles in the same piece. The characteristics of formal prose are: a) long, measured sentences, b) a learned vocabulary, c) a conservative grammar and usage, and d) a serious, impersonal tone.

In informal prose the style is greatly simplified: a) the sentences are fairly short and uncomplicated, b) the vocabulary is plain and may include idiomatic expressions, c) the grammar and usage are casual, and d) the tone is personal, often light and humorous.

Now compare examples of the two styles.

> Of all inorganic substances, acting in their own proper nature, and without assistance or combination, water is the most wonderful. If we think of it as the source of all the changefulness and beauty which we have seen in clouds; then as the instrument by which the earth we have contemplated was modelled into symmetry, and its crags chiselled into grace; then as, in the form of snow, it robes the mountains it has made, with that transcendent light which we could not have conceived if we had not seen; then as it exists in the foam of the current, in the iris which spans it, in the morning mist which rises from it, in the deep crystalline pools which mirror its hanging shore, in the broad lake and glancing river; finally, in that which is to all human minds the best emblem of unwearied, unconquerable power, the wild, various, fantastic, tameless unity of the sea; what shall we compare to this mighty, this universal element, for glory and for beauty? Or how shall we follow its eternal changefulness of feeling? It is like trying to paint a soul.
>
> *Ruskin's "Modern Painters," 1843*

> Vacation recipe: Mix equal parts of Rome, Madrid and Paris. Add a dash of San Francisco, a pinch of Monaco and sprinkle generously with a million people. Blend thoroughly. Place in the sun for a few centuries, basting occasionally with Moorish charm.
>
> The final concoction is Lisbon, the most delectable piece of real estate in Europe.
>
> For best results, digest slowly. Unfortunately, too many tourists in their haste to explore the more publicized cities of Europe make the mistake of breezing through Lisbon. One should allow plenty of time for the magic to jell.
>
> *Sunny, Exotic Charmer—That's Lovely*
> *Lisbon, by K. Pool*, L.A. Times
> (The Des Moines Register, *December 11, 1967*)

The selection from Ruskin's essay is obviously formal. The paragraph is dominated by a long and contrived middle sentence of some 150 words, the vocabulary is heavily imagistic—"modelled into symmetry," "deep crystalline pools," "tameless unity of the sea"—and the great abundance of carefully placed commas and semicolons is enough to indicate a conservative grammar. The tone is detached and lofty, clearly appropriate for Ruskin's topic and audience—a theory of esthetics written for intellectuals.

The travel piece on Lisbon is just as obviously informal. The sentences are short, the vocabulary is very plain and frequently idiomatic—"delectable piece of real estate," "breezing through Lisbon," "time for the magic to jell." The resulting tone is direct, personal, and light as befits a brief account of a tourist haven of interest to the general reader.

Since there is a range of styles and not two fixed categories, you will find it convenient in analyzing the following examples to use the terms *highly formal*, *moderately formal*, *very informal*, and so on. Also remember that level is determined by the subject matter, length, and occasion of the piece. Extended writing of a philosophic, scientific, or literary nature aimed at a select audience calls for a rather formal style, just as writing of a practical, utilitarian nature aimed at the general reader calls for a rather informal style.

> Whether or not man's history, his psychosocial evolution, the development of his social heredity could have been a gradual process, without spastic mutations, without the cyclic spiral of revolt, destruction, reimposition, and again revolt, we cannot say. It does not seem to have been possible in the past, though it is not impossible now, as this essay hopes to indicate. Up until now man does not seem to have been able to understand, consciously, and to cooperate, deliberately, with the life process that not only has brought him to his superanimal station but is still driving him on to higher achievement, greater powers, and greater comprehension.
>
> *Gerald Heard*, The Five Ages of Man, *1963*

> It is difficult to get mad at love, because love is whatever anybody wants it to be and is thus, by definition, absolutely perfect. Like Al Capp's famous love-animal the schmoo, it can turn into roast beef or chicken out of simple goodwill. So that if you don't like Sigmund Freud you can always try Irving Berlin; love comes in almost as may flavors as a successful politician.
>
> To the Christian, according to the parable of the Good Samaritan, love means binding the wounds of the stranger, which is tax-deductible these days. To the besotted consumer of pop fiction, it means the mechanical grappling hook that shoots out whenever good-looking people get together. To the worrier about foreign affairs, it is simply something that nobody feels deeply enough about Americans.
>
> *Wilfred Sheed, "We Overrate Love,"* Saturday Evening Post, *March 25, 1969*

> Sometimes, climbing among the western mountains, one crosses a long wind-lashed and snow-beaten shoulder of harsh broken rocks; and in a tiny hollow halfway across it, see, there is a tuft of bright flowers. Sometimes, from higher up, one looks down into a barren canyon, whose stony walls echo with the dull roar of the torrent below and with the crash of crumbling slabs and pinnacles above: there is not a patch of green, not a visible handful of nourishing earth; but halfway down those precipitous walls, raising its gallant head and spreading its hopeful arms, there grows a pine tree rooted in an invisible notch, and the birds flicker around it.
>
> *Gilbert Highet's,* Man's Unconquerable Mind, *1954*

Muzquiz, Mexico—All hope was abandoned Tuesday for 178 miners trapped underground when a gas explosion ripped through a coal mine near this northern village.

Fourteen bodies were recovered and an official of the Red Cross, which is coordinating rescue efforts, said there was no hope of any survivors.

Thirteen of the bodies recovered were of miners trapped near the mouth of the mine when fire-damp exploded and sealed off the two main shafts. The other was of a man living nearby who rushed into the pit mouth in search of a missing relative and was overcome by fumes.

Reuters, April 2, 1969
(*The Des Moines Register*)

The first selection on man's historical development is decidedly formal. The sentences are long, the language is technical, and the movement is slow. Since Heard is engaged in an analysis of a very complex nature, namely, the cultural evolution of man, we do not expect the prose to move as quickly as it does in the news report on the mine explosion in Mexico in which factual information is set forth in a simple and concise manner. Contrast the wording in the two pieces—"spastic mutations," "cyclic spiral of revolt," "superanimal station"; "178 miners trapped," "no hope of any survivors," "overcome by fumes." It should be obvious that the difference in subject and occasion accounts for the highly formal style of the one, and the everyday informal style of the other.

The same contrast is afforded by the paragraphs on love and the passage from Highet's book. The informal style of the first is apparent in the opening lines—"get mad at love" and "Al Capp's famous love-animal." Note the use of *so*, the contraction, the short sentences, and the mixing of allusions in regard to the Good Samaritan and tax-deductible. Although the writer's opinion on love may be new to most readers, he deals with it in an amusing, off-the-cuff fashion. Highet's paragraph is just the reverse: the familiar characteristics of literary diction, long sentences, and deeply serious tone stamp it as being very formal.

Having observed the differences between informal and formal prose, we must now examine the range of informal or everyday prose, since it is this stylistic level which is used in newspapers, journals, and job report writing. Briefly, everyday prose ranges from the moderately informal to the very informal, depending on the occasion. Moderately informal writing, as suggested earlier, is characterized by fairly short sentences, a simplified vocabulary, idiomatic expressions, freshly coined terms, and frequent references to the current scene. Prose which is very informal is exceedingly free and conversational. The writer uses many short, simple constructions, sentence fragments, and slang, and he ignores certain conventional grammatical distinctions. Add to this a penchant for satire, clever sallies, word play, and dialogue and you have a swinging free style, the ultimate in informal prose.

The examples which follow should make it clear that there is not a fixed "informal style" as such but rather varying degrees of informality in writing.

A pair of loud sonic booms shook the sky over the Atlantic Ocean last week, heralding the approach of Apollo 9 as it hurtled through the thickening atmosphere on its way home. Then, to the cheers of the sailors on the deck of the helicopter carrier *Guadalcanal,* the heat-charred spacecraft floated down through the cloud cover and splashed into the water only three miles away. The triumphant ending to the ten-day, near-perfect mission of Apollo 9 cleared the way for the final U.S. thrust toward a manned landing on the moon.

A worldwide TV audience had a close-up view of the astronauts when they splashed down and as they emerged from the bobbing spaceship they call Gumdrop. As the *Guadalcanal* moved to within 100 yards of the spacecraft, TV cameras on the deck zoomed in to show Astronauts David Scott, Russell Schweickart and James McDivitt tumbling into inflated rubber rafts—a surprisingly awkward operation after the precise maneuvers and sophisticated procedure of the space flight.

Time, *March 21, 1969*

This report on the landing of the Apollo 9 spacecraft is an example of moderately informal prose. Because of the familiar subject, simple word choice, and relatively short sentences, the delivery is plain and straightforward—which is not to say that the writing lacks impact. Phrases such as "hurtled through the thickening atmosphere" and "floated down through the cloud cover" convey very powerful images to the reader. But in overall effect the style is direct and business-like. The reporter has a story to tell and he tells it. He is not writing for the ages but for the modern reader who wants to sit down for a moment and catch up on the week's events. It is important to note that this writing style, in that it achieves dignity without straining after grammatical niceties, has become a kind of general purpose prose used by many newspaper and magazine writers.

College football is a better game than professional football. Better esthetically because there is more art and imagination to it, better technically because it is better coached, more entertaining, certainly more inspiring, more meaningful, more colorful.

Pro football is for fat linemen, quarterbacks who cannot run and coaches who never vary an offense. It is a pale imitation of the college game.

John Underwood, "The College Game Is Best," Sports Illustrated, *Sept. 20, 1965*

This excerpt on college football is considerably more informal. The sentences are very short and the language is unmistakably simple. You perhaps noticed the long sentence fragment in the first paragraph. Rather than say, "It is better esthetically . . .", the writer omitted the subject and verb so that he could repeat and emphasize the key word in his argument: "Better esthetically, better technically, better coached." As a short article written in defense of college football to be read by sports fans, there is no doubt that the strongly informal style is very effective.

"Hey! Look at me!" shouted little Billy, leaning over the side of his hospital crib. "I don't have any thumbs!"

At first you hoped it was a sick joke—a little 5-year-old hooking his thumbs under his fingers as he held them in the air. And then you remember where you are—the Shriners' Crippled Children's Hospital of Los Angeles. And you knew indeed there were no thumbs under those pathetically twisted fingers.

Even with thumbs, little Billy's hands won't be much. You see, they are attached at right angles to the wrists. Billy is a Thalidomide baby. He looks as if God made him in the dark. But he is as cheerful as if he were Mr. America.

Jim Murray, "A Sad Visit Into Despair"
(Des Moines Register, August 3, 1967)

These paragraphs taken from Jim Murray's column about crippled children are another example of everyday prose which is quite informal. Notice the abundant use of dialogue, the plainness of the language, the frequent use of the dash, and the second-person references: "At first you hoped," "Then you remember," "You knew indeed," "You see, they are attached." The author is writing as he would talk to the reader if they were face to face; hence, the sentences which begin with *and* and *but*, the contractions, and the short one-line similies such as, "He looks as if God made him in the dark."

It should go without saying that Murray required a highly informal style in working with this subject matter. To reach out and touch the reader, he needed the devices of idiom, dialogue, and second-person reference, and that is exactly why he used them.

We've breathed life into this one, so stand back! We call it "The Exterminator." It's a solid state powerhouse that comes on with a wall of sound—six speakers. Two 15, two 12, and two 7 inchers. It puts out a screaming treble that is almost unreal, and a bass that roars right through anything in its path. 250 watts of peak music power. That'll fill any room you're playing from gyms to sports arenas, all the way to open air coliseums.

"The Exterminator." It delivers! Try it![1]

To say that this advertisement represents prose which is extremely informal is to remark on the obvious. It would be difficult to miss the sentence fragments ("Two 15, two 12, and two 7 inchers"), the many contractions (we've, it's that'll), the colloquialisms (comes on, puts out, roars right through), and the simple metaphors (Exterminator, breathed life into, powerhouse).

We can learn something about the real nature of this highly informal writing by posing this question. How does the reader respond to it? Clearly, he responds very strongly—whether he decides to buy the product or not. In most instances the ad writer "gets through" to the reader. Why? Because the message is *condensed* and *dramatic*. Sentence fragments and contractions are condensed forms in themselves, and at least part of the appeal of colloquial expressions is their capacity to make an idea clear in the deft turn of a single phrase. As for metaphors (which are numerous in the Baldwin piece), they too compress by giving quick images rather than extended analyses.

Note the difference in dramatic effect in the examples below. The first para-

---

[1] Advertisement reprinted by permission of The Fred Gretsch Company, Inc.

graph is a rewrite in which the fragments, colloquialisms, contractions, and metaphors have been removed. The second paragraph contains the original language used in the ad.

> We have worked very hard on this amplifier, so you should not be surpised at the volume which you hear. We call it "The Model with the Volume." This amplifier is very solidly constructed and is quite powerful in volume because of the six speakers. There are two 15, two 12, and two 7 inch speakers. This machine offers the listener a treble which is unusually high and a bass which is very full and resonant.

> We've breathed life into this one, so stand back! We call it "The Exterminator." It's a solid state powerhouse that comes on with a wall of sound—six speakers. Two 15, two 12, and two 7 inchers. It puts out a screaming treble that is almost unreal, and a bass that roars right through anything in its path.

At this point we should note three questions which are commonly asked about language. First, is one stylistic level of writing better than another? The answer is no. There is no conflict between styles because each is appropriate in a given context. If a subject calls for a moderately formal style, use it. If another subject calls for a moderately informal style, use that. For example, a term paper which explores the mercantile theory of the seventeenth century would require a rather formal treatment whereas a letter to the editor of the school newspaper written in opposition to TV classes would probably warrant a rather informal style.

It is often supposed that scholarly writing heads the list and that excellence drops off as the prose becomes less formal. But the problem in regard to levels is one of determining appropriateness, not inherent superiority. It would be a mistake to use an extremely informal style in dealing with mercantilism just as it would be inappropriate to employ a highly formal style in a letter to the editor about TV classes.

As a second example, take the excerpt from Murray's column on crippled children which begins, " 'Hey! Look at me!' shouted little Billy." Can you imagine the consequences if Murray had attempted to use Ruskin's style in the passage which reads, "Of all inorganic substances, acting in their own proper nature. . ."? But then Ruskin could not have employed Murray's informal style, either. There is, then, no conflict between stylistic levels. The "best" style is simply the most "appropriate" style for a given context.

A second question frequently posed is, does "anything go" in highly informal writing? On the contrary, the only thing that goes in any level of writing is what works, and this rules out non-standard expressions such as "It don't," "I could of," and "That there book" as well as misspelled words, mispunctuated sentences, and awkward constructions. For example, in the Baldwin advertisement you will find fragments and colloquialisms used deliberately for dramatic effect, but you will not find misspelled words, clumsy phrasings, and non-standard expressions. Look at examples of highly informal prose in magazines and newspapers. It should not take you long to discover the great difference between highly informal prose which is artfully contrived and merely bad writing which is carelessly thrown together. Granted, if you search the national media for examples of bad informal writing, you can find them, but this fact will hardly justify your writing as carelessly as you can. It is only common sense to imitate the best, not the worst.

A third question frequently asked is, which style of writing should be used? In one sense this question has already been answered because the particular topic, occasion, and audience will determine stylistic level. Meanwhile, do not fail to observe that most student writing assignments call for a moderately formal to a moderately informal prose style. The subject matter being dealt with in the reports, analyses, and term papers which students submit to their professors suggests an informal or "general purpose" prose which falls between the extremes of the highly formal and the highly informal.

If you are still in doubt as to the nature and uses of the various stylistic levels, read magazines, newspapers, and trade journals with an eye to the language. For the perceptive student, these original sources constitute the best "text" ever written.

Authors and Audience

Since this text deals with workaday prose, that is, modern prose as it is written day to day in newspaper offices, business firms, and schools, it is a relatively simple matter to determine authors and audience.

The prose pieces which make up the national media are composed by journalists, staff writers, specialists, and free lance and lay writers. Reporters and staff writers handle news items, editorials, and feature stories on topics ranging from floods, fires, and famine to taxes, needed legislation, and the first day of spring. Specialists expound in columns on education, politics, and medicine; in reviews of art works, books, and film; and in articles on travel, farm problems, and organized crime. When the free lance writers who contribute heavily to the hundreds of small newspapers published throughout the country and the lay writers who compose most of the letters to the editor are added to the list, one can see that a great number of people are involved in producing the printed word.

How important are magazine and newspaper writers? To answer this question, one needs only to imagine our plight if we were suddenly cut off from all sources of written information concerning the war in Vietnam, the Israeli-Arab clash, the civil rights movements, union-management relationships, and reports on technology, agriculture, transportation, trade, and business investments. Clearly, it would be hard to survive without the informative-persuasive communications found in the national media.

The view that most magazine and newspaper writers are mere hacks is, then, absurd on two counts. First, analyses, news stories, and technical reports cannot be clearly and intelligently composed by hacks. In the second place, the journalists and specialists who write our newspapers keep us informed and thereby play a vital role in the world.

The question may now be raised: Who reads the informative-persuasive writing found in the mass media? It would be better to ask, who does not? It is easy to be fooled by the term "mass," which suggests a low level prose written for the uneducated. But today everyone is part of the mass citizenry and hence all citizens are dependent on the media to keep them up-to-date and knowledgeable. In this connection, it might be noted that the truth contained in Will Rogers' observation is amusing just because it is so often overlooked. "All I know is what I read in the papers," he remarked. In a very real sense this is all any of us know, because whether we are housewives, engineers, laborers, or students, we obtain our information from the mass media.

Although the student is usually aware of the importance of the popular media, he is often completely in the dark regarding a second source of informative-persuasive writing—the hundreds of business and professional journals which are published each month for special groups of readers. These magazines, called trade journals, are composed almost exclusively by and for specialists in the various fields.

The partial list below will reveal the extent to which trade journals keep business and professional people abreast of the lastest developments in their major area.

> Journal of the American Medical Association
> Progressive Grocer
> Gazette des Beaux-Arts
> Autolaundry News
> Botanical Review
> Today's Secretary
> Accountant's Digest
> Business Aviation
> Journal of Advertising Research
> American Bee Journal
> Product Engineering
> National Fisherman
> American Bar Association Journal
> International Trade Review
> Mortuary Management
> Career Model
> Journal of Philosophy
> Automotive News
> American Journal of Mathematics
> Farm and Power Equipment
> Music Journal
> American Forestry
> U.S. Steel News
> Tourist Court Journal
> American Physical Education Review
> Coins Magazine
> Progressive Architecture
> Outboard Boating

American Historical Review
Flower Grower

If you did not find your vocation, or avocation, represented in the above sample, rest assured that, whatever it is, there are a number of journals published on your subject. Experts in any given field must communicate with one another since this is, after all, the only way they can remain experts.

Business and professional writing also involves on-the-job prose—those reports, directives, letters, policy statements, and memos which are exchanged by the thousands in offices, shops, and plants across the country. There is certainly no difficulty in identifying writers and readers here: executives, doctors, ministers, engineers, civil servants, educators, and scientists write these communications and read them. It is because this kind of writing is so important—and often so little appreciated by the student—that we have provided a number of examples of on-the-job prose. The student writer all too often fancies that when he completes his degree in physics, education, or law he will make little use of his writing skills. Not so. As a physicist he will write project descriptions, progress reports, proposals, and letters. As an educator, he will submit lesson plans, curricula, committee minutes, and recommendations. As a lawyer he will write briefs, directives, warrants, and other correspondence. In fact, the higher he rises in his profession, the more use he will make of the written word. Logically enough, it is the leaders in each field who advise, guide, and innovate, and the chief means at their disposal is informative-persuasive prose.

College writing constitutes a third kind of everyday prose, and of course you are well aware of authors and audience in this category, since the student is the writer of book reports, literary analyses, and research papers and professors are the audience.

There are, by the way, several reasons why we have included in this text a section on college writing. Many students have a limited view of composition. They see very little connection between the themes they compose for their English teacher and the term reports, historical analyses, and essay-type tests they write for other instructors. But there is no difference in basic form between an English theme, a term paper, and an essay-type test. Each of these assignments constitutes a three-part writing sequence in which a thesis is established, supported, and concluded.

Not only does the student fail to relate theme writing to the papers assigned in his history, science, and art classes; he also fails to connect composition with popular, business, and professional writing. He supposes that college writing assignments are necessary evils in the system, and that there is no similarity between the prose he writes as a student and the prose written by journalists and professional people.

Of course, it is one thing merely to say that school and professional prose are basically alike and quite another thing to illustrate it. It is for this reason that we have provided in the last chapter of this book a section of readings on college writing assignments. By noting the similarities between these school papers and the professionally written pieces in this text, you should begin to see that the themes, literary analyses, and term projects you write today as a student are a realistic preparation for the reports, letters, and articles you will write tomorrow as a specialist.

2

The Writing Process

Topic

The following teacher-student dialogue takes place in composition classrooms across the country each fall.

"What shall I write about?"
"Write about your experiences."
"But I haven't been any place or done anything exciting."

As long as the term "experiences" is taken to mean visits to faraway places and exciting adventures, the typical apprentice writer certainly does not have any good topics for compositions. At eighteen, it is doubtful that he has played the tables at Monte Carlo, cavorted on the French Riviera, hunted big game in Africa, or dived for pearls off tropic islands. But if experience is considered in its full and legitimate sense, namely, as the sum total of what you have done, thought, observed, read, and heard, then there is no dearth of ideas for themes—even if you have never left your hometown. That life is full of countless topics for composition can be proved by noting the multitude of ideas dealt with in a single edition of a newspaper.

The items listed below were summarized from *The Des Moines Register*, June 10, 1969. In reading over the material, remember that this is not a mere exercise to illustrate the great miscellany of subject matter found in the national media. Rather it is designed to prove that a wealth of ideas for writing lies all around us. As you read, relate the various topics to your own personal experiences—your likes, dislikes, doubts, memories, convictions, preferences, opinions, hopes, disappointments, resolutions, fears, habits, and desires—any one of which could be developed into an informative or persuasive piece of writing:

The planned withdrawal of American troops from Vietnam, persons 65 years old issued half-fare subway and bus passes in New York City, new slaying at Ann Arbor, strike idles helicopter firms, government approves new measles vaccine, U.S. and Mexico officials meet to discuss drug traffic, psychiatrists name a new mental illness "crisis flight," closing of a major Catholic seminary in the state, blue suitcase ruled out as clue to whereabouts of missing girl, under-age children expected to hold prohibited jobs this summer, farm girl crushed in feed grinder accident, mummified sacred birds destroyed by fire in ancient Egyptian tunnels, doctors link deformed teeth to brain damage, construction accident results in hiring of additional state safety officers, eight ways to cut insurance costs, how to make a chocolate date cake, collectors pay thousands for rare antiques, Audubon club members sight 77 species of birds, two pro golfers make hole-in-one, fallen trees make good fishing spots.

The foregoing sample, incomplete as it is, constitutes a storehouse of ideas for writers. The headline on the planned withdrawal of American troops from Vietnam might suggest a theme in which you compare the thoughts of an American and a North Vietnamese soldier as they await the signal to move out. The story of the farm girl crushed in a feed grinder might remind you of an old idea of yours that farms can be death traps for unwary city children. And if cooking or fishing is your hobby, the items on baking a chocolate date cake and fishing near fallen trees could lead you to your own experiences on these topics.

It should be clear that you have at your disposal literally hundreds of topics on which to write, from politics, religion, economics, and business to sports, fashions, fishing, and cooking, and you have a dozen forms in which to write them—reviews, columns, articles, personality sketches, news analyses, interviews, and others. For the student who still thinks that composition is limited to the classroom and that what he did on his summer vacation exhausts his best ideas for themes, finding a good topic is indeed a problem. But the writer who sees the hundreds of informative-persuasive compositions on every hand has cleared this hurdle. He knows that he lives in a world of ideas and that any one of them is fair game for a paper.

Some writers keep a scrapbook of favorite newspaper and magazine clippings for future reference, and others keep a journal or notebook of their personal thoughts. What can be put into such a book? Anything you please—quotations, titles of books you want to read, notes from books you have already read, new concepts, bits of poetry, a summary of an article, an idea you intend to explore, new words and phrases, your first impressions of a college mixer, or a character sketch of the intellectual down the hall. The great value of a journal is that it is your slave. You can feed it whenever and whatever you wish, and throw caution to the winds as far as perfect writing form is concerned.

As with all good things, however, there are a few don'ts: a) don't forget to date each entry; in retrospect, you will want to know when you had a given thought, b) don't confuse a journal of ideas with a diary of your social life—who called up last night, why you cancelled a date, and so on, c) don't forget to document excerpted material such as lines taken from plays, poems, and books;

you cannot quote an idea or use it as a springboard if you neglected to get down the title and author's name, and d) don't mix class notes and assignments with journal entries; make a separate notebook of your journal.

Since a journal reflects its author's personality, interests, and moods, no two of them will read alike. But the samples which follow may shed some light on the art of journal keeping for those who are new at it.

April 8, 1969—Thoughts, like birds, must be caught or they fly away.—Hence this attempt at a journal.

April 10—Dr. Charles E. Winick believes that American young people are becoming desexualized. No sign of it yet on *this* campus. Get his book, *The New People*.

April 15—There were two news items in the paper this morning about "one car" accidents. Maybe I could do a piece on this topic, since I had a wreck like this myself. Would be interesting to interview some of the people who have been in one car accidents and find out some of the actual causes. Most drivers know why two car crashes happen, but the reasons for one car accidents are rarely discussed.

April 20—Mary Ellen is beautiful, poised, pleasant—and completely empty. How did she get that way? It must be a talent.

Two of my instructors waste valuable time haranguing the class on the importance of taking notes, reading the material, and attending each session. If they gave regular weekly quizzes there would be no need for all these warnings. To pass the quiz given every Friday, we would all have to attend class, take complete notes, and keep up in the text.

April 22—Read an amusing article in an old copy of *Reader's Digest* (Jan. 1967) called, "What We Can Learn from Children." Wechsberg talks about the thoughtful questions raised by his little girl—Do French dogs bark in French? and, How could a certain old gentleman be said to have one foot in the grave when she just saw him with both feet in his garden? Believe I could do a paper like this using some of my little brother's humorous observations and bent grammar.

April 27—I am going to sever my acquaintanceship with S_____. He's rude, crude, and treacherous. Friends like him I don't need. My error was in getting to know him. That was a mistake. Why I ever invited him on the trip I'll never know. What can I do about it? Nothing. I'm stuck with him.

April 29—Professor B_____ has an excellent memory. In discussing how our view of innocence has changed over the years, he recited from memory the following poem by Charles Kingsley.

A Farewell

My fairest child, I have no song to give you.
No lark could pipe to skies so
  dull and gray;

Yet, ere we part, one lesson I can
  leave you
For every day.

Be good, sweet maid, and let who will
  be clever.
Do noble things, not dream them, all
  day long;
And so make life, death, and
  that vast forever
One grand, sweet song.

April 30—There are three things I don't understand: 1) the meaning of the proverb, "Give him a horse who tells the truth," 2) the value of the 50 minute lecture, and, 3) my roommate.

In looking over these entries, you probably noticed that some have more potential than others as ideas for papers. For example, in the April 27 entry, the writer is just blowing off steam. There is more heat than light in his observation. But a number of his notations could be used as the basis for a composition and some might lead him to other ideas.

By way of a summary, we can say that finding topics for themes is not impossible if one is alert to the world around him and is willing to record his thoughts and impressions as they occur.

Prewriting

Prewriting, defined as the exploring and testing of a theme idea before it is written, is the most important and least understood phase in the writing process.

Professionals learn through long experience that a finished composition is never better than the original conception on which it is based. For this reason they never write out an idea in its final form until they have prejudged it as being effective in all ways. Inexperienced writers do just the opposite. They almost invariably select an idea in haste without considering whether it constitutes a sound approach to the topic. Although revision remains an essential part of the writing operation, it cannot solve problems such as an unrestricted thesis, lack of supporting detail, unimaginative content, and wrong focus. These errors, which are common in freshman writing, go to the bone of the composition and can only be removed if the writer is willing to throw out most of the completed material and begin again. The obvious solution is prevention, not cure; prevision, not revision.

The essence of prewriting, as we have said, is the early exploring and judging of the theme idea, but it has been variously defined as prejudging, as the meditative and reflective side of writing, and as the discovery stage. Any one of these definitions may be clearer than the term prewriting itself, since this expression suggests an activity which precedes all writing. But prewriting does not refer to what happens before any writing is done, but what happens before the final writing of the theme has been completed. As we will see in a moment, prewriting involves a great deal of writing in the form of jottings, lists, and other preliminary and purely tentative notes. It is wrong to assume, then, that the moment you put pen to paper you are no longer engaged in the meditative and discovery phase of writing. As long as you are exploring, testing, and judging material prior to the final writing of the composition, you are involved in prewriting.

It is important to note that the discovery stage of writing precedes the outline and rough draft, which are examined in the next section. The outline as conventionally treated consists of a sequence of thought in more or less final form, whereas prewriting, our present concern, deals with ideas which are tentative and fluid. This fact requires emphasis because the student often gets the cart before the horse. He tries to outline his thoughts before he has any thoughts to outline.

There are three elements involved in prewriting: 1) uncovering all of your ideas on a topic, 2) forming your most effective approach from a number of possibilities, and, 3) shaping the material into the desired sequence and noting the overall effect. Consider the following two themes on the same topic—one drawn up immediately in outline form without prewriting, the other prewritten on the basis of the foregoing three elements.

Suppose that the topic selected for your theme is a sentiment which you recorded in your journal—that you have trouble getting along with your roommate. If you outline your ideas at once without further thought, they would read something like this:

I can't get along with my roommate

1) He doesn't keep his half of the room clean.
2) He studies in the middle of the night.
3) He distracts me during the day by bringing in noisy friends.

It is not hard to see that the expanded version of this outline would consist of four or five meagerly developed paragraphs in which the reader would be told what he has heard in the same words a hundred times—that some roommates are hard to live with.

Would revision help this theme? No, because there is nothing there to revise.

What grade would the paper, as projected, receive? At the beginning of the course, perhaps a C or D, depending on the nature of the assignment and the quality of the grammar and diction. As the course progressed, such a theme would be failed as being dull and superficial and not up to college standards. Nor would this grade surprise the student writer. "Yes," he would say, "I knew the paper was empty. It was boring to write and must have been boring to read. But I couldn't come up with anything better. How else could I have written it?"

This question can be answered by submitting the same topic to the first step of the prewriting process, namely, uncovering your ideas on it. In listing, you make no attempt to order and connect the various facets of the topic. Your sole motive is to take a complete inventory of your thoughts just as they occur to you.

I can't get along with my roommate

1) He doesn't keep his half of the room clean.
2) Why can't we choose our own roommates?
3) Roommate relations are important in our mini room situation—10 x 20 foot cubicle, upper and lower bunk, one closet. I pity some of my friends who live three in a room.
4) How to combat territorial expansion in the form of his clothing, shoes, books, and golf equipment.
5) Can't study when he brings in his noisy friends during the day.
6) Freshmen need a course in roommate survival. Should be taught to high school seniors.
7) What are math and music majors supposed to have in common?
8) The inedible stuff he gets from home, like Aunt Martha's cream cake which almost killed me the last time.
9) He studies—when he studies—in the middle of the night.
10) The constant joking and sarcasm that goes on.—You said you were going to flunk out. Is that a promise? Can I have it in writing?

You're becoming an educated fool. Yes, but that's better than being a plain fool.

They named you Donald Loss but I think you'd better change it to Total Loss.

I'm interviewing fools. Tell me, have you been a fool all your life? No, I'm a part-time fool. You're a full-time professional.

11) I will say this for my roomie—he's got a photographic memory (but no mind).
12) How to smile when I'm asked for the nth time—"Are you still studying?"
13) How can a guy like that have such a doll for a sister?
14) He's got a million ideas for themes—all bad. The last ones he gave me were Summer Tan and Christmas Shopping for Mom and Dad. No wonder he majored in math!
15) You don't have to have the patience of Job to live with him—but it sure helps.

As compared with the original outline which represented only one corner of your thought, the above list lays out in full view all of your ideas on the topic. And now, with your material spread out before you, it is almost a pleasure to sort through the possible approaches and select the most effective one. This is the second step in the prewriting operation.

You could center your theme around the idea of needing the patience of Job to get along with your roommate, but look at some of the other slants. How about number 10—the joking and sarcasm which go on? This is good material but you may not want to use it as thesis. Item 6 on roommate survival looks promising—*Two weeks at this college have convinced me that freshmen need a crash course in roommate survival.* You could background this thesis by noting the arbitrary method used in assigning roommates, the crowded rooms and facilities, and then, in the body, you could tie all of your frustrations to the "survival" notion—how to combat territorial expansion, how to snore proof the top bunk, how to smile pleasantly when asked why you are still studying, and how to say no to another piece of Aunt Martha's cream cake. As another support, you could include the amusing material on exchanging sarcasms—how to defend yourself in verbal duels with your roommate. You could, in fact, close your theme with this idea. On the other hand, you might combine the thoughts in items 13 and 14 for your final paragraph—*Since there is little hope of adding a Crash Course in Roommate Survival to the catalogue, it appears that every man must fend for himself. As for me, I intend to try for a compromise. I won't force my roommate to live in the hall if he will promise to, 1) introduce me to his sister, 2) remain extremely silent if I ask him for some theme topics, and, 3) go fifty-fifty on a dorm room divider that is rumored to be on sale at the book store.*

On shaping your material into this sequence of thought, note that you have ample opportunity to prejudge its overall effect (the third step in the prewriting process). Is the informal approach effective or would a serious attitude toward the problem be more advisable? Do you want to treat the section on the verbal duel as a support, as the closing, or should you work it into the introduction as a good means of capturing reader interest? These and other questions will present themselves as you shape the idea, but then, they can be easily resolved because you have not yet written the theme. You are still in the prewriting stage of the operation, and hence it is a simple matter to backtrack, shift blocks of material, add ideas, and rephrase key notions.

A question commonly raised at this point has to do with time. The student grasps the logic of uncovering his thoughts on a topic, choosing the best thesis from a number of possibilities, and shaping the theme as a means of evaluating it, but he wonders if there are enough hours in the day for such an endeavor. But prewriting saves time. You can sort out your thoughts on a topic while you are walking across campus, waiting for a class to begin, or eating your lunch and, with a little practice, you can learn to develop and test out several approaches in your head. By the time you get your thoughts down in outline form on paper, few major changes are required because you have already worked out some clear ideas of what you want to do and how you want to do it. Compare this method with the dreary task of attempting to revise a hastily conceived, second-rate idea into an effective paper.

Some students object to prewriting on the grounds that they write best by composing the entire theme in one creative outpouring. Clearly, if one writes well by using the inspirational "turning on both faucets" method, he should certainly employ it. But if the technique leaves something to be desired in the final product, he should try prewriting his material.

A third point often raised concerns the extent to which prewriting is new. It is not new at all, nor is it peculiar to composition. The skilled photographer employs a similar process every time he takes a picture. He would not dream of clicking the shutter until he had examined and "prejudged" all of the relevant factors of his subject—background, angle, arrangement, distance, and lighting.

The musician engages in this same kind of initial testing. It is not uncommon for him to try out a melody in his head long before he goes near a piano or a score sheet.

Since young writers have always been urged to think through their material—to look before they leap—prewriting is not a new concept in composition. Meanwhile, as a key idea in the writing process, prewriting has not received the emphasis it deserves. The act of thinking through your thoughts before you write is not merely something you might do now and then but something you must never fail to do if you hope to discover your best ideas on a subject and the best means of expressing them.

As a means of further illustrating the value of prewriting, a second example of two themes composed on the same topic is given. We will assume that you have selected the fifty minute class lecture as your starting place and that, without additional thought, you write down in outline form your ideas on the topic.

I am opposed to the fifty minute lecture

1) It's outmoded and should be replaced by a new system which permits student participation.
2) The fifty minute lecture is dull and often covers material that can be read in the text.
3) The students need breaks such as class discussion, films, slides, and quizzes.

At first glance there appears to be a good theme here, but it is an illusion. Merely because you have written out a generalization followed by two or three points of discussion does not mean that you have constructed a logical base for a theme. A closer look at the outline reveals serious problems. Item 1 is listed as a supporting idea but it would serve better as a thesis. If you believe that the fifty minute class lecture is outmoded and should be replaced by a new system which permits student participation, then you should make that specific judgment your thesis rather than the broad statement with which you began.

But now a second problem presents itself. You described the new system as one which "permits student participation." But do not most instructors using the old system permit some student participation in the form of class discussion? To argue this point, you would have to acknowledge the fact that although there is currently some student participation in the classroom, it is not nearly enough. Now look at item 3 in the outline. Here is the bulk of the supporting material for your thesis, but it is crowded into one entry. Since class discussion, films, slides, and quizzes constitute the "new system" which is to replace the old lecture method, you must treat each of these elements separately and in great detail.

The simple truth is that your spur-of-the-moment outline is no outline at all but a jumble of first impressions which would have resulted in a jumbled theme. Can anything good be said of it? Yes, it represents a start, but only a start, in your thinking about the fifty minute class lecture.

Notice that the three items which composed the original outline constitute only a part of the complete list which follows, and be again reminded that in prewriting, the first objective is to uncover your thoughts on the topic; hence the ideas below were jotted down willy nilly as they presented themselves.

I am opposed to the fifty minute lecture

1) It's outmoded and should be replaced by a new system which permits student participation.

2) The fifty minute lecture is dull and often covers material that can be read in the text.

3) The students need breaks such as class discussion, films, slides, and quizzes.

4) Few professors have the skill to keep students alert during an unbroken fifty minute lecture and even fewer have the ability to do this week after week.

5) In using the fifty minute lecture, professors attempt the impossible. When they fail to hold the attention of the class, they blame the students and sometimes they question their own teaching ability.

6) Interview students and faculty on the long lecture as to problem and solution.

7) Should the lecture be thrown out completely? No, it is needed to give direction and goals to the course.

8) The straight lecture has some advantages. The teacher can talk from prepared notes and stay on schedule throughout the semester. But the mixed lecture, which includes class discussion, student reports, etc., can achieve these same ends: in both instances the teacher can be guided by notes.—Then what are the advantages of the straight lecture?

9) How about using the circle method? The chairs are arranged in a circle and the instructor acts as chairman. The students do most of the talking and thus teach themselves. The circle method is more effective used as an occasional technique than as the only technique; otherwise, the course would lose unity and emphasis, and become uninteresting.

10) Should the instructor include his own point of view as a means of injecting added interest or should he withhold this rather than risk brainwashing his class?

11) Variety is the spice of the college classroom. Instructors should audit one another's classes and meet together as a means of finding

effective classroom teaching devices. One teacher can know as much as eleven teachers if he is willing to learn from eleven.

12) Extremes should be avoided. Too little lecturing is as bad as too much.

13) As an example of the mixed lecture experts, mention Paul Samuelson, high school history teacher. He used surprise quizzes, challenging assignments (If Hitler had won, technology in America in the year 2070), rapid fire questioning, and his own experiences as a boy in the wilds of northern Minnesota, as a pilot in World War II, and as a family man (six kids).

Rather than attempt to discuss all of the benefits to be derived from this example of prewriting, we will limit our remarks to some of the most important ones. First of all, in forming your approach you would probably now reject item 1 as thesis because as you jotted down ideas a more convincing position became clear. Thus, rather than replace the old lecture system with a new one, you might argue that the old system should be retained but radically revised in regard to student participation. This view is supported in notes 7 and 12 in which you stated that some lecture is needed to give direction and goals to the material, and that a course which consisted of no lecture would be as bad as all lecture. An additional detail could be drawn from your observation on the circle method of teaching.

As build-up material in your opening paragraphs, you might wish to mention the natural limitations of the "straight" lecture and the fact that some professors blame themselves rather than the system when they lose rapport with their class. Having created reader interest, you are now ready to support your thesis by spelling out how the old system should be revised. Here you might be wise to follow your own lead and interview students and faculty as to the particular kinds of class discussion, films, and quizzes which could be used. Since these points will constitute the body of your theme, you need plenty of details on each. You would certainly include as a supporting idea the example of the high school "mixed lecture expert." An effective closing could be drawn by advising college teachers to audit classes and meet together as a means of achieving variety in their teaching.

At this point it is important to note the difference between prewriting a thesis and prewriting a subject. Thus far our analysis has dealt with theses. Beginning with a specific purpose idea such as the case against the fifty minute lecture, we have prewritten our thoughts in order to find the needed particulars. But in many instances the writer does not begin with a specific purpose idea. In this case he must explore a general subject to find a suitable thesis.

Let us suppose that you have been assigned the general topic of television for your next theme. Since you have no idea of a thesis and since the subject has innumerable possibilities, your first task is to divide it into smaller parts. Jotting down your ideas as they occur, you might prewrite a list something like this one.

Television

1) detective shows
2) cowboy movies
3) soap opera ("daytime serials" and the new "doctor shows")
4) give-away shows—panels and panelists
5) comedy—keep farm humor down on the farm
6) children's programs (mostly bad, especially those unimaginative and unending cartoon shows)
7) cliches in old Westerns—Let's head 'em off at the pass! and, Throw down that money box!
8) news reporters versus news analysts
9) TV of the future (kinds of programs)
10) European TV offerings
11) educational TV (is there such a thing?)
12) pay TV not discussed anymore
13) telephone-TV combination—see whom you're talking to
14) commercials—scourge of TV
15) ban the cigarette commercial on TV. Will it do any good?
16) color TV

In looking over your list you note that the items on detective shows and TV of the future are subjects in themselves which would require further division and that others such as your opposition to cartoon shows for children and TV cigarette commercials might make good theses as they stand. But your interest is caught by item 7—the cliches found in old Western movies.

To further explore the idea, you make this facet your new heading and prewrite your thoughts on it.

Cliches in Old Western Movies

1) Let's head 'em off at the pass! and, Throw down that money box!
2) No saddle tramp is going to marry my daughter!
3) This calls for a celebration, boys! Name your poison!
4) They're holed up in those rocks!
5) Outlaws trap hero and young school marm in old abandoned mine.
6) Saloon girl is shot in saving good guy from Dirty Dan who is hiding behind the staircase.
7) Hero rides off on Old Paint into the sunset.

8) Shifty-eyed bartender reaches sneakily for a rifle, ranchers vow to burn out peaceful sheep herders, and clean-cut newcomer in town stops unfair fight by stepping on bad guy's whip.

9) Sheriff and his deputy exchange silent glances as they come upon CIRCLING VULTURES.

10) Shot in the heart three times, the town doctor delivers a ten minute dying speech.

11) Indians who speak flawless English.

12) Rustler fires eight shots from a six-shooter without reloading.

It now becomes apparent that you have the material to write a humorous slant on old Westerns, but observe that your list has turned up, not merely additional cliches, but stereotyped scenes (the saloon girl, the shifty-eyed bartender, and the clean-cut newcomer) as well as classic boners (the ten minute dying speech, Indians who speak perfect English, and six-guns that shoot eight times). Your now expanded thesis could read, *No one should complain about TV's old Western movies. The cliches, stereotyped scenes, and classic boners which they offer provide endless entertainment.*

Observe that we began with a subject and prewrote our way through several lists to a specific thesis and the chief topics required to support it.

As proof that the technique of prewriting is not the exclusive property of composition teachers, and also to provide you with a very clear description of the discovery stage in writing, read the following exchange from Dr. T. I. Rubin's question and answer column, "A Psychiatrist's Notebook" (*McCall's*, July, 1967). Although Dr. Rubin does not use the term "prewriting," this is the very method which he recommends to the student.

QUESTION: I am twenty years old. I'm a junior in college, and my grades are fairly good. *But* I have a terrible time writing papers. Once I get started, I'm all right. But I can sit like a dunce trying to organize my thoughts, and hours (literally) go by, with nothing happening. Since I'm hoping to go to graduate school, I am terribly concerned. Have you any practical suggestions?

ANSWER: Try *not* to organize your thoughts into logical, complete patterns. If you wait until it is all in mind perfectly, you may wait a long time!

Remember that one thought brings on another, associations bring on more associations. Our goal here is to start the associative machinery working.

How? The trick is to start. The solution lies in the starting.

How? Write whatever comes to mind pertaining to the subject, and utterly disregard logic, organization, grades and teacher response. After, only after, there is considerable material—words on paper—take a look. Observe what you have. Do these thoughts lead to more thoughts? Are there any points of particular interest? Anything present deserving of more research? *After* this *start* has taken place, you may well find that a central theme presents itself, so that a logical assembly can now take place with relative ease.

It has perhaps now occurred to you that prewriting is really free writing, and it is this freedom which enables the writer to discover creative ideas and his own style of expression. Of course, outlines, and rough drafts have their uses too, as we will see in the section which follows.

Outlines and Rough Drafts

Some teachers regard the composing of the outline and rough draft as part of the prewriting process and some separate the two in order to emphasize the purely exploratory side of writing. The difference is probably academic: as long as you understand that the first step in composition is not a hastily conceived outline, but rather a careful exploration of your ideas on the topic, you should experience little difficulty in the initial planning of your themes. But since prewriting can affect the kind of outline and rough draft which you use and even the extent to which you use them, it is necessary to take a close look at these written plans as they are traditionally taught.

There are roughly two kinds of outlines—the formal and the informal. Perhaps the least useful is the formal "sentence outline" in which every idea in a projected theme is laid out and labelled as a major heading, a subheading of the first degree, the second degree, the third, and so on.

Sentence Outline

THESIS
I.
   A.
      1.
      2.
         a.
         b.
            (1)
            (2)
   B.
      1.
         a.
         b.
      2.
         a.
         b.

Since the sentence outline forces the writer to carefully order and subdivide his ideas, it can provide a step by step control of the material, particularly as applied to a long treatise which requires extensive research. But for most student compositions the formal outline is a hindrance rather than a help.

One problem is the many numbers and letters which are used in marking the divisions. Instead of weighing the relevance and clarity of a line, the writer often finds himself puzzling over whether to label it *A* or *a*.

A second problem is the illusion of completeness conveyed by the formal plan. What appears to be a fully worked out scheme is in fact an outline of the ideas in the body of the paper. The material needed for the two other vital parts—the lead and closing paragraphs—is usually excluded. It is doubtful that the writer will look for effective opening and closing statements in the prewriting stage if his outline does not make provisions for them.

A third problem occurs when the student, misjudging the completeness of his plan, tries to convert the formal outline into the finished theme simply by forming the material into paragraphs. This results in the familiar wooden, mechanical writing marked by graceless transitions and the absence of those nuances and sidelights which give prose its movement and style.

The limited sentence outline is more realistic. In this plan, the writer limits the division of his main topics to subheadings of the first degree, which leaves him free to add touches and new ideas to his outlined thoughts as he writes his theme.

Limited Sentence Outline

THESIS   I will never forget the happy days I spent as a boy at my grandfather's cabin on the Neosho River.
I. The approach to the cabin was an exciting world of sights and sounds.
    A. Birds of all kinds nested in the thick tangle of trees and brush.
    B. Rabbits, squirrels, chipmunks, and other small game scurried across the dirt road.
    C. As one approached the river, the deep droning of frogs blended with the bird calls to form a symphony.
II. The cabin was a home-made affair, small but serviceable.
    A. Grandpa boasted that he had made the cabin himself from river wood —and it looked that way.
    B. The six bunks and old lead wood table did not leave much elbow room inside.
III. The river had a morning, noon, and night appearance.
    A. In the early morning the river was viewed through a steamy mist which rose from its surface.
    B. At noon, the twists, inlets, riffles, and deep channels dominated the eye.
    C. The evening shadows created the impression that the river rolled on endlessly, having no beginning and no end.
IV. We caught fish of all sizes, shapes, and kinds.
    A. The largest fish were the catfish taken on trot lines.
    B. We also caught drum, crappy, bass, and perch.
    C. The strangest catches were the dogfish, gar, and hairfish.

The "topic outline" is a second kind of formal plan. It differs from the sentence outline only in that short phrases, rather than complete sentences, are used to mark the ideas.

Compare the topic version below with the sentence outline of the same section.

Topic Outline

I. The sights and sounds on approaching the cabin
    A. Birds of all kinds
    B. Small game
    C. Droning of frogs

Professional writers rarely employ formal outlines in their pure form. Instead they use a variety of informal plans: a mixed topic and sentence outline, a "scratch outline" of numbered points, or no outline at all if the prewritten list of material provides a clear idea of the pattern of thought which the writer wishes to employ. Since the original list of thoughts contains most of the details needed for the composition, the writer usually requires only a simple informal outline to give his ideas direction and coherence. He can, of course (and you may if you wish), write out a formal outline complete with labels which contains the full particulars for each heading and subheading in the paper, but usually this is not necessary. Aside from encouraging a choppy, artificial writing style in the finished theme, there is no need to repeat in an outline what has already been laid out in the initial list of your thoughts.

In a moment an example will be provided of a theme as it is composed through the various stages of the writing process. But first, be reminded that there are a dozen ways of planning a paper. The only right way is the technique which works for you, as evidenced by the excellence of the finished copy. Remember, too, that the plan which proved effective in one assignment may not fit another. The only constant in composition is prewriting, and even here practice varies. For example, impromptu theme assignments and on-the-spot writing situations will certainly prevent extensive prewriting. Also, writers differ in the kind and number of thoughts which they include in a prewritten list. Some prefer to jot down every conceivable idea in a two or three page list, some make several exploratory lists and omit the outline, and some prewrite in their heads so extensively that their first written effort takes the form of a rough draft.

To illustrate the composing of a theme as it is carried out through the prewriting, outline, and rough draft stages, let us assume that you have been asked to review a magic act to be given at your school. Armed with pencil and paper, you take a seat up front in the auditorium and await the arrival of "Marlowe, Master Magician."

The following list represents your prewritten observations as they occurred during the performance and those which you added later.

Marlowe the Magician

1) If Marlowe does the usual rabbit in the hat stuff, he'll have a tough audience on his hands. In a world of scientific marvels, these students won't be impressed with parlor tricks.

2) Marlowe gave a good opening comment about the two requirements of the ancient art of magic—a man skillful enough to fool you and people young enough at heart to enjoy being fooled.

3) Very effective first trick. Made a coin roll over his hand. Showed how "easy" it was by rolling two coins—one in each hand.

4) Went through impressive array of coin tricks—appearing, disappearing, multiplying coins.

   Good use of spotlight on M's hands (semidarkened stage).

   Got applause on the "coins from the air" routine in which he pulled silver dollars from nowhere—with rolled up sleeves.

   He's right in referring to his "ten talents" (ten fingers).

5) M. is short, medium build, dark hair. Seems taller because of commanding manner.

6) Knows how to handle students. Said he was sorry his act lacked political relevance, but he would vanish a Dean "if anybody had captured one lately."

7) Works well up close. Went down into the aisles, pulling coins out of students' hats and books.

   Managed to lift two watches, a wallet, and a belt from the audience.

   Asked owners to come on stage and claim their belongings.

8) M. is far better than other magicians I've seen. Why?

9) Interesting lecture-type intro to cards, the second half of his show. Spoke of history of cards—origin and changing design—and the names of famous card manipulators.

10) Beautiful sequence of card moves. In a five minute "warm up" exercise, M. did all the standard flourishes—the card waterfall, the boomerang (throws card into air and catches it, as it comes back) and the card fans.

11) Prestidigitator (?)

12) Got nods of approval from audience when he put on gloves before doing "the classic front and back hand palms" (made famous by Thurston, King of Cards).

13) Where are all the old tricks using guillotines, boxes, and trunks? Doesn't M. have an assistant?

14) For his next trick, M. asked student from audience to bring up new and still wrapped deck of cards and play poker with him.

M. at his best here. From deck shuffled and cut by student, M. dealt himself a royal flush and the student a hand of blank cards.

15) Last trick, M. observed that since he disliked carrying around heavy equipment, he restricted his act to "a few coins here in my pocket and this pack of cards—and I can get rid of it in a hurry." Made cards disappear one by one—saved last one, flipped it out into the audience as a souvenir, doffed his hat with a "Good evening," and the curtain came down on a first-rate performance.

16) Didn't hear catcalls and cries of "Fake!" from the audience. M. didn't do corny box tricks with false bottoms, springs, and mirrors. He relied upon sleight of hand—skill, not equipment ordered from catalogues.

17) Which came first in history of magic—sleight of hand or box tricks? Would make interesting research.

18) Hand magic deceives, but isn't false in the sense that box magic is, which has built-in gimmicks. Anybody can order the equipment from a catalogue and do the trick—but sleight of hand requires skill and talent.

19) Contrast M. with comic magicians who muff tricks for humorous effect, escape artists, mind readers, and stage hypnotists.

20) Just remembered M. didn't use music—always part of the act of old-style magicians. I remember the magic act I saw in high school.

Your prewriting effort has resulted in an abundance of detail which includes sidelights, your own observations, and a related personal experience. You can also see from your notes that the general divisions of the body of your review will probably follow the sequence of Marlowe's performance—you will divide your discussion into coin tricks and card tricks. But you are not ready to outline until you find an interesting slant, a focus which will attract and hold the reader.

The fact that you were very favorably impressed with Marlowe's show will not do as a thesis because it lacks specific purpose. In item 8 you asked why Marlowe was better than most magicians and in your later notes (items 16–20) you answered this question by showing that Marlowe is a superior performer because he presents hand magic, not box tricks. All of your thoughts on old-style magic and the skill required to perform sleight of hand can be assembled to support this view.

At this point you see your thesis as, *Marlowe's act was surprisingly good because he offered sleight of hand magic, not box tricks with built-in gimmicks.* Since you need an introduction which will make the reader sit up and take notice, you might include as background some details on old-style versus new-style magic.

For your closing, you could suggest that apprentice magicians should follow Marlowe's lead in doing hand magic.

Outlines and Rough Drafts   33

The outline below consists of a sequence of numbered parts, a mixture of topic, sentence, and paragraph entries, and provisions for the opening and closing. It may not look like the written plan which you have made in the past, but remember that this outline was composed from, and will be used with, a detailed list of prewritten ideas. Notice also the additions and other changes which have been made in some of the entries.

> THESIS: Marlowe's act was good because he offered sleight of hand magic, not box tricks with built-in gimmicks.
>
> 1) Lead—Those who attended Marlowe's magic show expecting to see the rabbit from the hat trick and other feats reminiscent of old-style magicians were in for a pleasant surprise. Marlowe presented a brilliant array of coin and card manipulations which held even the most cynical spectator spellbound during the fifty minute performance. (Get in reference to vanishing a Dean?)
> 2) Breaks ice with "young at heart" comment and "finger exercise" trick.
> 3) Describe coins from air sequence.
> 4) Get in incident about "solid objects" and President Malley.
> 5) Get in Marlowe's reference to his "ten talents."
> 6) Worked in aisles with audience.
> 7) Pick pocket routine (Lost and Found Department).
> 8) Lecture-type intro to cards.
> 9) Does standard card flourishes—the waterfall, etc.
> 10) At this point has held audience for 25 minutes without using any big stage equipment.
> 11) Put on gloves for classic front and back hand palms.
> 12) Highlight of card manipulation—poker game. Get in question which Marlowe asked the student.
> 13) Perfect closing number—vanishes cards, doffs hat.
> 14) Explain absence of hissing and cries of "Fake!" Show that charge of fakery doesn't apply to sleight of hand. Get in use of music to illustrate old-style magic.
> 15) Close with—Aspiring young prestidigitators can take a clue from Marlowe to travel light. All they need is a deck of cards, a few coins, and the ten talents of a master magician like Marlowe.

In composing the rough draft, the third stage of the writing process, you will work freely with your material, going from outline to prewritten list and back again, just as a painter dips his brush into one color and then another to achieve the desired effect.

And in shaping your theme you will draw from three sources: the prewritten list, the outline, and the ideas in your head. It is wrong to believe that because an idea was not included in your written plan, you cannot use it in the rough draft. If a good idea presents itself, put it in. As you have perhaps already discovered, prewriting works by association to lead you to ideas you never knew you had.

The rough draft also represents a refinement of the original material in content and style—lines are recast, missing details are added, transitionals are provided, and greater attention is paid to word choice. But we are still dealing with *rough* copy, as indicated by the crossed out passages and other changes in the draft which follows.

Marlowe the Magician Travels Light

Those who attended Marlowe's magic show/ were in for a pleasant surprise. Instead of the rabbit from the hat trick/ and other feats reminiscent of old-style magicians, Marlowe presented a brilliant array of coin and card manipulations which held even the most cynical spectator spellbound during the fifty minute performance. [last Tuesday night at the college auditorium; the levitation act]

The only reference to old-fashioned stage magic came early in the performance when Marlowe, noting that his show lacked political relevance, agreed to vanish a Dean "if anybody has captured one lately."

Marlowe broke the ice with his student audience by observing that there are two requirements of the ancient art of magic—a magician skillful enough to fool you and people still young enough at heart to enjoy being fooled. He then performed a "finger exercise" trick in which he made a coin roll/ over and under his hand. [obediently] To illustrate how "easy" it was, Marlowe rolled two coins simultaneously—one in each hand. The sight of the glittering coins revolving in the spotlight and the casual manner in which Marlowe performed got the show off to a good start.

The high point of the first half of the act came with the "coins from the air" routine. Marlowe—with his sleeves rolled up—pulled stacks of silver dollars from the air. A humorous incident occurred when the magician showed that he could pass a coin through a "solid object"—in this case the head of O. F. Malley, the president of the college. Marlowe then went down into the aisles and produced coins from students' hats and books, at which time he also cleverly managed to lift two watches, a wallet, and a belt. After the owners had claimed their belongings on stage, Marlowe chided them good naturedly by asking, "What do you think this is—the Lost and Found Department of the college?"

Marlowe introduced the second half of his show with a short lecture on the history of cards—their origin, original design, and the names of some famous card manipulators. This was followed by an impressive series of card flourishes—the waterfall, in which the deck of cards is sprung in an arc from hand to hand; the boomerang, which requires the skill to throw cards into the air and catch them as they spin back; and the beautiful card fans, which open and close, shrink and expand, at the flick of a wrist.

At this point in the show Marlowe had held his audience for twenty-five minutes without using a single piece of apparatus. All he needed, as he put it, was his "ten talents" (ten fingers).

There were nods of approval when the magician put on a pair of/gloves [felt] before doing "the classic front and back hand palms." These sleights, which involve concealing the cards behind the hand as it is turned front and back to the audience, were made famous by Thurston, King of Cards, who, according to Marlowe, also performed with gloves. The audience, obviously pleased with this portion of the act, asked for more.

The highlight of Marlowe's card work centered around a poker game with a student from the audience, who brought to the stage a new and still wrapped deck of cards. The two sat down at a card table and after the student had shuffled the deck and cut it repeatedly, Marlowe dealt himself a royal flush and the student a hand of blank cards.

Asked if he had learned anything, the student replied, "Yes, don't play poker with magicians!"

In preparation for his final trick, Marlowe observed that since he disliked carrying around heavy equipment, he restricted his act "to a few coins here in my pocket and this pack of cards—and I can get rid of it in a hurry." He then made the cards disappear one by one—except for the last one which he ~~signed~~/ [autographed] and spun into the balcony as a souvenir. Then, doffing his hat and bidding his audience good night, he signaled for the curtain—which came down on a first-rate performance.

There was a noticeable absence of hissing and cries of "Fake" from the audience which one usually associates with magic performances. This is because Marlowe did not offer box tricks with false bottoms, springs, and mirrors. He relied solely upon sleight of hand. Actually, hand magic deceives, but it is not false in the sense that box magic is, which has built-in gimmicks. Anybody who has the box can do the trick—but sleight of hand requires training and talent.

Also missing was the music which old-style magicians use to background their act. In the last magic show I saw, doves, rabbits, several untrained assistants who got in the way, Chinese rice bowls, collapsing bird cages, and parts for the guillotine number were all brought on stage to the accompaniment of a phonograph playing "The Sorcerer's Apprentice."

Aspiring young prestidigitators can take a clue from this excellent performance and "travel light." All they need are a few coins, a deck of cards—and the "ten talents" of Marlowe, truly a Master Magician!

The fact that the above copy does not include all of the material in the outline and prewritten list is another example to prove that the writer is not the slave of his written plan. The unused notes also reflect the fullness of the prewriting effort. As professionals say, if you don't have more material than you need, you don't have enough.

This concludes our examination of the preliminaries. You should now have some notion of what informative-persuasive prose is, and how it is written. In the next chapter you will be asked to apply your knowledge of form, language, audience, and the writing process to a very important type of everyday prose—the news story.

3

News Stories

A primary purpose of news stories is to inform us about current events; newspapers and news weeklies are perused to "get the facts."

But if the sources of news are really going to inform, then the writers themselves must know what they write about. This means that they must research their stories; they must dig for the information. They have to question relevant people or seek out significant written records. A news writer, for instance, may read up on a technicality in the law in order to understand a fine legal point, or he may discuss it with legal experts, but he has to know the law in question in order to do a good story on a trial. In fact, good research supplies both substance and quality to a story and the best are written by writers who can ferret out the facts.

Once a writer has gathered his material, he must organize it into an attractive whole. Most news stories follow some variation of a chronological order. They recount happenings which had a time sequence, so that the stories reflect that order of events.

There are a few news stories which follow a straight clock chronology, telling the details of a happening in the same sequence in which it occurred. A story about a lady's encounter with a bear in her back yard, in Warren, North Dakota, for one instance, can be told in this sequence: 1) Mrs. Gatling came out of her back door to hang up wet laundry, 2) She saw a bear in her back yard, 3) She chased the bear off with a broom.

More often, however, news stories do not follow a strict chronological order, because news writers like to start with an eye-catching preview of what will follow. They open with a lead—the salient features of the story contained in a paragraph or two.

It is sometimes said that the lead should answer several basic questions: who? what? when? where? why? and how? Of course, not many leads can answer all those questions, but they usually provide answers to some of them.

The story about Mrs. Gatling and the bear, for example, might start with a brief mention of the climax of the event: the fact that she chased the bear away with a broom. After such an opening, a writer might then return to a chronological sequence to relate the incidents which led up to that conclusion.

Notice, too, that any aspect of the bear story, such as background material or sidelights, might be developed in detail. A writer might wish to go into the possibility that Mrs. Gatling may be a fearless woman who has shown her courage on other occasions, or he might wish to pursue the recent history of other bear encounters near Warren, North Dakota. And the further development of any such peripheral points can be added to the story after the main features of the event have been told.

Whatever the pattern of organization, most news stories have a rather distinctive style. For one thing, they are often liberally decorated with dialogue. Statements by participants usually appear throughout the piece. The vocabulary is generally not technical or academic and the sentences tend to be short, with a subject, verb, object, order. And a most distinctive feature is that the short paragraphs, sometimes only a sentence or two in length, are designed to break up the column of type, because readers may be turned away by forbidding solid blocks of print.

How long should news stories be? The answer depends on the expected audience. The local news weekly in Warren, North Dakota, would probably carry a more elaborate account of Mrs. Gatling's bear baiting than the two or three paragraphs that might appear in an urban daily, because a local audience would be more interested in the details of their neighbor's curious experience than those who do not know her.

If a news story reflects the writer's research as well as his judgment of what is important, then news stories can never be strictly objective. The writer's judgment, his point of view, and his values, will inevitably color his account. For this reason, news stories may be considered persuasive as well as informative. They give us the writer's view of the world, his notion of what is important. And the more skilled the writer, the more the reader is apt to be persuaded by his account.

To conclude this brief survey of the news story, we can see that any story must first be researched and then carefully structured. There are many ways to do this, as you will see when you examine the actual news stories which follow. The samples will illustrate the principles discussed here, but do not end your study of news stories with these few illustrations. Learn to look closely at your own news sources in order to see just how these writers fashion their informative-persuasive prose.

Kennedy Is Killed by Sniper as He Rides in Car in Dallas; Johnson Sworn In on Plane

TOM WICKER

Dallas, *Nov. 22*—President John Fitzgerald Kennedy was shot and killed by an assassin today.

He died of a wound in the brain caused by a rifle bullet that was fired at him as he was riding through downtown Dallas in a motorcade.

Vice President Lyndon Baines Johnson, who was riding in the third car behind Mr. Kennedy's, was sworn in as the 36th President of the United States 99 minutes after Mr. Kennedy's death.

Mr. Johnson is 55 years old; Mr. Kennedy was 46.

Shortly after the assassination, Lee H. Oswald, who once defected to the Soviet Union and who has been active in the Fair Play for Cuba Committee, was arrested by the Dallas police. Tonight he was accused of the killing.

SUSPECT CAPTURED AFTER SCUFFLE

Oswald, 24 years old, was also accused of slaying a policeman who had approached him in the street. Oswald was subdued after a scuffle with a second policeman in a nearby theater.

President Kennedy was shot at 12:30 P.M., Central standard time (1:30 P.M., New York time). He was pronounced dead at 1 P.M. and Mr. Johnson was sworn in at 2:39 P.M.

Mr. Johnson, who was uninjured in the shooting, took his oath in the Presidential jet plane as it stood on the runway at Love Field. The body of Mr. Kennedy was aboard.

Immediately after the oath-taking, the plane took off for Washington.

Standing beside the new President as Mr. Johnson took the oath of office was Mrs. John F. Kennedy. Her stockings were spattered with her husband's blood.

Gov. John B. Connally Jr. of Texas, who was riding in the same car with Mr. Kennedy, was severely wounded in the chest, ribs and arm. His condition was serious, but not critical.

The killer fired the rifle from a building just off the motorcade route. Mr. Kennedy, Governor Connally and Mr. Johnson had just received an enthusiastic welcome from a large crowd in downtown Dallas.

Mr. Kennedy apparently was hit by the first of what witnesses believed were three shots. He was driven at high speed to Dallas's Parkland Hospital. There, in an emergency operating room, with only physicians and nurses in attendance, he died without regaining consciousness.

Mrs. Kennedy, Mrs. Connally and a Secret Service agent were in the car with Mr. Kennedy and Governor Connally. Two Secret Service agents flanked the car. Other than Mr. Connally, none of this group was injured in the shooting. Mrs. Kennedy cried, "Oh no!" immediately after her husband was struck.

Mrs. Kennedy was in the hospital near her husband when he died, but not in the operating room. When the body was taken from the hospital in a bronze coffin about 2 P.M., Mrs. Kennedy walked beside it.

Condensed from *The New York Times*, November 23, 1963, © 1963 by The New York Times Company. Reprinted by permission.

Her face was sorrowful. She looked steadily at the floor. She still wore the raspberry-colored suit in which she had greeted welcoming crowds in Fort Worth and Dallas. But she had taken off the matching pillbox hat she wore earlier in the day, and her dark hair was windblown and tangled. Her hand rested lightly on her husband's coffin as it was taken to a waiting hearse.

Mrs. Kennedy climbed in beside the coffin. Then the ambulance drove to Love Field, and Mr. Kennedy's body was placed aboard the Presidential jet. Mrs. Kennedy then attended the swearing-in ceremony for Mr. Johnson....

Mr. Johnson was sworn in as President by Federal Judge Sarah T. Hughes of the Northern District of Texas. She was appointed to the judgeship by Mr. Kennedy in October, 1961.

The ceremony, delayed about five minutes for Mrs. Kennedy's arrival, took place in the private Presidential cabin in the rear of the plane....

Mrs. Johnson, wearing a beige dress, stood at her husband's right.

As Judge Hughes read the brief oath of office, her eyes, too, were red from weeping. Mr. Johnson's hand rested on a black, leather-bound Bible as Judge Hughes read and he repeated:

"I do solemnly swear that I will perform the duties of the President of the United States to the best of my ability and defend, protect and preserve the Constitution of the United States."

Those 34 words made Lyndon Baines Johnson, one-time farmboy and schoolteacher of Johnson City, the President.

JOHNSON EMBRACES MRS. KENNEDY

Mr. Johnson made no statement. He embraced Mrs. Kennedy and she held his hand for a long moment. He also embraced Mrs. Johnson and Mrs. Evelyn Lincoln, Mr. Kennedy's private secretary.

"O.K.," Mr. Johnson said, "Let's get this plane back to Washington."

At 2:46 P.M., seven minutes after he had become President, 106 minutes after Mr. Kennedy had become the fourth American President to succumb to an assassin's wounds, the white and red jet took off for Washington.

In the cabin when Mr. Johnson took the oath was Cecil Stoughton, an armed forces photographer assigned to the White House.

Mr. Kennedy's staff members appeared stunned and bewildered. Lawrence F. O'Brien, the Congressional liaison officer, and P. Kenneth O'Donnell, the appointment secretary, both long associates of Mr. Kennedy, showed evidences of weeping. None had anything to say.

Other staff members believed to be in the cabin for the swearing-in included David F. Powers, the White House receptionist; Miss Pamela Turnure, Mrs. Kennedy's press secretary, and Malcolm Kilduff, the assistant White House press secretary.

Mr. Kilduff announced the President's death, with choked voice and red-rimmed eyes, at about 1:36 P.M.

"President John F. Kennedy died at approximately 1 o'clock Central standard time today here in Dallas," Mr. Kilduff said at the hospital. "He died of a gunshot wound in the brain. I have no other details regarding the assassination of the President."

Mr. Kilduff also announced that Governor Connally had been hit by a bullet or bullets and that Mr. Johnson, who had not yet been sworn in, was safe in the protective custody of the Secret Service at an unannounced place, presumably the airplane at Love Field.

Mr. Kilduff indicated that the President had been shot once. Later medical reports raised the possibility that there had been two wounds. But the death was caused, as far as could be learned, by a massive wound in the brain.

Later in the afternoon, Dr. Malcolm Perry, an attending surgeon, and Dr. Kemp Clark, chief of neurosurgery at Parkland Hospital, gave more details.

Mr. Kennedy was hit by a bullet in the throat, just below the Adam's apple, they said. This wound had the appearance of a bullet's entry.

Mr. Kennedy also had a massive, gaping wound in the back and one on the right side of the head. However, the doctors said it was impossible to determine immediately whether the wounds had been caused by one bullet or two. . . .

The details of what happened when shots first rang out, as the President's car moved along at about 25 miles an hour, were sketchy. Secret Service agents, who might have given more details, were unavailable to the press at first, and then returned to Washington with President Johnson.

KENNEDYS HAILED AT BREAKFAST

Mr. Kennedy had opened his day in Fort Worth, first with a speech in a parking lot and then at a Chamber of Commerce breakfast. The breakfast appearance was a particular triumph for Mrs. Kennedy, who entered late and was given an ovation.

Then the Presidential party, including Governor and Mrs. Connally, flew on to Dallas, an eight-minute flight. Mr. Johnson, as is customary, flew in a separate plane. The President and the Vice President do not travel together, out of fear of a double tragedy.

At Love Field, Mr. and Mrs. Kennedy lingered for 10 minutes, shaking hands with an enthusiastic group lining the fence. The group called itself "Grassroots Democrats."

Mr. Kennedy then entered his open Lincoln convertible at the head of the motorcade. He sat in the rear seat on the right-hand side. Mrs. Kennedy, who appeared to be enjoying one of the first political outings she had ever made with her husband, sat at his left.

In the "jump" seat, directly ahead of Mr. Kennedy, sat Governor Connally, with Mrs. Connally at his left in another "jump" seat. A Secret Service agent was driving and the two others ran alongside.

Behind the President's limousine was an open sedan carrying a number of Secret Service agents. Behind them, in an open convertible, rode Mr. and Mrs. Johnson and Texas's senior Senator, Ralph W. Yarborough, a Democrat.

The motorcade proceeded uneventfully along a 10-mile route through downtown Dallas, aiming for the Merchandise Mart. Mr. Kennedy was to address a group of the city's leading citizens at a luncheon in his honor.

In downtown Dallas, crowds were thick, enthusiastic and cheering. The turnout was somewhat unusual for this center of conservatism, where only a month ago Adlai E. Stevenson was attacked by a rightist crowd. It was also in Dallas, during the 1960 campaign, that Senator Lyndon B. Johnson and his wife were nearly mobbed in the lobby of the Baker Hotel.

As the motorcade neared its end and the President's car moved out of the thick crowds onto Stennonds Freeway near the Merchandise Mart, Mrs. Connally recalled later, "we were all very pleased with the reception in downtown Dallas."

APPROACHING 3-STREET UNDERPASS

Behind the three leading cars were a string of others carrying Texas and Dallas dignitaries, two buses of reporters, several open cars carrying photographers and other reporters, and a bus for White House staff members.

As Mrs. Connally recalled later, the President's car was almost ready to go underneath a "triple underpass" beneath three streets—Elm, Commerce and Main—when the first shot was fired.

That shot apparently struck Mr. Kennedy. Governor Connally turned in his seat at the sound and appeared immediately to be hit in the chest.

Mrs. Mary Norman of Dallas was standing at the curb and at that moment was aiming her camera at the President. She saw him slump forward, then slide down in the seat.

"My God," Mrs. Norman screamed, as she recalled it later, "he's shot!"

Mrs. Connally said that Mrs. Kennedy had

reached and "grabbed" her husband. Mrs. Connally put her arms around the Governor. Mrs. Connally said that she and Mrs. Kennedy had then ducked low in the car as it sped off.

Mrs. Connally's recollections were reported by Julian Reade, an aide to the Governor.

Most reporters in the press buses were too far back to see the shootings, but they observed some quick scurrying by motor policemen accompanying the motorcade. It was noted that the President's car had picked up speed and raced away, but reporters were not aware that anything serious had occurred until they reached the Merchandise Mart two or three minutes later.

RUMORS SPREAD AT TRADE MART

Rumors of the shooting already were spreading through the luncheon crowd of hundreds, which was having the first course. No White House officials or Secret Service agents were present, but the reporters were taken quickly to Parkland Hospital on the strength of the rumors.

There they encountered Senator Yarborough, white, shaken and horrified.

The shots, he said, seemed to have come from the right and the rear of the car in which he was riding, the third in the motorcade. Another eyewitness, Mel Crouch, a Dallas television reporter, reported that as the shots rang out he saw a rifle extended and then withdrawn from a window on the "fifth or sixth floor" of the Texas Public School Book Depository. This is a leased state building on Elm Street, to the right of the motorcade route.

Senator Yarborough said there had been a slight pause between the first two shots and a longer pause between the second and third. A Secret Service man riding in the Senator's car, the Senator said, immediately ordered Mr. and Mrs. Johnson to get down below the level of the doors. They did so and Senator Yarborough also got down.

The leading cars of the motorcade then pulled away at high speed toward Parkland Hospital, which was not far away, by the fast highway.

"We knew by the speed that something was terribly wrong," Senator Yarborough reported. When he put his head up, he said, he saw a Secret Service man in the car ahead beating his fists against the trunk deck of the car in which he was riding, apparently in frustration and anguish.

MRS. KENNEDYS REACTION

Only White House staff members spoke with Mrs. Kennedy. A Dallas medical student, David Edwards, saw her in Parkland Hospital while she was waiting for news of her husband. He gave this description:

"The look in her eyes was like an animal that had been trapped, like a little rabbit—brave, but fear was in the eyes."

Dr. Clark was reported to have informed Mrs. Kennedy of her husband's death.

No witnesses reported seeing or hearing any of the Secret Service agents or policemen fire back. One agent was seen to brandish a machine gun as the cars sped away. Mr. Crouch observed a policeman falling to the ground and pulling a weapon. But the events had occurred so quickly that there was apparently nothing for the men to shoot at.

Mr. Crouch said he saw two women, standing at a curb to watch the motorcade pass, fall to the ground when the shots rang out. He also saw a man snatch up his little girl and run along the road. Policemen, he said, immediately chased this man under the impression he had been involved in the shooting, but Mr. Crouch saw he had been a fleeing spectator.

Mr. Kennedy's limousine—license No. GG300 under District of Columbia registry—pulled up at the emergency entrance of Parkland Hospital. Senator Yarborough said the President had been carried inside on a stretcher.

By the time reporters arrived at the hospital, the police were guarding the Presidential car closely. They would allow no one to approach it. A bucket of water stood by the car, suggesting that the back seat had been scrubbed out.

Robert Clark of the American Broadcasting Company, who had been riding near the front of the motorcade, said Mr. Kennedy was motionless when he was carried inside. There was a great amount of blood on Mr. Kennedy's suit and shirtfront and the front of his body, Mr. Clark said.

Mrs. Kennedy was leaning over her husband when the car stopped, Mr. Clark said, and walked beside the wheeled stretcher into the hospital. Mr. Connally sat with his hands holding his stomach, his head bent over. He, too, was moved into the hospital in a stretcher, with Mrs. Connally at his side.

Robert McNeill of the National Broadcasting Company, who also was in the reporters' pool car, jumped out at the scene of the shooting. He said the police had taken two eyewitnesses into custody—an 8-year-old Negro boy and a white man—for informational purposes.

Many of these reports could not be verified immediately.

EYEWITNESS DESCRIBES SHOOTING

An unidentified Dallas man, interviewed on television here, said he had been waving at the President when the shots were fired. His belief was that Mr. Kennedy had been struck twice—once, as Mrs. Norman recalled, when he slumped in his seat; again when he slid down in it.

"It seemed to just knock him down," the man said. . . .

The speech Mr. Kennedy never delivered at the Merchandise Mart luncheon contained a passage commenting on a recent preoccupation of his, and a subject of much interest in this city, where right-wing conservatism is the rule rather than the exception.

"Voices are being heard in the land," he said, "voices preaching doctrines wholly unrelated to reality, wholly unsuited to the sixties, doctrines which apparently assume that words will suffice without weapons, that vituperation is as good as victory and that peace is a sign of weakness."

The speech went on: "At a time when the national debt is steadily being reduced in terms of its burden on our economy, they see that debt as the greatest threat to our security. At a time when we are steadily reducing the number of Federal employes serving every thousand citizens, they fear those supposed hordes of civil servants far more than the actual hordes of opposing armies.

"We cannot expect that everyone, to use the phrase of a decade ago, will 'talk sense to the American people.' But we can hope that fewer people will listen to nonsense. And the notion that this nation is headed for defeat through deficit, or that strength is but a matter of slogans, is nothing but just plain nonsense."

Questions

1. Why does the story of the President's assassination open with these particular short paragraphs?
2. Does the author supply us with more details about those same events later on in the account?
3. Discuss the effective use of quotations in the story by noting three examples.
4. Is the story told chronologically? Why?

5. In Chapter 17, the following common problems are discussed: a) failure to create reader interest, b) missing *who, what, where, when* and *why* information, c) unclear topic sentences, d) missing examples, explanations, and facts, and e) lack of completeness in the closing section. On the basis of any *one* of these problems, show how a beginning writer might have gone wrong in reporting the Kennedy assassination. Use the news story in the text to illustrate your points.

Man Walks on Moon!

Man landed on the moon and walked its dead surface Sunday, July 20, 1969.

Two men, wearing American flags sewn to their left shoulders, landed on the Sea of Tranquillity at 3:17 p.m. (Iowa time). One of them, Neil A. Armstrong, 38, of Wapakoneta, Ohio, was the first to set foot on its alien soil warming in the lunar sunrise.

His first words at that moment, 9:56 p.m. were: "That's one small step for man, one giant leap for mankind . . ."

"The surface is fine and powdered, like powdered charcoal to the soles of my boot . . . I can see my footprints of my boot in the fine particles."

He was soon joined by Edwin E. Aldrin, jr., 39.

The television camera on the side of the Eagle was on them constantly.

Armstrong stepped first onto one of the four saucer-like footpads of his spacecraft. Then the moon. He was in the bitter cold of lunar shadows as the camera caught the sight of his left foot, size 9½, pressing into the lunar soil.

Armstrong said the spacecraft's footpads had pressed only an inch or two into the dusty soil. His foot sank only a "small fraction—about an eighth of an inch" into it, he said.

His first steps were cautious in the one-sixth gravity of the moon. But he quickly reported: "There is no trouble to walk around."

Armstrong was not visible to the third Apollo 11 astronaut, Air Force Lt. Col. Michael Collins, locked in a lonely patrolling orbit in the command ship Columbia, some 69 miles above them.

"It has a stark beauty all its own," Armstrong said. "It's different. But it's very pretty out here."

PLENTY OF ROOM

When first Armstrong emerged from the spacecraft, slowly, cautiously, backing out, the world waited, and waited. He took repeated instructions from Aldrin, "Plenty of room to your left."

"How am I doing?" he asked. "You're doing fine," he was answered. Then he told mission control, "Okay, I'm on the porch." It was 9:51 p.m.

After he tripped the television camera, the picture of his foot swinging, tentatively

---

The Des Moines Register, July 21, 1969. Reprinted by permission of The Des Moines Register and Tribune.

groping for the ladder rungs, could be seen clearly.

Minutes later as he scouted the surface for rocks and soil samples he appeared phosphorescent in the sunlight, his white suit blinding.

His movements were sort of gross, abnormal leaps, almost like a slow-motion kangaroo. Repeatedly he returned to the spacecraft to perform his many duties.

Armstrong and Aldrin had been impatient to be out—to complete man's ancient dream. They asked, and received permission, to make their walk early.

AWAITING REUNION

Eagle landed on the moon while Collins —in the mother ship that brought them— continued to girdle the moon awaiting their reunion 22 hours later.

"Houston," Armstrong's voice called out in the first human communication from the moon. He paused a full two seconds. "Tranquillity Base here. The Eagle has landed."

"Fantastic," said Collins on his lonely orbital perch some 69 miles above.

Later Aldrin sent a message "ask every person listening, wherever they may be, to pause for a moment and contemplate the events of the past few hours and to give thanks in his or her own way."

The events that brought them here were already inventoried, and the hazards known.

As Eagle neared the surface of the moon, Armstrong saw that the computerized automatic pilot was sending the fragile ship toward a field scattered with rocks and boulders in the projected landing site on the moon's Sea of Tranquillity.

GRABBED CONTROL OF SHIP

He grabbed control of his ship, sent it clear of the area where it would have met almost certain disaster, and landed four miles beyond the original landing point.

It was a costly maneuver. It cut the available fuel short. When it landed Eagle had barely 49 seconds worth of hovering rocket fuel left, less than half of the 114 seconds worth it was supposed to have.

The landfall on the moon was the fruition of a national goal declared by the late President John F. Kennedy. The fulfillment cost $24 billion.

"The auto targeting was taking us right into a football field-sized crater with a large number of big boulders and rocks," Armstrong said. "And it required us to fly manually over the rock field to find a reasonably good area."

They landed just north of the moon's equator. In the original landing site, Armstrong said, there were "extremely rough craters and a large number of rocks. Many of them were larger than 10 feet."

Tranquillity Base

President Nixon, who watched the news of the landing from his working office in the Executive Office Building next door to the White House, sent his personal congratulations.

Immediately after Eagle touched down, mission control dropped the radio call sign Eagle and referred to the Americans on the moon as Tranquillity Base.

SIGHTS NOT SEEN BEFORE

The first hour was full of descriptions of sights no one had ever seen before.

"From the surface," Aldrin reported, "we could not see any stars out of the window. But out of the overhead hatch, I'm looking at the earth, big, round and beautiful."

Just after landing, mission control called up: "Be advised there are lots of smiling faces here and all around the world."

"There are two up here also," Armstrong beamed back.

"Don't forget the third one up here," added Collins from the orbiting command ship.

Then he added his compliments. "Tranquillity Base, you guys did a fantastic job," he said.

"Just keep that orbiting base up there for us," said Armstrong on the moon.

"Some Angular Blocks"

"We are in a relatively smooth plain with many craters five to 50 feet in size," Armstrong said. "We see some ridges. And there are literally thousands of little one- and two-foot craters. We see some angular blocks some feet in front of us, about two-to-three feet in size.

"There's a hill in view on the ground track ahead of us. It's difficult to estimate, but it might be one-half mile or a mile away." Normally, the lunar horizon could be as much as two miles away.

When he heard his fellow crewmen on the moon describing the scene around them, Collins interrupted to say: "Sounds like it looks better than it did yesterday. It looked rough as a cob then."

"The targeted area was very rough," Armstrong told him. "There were many large boulders and craters there."

"When in doubt," Collins said, "land long."

"So we did," Armstrong replied.

"ALMOST EVERY VARIETY OF ROCK"

The sun appeared to alter the color of the rocks around them. Aldrin said: "Almost every variety of rock you could find. The color varies, depending on how you're looking at it. Doesn't appear to be much of a general color at all."

Armstrong then described what he said were rocks fractured by the exhaust of Eagle's rocket plume.

"Country Basalt"

"Some of the surface rocks in close look like they might have a coating on them," he said. "Where they're broken, they display a very dark gray interior. It looks like it could be country basalt."

The voices of Armstrong and Aldrin were always tightly under control despite the excitement of the moment.

Even during the powered descent, they read off their altitude figures with the dispatch of a broker reading stock market quotations.

The descent rocket burned for some 12 minutes, the controls in Armstrong's right hand, as Eagle followed the long arc over the lunar surface and came down like a hovering helicopter.

Busy Silence

Just after landing, there was a busy silence while the men quickly set up the spacecraft for an emergency takeoff if necessary. The first minutes were devoted to making the decision whether to stay.

The dust was still settling. The rocket kicked up clouds of dust from the moment it reached a point 40 feet over the lunar surface.

The men on Tranquillity Base, accustomed to the weightless state of space flight, were suddenly subjected to the moon's gravity, one-sixth as strong as earth's. They felt as though they weighed about 30 pounds.

"It's like being in an airplane," Armstrong said. "It seems immediately natural to move around in this environment."

At a news conference at the Manned Spacecraft Center, Dr. Thomas O. Paine, head of the space agency, told newsmen:

"We have clearly entered a new era. The voices we hear coming back from these brave men are hard to believe. But it's true. It's raised spirits of men around the world."

He said he had spoken to the President who was watching the news with Frank Borman, spacecraft commander of Apollo 8. Paine said they discussed the gripping excitement and wonder that held the White House group.

"THE EAGLE HAS WINGS"

When the astronauts began their dangerous descent at 2:09 p.m., Eagle was coming around the backside of the moon for the fourteenth time. "Everything is going along just swimmingly," said Collins in the command ship.

His spaceship acted as a communications relay when there was some temporary difficulty talking to the astronauts on their own.

On Their Own

Before that, they separated from Columbia, and they were in Eagle.

"The Eagle has wings," reported Armstrong.

After landing, the astronauts immediately began preparing for an emergency liftoff. But that procedure ended when mission control assured them that Eagle was healthy and able to spend at least two more hours on the lunar surface.

Armstrong and Aldrin conducted a simulated countdown to liftoff, as planned, until they received the go-ahead to stay.

The spacemen then took off their helmets and gloves and started eating man's first meal on the moon. Eagle's larder included a choice of breakfast-style and dinner-style food. The spacemen didn't say which they selected.

Soviet Craft

Meanwhile Eagle, the lunar taxi, was being shadowed by the unmanned Soviet craft Luna 15. Scientists at Britain's Jodrell Bank Observatory, tracking the Soviet ship, reported it had changed its orbit as Apollo 11 set for its landing.

It could only mean, they said, that Luna 15 was preparing to land, or intending to watch and photograph the Apollo 11 landing.

The Soviet news agency Tass said the robot satellite had dropped to within 10 miles of the moon at the low point of its orbit.

"SOMEBODY'S UPSIDE DOWN"

Armstrong and Aldrin in Eagle cast off from the command ship, Columbia, at 12:47 p.m. They were behind the moon, out of radio contact. When they emerged from their thirteenth pass, they confirmed separation.

Collins pressed a button in the command ship releasing latches, and a powerful spring shoved the two ships apart.

"Looks like you've got a mighty good-looking flying machine there, Eagle, despite the fact you're upside down," Collins said.

Big Engine

"Somebody's upside down," said Eagle in a world without a right-side-up.

Twenty-five minutes later, Collins fired his big spacecraft engine, and shot two miles ahead of Eagle.

"See you later," he said, later being some 30 hours and man's most dramatic moment away.

"You're going right down U.S. 1 Mike," said Armstrong watching Columbia dash ahead on course over one of the rilles of the moon, a river-like depression so straight the astronauts nicknamed it after a major highway serving Cape Kennedy, Fla.

Meanwhile, Collins would keep his lonely vigil in Columbia, patrolling the moon in an orbit between 62 and 75 miles above, standing by to take them home.

Strange Craft

Aldrin, the pilot of the spidery lunar lander was the first into that strange craft, linked nose to nose with the mothership.

He entered at 8:20 a.m. through the tunnel connecting the two ships.

About an hour later, spacecraft commander Armstrong slipped through to join him. From then on Armstrong and Aldrin carried the radio call sign Eagle. Collins became Columbia.

At 11:32 p.m., they pushed a button that extended the landing legs of the lunar landing craft, the legs that took the impact of the landing, a four-foot free fall to the surface with the engine shut down.

SHORTEST REST PERIOD

The astronauts awakened at 6:02 a.m. They took half an hour for breakfast. Then Armstrong and Aldrin donned the heavy protective suits they would wear for their moon walk.

Both ships were in top condition, they reported. Armstrong had five and a half hours sleep Saturday night, Collins six, and Aldrin five. It was the shortest rest period on their flight plan.

Quickly Fixed

It was delayed more than 90 minutes while flight controllers on earth tracked down a pesky communications problem. They found the root of their problem in the aim of an antenna. It was quickly fixed.

Then, just after midnight, they were given a goodnight to rest for the adventure ahead, three men facing man's first visit to another body in space.

Even as the big moment approached, spirits were light although the men were busy. Mission control beamed up a brief report on the activities of the astronaut families and the morning news.

Aldrin's son, Andy, was given a tour of the space center, Saturday, along with an uncle, Robert Moon, brother of Aldrin's late mother whose maiden name was Marian Moon.

Otherwise, the work was fast and deadly serious. On earth, 240,350 miles away, half a world offered prayers for their safety.

A PERFECT LAUNCH

Apollo 11 blasted off from Cape Kennedy at 8:32 a.m. Wednesday, July 16, 1969, a perfect launch just a split-second late. The events that followed were just as perfect. The problems that cropped up were small and easily surmountable.

The color television pictures of the shrinking earth and the approaching moon were sharp and unforgettable. Both planetary images took on new meaning, embellished with the aim of Apollo 11.

Less Busy

Thursday and Friday whipped by, the flight plan less busy than on previous shots, to keep the astronauts fresh for the strenuous and daring moments to come.

Then at 12:22 p.m. Saturday, July 19, they fired their big spacecraft engine in the direction of their flight, slowing their speed and falling into orbit around the moon.

Aldrin entered Eagle briefly Saturday to ready some of its systems.

"Everything is beautiful in here," he said.

"Everybody is happy as a clam down here," replied earth.

Each pass around the moon, the astronauts studied the pocked and cratered southwestern edge of the Sea of Tranquillity where they were to land.

Then for 35 minutes they telecast the breathtaking lunar landscape below them. Crisply they described for the people at home the landmarks they saw on the surface.

The sun played games with the colors of the moon. "At these low sun angles, there's no trace of brown in the moon's color," said Collins from some 62 miles up. "It's now returned to a very gray appearance and like the Apollo 8 crew said, it has the look of plaster of paris to it at this sun angle."

At the boundary line between sunlight and shadow, Armstrong said, "It's ashen gray. As you get away from the terminator, it gets to be a lighter gray. And as you get closer to the sun-solar point, you can definitely see tans and browns on the ground."

Directed by the curiosity of men on the earth, they peered deep into the crater Aristarchus. "It seems to have a slight amount of fluorescence to it." Armstrong reported. "The area in the crater is quite bright."

Some earthbound telescopes have seen bright spots in the area which astronomers believe may be signs of volcanic activity.

Today after the scheduled 22 hours on the moon, the Apollo 11 astronauts are to blast off from the lunar surface to rejoin Collins in the mother ship.

Then Tuesday, just after midnight, they are to fire their spacecraft engine again and head for home and a splashdown Thursday in the Pacific, their spacecraft and their minds loaded with new clues to the moon.

Questions

1. Does the lead in this piece reflect the greatness of the occasion? To answer this question, examine the first five paragraphs in regard to style and content.
2. Did the journalist write this story in a simple chronological fashion, from the launching of the spacecraft at Cape Kennedy to the landing on the moon, or did he employ a number of flashbacks? Why? Use concrete illustrations.
3. Since this story concerns a history-making event, was the use of humor appropriate? Base your argument on specific examples.
4. Speculate on the various sources used by the writer in researching this piece.
5. Analyze the stylistic level of the language and the use of colloquialisms, space terms, and figures of speech.

Queens Woman Is Stabbed to Death in Front of Home

A 28-year-old Queens woman was stabbed to death early yesterday morning outside her apartment house in Kew Gardens.

Neighbors who were awakened by her screams found the woman, Miss Catherine Genovese of 82-70 Austin Street, shortly after 3 A.M. in front of a building three doors from her home.

The police said that Miss Genovese had been attacked in front of her building and had run to where she fell. She had parked her car in a nearby lot, the police said, after having driven it from the Hollis bar where she was day manager.

The police, who spent the day searching for the murder weapon, interviewing witnesses and checking automobiles that had been seen in the neighborhood, said last night they had no clues.

The New York Times, March 14, 1964. © 1964 by The New York Times Company. Reprinted by permission.

38 Who Saw Murder Didn't Call Police

MARTIN GANSBERG

For more than half an hour 38 respectable, law-abiding citizens in Queens watched a killer stalk and stab a woman in three separate attacks in Kew Gardens.

Twice the sound of their voices and the sudden glow of their bedroom lights interrupted him and frightened him off. Each time he returned, sought her out and stabbed her again. Not one person telephoned the police during the assault; one witness called after the woman was dead.

That was two weeks ago today. But Assistant Chief Inspector Frederick M. Lussen, in charge of the borough's detectives and a veteran of 25 years of homicide investigations, is still shocked.

He can give a matter-of-fact recitation of many murders. But the Kew Gardens slaying baffles him—not because it is a murder, but because the "good people" failed to call the police.

"As we have reconstructed the crime," he said, "the assailant had three chances to kill this woman during a 35-minute period. He returned twice to complete the job. If we had been called when he first attacked, the woman might not be dead now."

This is what the police say happened beginning at 3:20 A.M. in the staid, middle-class, tree-lined Austin Street area:

Twenty-eight-year-old Catherine Genovese, who was called Kitty by almost everyone in the neighborhood, was returning home from her job as manager of a bar in Hollis. She parked her red Fiat in a lot adjacent to the Kew Gardens Long Island Rail Road Station, facing Mowbray Place. Like many residents of the neighborhood, she had parked there day after day since her arrival from Connecticut a year ago, although the railroad frowns on the practice.

She turned off the lights of her car, locked the door and started to walk the 100 feet to the entrance of her apartment at 82-70 Austin Street, which is in a Tudor building, with stores on the first floor and apartments on the second.

The entrance to the apartment is in the rear of the building because the front is rented to retail stores. At night the quiet neighborhood is shrouded in the slumbering darkness that marks most residential areas.

Miss Genovese noticed a man at the far end of the lot, near a seven-story apartment house at 82-40 Austin Street. She halted. Then, nervously, she headed up Austin Street toward Lefferts Boulevard, where there is a call box to the 102d Police Precinct in nearby Richmond Hill.

'He Stabbed Me!'

She got as far as a street light in front of a bookstore before the man grabbed her. She screamed. Lights went on in the 10-story apartment house at 82-67 Austin Street, which faces the bookstore. Windows slid open and voices punctured the early-morning stillness.

Miss Genovese screamed: "Oh, my God, he stabbed me! Please help me! Please help me!"

From one of the upper windows in the apartment house, a man called down: "Let that girl alone!"

The New York Times, March 27, 1964. © 1964 by The New York Times Company. Reprinted by permission.

The assailant looked up at him, shrugged and walked down Austin Street toward a white sedan parked a short distance away. Miss Genovese struggled to her feet.

Lights went out. The killer returned to Miss Genovese, now trying to make her way around the side of the building by the parking lot to get to her apartment. The assailant stabbed her again.

"I'm dying!" she shrieked. "I'm dying!"

A City Bus Passed

Windows were opened again, and lights went on in many apartments. The assailant got into his car and drove away. Miss Genovese staggered to her feet. A city bus Q-10, the Lefferts Boulevard line to Kennedy International Airport, passed. It was 3:35 A.M.

The assailant returned. By then, Miss Genovese had crawled to the back of the building, where the freshly painted brown doors to the apartment house held out hope of safety. The killer tried the first door; she wasn't there. At the second door, 82-62 Austin Street, he saw her slumped on the floor at the foot of the stairs. He stabbed her a third time—fatally.

It was 3:50 by the time the police received their first call, from a man who was a neighbor of Miss Genovese. In two minutes they were at the scene. The neighbor, a 70-year-old woman and another woman were the only persons on the street. Nobody else came forward.

The man explained that he had called the police after much deliberation. He had phoned a friend in Nassau County for advice and then he had crossed the roof of the building to the apartment of the elderly woman to get her to make the call.

"I didn't want to get involved," he sheepishly told the police.

Suspect Is Arrested

Six days later, the police arrested Winston Moseley, a 29-year-old business-machine operator, and charged him with the homicide. Moseley had no previous record. He is married, has two children and owns a home at 133-19 Sutter Avenue, South Ozone Park, Queens. On Wednesday, a court committed him to Kings County Hospital for psychiatric observation.

When questioned by the police, Moseley also said that he had slain Mrs. Annie May Johnson, 24, of 146-12 133d Avenue, Jamaica, on Feb. 29 and Barbara Kralik, 15, of 174-17 140th Avenue, Springfield Gardens, last July. In the Kralik case, the police are holding Alvin L. Mitchell, who is said to have confessed that slaying.

The police stressed how simple it would have been to have gotten in touch with them. "A phone call," said one of the detectives, "would have done it." The police may be reached by dialing "O" for operator or SPring 7-3100.

The question of whether the witnesses can be held legally responsible in any way for failure to report the crime was put to the Police Department's legal bureau. There, a spokesman said:

"There is no legal responsibility, with few exceptions, for any citizen to report a crime."

Statutes Explained

Under the statutes of the city, he said, a witness to a suspicious or violent death must report it to the medical examiner. Under state law, a witness cannot withhold information in a kidnapping.

Today witnesses from the neighborhood, which is made up of one-family homes in the $35,000 to $60,000 range with the exception of the two apartment houses near the railroad station, find it difficult to explain why they didn't call the police.

Lieut. Bernard Jacobs, who handled the investigation by the detectives, said:

"It is one of the better neighborhoods. There are few reports of crimes. You only get the usual complaints about boys playing or garbage cans being turned over."

The police said most persons had told

them they had been afraid to call, but had given meaningless answers when asked what they had feared.

"We can understand the reticence of people to become involved in an area of violence," Lieutenant Jacobs said, "but where they are in their homes, near phones, why should they be afraid to call the police?"

He said his men were able to piece together what happened—and capture the suspect—because the residents furnished all the information when detectives rang doorbells during the days following the slaying.

"But why didn't someone call us that night?" he asked unbelievingly.

Witnesses—some of them unable to believe what they had allowed to happen, told a reporter why.

A housewife, knowingly if quite casual, said, "We thought it was a lover's quarrel." A husband and wife both said, "Frankly, we were afraid." They seemed aware of the fact that events might have been different. A distraught woman, wiping her hands in her apron, said, "I didn't want my husband to get involved."

One couple, now willing to talk about that night, said they heard the first screams. The husband looked thoughtfully at the bookstore where the killer first grabbed Miss Genovese.

"We went to the window to see what was happening," he said, "but the light from our bedroom made it difficult to see the street." The wife, still apprehensive, added: "I put out the light and we were able to see better."

Asked why they hadn't called the police, she shrugged and replied: "I don't know."

A man peeked out from a slight opening in the doorway to his apartment and rattled off an account of the killer's second attack. Why hadn't he called the police at the time? "I was tired," he said without emotion. "I went back to bed."

It was 4:25 A.M. when the ambulance arrived for the body of Miss Genovese. It drove off. "Then," a solemn police detective said, "the people came out."

Questions

1. Give evidence to show that in the first story about the Queens murder, the opening paragraph constitutes a typical lead.
2. Is there any connection between the routine police activity described in the final paragraph of the first account and the follow-up story, "38 Who Saw Murder Didn't Call the Police"?
3. The murder of Kitty Genovese occurred on March 13, but the follow-up story was not printed until March 27, two weeks later. Why?
4. What is the main idea of the second story as set forth in the first five paragraphs?
5. Show the great amount of research which went into the writing of this story. Use specific illustrations.
6. Indicate two quotations which you believe are particularly effective in revealing the reluctance of the witnesses to become involved.

2 Accept Medals Wearing Black Gloves

Tommie Smith wore a black glove on his right hand tonight to receive his gold medal for winning the final of the Olympic 200-meter dash in the world-record time of 19.8 seconds.

John Carlos, his American teammate, received the third-place bronze medal wearing a black glove on his left hand. Both appeared for the presentation ceremony wearing black stockings and carrying white-soled track shoes. The two had said they would make a token gesture here to protest racial discrimination in the United States.

While the "Star Spangled Banner" was played, these most militant black members of the United States track and field squad bowed their heads and raised their black-gloved hands high.

Doubted He Could Run

The right-hand glove and the left-hand glove represent black unity, Smith explained later. "Black people are getting closer and closer together," he said. "We're uniting."

Smith, who suffered a thigh injury while winning his semi-final earlier in the day, said it had been "80 per cent doubtful" he would be able to start in the final.

"When I was on the stretcher, I was really wondering if I could run," he said. "But this meant everything to me. The doctor taped me up. It was okay."

Both San Jose State sprinters demonstrated a togetherness that apparently extended to the gold medal. Explaining why he had glanced to his right near the finish, Carlos said:

"The upper part of my calves were pulling pretty hard. I wanted to see where Tommie was, and if he could win it. If I thought he couldn't have won it, I would have tried harder to take it."

He Voices Pride

The bronze medal dangled by its green ribbon from Carlos's neck. The gold medal around Smith's neck was tucked inside his sweatsuit.

"We are black," Smith said, "and we're proud to be black. White America will only give us credit for an Olympic victory. They'll say I'm an American, but if I did something bad, they'd say a Negro. Black America was with us all the way, though."

Carlos said:

"We feel that white people think we're just animals to do a job. We saw white people in the stands putting thumbs down at us. We want them to know we're not roaches, ants or rats."

Switching metaphors, Carlos likened the white attitude toward black athletes to the relationship between trainers and show horses or elephants.

"If we do a good job," he said, "they'll throw us some peanuts or pat us on the back and say, 'Good boy.'"

The New York Times, October 17, 1968. © 1968 by The New York Times Company. Reprinted by permission.

Questions

1. What is the important aspect of this story, our athletes winning gold and bronze medals or the black protest?

2. Does the author reveal his own attitude toward the protest of the black athletes? Explain.
3. Why did Smith and Carlos bow their heads while the "Star Spangled Banner" was played?
4. Why are Smith and Carlos quoted so extensively?
5. In your opinion would this account help or hurt the black cause?

Negroes in Detroit Defy Curfew and Loot Wide Area

Thousands of rampaging Negroes firebombed and looted huge sections of Detroit last night and early today. Gov. George Romney ordered 1,500 National Guardsmen, backed by tanks, to quell the riot.

Violence spread uncontrolled over most sections of the city. Destructive fury swept along three-mile and four-mile sections of streets crisscrossing the heart of Detroit and ranging seven miles outward almost to the city limits.

A warm, sultry wind fanned scores of fires, and in at least one area the fire ranged in a solid sheet for more than 10 blocks.

[At least four persons were reported killed, according to United Press International.]

The police arrested more than 600 adults and 100 juveniles.

But thousands more ignored a curfew of 9 P.M. to 5.30 A.M. imposed by Mr. Romney and Detroit's Mayor, Jerome P. Cavanagh. Officials ordered all schools closed today.

"It looks like a city that has been bombed," Mr. Romney said while sweeping by helicopter over areas laid to waste by looters and arsonists.

Scores were injured, many from stabbings, but no deaths were reported early today. Sporadic gunfire was heard in the city.

A first wave of 700 National Guardsmen, 200 State Police troopers and 600 Detroit policemen failed to slow the outbreak.

Destruction spread from a West Side area where it began early yesterday and ignited flareups throughout the day and night that reached into East Side neighborhoods.

The trouble began when the police raided a "blind pig," or after hours drinking spot, on 12th Street near Clairmount and arrested 73 persons.

Mr. Romney declared a state of public emergency in Detroit and its two self-contained suburbs, Highland Park and Hamtramck.

He ordered sales halted on all liquor, beer and other alcoholic beverages as groups of Negroes grabbed liquor from stores and drank beer on some of the city's main streets.

"The disturbance is still not under control," the Governor said shortly before midnight.

The police at first were ordered to withhold gunfire, but Mr. Cavanagh said later: "Their safety is at stake and if they must return fire, it must be."

The New York Times, July 24, 1967. © 1967 by The New York Times Company. Reprinted by permission.

Questions

1. This story of an urban riot contains several dramatic and vivid details (like the description of a police helicopter). Identify several such incidents.
2. Are Governor Romney's comments an important addition to the story? Why?
3. Can you improve on the closing?
4. Do you think that the story about one block club protecting the firemen adds to the account of the riot?
5. What sort of detail is left out of this story which might be included? For example, do you think there should be a fuller account of the incident at the "blind pig"?

Accused of Rape, Man Lives a 13-Day Nightmare in "Mistaken Identity" Case

They arrested Danny Brew just before dawn.

He was taken to jail, fingerprinted and photographed.

He took a lie detector test. He was put in a police lineup. He was identified. And he was charged with rape.

That was the beginning of a nightmare for the 26-year-old machinist that began March 25. It lasted 13 days. Authorities say now he is innocent.

It was, police say, a case of mistaken identity. It was a matter of being in the wrong place at the wrong time. For Danny Brew, it was hell.

Hard on Wife, Parents

It was no better for his wife, Linda, 24. Or his parents.

"It's really indescribable, I guess," said Danny, back at work at his job in an oil equipment firm. "It is a hard emotion to explain. Helplessness, I guess.

"I couldn't believe it. That kept running through my mind. I couldn't believe this was happening."

Here's His Account

But it did. Here's how Danny tells it:

He got off work at 3 o'clock that morning. He "piddled around" an hour or so at his home in suburban Everman, then started across town to pick up his wife at the home of a relative.

A patrol car stopped him.

"I didn't know what it was. They said I wasn't using a right turn signal or something."

He was directed to the patrol car.

"I heard an announcement over the radio

Waterloo Daily Courier, April 9, 1969. Reprinted by permission of the Associated Press.

A battalion of 800 National Guardsmen was ordered from Grand Rapids, 150 miles northwest of Detroit, to assist the 700 on duty as Mr. Romney declared the riot out of control.

Helicopters equipped with floodlights and manned by officers armed with submachine-guns whirred through the fire-streaked darkness in search of rooftop snipers.

Mr. Romney said, "It's a case of lawlessness and hoodlumism and apparently not organized. Disobedience to the law cannot and will not be tolerated in Michigan."

"I will supply whatever manpower the city needs to handle the situation."

Fires raged through tenement buildings, businesses and individual residences in a mile-square section of the city's near West Side. More fires erupted in the Northwest Side.

National Guardsmen and state troopers encircled various police stations.

Inside, officers scurried up and down hallways with armloads of .38-caliber ammunition for police revolvers.

The police, however, were ordered to hold their fire. This apparently was the reason that injuries were kept to a minimum and no deaths were reported.

Fifteen of the injured were policemen, who, throughout the day-long disturbance, gave ground to the Negroes and ignored most looting.

As National Guardsmen rolled into areas of violence in Army trucks and city-owned buses, violence sprang ahead of them, surging into new areas.

The police, meanwhile, brought in carloads of guns picked up from gun stores and pawn shops in and around the riot areas and throughout the downtown section near police headquarters.

The headquarters itself was ringed with armed policemen.

Great clouds of smoke from flaming tenements and shattered businesses and homes lay over much of the city as dusk came, and the smell of smoke pervaded the night air.

A four-mile section of Woodward was plundered by looters, and a three-mile section of Grand River was hit by looting and firebombing, which raged along 18 blocks of 12th Street.

A 20-block area of Grand River was almost solidly aflame.

During the violence along 12th Street, some looters raced past weary firemen and dropped off two six-packs of beer as a prankish gesture.

At one point, beleaguered firemen pulled out of the blazing areas, saying that they had insufficient protection from bricks, bottles and other debris thrown at them.

They left their hoses in the streets.

Block-long sections of tenements and small businesses went up in smoke.

Later, firemen moved back into the areas, sometimes with the protection of residents of the burning areas.

About 20 Negro members of one block club armed themselves with rifles and deployed around firefighters to protect them from harassment.

"They say they need protection," said Lennon Moore, one of the block club members, "and we're damn well going to give it to them."

The outbreak was the worst in Detroit since the city's race riots in 1943. Major parks, including Belle Isle, an island park, where the 1943 riot began, were closed this afternoon.

Looters roamed freely within swirls of smoke in the embattled area, carrying clothes, lamps, golf bags and other goods from flaming shops and stores with their fronts bashed in.

Detroit policemen were ordered on 24-hour duty.

Questions

1. This story of an urban riot contains several dramatic and vivid details (like the description of a police helicopter). Identify several such incidents.
2. Are Governor Romney's comments an important addition to the story? Why?
3. Can you improve on the closing?
4. Do you think that the story about one block club protecting the firemen adds to the account of the riot?
5. What sort of detail is left out of this story which might be included? For example, do you think there should be a fuller account of the incident at the "blind pig"?

Accused of Rape, Man Lives a 13-Day Nightmare in "Mistaken Identity" Case

They arrested Danny Brew just before dawn.

He was taken to jail, fingerprinted and photographed.

He took a lie detector test. He was put in a police lineup. He was identified. And he was charged with rape.

That was the beginning of a nightmare for the 26-year-old machinist that began March 25. It lasted 13 days. Authorities say now he is innocent.

It was, police say, a case of mistaken identity. It was a matter of being in the wrong place at the wrong time. For Danny Brew, it was hell.

Hard on Wife, Parents

It was no better for his wife, Linda, 24. Or his parents.

"It's really indescribable, I guess," said Danny, back at work at his job in an oil equipment firm. "It is a hard emotion to explain. Helplessness, I guess.

"I couldn't believe it. That kept running through my mind. I couldn't believe this was happening."

Here's His Account

But it did. Here's how Danny tells it:

He got off work at 3 o'clock that morning. He "piddled around" an hour or so at his home in suburban Everman, then started across town to pick up his wife at the home of a relative.

A patrol car stopped him.

"I didn't know what it was. They said I wasn't using a right turn signal or something."

He was directed to the patrol car.

"I heard an announcement over the radio

Waterloo Daily Courier, April 9, 1969. Reprinted by permission of the Associated Press.

describing somebody. I didn't know who. But it fit me: 5-8, blond and dirty—I'd just got off the job and I was dirty.

"I knew something was up.

"A couple of police cars pulled up about that time. They proceeded to search my car. They found my pistol. That was the big foul-up."

He said he had carried the pistol five years.

Taken to Jail

They took him to the city jail: "I thought it was just for carrying a pistol . . . I was kinda in a state of shock after I was told I was up for rape."

Then came the lie detector test. "All I know is that it didn't turn out right for me."

Then with his wife crying out something like, "He didn't do it," Brew was put in a police lineup. And the victim, a 25-year-old school teacher, picked him out.

She identified him as the man who attacked her at gunpoint in her apartment between 3:30 and 4 A.M.

"I Couldn't Believe It"

"I couldn't believe it.

"When they transferred me to county jail, I think I really woke up to what had happened and could happen. Having 15 doors close after you really wakes you up in a hurry.

"More than likely, I figured, this would ruin us. My wife would have had to change her name and start all over, I guess.

"And that awful feeling of being sent up for something you didn't do."

FREED ON BOND

After he spent nearly 36 hours in custody, his lawyer won his release on bond, $10,000 on the rape charge and $1,500 for carrying the pistol.

Police meanwhile had arrested a suburban Hurst youth, Robert Wayne Black, 17. They charged him with three cases of rape.

The school teacher spotted Black in news photographs and on television. She decided she might have been wrong in her identification and told the district attorney's office so.

SECOND LINEUP

A second lineup was arranged, this time with Black and Danny side by side.

"He was No. 2. I was No. 3. We resemble each other vaguely. I guess I was kinda in a state of shock. Needles and pins. A lot of people wouldn't own up to being wrong. . . .

"I heard her say 'No. 2' . . . I don't know how I felt. I felt pretty damn good, I guess."

The district attorney said he would drop the case against Danny.

With bondsmen, lawyers and other expenses, Danny said, the ordeal will cost him "roughly $3,000."

"MY MAIN CONCERN . . ."

"My main concern," he said " is clearing my name . . . They're really down on you, the general public. In the back of their minds, well, 'He could have done it.' "

And the rape victim who identified him?

"She said she was sorry."

Questions

1. What are the basic facts in this story? Are they introduced at the outset?
2. What would you miss in the story if you read no further than the first five paragraphs?
3. What makes the closing effective?

4. Do the comments by Danny Brew make it more likely that a reader will identify with the boy?

5. Does this story raise any serious questions about the effectiveness of our system of due process: the validity of lie detector tests, the bail system, or the validity of identification by the victim?

Students—Signs of Suicide

The high rate of suicide among college students has long been recognized as one of the more ominous statistics of higher education. Last week Harvard Psychiatrist Mathew Ross reported that the college-age group runs a 50% higher suicidal risk than non-students in a similar age group, and he scolded the American College of Physicians at its meeting in Boston for not doing more to prevent such deaths. Individuals contemplating suicide normally signal their intention, he said, and doctors must be alert to the message. The most common clues:

▶ A "posture of depression" in which the student becomes withdrawn, "seldom leaving his room, which has, like himself, become increasingly unkempt and uncared for." This may be accompanied by lack of appetite, headaches, constipation and loss of weight.

▶ A decline in self-esteem, which shows up in daydreaming, procrastination in schoolwork, inability to concentrate on reading material, apathy and fatigue.

▶ A loss of interest in academic work. The student may prefer "to thumb idly through magazines and science fiction, haunt movies, sit about all day listening to hi-fi or just languishing."

▶ Suicide threats and notes, which "should always be taken seriously."

A teacher or close personal friend should not delude himself into thinking that he can cope with the potential suicide, Ross warned. The disturbed student must have medical help, most often hospitalization, and exploratory psychotherapy. Even then, he should not be discharged to return "to an empty dormitory room," where "solitary residence" can aggravate his problem.

. . .

Another Harvard psychiatrist expressed concern last week about another form of student behavior. Speaking to the Maternity Center Association in Manhattan, Dr. Graham B. Blaine Jr., said that illegitimate births in the U.S. have tripled in the past 25 years. He placed a major share of the blame on college officials who, by allowing men and women to visit each other in dorms, have encouraged intimacy both on and off campus, and "are actually giving tacit consent to premarital sex." This "puts an unhealthy degree of pressure on those who wish to curb their natural impulses," he said. But Blaine saw brighter prospects ahead. He reported on a poll of Harvard undergraduates, most of whom indicated that they hope their future children will live by a stricter moral code than they have.

Time, April 12, 1968. © 1968, Time Inc. Reprinted by permission.

Questions

1. In the first two lines of the lead paragraph, the writer goes from a general to a specific statement. Explain.
2. Why does the author use incomplete sentences in listing the clues given by potential suicides?
3. This report is divided into two general parts. Identify them.
4. Produce two examples of the effective use of statistics as supporting detail.
5. Does this piece end on a positive note?

Things That Go Bump in the Night

TOM TIEDE

The house is small and aged. The plaster is flaking and the eaves drip with spider weavings. Long fingers of foliage scrape menacingly against some of the higher windows.

Fay Cook lives here.

And so, she says, does "that darned ghost."

Mrs. Cook isn't spoofing about the spook. She claims her house is haunted by its previous owner, a man who died in bed 25 years ago.

According to legend, the previous owner succumbed in anguish. A murder had been committed in the neighborhood at the time and the man was personally connected with both the victim and the slayer.

"It must have really shook him," says Mrs. Cook.

In fact, it did more than that. The man was so bothered by it all that one evening he climbed into an attic bedroom, laid down, fell asleep and was never heard from again . . . that is, until recently.

"He started moving around a short while ago," explains Mrs. Cook. "At first I could hear things in the attic. Then once in awhile I felt somebody or something touch me when I was all alone.

"Then one night he came right out in the open. I was in bed and I saw his eyes here in this very room. It's true. I could see his eyes very plainly . . . looking right at me in the dark."

Since then, the ghost has been a regular terror.

He moves around the house at will, Mrs. Cook says. Sometimes he bumps a hanging lamp and it wiggles in his wake. Sometimes he slams a door or moves a chair or lets out a funny little sound.

He is generally quiet during the day. But at night he is restless and the floors often creak under his pacing, thumping feet.

The Des Moines Register, October 24, 1967. Reprinted by permission of Newspaper Enterprise Association (or NEA).

"I know it sounds strange," Mrs. Cook admits. "It's hard for me to believe it all myself. I used to wonder if I was having hallucinations and I tried to figure out natural causes for everything.

"But I don't try to figure it out any more. Too many things happen in this house. I have no doubt that it's really being haunted."

Mrs. Cook is not alone in her opinion. Dozens of the curious have inspected her premises and several have confirmed her suspicions.

Some examples:

Glenda Christianson, a housewife who explores the supernatural, says she has experienced "tremendous blasts of cold air" in the attic deathroom, even though outside temperatures were over 90 degrees.

Another believer, a self-hypnotic student, insists he has communicated with a deceased "Uncle Marvin" who warned him and others to "get the hell out" of the attic bedroom and the house itself.

A third young man entered the house a month ago and immediately began screaming that he saw "my dead grandmother." He lost control, had to be forcibly quieted, and broke down in tears.

But the most talked-about incident in Mrs. Cook's house occurred recently when a local radio personality, Tom Carlin, agreed to conduct an hour-long experiment in the "afflicted" room.

Before entering, Carlin was given a sheet of infrared Polaroid film by a University of Utah instructor who remained with the radioman throughout the test. A dozen others also witnessed the episode.

Carlin's film was factory-wrapped in thick layers of paper. It had been presealed and never opened. The radioman's task, of course, was to get some ghostly communication on the packaged film.

"I was," says Carlin, "very skeptical."

The skepticism, however, was shortlived. Inside the room he had a number of strange sensations, one being an overwhelming odor of bay rum, although a subsequent search failed to uncover any source.

When he finally emerged from the attic, the radioman opened his package of film in the presence of his companions. The film was exposed with the imprint of a single, shakily written word: "Danger".

"It's the truth," says Carlin, "so help me."

"I realize I can't prove that darned ghost is really here," says Mrs. Cook, "but on the other hand, nobody can prove he really isn't."

Questions

1. Explain why this piece could be classified as a human interest story.
2. Do you think you could write a more effective lead paragraph?
3. Is there any evidence to suggest that the author is skeptical about ghosts?
4. Why does the story contain so many comments by Mrs. Cook?
5. If you had written the story, would you have included the experiences of the other persons who visited the house?
6. What does the introduction of Tom Carlin's experience add to the account?

Strippers "Busty"—That's News?

Professional strippers are taller, hippier and heavier than most other American women, two sociologists reported Tuesday in a unique study.

Strippers tend to have "extremely well-developed busts, several approaching astronomical proportions," the researchers added, apparently in the belief it was news.

In the first known sociological study of stripteasers, Professors James K. Skipper, jr., and Charles H. McCaghy of Case Western Reserve University studied 75 strippers in major cities.

They found the stripper is lured to the stage primarily by the high income—from a minimum union wage of $175 weekly up to $1,500 weekly for headliners. A number of girls also moonlight as prostitutes, the sociologists found.

The Des Moines Register, September 3, 1969. Reprinted by permission of The Des Moines Register and Tribune.

Questions

1. Since this material is based on a scholarly report—"the first known study of stripteasers"—was the journalist justified in giving it a "human interest" slant?
2. A good follow-up story on this item might be based on an interview of the two sociologists. Explain.
3. Although the write-up is very brief, show that the journalist did try to give the reader the gist of the published report.
4. Comment on the effectiveness of the headline and the closing.

Hero: What Does He Look Like?

GAVIN SCOTT

"He got pretty salty at times. He was a typical Navy Chief. He enjoyed the Navy. He only had a couple of more years to go . . ."

This was one friend's description of "Old Salt" Charles Cannington, the 38-year-old petty officer who lost his life saving 10 shipmates aboard the destroyer Frank E.

The Record, Cedar Falls, Iowa, June 26, 1969. Reprinted by permission of the Associated Press.

Evans after it was cut in two in a collision with the Australian aircraft carrier Melbourne June 3 in the South China Sea.

Cannington's exploit was read into the record at Subic Bay in the Philippines, where a board of inquiry is probing the collision.

CPO Larry I. Malilay, 42, told the board he and Cannington, a slender 6-footer with a southern drawl, found themselves in a darkened compartment with nine other men after the ships collided.

Using his flashlight, Cannington, a hospital corpsman on the Evans, lined the other men up in front of the compartment's only hatch. Then he took his place at the end of the line and helped the men crawl to safety from the forward section of the severed ship.

Cannington was the only man who didn't make it out of the hatch, Malilay said. He was lost with 73 other Evans crewmen.

In Orange Park, where Cannington made his home, friends and neighbors remember him as a gruff, but friendly man who enjoyed golf and bowling after duty at the nearby Jacksonville Naval Air Station.

His wife works in a logistics office at the air station, but has kept to herself since learning of her husband's death.

"She doesn't want to talk with anyone," explained her boss, Commander F. J. Klinker.

One of the couple's neighbors described Cannington as "a very nice person. But I couldn't say I would think of him as the type to be a hero."

However, Lt. R. E. Smith, head of the records section at the base hospital, where Cannington once worked, had a different thought about heroism.

"It's hard to say what a hero looks like," he said. "How do you know ahead of time?"

Questions

1. Explain the importance of the headline in relation to the first paragraph of this piece.
2. Is this write-up an exception to the practice of establishing the particulars in the lead paragraphs?
3. The gist of the story is found in the fourth, fifth, and sixth paragraphs. Explain why the writer did not begin with this material.
4. Should this piece be classified as straight news or as human interest?
5. Show how the author ties together the last two quotations to form an effective closing.

Small-Time Gardener Rolls Out the Barrow

You've heard of truck gardens? Gilbert E. Krueger of Marshalltown has a wheelbarrow garden.

Krueger has planted two rows of lettuce and two rows of radishes in a wheelbarrow filled with soil.

"I'm a putterer," Krueger said. "I didn't want to dig up my lawn for a large garden, so I filled a wheelbarrow with dirt.

"If I want to expand my operation, all I have to do is buy another wheelbarrow," he laughed.

Going first class, Krueger went to a local nursery and bought the best soil he could find for his wheelbarrow garden. His painstaking care has brought results.

"I water the 'garden' regularly with warm tap water," he said. "This aids germination. I also take it inside each night so the cold temperatures won't hurt it, then run it out in the sunlight each morning.

"I planted the crop Apr. 12, and the plants are out of the soil more than an inch and a half.

"At this rate, I think I can get three crops a year from one wheelbarrow." The wheelbarrow holds three cubic feet of garden.

The Des Moines Register, April 27, 1969. Reprinted by permission of The Des Moines Register and Tribune.

Questions

1. Where does the writer make use of a pun?
2. Identify the *who, what, where* and *why* details which are established in the opening.
3. Why are single quotation marks used with the word *garden* in the sixth paragraph?
4. What explanation can you give for the fact that this item consists mostly of quotation?
5. One student critic pointed out that the last line is an anticlimax, and that the account should end with the quotation about geting three crops a year. Do you agree?

Sailor: Sea Turtle Saved Me

It took a whale to save Jonah from the briny deep. Chung Nam Kim says he made it with a turtle, and he's got witnesses.

Kim, a 27-year-old South Korean sailor, told Wednesday how a turtle kept him afloat after he fell from the deck of a merchant ship in the Pacific Ocean.

Hours after his strange adventure began, he was picked up by a Swedish freighter, The Citadel.

Waterloo Daily Courier, September 28, 1969. Reprinted by permission of the Associated Press.

Crewmen of the freighter said Kim was swimming with one arm on a turtle's back, and one of them took pictures to prove it.

Tells His Story

Kim related his story in a radio-telephone interview aboard The Citadel, which is due here Friday.

He said he left his parents and brothers and sisters in Pusan, went to Japan last October and got a job as deckhand aboard the Federal Nagara, a Liberian ship headed for New York.

As the ship sailed about 100 miles off Nicaragua last Friday, Kim said, he got a headache. It was about 2 A.M. and he couldn't sleep.

So he walked out on the deck for some fresh air, he said, and "one foot went off—and then I went off. Nobody saw it." He started swimming.

"I had been swimming it seemed like 13 hours," he said, when he saw an animal. "I thought it was a shark, then I could see it was a turtle.

"I threw an arm around it and we swam, very slowly, very slowly, for about two hours."

The water was cold, Kim said, and "I was very afraid. I thought I was dying."

Finally he spotted The Citadel. He waved. The crew waved back.

Capt. Horst Wedder of The Citadel said he could see the turtle, three or four feet long. One member of his crew took pictures of it, Wedder said. "I don't know yet what they show, but what you could see from a distance was the round back."

Sailors of the freighter threw Kim a lifebelt. He grabbed it and they pulled him out.

Saw Turtle Disappear

Kim said he looked back and saw the turtle disappear under the water. Nobody on the ship saw it again.

Wedder said Kim "has a lot of marks on his skin like he was bitten by some little animals. They're mysterious marks. I don't know what kind of animal could have made them."

Another Mystery

That isn't the only mystery. Why did the turtle play Good Samaritan?

A sea turtle is normally very sensitive and dives when it's disturbed, said a marine biologist, Malcolm Gordon, of the University of California at Los Angeles.

"It's awfully unlikely," Gordon said, "that a guy would be able to use one for a life raft."

Questions

1. Discuss the effectiveness of the title.
2. How does the writer background his story in the opening paragraph?
3. Why does the author use narration in the body of this piece?
4. Is quotation important in this write-up?
5. Did the writer include the marine biologist's statement in order to throw doubt on the truth of Kim's story?

Suggested Writing Assignments

1. Write a news account which could be published in your school paper on some item of current interest: a student government meeting, a fund-raising project, an election, a visiting speaker, an administrative action, and so on. Your opening paragraphs should create reader interest and convey the who, what, where, when, and why information needed to clarify your topic. Study the text selections for other clues in writing an effective news report.

2. Write two human interest pieces which could be published in your local paper. As illustrated by the examples in the text, readers are interested in people and events which are unusual or humorous in some way. And don't overlook the tricks of the trade—the use of suspense, quotation, puns, irony, figures of speech, and eye-catching titles.

3. As a means of gaining insight into the problem of objectivity in journalism, write up the same political event from two divergent points of view. For example, attend a political rally or a political speech and write your report as it might be written by a right wing reporter and then by left wing reporter. Perhaps several members of the class could write different slants on the same material.

4. Compare and contrast any two of the news stories in this text in the matter of organization, use of detail, and language.

4

How-To Articles

The myriad "how-to" articles which appear in our media are evidence of a vast and unceasing effort at public education. Magazines and newspapers contain articles telling us how to cook, how to invest our money, how to play Bridge, how to raise our children, or how to eliminate poverty. All such pieces are how-to articles and they command a large and attentive audience. Most how-to articles are of two kinds: (1) practical pieces designed to show us *how we can do something* and (2) those purely informative pieces designed to tell us *how something is done*. In the first category we can find such diverse subjects as how to lose weight or how to gain weight, how to invest money or how to spend it, how to choose a college or how to educate yourself, how to buy a house or how to sell one, how to ask for a raise or how to live within your income, how to be popular with the opposite sex or how to live alone and like it, and how to choose a doctor or how to get along without one. One author even came up with an article on "How to Spend More Than You Make and Still Stay Out of Jail," and another wrote a book on "How To Read A Book."

The second kind of how-to piece, the purely informative article, tells us how something is done by experts, not how the reader can do it. Here the writer wants to inform rather than direct. For example, articles on "Handling Poisonous Snakes," "Driving the Indianapolis 500," or "Playing Professional Football" tell us what experts do. We want to know, even though we do not plan to try it ourselves.

And there is also the more general how-to article which, again, is not fashioned to guide our action, but merely to add to our information. For example, there are articles on "Protecting Natural Resources," on "Slowing Inflation," or on "Preventing Teenage Crime." All of these simply broaden our understanding of the problems. The general public is not likely to be in a position to fashion policy on such large problems and yet we like to know what steps one might take. In fact, our knowledge of such issues is an important part of being a good citizen.

But whether a how-to piece is designed to guide us or merely inform, it contains several distinguishing characteristics. In most how-to pieces the writer must constantly keep in mind the fact that his audience is intelligent yet uninformed. Often persons will try to explain by referring to things they think the reader already knows. When you are lost in a strange city, for instance, and ask how to reach your destination, an inept citizen will tell you that you must go right on past the Baptist Church and turn right at the Elks Club. Such directions are fine for him, because he knows where the Baptist Church and the Elks Club are, but you may find them difficult to follow, because you don't know those "obvious" landmarks. A better explanation will give directions that even a stranger can follow. A more practiced explainer will tell you "go straight ahead for four blocks and then turn right." If you can count, you can follow his advice.

In fact, being conscious of what your audience *does not know* is a most important part of explaining. A successful author of a how-to article, therefore, must put himself in the uninformed reader's place in order to judge his own explanation. If a writer assumes that "it's really quite simple" or "you can't miss it," then he will probably not be very helpful. In addition, any explanation must have a logical beginning, middle and end. If an explanation starts in the middle of the process and then jumps to the beginning, and so on, it will be less useful than if it starts at a reasonable beginning and completes that phase of the explanation before going on to the next. If you are going to explain how to build a Dune Buggy, for instance, you should start with the main frame, not the floor plate.

Another characteristic of how-to articles is that they often warn us against wrong moves. They may contain, therefore, *don'ts* as well as *do's*. If you want to protect your home against burglars when you are on vacation, you may be advised not to draw the blinds or turn off lights.

One last feature of how-to articles is that they are often supported by visual aids to learning: diagrams, photographs, charts, and illustrations of the various phases. If you are writing about how to grow tomatoes at home you can clarify the piece by illustrations which show how to set the plants, how to tie them to a support trellis, and how to protect them against insects.

As for the style of a how-to article, it should fit both the subject and the audience. If you try to advise young boys on how to improve their batting average, the style will probably be informal; but if you write to advise adults on how to draw up a will, then the style will be more formal.

Both the audience and the subject can determine the proper length of how-to articles. Most newspaper pieces are brief; those in magazines tend to be longer. If you have an audience of specialists that appreciates detail, then your exposition can be extended. Newspaper readers will merely glance through a column on how to invest money in the stock market, but readers of *Fortune* magazine will give more careful and extended attention to the same subject. Authors of how-to pieces get the information they need either from their own experience or from their research, but the author's actual experience certainly adds impressive authority to the piece. If an ex-pickpocket tells us how to protect ourselves, we are apt to be more impressed than if the author of such a piece gathered his information from books and interviews.

Most of us have experiences that will make effective how-to articles. An enterprising housewife, for instance, already knows enough to write on "How To Shop for Groceries" or "How To Bake a Layer Cake," and a householder probably knows such things as "How To Fix Household Appliances" or even "How To Build a Patio." Thus, the author with actual experience has an advantage, and yet there is no good reason why a careful researcher cannot come up with interesting information on any topic. Finding answers is the trick, and one can do it either by going to the people who know or going to their articles and books. If you have ordinary library resources, you can learn enough to write on such topics as "Stretching Your Income" or "Caring For the Uncommon Cold."

If you learn how to do it and also how to explain it, you will have an audience for your effort. Readers want to know.

Five Common Frauds, and How To Avoid Them

DON WHARTON

What are the chances in just one month that a typical homeowner will be the target of some shady or fraudulent scheme? About even, says one experienced investigator. You're vulnerable any time you open your mail, look at TV, answer the phone or go to the front door. As many as a dozen times a year, you may actually be brought into direct contact with the swindlers. Sometimes they're trying to take you for a few dollars, sometimes for thousands.

Here are five widespread schemes which, according to a coast-to-coast survey by 134 Better Business Bureaus in the United States and Canada, are tricking honest people out of substantial sums.

Phony Bank-Examiner Swindle. This fraud almost always costs the victim $1000 or more. It has many variations, but it usually develops this way: Confidence men, working as a pair, set out to learn the banking habits of some woman—preferably elderly, living alone. They line up behind her at a teller's window, find out about her deposits, get her account number, sometimes her balance. They follow her home, determine her name and address, later phone her. Posing as a bank examiner or FBI agent, one of them tells her that shortages have been found at the bank and asks for her coöperation in trapping a suspected employe. All this is said with dignity, an impressive voice and promise of reward.

When she agrees to help, she is instructed to go to the bank, make a cash withdrawal (a sum usually just under her balance) and take the money home. "We will send one of our investigators to pick it up and redeposit it in your account, with a $500 bonus in appreciation of your coöperation." This way,

---

The Reader's Digest, December, 1967. Reprinted with permission from the December 1967 Reader's Digest. Copyright 1967 by The Reader's Digest Assn., Inc. Condensed from Contemporary.

in a single week last February, two gangs extracted $55,000 from elderly women in Los Angeles.

Better Business Bureau advice: Give no money and no information about your banking affairs to anyone identifying himself as a bank examiner, security officer or government agent. Take his number if he'll leave it, then call the police or FBI. If he won't, just hang up.

Home-Improvement Gyps. The itinerant home repairman is one of the worst schemers. He gyps Americans out of an estimated $500 million a year. Despite repeated warnings, homeowners still fall for his standard swindles such as the fake furnace "inspection," whereby he tricks you into buying an exorbitantly over-priced furnace. Or the driveway-resurfacing gimmick, where you pay for asphalt but get old crankcase oil. Or phony "termite control," which begins with an "inspection" by "experts," continues through costly "checkups" to a final expensive "touch-up."

Variations of these old schemes crop up all the time. Recently New England homeowners were flooded with letters about an alleged big advertising campaign for new plastic siding: "Be the first house to be plasticized in your neighborhood." They were told this would put them "in line" for a "profit-sharing bonanza" and an "additional bonus of a brand-new color TV." These were empty promises, simply a slick scheme to peddle overpriced plastic siding, devised by men who, without any authorization, had used the insignia of one of the nation's top corporations. Meanwhile, in Georgia, carports constructed at above-normal prices are turning out to be so flimsy that ropes have to be attached to keep them from falling apart. Around Yakima, Wash., one high-pressure group sold 137 fire-alarm systems. Typically, a system that cost the outfit $225 was unloaded on the homeowner for $1187.

When you need repairs, get bids in writing from reputable local firms. Avoid all gimmicks, including the repairman who "just happens" to have material left over from another job. Order self-styled "inspectors" off your property. Above all, don't deal with itinerants.

Dishonest Telephone Solicitations. Telephonic chicanery has increased so much that laws have been introduced in several state legislatures requiring agents selling merchandise by telephone to be licensed.

Some schemers employ a recorded message: your answer starts a slick, tested, minute-long hard-sell. Then a live voice asks if you will allow a man to come to see you. Saying yes can be costly. Last January, a firm peddling carpets made appointments over the phone in Rhode Island and Massachusetts. Customers were promised free carpeting in return for the names of potential rug buyers in their neighborhood. Somewhere along the line a contract was signed and many of the victims actually wound up paying $30 a yard for their "free" carpeting.

Fake "market surveys" by telephone are another favorite gimmick to get a salesman into your home. Questions are asked about your furnishings; then you are told that a man will be around to appraise your furnishings as part of a survey to determine the potential size of the local furniture market. Of course, he turns out to be a salesman—of over-priced, misrepresented goods.

Sometimes the voice over the phone will ask an easy question ("What's the hardest natural mineral—often used in engagement rings?") When you answer correctly, the voice will ask when his firm can deliver your prize, perhaps a set of steak knives. The delivery man will be a specialist in high-pressure selling of vacuum cleaners or books or home improvements.

Or the call may be from a dance studio, and aimed at lonely women: "You are the lucky winner of an hour's free dance instruction." Then at the studio the con men turn on the flattery, sell "lifetime" memberships providing thousands of hours of instruction. In Oakland, Calif., one widow signed contracts totaling $5485.

Once you detect deception—and it's probable if the caller uses the words "free," "no cost to you," "contest," "winner," or "gift" —interrupt the spiel, tell the caller to send you a letter, and hang up. If the case seems flagrant, report immediately to your BBB or to the consumer-protection division in your state attorney general's office.

Questionable Charities. Of the $10.6 billion that individuals in this country give annually to charity, some $100 million goes to phonies—usually to swindlers soliciting for fake charities or to professional fund-raisers who absorb most of your contribution. Early this year, for example, a District of Columbia charity raised $7684 for a Thanksgiving dinner for the needy and spent $116 on the dinner. A California group aiding a children's foundation collected $3,978,-000 and withheld 82 percent to cover fund-raising costs. Although 28 states and many cities attempt some kind of control over solicitations, questionable operations still get through.

So don't respond hurriedly to any telephone or telegram appeal. Ask that pertinent facts about the organization be sent you in writing. Be on guard against organizations which you have never heard of—even those which decorate their appeals with prominent names (sometimes without authorization). If you have doubts, check with your local BBB or Chamber of Commerce.

Pre-Financed Funeral Plans. One of the most despicable current schemes is high-pressure selling of funeral plans that supposedly provide caskets, mortuary facilities and often a cemetery plot. Promoters persuade prospects to pay for the plan years and even decades in advance of the purchaser's prospect of death—as a hedge against inflation. The total take runs into millions. The plans are sold door to door, often on the installment basis, by a professional type of promoter who has no mortuary and little financial responsibilty, but does have a glib tongue. In Colorado, where reportedly $8 million in contracts have been sold in a year, a woman attending a funeral noticed a stranger writing down auto-license numbers. Three days later she got a phone call from a funeral-plan salesman.

The major problem has been the difference between what the salesman says and what is printed in the contract. For instance, victims in New Mexico bought $637.50 contracts, believing they covered an entire funeral service—only to discover that all they got was a casket (which, incidentally, the promoters secured for $96.50). Buyers are led to think that the funeral service will be provided by a mortician of their own choosing anywhere in the United States and Canada. One Carlsbad couple signed up for two $1324 contracts, then found that the contract provided for use of the funeral home dictated by the seller; a different one would cost them $400 extra.

Another deception involves what happens to the money paid in advance. Many states have laws requiring that such funds be deposited in approved financial institutions. But evidence indicates that this is rarely done, even though the salesmen almost invariably refer to "escrow" or "escrow plan." In New Mexico, one firm took in $32,923 without depositing a penny. Another firm collected $18,000 and put $800 in escrow.

As the Association of Better Business Bureaus asks, "If you are 40 or 50 years of age, how sure can you be that the exact funeral services and the funeral home designated will be available when you're 70 and the need arises?" And the Supreme Court of Illinois has observed: "In the long interval between full receipt of the purchase price and contract performance, the opportunities for fraud are great and risk of insolvency, with consequent inability to perform, apparent." In light of all this, most people would be well advised to refrain from talking to any funeral-plan salesman.

Here, as in the case of almost all other deceptive schemes, the first line of defense is to curb your desire for a bargain. The second line to to curb any thought that you can outwit the schemers.

Questions

1. Does the title of this article throw any light on the thesis?
2. Why are subheadings used to introduce the points in the discussion?
3. Are statistics important in this write-up? Base your answer on some actual examples.
4. Why does the writer take pains to describe each of the frauds before he deals with the how-to aspect?
5. What technique does the author employ in his lead paragraph to create reader interest?

There's More to the Dinner Party Than Dinner

BOKARA LEGENDRE

LADIES ARE EXEMPT from the draft, but their dinner party drill requires all the guts of a Green Beret and the flair of a field marshal.

Their weapons are wine and wit and the lurking enemy is boredom. Hostesses require enormous optimism and imagination to combat it.

Now that the sunny months have ended and the poolside parties have had their last splash, at-home entertainment moves from the barbecue pits to the more confining and protocol-bound quarters of the dining room.

Since the diversions of sunsets, sand and mosquitoes are over, more than ever it is the guests who must generate the mood and the gaiety.

How is the hostess to turn her little dinner party into success? For most modern hostesses, proud possessors of casseroles and time ovens, the maneuvering of guests provides more of a problem than the complexities of cooking. If fate is on her side, her friends will have just finished reading the same book and walked out on the same film. They will cheerfully engage in friendly banter while she tussles with the entree and later she can manipulate the chatter.

Whatever her proficiency in culinary art, common sense seems to preclude trying out esoteric masterpieces for the first time. The classic—if not unusual—story of a young society lady newly married to a gentleman from New Orleans comes to mind.

In a desperate attempt to impress her southern friends, she whipped up a Creole Gumbo for the occasion and when it reached the ideal simmer tossed in the last ingredient of the recipe.

She served the chowder-like dish to her horrified guests amid gales of puzzled laughter.

In the middle of the bowl floated a large raw steak. For weeks the jars of a little herb

---

The Des Moines Register, October 16, 1968. Reprinted by permission of the North American Newspaper Alliance.

called Filet poured in from her southern friends.

So, if you must experiment with some rara avis, try it out first on your husband or your boy friend as the case may be.

Each dinner party has its own special character; sometimes a party requires props, sometimes just lots of ingenuity. If an arty evening complete with "Culture Vultures" and "Unknown Artists of Great Promise" is in the cards, it's well to have a few examples of the art in question somewhere visible.

Many a desperate lady has quickly picked up a coffeetable "Art Book" as she rushed home from the deli.

In a raucous political gathering, especially in this Year of Universal Fury, it is sometimes necessary to take extreme measures—like dropping a plate to keep someone else from throwing one.

Even at a purely social, frivolous dinner party, hostesses must be ready for hazards of the most unexpected nature. At a dinner party given for circus impresario John Ringling North, a lady fainted—or rather successfully feigned a faint—in the middle of dinner in a fit of pique at not being seated next to the guest of honor.

Injury followed insult in this case, when the hostess later discovered that she had inadvertently asked the wrong North.

It's often been said that talk flows best around a round table, and certainly for small groups it seems to be the case, as it makes for an easy interchange of chatter. If a larger group is expected and the hostess must use a long table, it's a good idea to put the serious talkers at one end and the frivolous funsters at the other. This may work, but it's vital to break it up at the end of dinner as bores bedevil one another too.

Sometimes even the most experienced hostesses blunder at the seating problem. I attended a dinner for the acidly witty Lady Nancy Astor at an English country house. The first woman member of Parliament annihilated a few guests by leaning down the dinner table and commencing a conversation with a gentleman seated 11 people away on the hostess's left.

"Nancy," cried out the hostess, "why can't you talk to the people at your end of the table?"

"Because," replied Lady Astor, "the people at my end of the table are so boring that I would rather talk to the ones at your end."

Women and wine—both of them in quantity and quality (but not necessarily vintage)—are highly desirable at dinner parties. Prolonged cocktail time not only produces loss of taste and appreciation of food, but can produce total indifference to the dinner itself.

Too many times a three-martini guest has sat through dinner with one of those silly grins and moronic states of mind, adding as much elegance to your table as a paper napkin.

Hostesses who don't or won't invite beautiful women to their dinner parties are committing a grave error. Not only does the glow of a pretty woman surface the genius in most men, but a beauty can change the course of a conversation without an apparent flank movement. Such a lady, when strategically seated, can provide a light touch to a serious debate without in any way stifling it or diminishing the exchange.

Beware of whisperers, however; there is nothing so contagious and the whole party will start to sound like a seance.

Anything worth saying at a dinner party is worth saying loud and clear.

"What shall I wear?" is a familiar wail. "I think women should always look terribly glamorous, and men should be tidy and comfortable," an actress told me, and it appears to be pretty good advice.

One of the great contributions that American entertaining has made to the world is to dispense with black ties except at large functions. Most men are overjoyed, and it doesn't put many limits on what the girls can wear.

It should also be remembered that not

everbody in the world is on a diet and that one of the pleasant purposes of a dinner party is to eat—and eat well.

Those who are on diets should be allowed to wrestle with their own problem in silence while the others can have yet another serving.

Actress Sarah Bernhardt was famous for the excellent table she kept in Paris at the height of her career when she entertained the leading celebrities of the era. She never ate anything herself, just a morsel or a sip, but her guests gorged to their stomachs' delight, without ever being aware of the abstemiousness.

Dividing the gentlemen from the ladies after dinner is outdated and unprofitable. "No one wants to talk about decorating or babies any more," says one New York hostess.

Women display an increasing interest in the stock market and politics, and men usually like largish audiences anyway. If, for any reason, the company does break up and the hostess wants to discreetly lure someone from one room to the other, it can generally be done by a tempting brandy.

The method has been used on countless recalcitrant animals for years, and it is almost foolproof.

Unless like Mrs. Robert Bacon, one of the grande dames of Washington, D.C., one can have Artur Rubenstein play a little sonata just for you, or like the ex-French Ambassador Herve Alphand one can summon the visiting corps de ballet, entertainment is generally disastrous at dinner parties.

It serves only to break the ambiance and interrupt conversation. Unless the invitation called for cards or gambling, games, likewise are death. A clever hostess can maneuver conversation so that it not only suffices but transcends any other variety of diversion, stimulation or humor.

A hostess must be ready for any contingency, even missing guests. To have a gentleman fail to attend is a tragedy, a lady's absence is generally rated only a great inconvenience. In either case no amount of florist's fare or apologies quite mitigates the sin of the *Crime of the Missing Guest.*

Misbehavior is equally hard to foresee. British journalist and author James Cameron tells a story in his book "Point of Departure," about going to newspaper tycoon Lord Beaverbrook's for dinner with Aristotle Onassis and Sir Winston Churchill.

The Prime Minister, then very old, slept through dinner. Old British prime ministers can get away with this. The rest of us can't.

The worst thing about giving a madly successful dinner party is that nobody will leave. When the situation reaches desperate proportions, there are various possibilities:

1) Go to bed.
2) Wake the children, and then have them all say good night again.
3) Straighten up the entire house, busily emptying ashtrays, etc.
4) Take the dog out for a walk (even the canary will do).
5) Plan the breakfast menu.

Questions

1. Does this article tell the ordinary housewife how to give a dinner party?
2. Block out the supporting ideas which Legendre provides in support of his thesis.
3. Evaluate the effectiveness of the opening and closing paragraphs.
4. Discuss the stylistic level of the language and the writer's use of anecdote and humor.

5. It is often observed that some writers throw as much light on themselves as they do on their subject matter. Does this piece tell us anything about the author's outlook and way of life?

How to Make Housework Easier

JOSEPH H. QUICK

Can the housewife apply modern business techniques to her daily chores to get more done in less time?

Based on my experience as senior vice president of Wofac Company, management consultants, Moorestown, N.J., I offer the following tips to every housewife who has had to decide which to do first—the breakfast dishes or the beds.

Have a morning timetable
Household mornings are usually hectic, with everyone rushing around while mother tries to keep peace and provide a substantial breakfast. Because of last-minute sleepers, bathroom and breakfast-table traffic frequently jams up.

Stagger the getting-up time, the slowpoke starting first; avoid morning clothes emergencies by training youngsters to lay them out the night before.

Get more help from your children
Youngsters potentially are a source of help, but most mothers complain that they need so much urging that "I'd rather do it myself."

Try the incentive system. If it works in industry, it will work at home. Decide on a fair allowance, and have it understood for *what* chores it is being paid. Then offer a weekly bonus for doing the work *without* prodding.

Plan a month ahead
Try the fundamental business technique of planning. The first of every month, with a calendar, map out major chores or projects you want to accomplish—a vacation trip, a child going to camp, redecorating a room, giving a big party. Assign a specific time allotment to each.

As businessmen do, check yourself at the end of the month. If the planned projects were not completed, figure out what went wrong and make a more realistic schedule next time.

Start an efficient file system
Do you make an extensive search for a receipted bill or the vacuum-cleaner maintenance manual? Every home should have an alphabetized accordion file, making important records readily available. Cancelled checks, which serve as receipts and should be kept for at least six years, can be stored in a less accessible place.

Paste magazine recipes that you wish to keep on cards and keep them alphabetized in a file box in the kitchen.

Family Weekly, June 29, 1969. Reprinted by permission from the June 29, 1969, issue of *Family Weekly* Magazine.

Schedule your leisure time

Realistically calculate the time a bridge game, say, will take, to avoid rushing home to start dinner. With family outings, be initially generous with driving time, then add more to cover the inevitable delays and side excursions which often occur.

To get the most out of public recreational facilities—neighborhood bowling alley or town pool—check with attendants, then plan to go when they are least crowded.

Persuade your husband to take part of his vacation in single days, so excursions can be made on uncrowded weekdays.

Do you and your husband often stay at a party longer than intended, then get a late, tired start for the next day's activities? Agreement on departure time beforehand will avoid this, and the next morning will start easier and happier.

How to do your chores faster

One of Parkinson's Laws says that a given job will expand to take all the time allotted to it. Production managers have learned how to get around this phenomenon. You can profit by their technique.

Think of your working day as divided into 15- or 30-minute segments. If you decide to do the breakfast dishes between 8 and 8:15 and the beds between 8:15 and 9, the jobs will get done in the allotted time. Otherwise it is easy to wander, without finishing any one job.

Why not try some of these proved techniques that help your husband to accomplish more in less time on his job?

Questions

1. What is the author's thesis? Does he state it openly or merely imply it?
2. Do you think the author's advice is too demanding for the average housewife to follow?
3. Does the author give enough concrete illustrations for his thesis?
4. How does the writer establish the fact that he is something of an authority on the subject?
5. Evaluate the audience appeal of the opening and closing sections.

Enter: The Volks/Roadster/Street Rod/Dune Buggy

ED ORR

HEY! How about a combination Volks-Rod, Street Roadster and Dune Buggy? With good old-fashioned jan-u-ayn street roadster rear suspension and good old-fashioned jan-u-ayn Dune Buggy, VW front end. It'll take a Volkswagen mill and transaxle and any fiberglass dune buggy body made.

"Hark," you may ask, "Who has done

Rod & Custom, May, 1969. Reprint courtesy of *Rod & Custom* Magazine.

Pirate a VW for front end, engine and transaxle, screw it all together and you've got the makings of a very streetable rod or a charging dune buggy.

PSI doesn't make their own body, but distributes the Sand Rover which, like most available bug bodies, affixes easily to PSI frame and floor. Body here is "A" kit. "B" kit includes windshield, other goodies for legal street use. Tires/wheels are your choice; here is sand setup.

this strange and wondrous thing?" And I say to you, "It is none other than a company called PSI that is to be found at 9107 E. Garvey Blvd., in Rosemead, California. They are a division, or subdivision, or something, of a company well known to R&C readers—Antique Auto Parts.

"So, big deal," you say, "Who needs a substitute Vee floorpan?" Well, brother, if you intend to build a VolksRod or dune buggy, you do. Tried buying the real thing lately?

What with the jillions of guys discovering that VW's are really sauerkraut flavored Model A's and thus have all the rodding potential you could wish for, the picture on wrecked VW's is getting pretty grim. Volksy floorpans in junk yards now come in three conditions; folded, bent or so bloody expensive you need a government subsidy to start the project. Several buggy manufacturers who build complete cars for sale have found to their surprise that it is actually cheaper to buy brand new cars, strip them for the pans and mills, and sell what's left over than it is to buy wrecks! This may be neat if your name is Joe Gotrocks but for the average Herm it is a tad steep.

So here (just going into the last reel) comes PSI with bugles blaring, to the rescue. The total cost for their frame is less than three big ones and that includes all the hardware goodies. You don't even need a torch. They do all the cutting and welding. And it isn't just garden variety welding, either. Every joint is heli-arced.

The main frame members are rectangular tubing made of 219 mild steel with .125-inch walls. The cross members are also mild steel tubing but they are round. The wall thickness is the same and they have a two-inch O.D. The bare frame weighs but 40 pounds which means it is both stronger and lighter than the stock VW pan. Up front are four brackets that bolt directly to a VW front end. These can be ordered in two sizes depending on whether you are using the early front end of the '66 and later ball joint unit which has the torsion tubes spaced further apart.

But it is at the rear of the frame that the real surprise comes. Here is the old, familiar single transverse leaf arrangement so dear to the hearts of the roadster crowd. PSI figures this is an improvement all the way around. It weighs less, gives a softer ride and should handle better. Cost of the plain frame with hardware is $195.00. Add $99.50 for a complete rear suspension kit and you have $290.50. Match that at your local junketeria.

In case you have been looking at those open rails and wondering which pocket your feet go in, PSI has an answer. For around $80.00 they will supply a feather light, fiberglass floorpan that bumps and bulges in all the right places to mate up with your dune buggy body. Formed in to its shape are mounts for the pedal assembly and a tunnel to carry the shift rod and control cables. And they will even provide the body if you like.

While it is not of their own manufacture, PSI handles a Manx-like buggy body called the Sand Rover. It is made by Poty Enterprises in Santa Fe Springs, California. The "A" or plain body kit is $245.00 and the "B" kit weighs in at $325.00 The latter is much the better deal. It includes roll bar, headlights, windshield, all the little nuts and bolts, and so on.

Your choice of tires will decide what the finished product will be. A set of fat sand skins on the rear and it is a dune buggy. Swap them for eight-inch mags and a pair of wide ovals and you are ready for the street in your Volks/Roadster/Street Rod/Dune Buggy. ◄

Questions

1. What is the main point of this article?
2. How does the writer create reader interest in the opening paragraphs?
3. Explain how the audience for this piece affected the writer's word choice and style.
4. Comment on the diagrams and on the explanatory material which accompanies them.
5. What techniques does the writer employ to relieve the monotony of a routine do-this-then-do-that explanation? Provide concrete examples.

How We Are Fighting the Bank Robbery Boom

BILL SURFACE

In Nashville, Tenn., two gunmen strolled into the First American National Bank, sprayed blinding chemical Mace into faces of every employee and customer, then escaped with $169,950.

In Northlake, Ill., three masked gunmen robbed a bank of $83,000 and fired such an intense barrage of bullets from their submachine guns that they killed two policemen and wounded two others—before two of them were shot.

In Seabrook, Md., three armed men forced 16 of the Equitable Trust Company's employees and customers to lie on the floor while they emptied the cash drawers. Then they threw a tear-gas grenade into the bank and drove off at speeds of up to 110 mph for 11 miles before police shot out their tires and captured two of them.

Violent incidents from the Roaring 20s? A typical day in the lives of Bonnie and Clyde? Not at all! Bank robberies such as these now occur an average of 10 times every weekday in the U.S. Another statistic underscores this disquieting trend: robberies of banks and savings-and-loan associations rose an astonishing 278 percent between 1957 and 1967 and last year nearly doubled over the previous year. The increase in bank robberies is *five* times higher than the nationwide rise in all other types of serious crime.

Specifically, a bank in Oxon Hill, Md., that was equipped with new, sophisticated alarm systems was robbed so many times (six) in a two-year-period that 1) its employees eventually refused to work any longer; 2) many customers withdrew their deposits; 3) the insurance company cancelled its coverage of the bank; 4) as a result, the bank was forced to close.

This bank is not an isolated example. Branches of the Bank of America in San Francisco have been robbed with such alarm-

---

Family Weekly, March 2, 1969. Reprinted by permission from the March 2, 1969, issue of *Family Weekly* Magazine.

ing frequency that the bank now purchases full-page newspaper ads offering $1,000 rewards for information leading to the arrest and conviction of any of its "five most-wanted bank robbers."

Asking why men rob banks has been futile since Willie Sutton, the master bank robber, explained, "Because that's where the money is!"

But there is reasonable agreement among law-enforcement personnel on one reason why bank robberies have multiplied. The number of suburban banks and branch offices have doubled in the last 10 years. Such banks, which account for 40 percent of all bank robberies, are structurally esthetic but often more vulnerable to armed bandits.

Furthermore, it is easier for would-be robbers to "case" these banks, then park their automobiles and subsequently escape onto an uncrowded six-lane superhighway.

At the same time, however, armed robbers have intensified their assaults on banks located in the most congested downtown areas. FBI statistics show that, in one 12-month period, 586 bank robbers apparently sensed that roads were too crowded and simply *walked* away from the banks that they robbed. Four such robbers escaped on bicycles or motorcycles, two quickly abandoned their panel truck and escaped by motorboat. One even used the subway.

A second reason for the increase is the unprecedented emergence of both organized criminals and "amateurs" as bank robbers. John "Sonny" Franzese, for example, who the FBI calls "a ranking member of the Cosa Nostra," was recently sentenced to 50 years in prison following his conviction for masterminding six bank robberies in New York, Massachusetts, and Utah.

By contrast, the novices have included a 21-year-old barefoot man who wore Bermuda shorts as he nervously robbed a bank in Delaware; a 68-year-old pensioner who robbed an Eastern bank of $3,637 and left in a cab; and two college students and their girl friends who took $59,441 from three banks before being apprehended.

What type of person is committing the vast majority of these robberies? As FBI Director J. Edgar Hoover maintains: "There is no single person we could point to and say he is a typical bank robber, just as there is really no typical bank robbery or method of solution."

A remarkable uniform profile of bank robbers' working habits, though, has emerged from the FBI's study of 2,200 recent bank robberies. Most bank robbers are men between the ages of 26 and 36 who, in 53 percent of the cases, prefer to work alone and, in 75 percent of the robberies, walk into a bank between 10 a.m. and 2 p.m. on a Friday, wearing either sunglasses, phony mustaches, or ski masks as disguises. Almost 55 percent of the robbers are armed with pistols, and 86 percent of them leave with money—with an average haul of $5,951.11 each.

There was little similarity, though, in the FBI's techniques of identifying bank robbers and recovering $2,715,216 stolen from banks in fiscal year 1968. Consider the case that began when a man wearing a stocking over his face robbed a drive-in bank in Council Bluffs, Iowa, and left with $12,513 in a brown shopping bag. An FBI agent detected a resemblance between the description of the robber and Steven Orval Stiles, a convicted car thief and escapee from a Federal penitentiary.

The FBI's suspicion was heightened the next morning when 17 fingerprints matching those of Stiles were found on shopping bags inside a stolen automobile that had been recovered. A review of Stiles' background, meanwhile, showed that he enjoyed being a big spender in Omaha, his home town. Interviews with clerks and cab drivers confirmed this. Furthermore, one driver said he took Stiles to an apartment house.

The building's superintendent said that a man who "sounds like your fellow" did have a small apartment and had telephoned that he would "wire the rent first thing tomorrow morning." By this time, FBI agents had learned that a man matching Stiles' description had purchased a plane ticket to Los Angeles. Whereupon, FBI agents hid in every Western Union office in Los Angeles and arrested Stiles within five hours. He was convicted of bank robbery and sentenced to 15 years in prison.

Stories of FBI investigations such as this are legend. But what is being done to stop bank robberies *before* they take place?

Perhaps the most successful method of reducing them has been for police to urge bank employees to report any suspicious-looking person seen in the vicinity of a bank. Simply consider the results of such a report in downtown Washington, D.C. Two patrolmen used the "stop-and-frisk" law to question three "suspicious-looking" men as they approached the Independent Savings and Loan Association and arrested them for illegally carrying three .38-caliber revolvers and a tear-gas gun.

Even more protective steps are being taken inside banks. The Federal Reserve Board, for example, has just stipulated that any new vault constructed within a bank under its jurisdiction must have doors constructed of special "drill and torch resistant materials."

Many banks are suddenly augmenting their security systems by 1) employing more armed uniformed guards with their revolvers plainly visible; 2) hiring former FBI agents to review their security measures and determine how vulnerable they are to robbers; 3) keeping only a small amount of currency in the tellers' drawers; 4) installing bulletproof glass on tellers' windows.

Such banks, moreover, have followed J. Edgar Hoover's advice that nearly all banks are thoroughly "cased" before they are robbed, and, therefore, employees should be trained to watch for "loiterers and suspicious-looking individuals who seek change or attempt to open small savings accounts and even uniformed workmen who don't offer proper identification when they request access to restricted bank space."

Law-enforcement agencies have encouraged many banks to stage mock robberies in order to alert tellers to the *modus operandi* of actual bandits and, significantly, what to do if a bank robbery does occur. Employees are shown how to give a robber "bait" money in which the serial numbers have been recorded without taking an unnecessary risk that might provoke the bandit into firing his weapon. Then, while obeying a robber's orders, employees are taught how, if possible, to keep the robber's note and observe facial features, clothing, and any scars or unusual markings, that would help police or FBI in identification.

A variety of implements that eject tear gas are being installed, too. Some smaller banks already use money wrappers that discharge tear gas.

Another new device being used is clear plastic vials hidden in money wrappers that, if secretly broken by tellers during a robbery, cause the money to emit a sickening odor when it is carried outdoors.

After the chemical was used in a robbery of $1,600 from a West Coast bank, the two robbers' getaway car smelled so badly that they abandoned it and ran. Though the men were not immediately caught, bank officials maintain that the money "smells so awful that it will never be spent."

Furthermore, Congress' new Bank Protection Act, and subsequent orders on Jan. 6, 1969, by four Government agencies, will *require* all Federally insured banks and savings-and-loan associations to take certain protective steps that, surprisingly, had not always been done:

1. Install, repair, and maintain equipment that can secretly notify police if a robbery occurs during banking hours or if someone breaks into a building at night. Many bank officers assumed their burglar alarms functioned properly—until they were robbed!

After the banks were robbed a second time, police frequently found that the banks hadn't connected the alarm after the first robbery.

2. Use lighting devices that will illuminate lobbies and entrances to vaults at night.

3. Install cameras that photograph anyone who walks up to a bank teller's window.

Although such photographic equipment doesn't necessarily frighten away all bank robbers, it has brought legal dividends when the bandits have been apprehended. Take, for example, the recent case of 27-year-old Raymond Clardy who entered a plea of "not guilty" in a Boston court to the charge of robbing the Suffolk-Franklin Savings Bank.

Whereupon, the prosecutor requested permission to show a film of the robbery. After Clardy watched himself leave the bank with a pistol in his right hand and a bag of money in his left, he changed his plea to guilty and was sentenced to a term of six-to-ten years in Massachusetts State Prison.

Questions

1. Which of the two kinds of how-to writing does this article illustrate?
2. The actual how-to information is not presented until the middle of the article. Why?
3. Is the opening designed to catch reader interest?
4. What techniques does the writer use to make the statistics more interesting?
5. Does the writer provide vague topic sentences in setting forth the devices used to prevent bank robberies, or does he identify them clearly? Base your answer on specific references to the article.

How To Write Effectively to Congress

WILLARD CLOPTON JR.

Washington, D.C.—Writing your congressman can be a pretty meaningless exercise if it's done the wrong way. If it's done right, it can be a valuable part of the legislative process.

Representative Morris K. Udall (Dem., Ariz.) who among other things has been an Air Force captain and a pro basketball player and is now chairman of the House subcommittee that deals with civil service pay, recently put together a list of "do's" and "don'ts" for his prospective correspondents.

The Des Moines Register, August 17, 1969. Copyright, The Los Angeles Times/Washington Post News Service. Reprinted with permission.

The suggestions were aimed at his own folks back home, but they make good advice for constituents anywhere.

Correct Address

First of all, he says, address the letter correctly. Send it to Honorable Joe Smith, House Office Building, Washington, D.C. 20515 (or if to a senator, the Senate Office Building, Washington, D.C. 20510).

This may sound pretty basic, but the congressman once got one that began: "Mr. Morris K. Udall, U.S. Senator, Capitol Building, Phoenix, Arizona."

Identify the bill you're writing about. About 20,000 are introduced each year. If you don't know its number, give some description, such as "Truth in Lending."

Write in time to do some good. Often a bill is out of committee or has already passed the House before a congressman receives your helpful ideas.

Don't bother writing any representatives or senators but your own.

Your letter will probably have greater impact if it's kept reasonably brief. Don't worry about grammar, spelling or form. It needn't be typed—merely legible.

Give your own views. A personal letter is more valuable than a signature on a petition.

Give reasons for your position. Phrases like "I'm bitterly opposed" don't help much, unless you go on to say, "H.R. 100 will put small dealers like me out of business."

Needs Experts

If you have specialized knowledge on some issue, by all means write. A congressman is a layman on most matters and is always glad to know what the experts think.

Be constructive. Don't just say what's wrong with a bill. State what you think is the right way. And don't just write when you're mad. If your man votes the way you like, send him a "well done" occasionally.

Don't threaten to campaign or vote against your man if he doesn't do what you want. Such remarks, says Udall, "rarely intimidate a conscientious member, and they may generate an adverse reaction."

And don't bother calling him names.

Don't pretend to have vast influence.

Don't become a constant "pen pal." Write often if you like, but be pertinent and brief.

Don't demand that he take a public stand before he has all the facts.

"On major bills there usually are two sides to be considered, and you may have heard only one," says Udall.

Udall's advice is a good answer to the often-asked question, "What can one mere citizen do?" Clip and save this article.

Questions

1. Identify the elements which make the introduction effective.
2. What device does the writer use to emphasize his topic sentences?
3. Sometimes the writer illustrates his point and sometimes he doesn't. Why?
4. Show that the informality of the language is appropriate for the topic and audience.
5. One way to judge the effectiveness of an article is to see how much of it sticks. Without rereading, how many do's and don'ts can you remember from this how-to piece?

How To Pick Ripe Melons

GENE LOGSDON

Science has discovered an intricate process for changing the number of chromosomes in a watermelon, but not how to tell when the blamed thing gets ripe. There are the time-honored methods, of course, but I can tell you: none of them work.

The Thumping Technique

Snap your fingernail against the melon and listen. If you hear a metallic *tic-tic-tic*, the melon is still green. In a few days, the tic changes to a *tock* and you know the melon is nearly ripe. When the sound becomes a dull *thunk-thunk-thunk*, the melon is rotten.

The Squeeze Trick

Place the palms of your hands at either end of the melon with your ear against it. Apply bear-hug pressure. If you hear a crackly, wheezy noise, the melon is ripe. If you lack the double-jointed dexterity to perform this operation without falling flat on your face or pulling the melon loose from the vine, try dropping a 4-lb. rock from a height of 3' on the melon. If the rock bounces off and barks your shin, the melon is not ripe. If the melon smashes into smithereens, it was ripe.

Skin Scraping Method

Scratch the hide of the melon with your fingernail. If the outer skin peels off easily, the melon should be ripe. If the skin is difficult to peel, you've made a nice entrance for slugs.

The Color Test

This method requires an eye for subtle shades of color that would make Da Vinci green with envy. When the melon turns from a light to a dark shade of green, and its bottom from ivory to yellow, color it ripe. When you cut the melon open and it is still whitish-pink instead of red, color yourself purple with rage.

The Dried Curlicue Theory

Pay close attention to the *three* tendrils on either side of the stem of the melon you wish to pick. When these curlicues turn brown, the melon is supposed to be ripe. If the melon is still green, you have a bad case of fusarium wilt.

The only sure way to tell a mature melon is to let the groundhogs do it for you. When you find a melon with a big hole gnawed in its side, you should have picked it yesterday.

Farm Journal, October, 1968. Reprinted, by special permission, from October 1968 issue of *Farm Journal*. © 1968 Farm Journal, Inc.

Questions

1. Explain how the writer piques our curiosity in the opening paragraph.
2. Would you characterize the language of this piece as being moderately, or highly informal.

3. Pin down the humorous approach which the writer uses in discussing each of the "time-honored methods."
4. Is this how-not-to article pure spoof, or do we learn something about picking ripe melons?

Suggested Writing Assignments

1. In preparation for the composing of a how-to paper, prewrite a list of your thoughts on a topic of your own choosing, such as your hobbies, jobs, and special skills. Discuss your list with your classmates and instructor as a means of finding an effective how-to slant. You may find it necessary to prewrite several topics in order to discover a suitable thesis. In writing your paper, make use of the techniques which are employed in the text selections.
2. Write a paper in which you compare any two of the how-to selections in the text on the basis of form, the use of details, stylistic level of the language, audience, and other factors. Depending on the choice of selections, you may want to show that one piece is better written than the other or that they are equally effective.
3. Present a complete analysis of a how-to piece which is not included in the text. As a preliminary search will reveal, how-to articles abound in magazines and newspapers. You may wish to use a selection from your scrapbook of informative-persuasive clippings. In composing your paper, be guided by the text discussion of how-to writing and the basic elements of form and the use of detail, as described in assignment two above.

5

Editorials

       Although editorial writers suffer stiff competition from nationally syndicated columnists, still they write a widely read form of modern prose.

  Occasionally, editorials are signed by the authors, and we know whose views we are getting. But more often they are unsigned and reflect only the ideas of the familiar and anonymous "editorial we." An editorial, then, may represent only the opinions of the publisher. It may, however, reveal the attitudes of an editorial board, a policy-making group, or the ideas of a single editor.

  As for the subject matter of editorials, there is no limit. While they may deal with educational, military, political, moral, economic, or literary aspects of our lives, they are usually designed to catch the interest of a particular audience. What this means, in practice, is that most editorials, in your school or hometown papers, are probably devoted to such local matters as a campus or community problem. Of course, some editorials deal with larger, national questions and a few turn to truly international issues.

  While editorials may be satiric and even comic, they are, in the main, formal, rather serious essays. The audience for editorials, as a consequence, tends to be more thoughtful, more perceptive, and more discriminating than average readers. They are persons who like to see what others think in order to form and test their own opinions.

  Of course, one can also learn from editorials, because they may analyze current happenings or give us background. If our president makes a formal visit to Latin America, we can expect editorials which will go beyond the news of the event to explain why he made this trip or to tell us about earlier South America trips by American presidents.

  But in addition to clarification and analysis, editorials often evaluate current events. They comment, for instance, on whether the president ought to make a particular trip and, once made, whether it was successful.

Apparently, editorials used to be more vigorously controversial than they are today. Many modern publications seem to avoid sharp differences of opinion with their readers, evidently fearing they will alienate some of them. And since publications depend on advertising for their revenue, editors sometimes shy away from expressing a view contrary to the message in the ads.

Whatever the reason, editorials are often bland, noncontroversial bits of verbal cotton candy. Many of them dwell on such generally agreed upon topics as the dignity of motherhood or the desirability of patriotism. Such editorials neither arouse nor offend. They merely fill space.

A few publications, however, both newspapers and magazines, still fire away with militant editorials which champion causes. Yet, even here, the editorial style tends to be restrained and dignified.

Perhaps the most striking characteristic of editorials, whether bland or blazing, is that they usually have a carefully designed unity. Although relatively brief, from 150 to 800 words, they are precisely cut and pruned pieces, placed in a special part of the publication, on the editorial page, or boxed in bold, black lines to set them off.

With their brevity, editorials are ordinarily devoted to only one subject or to one facet of a larger issue. Editorial writers, then, must plunge directly to the main point and must quickly bring in carefully selected illustrations and persuasive support. In short order, they must tie the whole together and finish with a distinct close.

Of course, conventional editorials can be constructed out of wilted cliches. But when editorials are intelligently done, they contain some of our best prose. For this reason, among others, they still hold the attention of discriminating readers.

Reflections on Moon Trip

Watching man's landing on the moon one could not help a feeling of awe, of wonder and excitement, and of pride in this accomplishment by his country.

By means of another technological marvel, television, one could have a sense of involvement, of almost being there, of being a participant in this great adventure.

It was truly an achievement worth celebrating.

But as one watched he had other thoughts, too, and questions. Among them were these:

Surely a people who can accomplish this can find other ways for settling disputes than by killing other people and destroying other countries.

Surely a nation that can utilize science to achieve this milestone can find a way to eliminate poverty and hunger and disease from its land and the land of its neighbors on earth.

Surely a nation that can concentrate its skills and money for such a physical feat can find a way to end the pollution of its own land and people.

We do not share the optimism of many

The Pilot (Southern Pines, N.C.), July 30, 1969. Reprinted by permission.

people who see great benefits from landing a man on the moon. Of course we will acquire additional information that will add to our knowledge of outer space. But there is no evidence that other gains and benefits can be claimed.

It may well be, as the economist-historian Robert L. Heilbroner says: "After making this tremendous effort, many people are going to reflect upon it and think: 'So what?' Many may come to the conclusion that the moon landing is hardly more than a TV spectacular. We may have that morning-after feeling and, in a penitent mood, decide to start looking after our worldly problems."

Some may even feel as Lewis Mumford, the writer-philosopher, feels that the moonshot is simply modern man's equivalent of the pyramids of Egypt, those massive stone monuments which were the medium for taking the pharaohs to their god. Mumford is fearful that the moonshot, which was conceived to prove military superiority, "will only reinforce the military-industrial-government complex. It will give the complex more funds and power, and divert attention from the pollution that is destroying society."

These are pessimistic expressions, but perhaps they are needed to dampen to some degree the exhilaration Americans feel over the physical achievement. Perhaps they are needed more to turn our attention to our earthly problems of war and hunger and disease.

For though there may be more frontiers of space to conquer, there are even more and even greater frontiers of the mind and spirit here on earth which call for our concern and the best efforts of mankind.

Questions

1. What is the function of the first four paragraphs?
2. As discussed in Chapter XVII, one of the common errors made by the novice writer is his failure to provide clearly stated topic sentences, with the result that the reader gets lost. Show how this experienced writer avoided that error by using "sign-post" sentences to mark each of the main parts in the editorial.
3. Do you agree with Heilbroner's observation?
4. Comment on the appropriateness of Mumford's analogy between the Egyptian pyramids and the moon shot.

College Co-operation With FBI

What is the obligation of college authorities to co-operate with FBI investigations of their students?

At Simpson College in Indianola, college administrators refused to give to the FBI the names of students responsible for an anti-

---

The Des Moines Register, October 31, 1969. Reprinted by permission of The Des Moines Register and Tribune.

Vietnam war rally and refused to answer FBI questions about students regarded as "radicals" and "agitators."

At Grinnell College, administrators agreed to act as intermediaries for the FBI and called in students for questioning by FBI agents investigating a violent demonstration in Chicago in which some Grinnell students were arrested. The college also made available its facilities for the questioning. Grinnell officials now seem to think they made a mistake and doubt that the college's intermediary role will be repeated.

The Simpson and Grinnell situations are dissimilar and do not justify the same non-co-operation in each case.

The rally at Simpson was sanctioned by the college. There was no suggestion that students had engaged in illegal conduct. The questions directed at college administrators by the FBI amounted to a fishing expedition and request that they act as political informants about their students. Colleges have a responsibility to refuse to spy and report on the political views and activities of their students when no illegal conduct is involved.

Grinnell administrators did not question students, and they deny that information was given to the FBI about the students. All the college seems to have done was facilitate the FBI investigation of the Chicago disorders by locating students the FBI wanted to see.

The FBI could have made the contacts itself, but it seems to us to be no breach of a college's obligation to its students to accede to an FBI request that it arrange the meetings. The FBI might well have been criticized if it had searched out students on the campus without going through college channels.

The FBI sometimes takes a too-sinister view of campus activities. The agency was clearly over-zealous and out of line in its probe at Simpson College. But that doesn't make every FBI bid for co-operation unacceptable. Grinnell's co-operation with the FBI, which is, after all, a duly recognized law enforcement agency, was minimal and proper.

Questions

1. Comment on the effectiveness of opening with a question.
2. Is the overall purpose of this editorial to shape college policy or is it merely to analyze two particular events?
3. What significant differences does the writer find between the situations at Simpson College and at Grinnell?
4. To what extent is this editorial critical of the FBI?

Leadership Needed

This has been a poignant week in Cedar Falls since the parents of a 17-year-old youth blamed his death on LSD.

For a time the community virtually was one in its willingness to meet this problem head on.

That's why we were disappointed to see some public school officials seem to drop the

---

The Record (Cedar Falls, Iowa), November 28, 1969. Reprinted by permission.

ball . . . to fail to move ahead toward closer community cooperation in meeting the problem.

At a meeting of officials Wednesday, Assistant Supt. Marvin Ziesmer seemed doubtful there is a problem. No plan for closer cooperation was worked out between officials.

A youth is dead. Facts point to the conclusion that someone supplied him with a dangerous drug that led to his death.

What can be done to help prevent such occurrences in the future?

We had hoped that there would be closer coordination planned between school and law enforcement officials. When a youth is believed to have taken drugs, authorities should be called into the case.

We repeat: we are not interested in busting every kid who has come into contact with drugs. But an intense effort should be made to arrest the suppliers of dangerous drugs.

Some say this action only drives the problem underground. This statement is nonsense. The drug world IS underground now. It's as hush, hush as mental illness was 50 years ago.

Let's bring it out into the open. Let's help the kid who has gotten himself mixed up with drugs. But let's make this a decidedly unhealthy place for the supplier of dangerous drugs.

And let's not go mushy on that point. The solution is going to require the cooperation of parents, students, school officials, counselors and law enforcement authorities. The latter need witnesses if they are to be effective.

The drug problem is a complex sociological matter, this is true. Kids who feel a sense of purpose and self confidence aren't as likely to be attracted to drugs.

But the Markle case showed that any kid from any family might become involved if drugs are around.

We think the kids understand this better now.

They have no reason to protect any one who would profit from crippling or killing one of their friends.

Now, they are waiting for more positive leadership. Where is it?

Questions

1. What is the main point of the editorial?
2. How would you characterize the tone of this piece?
3. Do you think that the editorial might result in stronger community action on the drug problem?
4. How would you describe the language used by the writer? Provide examples.
5. One of the insights which this book hopes to convey is that all of the various kinds of modern prose have a common *form* and *motive*. Support this view by showing that this editorial consists of a beginning, middle, and end, and is written to inform and persuade.

We Are Concerned

Ald. A.A. Rayner has asked this question on a number of occasions: "Why aren't black people involved in anti-war campaigns?" The question, of course, raises an interesting point. Since almost 40 per cent of the casualties in Vietnam are black, it seems, according to Rayner, that blacks should be involved.

To answer this question directly would be like solving the problem: "What came first, the chicken or the egg?" Of course blacks are concerned about the Vietnam war, but we are also concerned about the battle for survival and equal rights. To say that blacks are not concerned is like pouring salt into an open wound.

We have determined that fighting the war will not give us first class citizenship, nor will it have any significant effect on the racist attitudes of whites. Nothing thus far has. For centuries black people have lived beneath a shroud of terror, hatred and hunger; betrayal, deprivation and murder. Killing black soldiers in Vietnam is no better nor worse than killing blacks in our own homeland.

Yes, black people are concerned about the Vietnam war, but we are also concerned about the killings, police brutality and the degradation which exists in our own communities. The only difference between a dead black soldier in Vietnam and a dead black youth on the streets of Chicago is the assassin.

Our fight is a total fight, not confined to Vietnam or the streets of Chicago or any other town or village. When we rid ourselves of the monster which has created the dependency, that contemporary slavemaster who now controls his flock with a gun, then we will be able to rid ourselves of all the Vietnams which threaten our existence.

The New Pittsburgh Courier, November 8, 1969. Reprinted by permission.

Questions

1. At what point in the editorial do we learn that the writer is black?
2. What is the writer's main point and how does he create reader interest in it?
3. In your opinion, does the editor give a convincing answer to Rayner's question?
4. This editorial was taken from a newspaper written by and for blacks. If the editor had written the piece for a white audience, would he have answered Rayner's question in the same way?

Summer in Blossom

By the first week in July the day lilies at the roadside and the brown-eyed Susans in the old pastures splash the countryside with Van Gogh orange. The hot, tropical shades leave no doubt about the season. Tawny hawkweed might have been imported from a Mexican landscape, and even its rather pale yellow cousin, Canada hawkweed, has a hot-climate look.

The elderberry bushes are frothed with white blossoms, to be sure, and the daisies that still claim their share of the waste places are white and gold, a cool combination against the lush green of trees. But that sun-color, that warm weather yellow, is everywhere. The evening primroses spread their petals in late afternoon, to lure the moths. Butter-and-eggs, the wild snapdragon, combines the yellow and orange in blooms that lure the bumblebees. Jewel-weed, both the pale yellow and the red-spotted, lifts its succulent stem and opens its pouched flowers for bumblebees and hummingbirds. Half a dozen cinquefoils make the back roads and the old meadows sparkle with their variety of hot-sun yellows.

And now the sunflowers, big and little, tick-seed and plain, tuber-rooted and everyday, come to bloom, the apotheosis of that yellow response to July, that mid-spectrum color which is like the midday sun itself, summer come to full flower.

The New York Times, July 6, 1969. © 1969 by The New York Times Company. Reprinted by permission.

Questions

1. Since most editorials deal with local, state, and national problems, is this one on an acceptable subject?
2. Does the writer display a considerable knowledge of nature? Illustrate by concrete reference to the piece.
3. Comment on the choice of words. Look at the verbs and adjectives.
4. This selection is deceptive in structure. At first glance, one might suppose that there is no central point or main idea, but on closer analysis the key idea of "warm weather yellow" emerges. Explain how this idea gives unity to the piece.

The Chance To Invest in Survival?

If it is true, as a recent Gallup Poll suggests, that only 4% of the American people consider pollution a major problem facing this country, then America is in deeper trouble than even Mr. Nixon thought when he devoted a portion of his State of the Union message to a concern with the destruction of our natural environment. It is one thing for a leader to point to a problem; it is something else to persuade two-hundred-million followers that the problem deserves their serious attention. Ian McHarg begins his lectures to college audiences by telling them: "Yours is the first generation in history *which has no future*." Other conservation spokesmen have proposed that to arrest and reverse the processes which are making the earth unlivable might cost as much as 50 billion dollars a year. The American people —both as members of the human family and as suffering taxpayers—have never been confronted by a prospect so bleak as the choice between ecological suicide and the enormous cost of survival.

Because we believe that we must choose to survive, and that we must so choose *at once*, The North American Review proposes a modest first step—a first step which is not only within the power of the people and their elected government, but which can at the same time help to persuade that unawakened 96% of Americans of the severity—of the *finality*—of our environmental problems.

The North American Review proposes that the Federal Government begin selling "U. S. Conservation Bonds" under a system exactly parallel to the existing sale of U. S. Savings Bonds. That is, we ask that the Government issue Conservation Bonds in face amounts of $25, $50, $100, $500, etc.; that the Government set up "Payroll Conservation Plans" identical to the present Payroll Savings Plans; that the Government sell "Conservation Stamps" to school children; that all moneys received under this Conservation Bond plan be earmarked for investment in the fight against the contamination of our water, the pollution of our air, and the rape of our lands, and *for no other purpose*. We ask that the Government devote the same ingenuity to the advertising and promotion of the Conservation Bond plan as it presently devotes to the selling of Savings Bonds. We suggest that as Savings Bonds display the portraits of Presidents and Statesmen, Conservation Bonds might display the portraits of great conservationists or scenes of America's dwindling natural splendor. Finally, we ask that this Conservation Bond campaign be put into operation *immediately*.

We have no illusions about this plan. We do not delude ourselves into the belief that it can raise 50 billion dollars annually, nor do we believe that the sale of Conservation Bonds can, by itself, make any deep impact on healing the terrible wounds America has already inflicted upon its natural resources. We *do* believe that the availabilty of Conservation Bonds will give to the American people the live option of saving their environment, and that it will remind them of how pressing are the problems of environment which confront us. We further believe that a considerable acceptance of Conservation Bonds, as measured by the dollar value of their sale to the people, will serve as a

---

Reprinted with permission from *The North American Review*, Spring 1970. Copyright © 1970 by the University of Northern Iowa.

model and a spur to the anti-pollution askings of the Administration and the anti-pollution appropriations of the Congress.

We are anxious for the preservation of this society and this civilization. We believe the small step of issuing Conservation Bonds may lead America to giant steps in the direction of such preservation. A decision by the Federal Government to begin to sell Conservation Bonds will feed the hunger of our optimism.

Questions

1. Just how does the first paragraph bring the problem to the reader's attention?
2. Is the analogy between Savings Bonds and Conservation Bonds a good one for the editor's argument?
3. Does the editor say that the sale of bonds will solve the problem of the abuse of nature?
4. If not, then what will the value of the bond sale be?
5. Do you favor this plan? Explain your answer.

Suggested Writing Assignments

1. Assume that you are the editor of the school paper. Write an editorial on a topic comparable to one of these: required courses, tuition costs, a visiting speaker, traffic congestion, a potential riot area, or park upkeep. Remember to slant your material for a particular audience.
2. Assume that you are the editor of a big metropolitan newspaper. Write an editorial on a national or international issue: the war, overpopulation, religion, education, or space exploration.
3. Analyze any two or three of the editorials in the text. Look at subject, tone, detail, and language. Do not hesitate to examine other interesting elements which may have come to your attention.

6

Letters to the Editor

We all have a few outlets for our opinions. We can sound off to our family or to our friends, but, even better, if we are really serious about our views we have a chance to see our ideas in print in the "Letters to the Editor" section of newspapers and magazines. This constant parade of public opinion has become one of the most sprightly and closely followed features of our media.

Letters to the editor sparkle with oddities of opinion and the sharpness of controversy. One writer blasts the national administration for its welfare policy, another berates the mayor for his failure to plan adequate flood control, and still another praises the city for its friendliness to newcomers. The subjects and opinions of all these letters to the editor are as various and diverse as the authors. The best letters are usually quite short, not more than a few hundred words. In fact, many magazines and newspapers will not print longer letters. This restriction on length places a serious burden on the writer to limit his attention to a single subject: a change in the exam schedule, a new policy, or a more precise use of certain words.

We have all seen letters which so scatter their shot that nothing is hit. There are letters to the editor which change the subject in almost every line, opening up, for example, with an objection to the present system of foodstamps, bewailing the loss of a ball game, blaming politicians for high taxes, applauding ministers for their work, and ending by asking that we read our Bible. Such letters are perhaps more amusing than effective.

The more impressive letters to the editor usually focus their fire. They make their point in the opening paragraph, usually the opening sentence or two, and follow that with a minimum of support and illustration. For example, a letter asking for an improvement in the local ball team might open with the writer's objections to the present squad and go on to show how those ills might be cured by a few intelligent purchases of new players. Such a letter might close with a brief reference to one of the advantages of having a winning team: it would bring more business to the community.

Only good taste and libel laws limit the subject and the tone of letters to the editor, but restraint is usually more effective than free swinging passion. The ranting, intemperate letter may be eye catching and even funny, but little more. The writer who is so fed up with City Hall that he advocates that we refuse to obey all laws and refuse to pay all taxes may have found an outlet for his anger, but he is not very persuasive. A more modest, more pointed letter about the city administration would be more effective.

"Realistic" Policy

To the Editor:

As a member of President Nixon's "silent majority," my thinking on the Vietnam question is guided by four basic considerations:

Tactics of intimidation must never be appeased and, in effect, rewarded. The revolutionary methodology being manifested in Vietnam is as much or more of a threat than is Communist ideology, per se. These two things commonly tend to be identified with each other, but it is quite important to make the distinction between them and to identify insurgent methodology as perhaps the greater danger. It must be demonstrated that the method does not necessarily work.

It is essential to our self-interest and to the continued relative stability of the world at large that the United States should not emerge from this conflict with a "loser" image. Any notion that world opinion would view unilateral United States withdrawal as noble, courageous and self-effacing is largely wishful thinking.

The war is indeed a serious liability, and it has to be liquidated as soon as possible. It can be resolved only from a position of relative strength, and only on terms that do not amount to an eventual assured "giveaway."

Anyone who is capable of separating the reporting of news from the reporting of opinion can see for himself that we already have a position of relative strength. Why give it away?

It is abundantly clear that the several prominent and vociferous "doves" in this country—some of them in the Senate—have already severely damaged our national image, wounded our national sense of purpose and identity, and immeasurably impaired the quest for a genuine peace in Southeast Asia. These dissident voices would lead us nowhere except into a "peace to end all peace."

It is time for thinking people to stand up and recognize the more realistic and rational leadership provided in our President's Nov. 3 Vietnam policy statement.

GENE A. MARKEL

The New York Times, November 9, 1969. © 1969 by The New York Times Company. Reprinted by permission of The New York Times Company and Gene A. Markel.

Questions

1. Is the overall organization of this letter clear? Can you, for example, quickly identify the "four basic considerations" referred to in the opening sentences?
2. Which of the main arguments are the most convincing?
3. Could the close of this letter serve just as well as an opening sentence?
4. What level of language does this writer employ? What sort of audience does he address himself to?

Children Riding

To the Editor:

I am a newcomer to Cedar Rapids and to Iowa. I came here from California and Nevada.

I have noticed, and been horrified by, the habit of some local parents allowing their small children to stand up in the seats of their vehicles without safety devices of any kind, and felt I must write this in hopes that at least some parents will read it and take heed.

About five years ago I was driving along a country road in northern California—not a heavily trafficked road—when I was passed by a sedan containing a small family which, like many others on that first good day of spring, was simply out to enjoy the air.

Standing in the back seat was a very lovely 21-month-old baby girl, her hair floating out behind her in the breeze, her eyes sparkling with pleasure.

A mile and a half farther on I came upon that car again, smashed into the rear end of another car. It seems the first driver had stopped suddenly to avoid hitting a little boy who had darted into the road ahead of him. Being on a curve, the driver following didn't see the first car in time to stop.

Damage to the first car: Rear lights broken, turtle back and bumper smashed in. Damage to second car: Headlights broken, grille, hood and bumper smashed, windshield smashed.

Crumpled on the floor of the second car was the body of a 21-month-old baby girl, her features hardly recognizable. . . . It was not the impact of the two autos that had broken the windshield.

MRS. MARY MANLEY

The Cedar Rapids Gazette, April 19, 1969. Reprinted by permission.

Questions

1. What is the connection between the writer's main point and a car wreck which occurred five years ago?
2. The description of the wreck could have been written in twenty-five words. Why did the writer expand on the incident?
3. Is the closing effective? Explain.

President's Critics

To the Editor:

In recent weeks, a former Democratic Secretary of State (who has just made a brilliant debut as a historian), the editorial writer of a New York financial daily and a couple of conservative columnists have propounded an interesting doctrine.

These men argue that, in its own interest, the country must simply stop criticizing President Nixon. They point out that he is the only President we will have (God willing) till 1973, and they contend that the weakening of his authority and prestige will only imperil the whole nation. Playing on the title of Theodore H. White's quadrennial dramas, they talk about "The Breaking of the President—1969."

This argument is plainly at odds with our national traditions. The Founding Fathers, in establishing the American Government, rejected the ancient idea that the king could do no wrong. Indeed, at a time when the republican experiment was struggling for survival, George Washington did not claim, and was not accorded, immunity from criticism (though criticism made him, as it has made all succeeding Presidents, exceedingly unhappy).

Historically, Americans have been in the school, not of the royal prerogative, but of Montaigne: "Sits he on never so high a throne, a man still sits on his bottom."

But those concerned about "the breaking of the President" would perhaps rejoin that they do not say that Mr. Nixon can do no wrong—only that he is working as hard as he can, that his policy requires the united backing of the American people for its success and that the strength of the Presidency is vital to the effectiveness of our system.

Even in this modified form, the plea to suspend criticism implies that the President's problems are largely the creation of his critics. Is this really very plausible?

Moreover, the doctrine is not altogether novel; it was also proposed in the 1950's when General Eisenhower was President. Considering this fact, one wonders why it is invoked only to protect Republican Presidents.

One remembers the savage and unrelenting assault on Franklin Roosevelt, Harry Truman, John Kennedy and Lyndon Johnson; but one does not remember The Wall Street Journal or David Broder and Joseph Alsop saying that such criticism must forthwith stop lest it weaken the Presidential authority. Nor did such consideration ever

---

The Washington Post, October 29, 1969. Reprinted by permission.

notably deter Mr. Nixon when he was in the opposition.

Does the "breaking of the President" portend national disaster only when a Republican is in the White House?

Even if the doctrine were applied to all Presidents, the notion that it is in the national interest to stop criticizing Presidents does not make much sense. Surely it is not even in the President's interest thus to insulate him from the realities of national opinion. If President Nixon believes in government by consent, it would certainly help him if he knew better what his problems in winning consent might be.

When the President's friends advance this weird idea that criticism must cease, they might be invited to recall—how in heaven's name could Dean Acheson, of all people, ever forget?—the way President Truman disposed of the issue: "if you can't stand the heat, get out of the kitchen."

ARTHUR SCHLESINGER, JR.

Questions

1. Show that this letter to the editor is a tightly structured little essay in which a thesis is presented, supported, and brought to a close.
2. Which of the arguments advanced by Schlesinger did you find the most convincing?
3. The text distinguishes between letters which "scatter their shot" and those which "focus their fire." In which category would you place this piece?

Does Cardinal Cuddle Bluejay?

Evansdale—
To the Editor:

Here in our front yard, on many a bright sunny, summer day, I have sat outdoors and watched and listened to all the beautiful birds flying in and out of our weeping-willow tree.

At times there might be a robin, a blue-jay, a cardinal and a darling little wild canary, all at the same time in the same tree; happily singing and getting along beautifully.

But never, never have I seen a little wild canary fly out of that tree with its wings around a robin or have I seen a cardinal cuddling close to a blue-jay.

Perhaps God, in all His wisdom, is trying to tell us something here, if we all but look and listen.

MRS. D. W. CARR

Waterloo Daily Courier, March 6, 1969. Reprinted by permission.

Finds Miscegenation Philosophy "Interesting"

Waterloo—
To the Editor:

While reading Thursday night's Courier, I was interested by Mrs. D. W. Carr's discerning analogy between the events in her willow tree and the subject of miscegenation. Mrs. Carr pointed out that she has never observed song birds breeding outside their own species, thereby meaning to imply (I assume) that interracial dating and marriage are somehow against "the will of God." I thought it might be reassuring for you to know, Mrs. Carr, that you are not alone in placing credence in this observation. In fact, one of this century's most famous political analysts drew the same parallel some 40 years ago. He writes:

"Every animal mates only with a representative of the same species. The titmouse seeks the titmouse, the finch the finch, the stork the stork, . . . etc."

This author of an international best-seller continues.

"Just as little as Nature desires a mating between weaker species and stronger ones, far less she desires the mixing of a higher race with a lower one."

I quote, of course, from the writings of Adolf Hitler in "Mein Kampf." Herr Hitler's philosophy was quite popular in his country some years ago. Perhaps this philosophy will catch on in our country some day.

ALAN M. RUSSELL

Waterloo Daily Courier, March 10, 1969. Reprinted by permission.

Questions

1. What is the main point that Mrs. Carr makes in her letter? Does she state it openly or merely imply it?
2. Why does Mrs. Carr suggest that God is trying to make the same point that she is advancing?
3. What rhetorical device does she use to present her opinion? Is the device effective?
4. Show how Mr. Russell uses irony in his letter of reply to Mrs. Carr.

Communist Influence Everywhere

Dear Sir:

It seems apparent that communist influence is stronger than ever before. Moscow, the center for this vile world conspiracy, is like a giant octopus with an infinite number of tentacles, which reach out into every facet of our lives.

Our schools and colleges have always been a prime target for the communist influence, but the effects are more evident than before. Wild-eyed, bearded, and radical students now plot the overthrow of the university itself. They take over buildings, break windows, and throw firebombs. Their unreasonable demands on their professors and the administrators amount to educational suicide. They want everything—for nothing.

The labor unions too were an early target for communist control and they still are. Clever and hidden communists in the unions persuade laboring men to ask for such ridiculously high wages that they threaten the capitalistic system. If communist influence drives prices any higher, our economy will be brought to a halt. Overburdened and underpaid consumers will not have the ability to pay.

Even our churches show signs of communist influence. A kind of militant secularism has crept into the pulpit itself, and ministers now cry for nothing but socialized reform. The saving of souls is out of date.

The government itself seems in the grip of communist influence. In the name of half-heartedly fighting communism in Asia, our country is being so weakened that we are going to fall easy victim to a communist plot. Naturally, Black militants stand around waiting for the fall. They have been brainwashed into wanting to bring down our system and raise, in its stead, a socialized dictatorship. Unless Americans wake up, we are lost.

OSCAR TIMMONS

Clarion (Tuppawa, Nebraska), April 23, 1969.

Questions

1. Does the writer support his claim that the communist influence is growing stronger?
2. What evidence would reinforce the writer's claim that campus violence is occasioned by communist influence?
3. How many different kinds of causes are there for labor's bid for higher wages?
4. Try to describe the general political and social beliefs of the author of this letter.

Protests Nude Paintings

Dear Sir:

Let me as one citizen, with too small a voice, protest the paintings by Miss Doris Fairchild which were hung in the Newman Gallery last week. It seems that there is practically no one left who will defend decency. Stark and raw nudity now parades on the stage and appears in our magazines and newspapers, but I would like to be free of this kind of degeneracy when I go to an art exhibit. Is no place safe from the degrading influence of such vulgarity?

Miss Fairchild's paintings, and I am ashamed to admit that she is a woman, contain not just nudity but actual pornography. Some of the classical artists, it is true, depict the nude female figure tastefully. Miss Fairchild, however, is not interested in such a mild and traditional display. The antics of her nude figures, their postures, their looks, their gestures, make her work fall into the category of pornography rather than true art. The leering and suggestive poses are just indecent. Freedom for the artist has become licentious license.

MRS. RALPH HARLINGTON

Gazette (Wallingham, Texas), June 17, 1968.

Questions

1. What unexpressed ethical assumptions do you think this writer might hold?
2. Would the letter increase or decrease attendance at the art exhibit in question?
3. What conception of women does the writer hold that would make her ashamed that the artist is a woman?
4. Do you think the letter would be persuasive?

Recalls Life in a Sod House

To the Editor:

A few days ago a friend in Iowa sent me a clipping from the Feb. 16 Sunday Register headlined "Conduct a Survey of Sod Houses" and asking for the names of persons who lived in them. The article started a train of

---

The Des Moines Register, March 30, 1969. Reprinted by permission of The Des Moines Register and Tribune and Myrle Tabler.

nostalgic memories for I lived in a sod house.

About 1905, my father, George Middleton, built a three-room sod house six miles north of Bartlet, Neb., and moved into it with his wife and five children. . . We lived there for five years until he moved up on the 640-acre homestead.

Ours was one of the "better" soddies, having good board floors and plastered interior walls, which gave ample protection from the prairie wind's icy breath and from summer heat untempered by shade trees. . . .

Life was hard in sod house days. It was a mile and a half to the nearest neighbor and the same distance to the one-room school. We froze our feet and fingers walking to school, yet I remember earning perfect attendance certificates.

Sometimes small creatures took refuge under the soddy's roof and got inside where the walls made a deep ledge. Once we sighted a large bull snake just above where my baby sister was sleeping. Mama and I managed to get him out without waking her.

Those walls also often echoed with happy laughter and social good times. Nebraska prairie people are friendly folk and liked to get together anytime. In winter it was dances —a bit of paraffin for floor wax and the neighborhood fiddler for music were all that was needed. In summer it was picnics and watermelon feeds. . . .

We didn't have an organized church or a preacher, but we held Sunday School in the school house, where we learned the Ten Commandments and believed in them.

Winter evenings we played games, and who needed a TV? Later, snuggled down in feather beds, through the soddy's walls we could hear the weird, spine-chilling but strangely beautiful coyote chorus. And when spring came, through the open door, we could hear the booming mating call of the prairie chicken and sandhill crane. And overhead, unobstructed by skyscraper or highrise apartment housing, we could see the wild geese winging northward.

Yes, life was hard in those days, but much of it was wholesome, too, and a good environment to grow up strong, honest and free.

MRS. MYRLE TABLER

Questions

1. Illustrate the use of descriptive detail in this letter.
2. Explore the motive of the letter. Was it written to provide information about sod houses, or did the writer also wish to persuade the reader?
3. A student critic observed that paragraph seven could be omitted because it is not related to the central point about sod houses. Do you agree?

Suggested Writing Assignments

1. Compare and contrast any three of the letters to the editor given in the text. Your discussion should deal with subject, audience, language, and other pertinent elements.

2. Write your own letter to the editor on any current article not in this text. Submit the article along with your letter so that the effectiveness of your answer can be judged.

3. Write an answer to one of the letters in the text. Since the reader may not remember or may not have read the previous letter, it is usually a good idea to begin with a statement which briefly summarizes the point which you want to answer.

4. Write a letter to the editor on any current issue which you consider significant. Present your point of view clearly and briefly.

7

The Interview

An interview, usually focused on a single individual, contains a generous amount of quotation of his remarks. Of course, quotes may appear in any kind of article, but when the piece is dominated by the subject's ideas and by his own words, then we have an interview.

Interviews appear almost everywhere: in trade journals, popular magazines, and newspapers. Certainly one reason why they are so popular is that they seem to bring the reader into direct contact with another human being. In an interview one learns precisely what a policeman, a prostitute, or a politician says. An interview, therefore, has an immediacy, an appealing dramatic effect.

Compare, for instance, the experience of reading that a police officer is charged with brutality with the quite different experience of reading the policeman's own account of the incident. In the first instance, we read that "A street gang leader charged yesterday that he was the victim of police brutality . . ." and so on.

In contrast to that kind of news story, an interview can give us the policman's own words. The officer might argue, for instance, "Sure, I know cops are supposed to be brave, but they aren't any braver than anybody else and when I came up on this guy, he drew back and reached around as if he was going to draw a gun or a knife. I figured I didn't have time to talk it over, so I put him on the ground as quick as I could and I held him there."

Or compare the experience of reading about a conscientious objector who spoke before a local draft board with the experience of reading an interview with the young man. In the first case, you are relatively removed from the incident and get only the bare bones of a report. In the interview, however, you may learn directly about the boy's religious convictions, his patriotism, or his youthful seriousness. He can point out, "I want to serve my country, but I can't serve in a way that runs contrary to my deepest moral convictions."

Sometimes the person being interviewed is so well known, either locally or nationally, that his name is of some significance. If this is the case, then *who* he is helps to make *what* he says important. And, beyond this, if what he says has news value, then the interview will hold an audience. For instance, we follow carefully when the Secretary of Defense speaks on Russia's war potential, and we pay attention when an automobile manufacturer talks about auto safety.

But even if the person being interviewed is relatively unknown, an interview can capture widespread interest. A person's experiences *in his own words* can make his ideas attractive. We are curious, for example, about the Mafia, about hippies, and about beauty contest winners. We will closely follow what a mafia member says about the mob or what the new beauty queen thinks about her boy friends.

In much the same way, we will read what a relatively unknown scientist says on an important defense issue. Even though we do not know exactly who the speaker is, his position gives his words authority. If he comments on whether this country should build more missile bases, we may learn that he thinks such bases do not endanger our citizens and are an important addition to our security.

Thus, whether the person being interviewed is a celebrity or not, the interview can be interesting, but the success of the interview depends ultimately on the skill of the interviewer-author. And one of the first things a writer often has to decide is whether he should do a personality sketch or an interview, because the two are so nearly alike that one may shade into the other.

Indeed, the difference between a personality sketch and an interview is only a matter of emphasis. A personality sketch tends to dwell on the subject's personal life, including his background, his family, his job, or his relation to his community. An interview, on the other hand, tends to let the subject speak for himself, so that the reader gets a first-hand impression.

We should also note that the term "interview" can refer to two phases of the operation: either, (1) the question and answer session or, (2) the write-up itself. Consider, first, the question and answer session. If one can choose the place where the questioning is to occur and can also plan his queries, then he has a most desirable control over the situation.

But even if he has a series of prepared questions, the interviewer should know how important it is not to slavishly follow the plan. Once he starts the interview he may find that the subject wants to range into areas which he has not anticipated and these may be better than anything he foresaw.

Where the skill of the questioner is also crucial is in an impromptu question and answer session. In this kind of interview, the questioner has not had a chance to plan either the questions or the encounter. Under these conditions, his wit and experience must carry him along.

No matter what the conditions, however, the interviewer's own ideas about the person being interviewed and what is said provide the frame. For example, some interviews are straight questions and answers, recorded on the spot and written up later, with a minimum of editing; but, even so, a questioner can direct the dialogue to what he considers to be the interesting facets and he can evaluate the answers by the kinds of questions he asks. In this fashion, an interviewer can subtly or overtly display his approval or disapproval of a campus militant, a professor, or a college trustee.

The author-interviewer takes an even more active role when he chooses to set the stage and to describe the subject. Here he is clearly the master. He can picture the place where the interview occurred or probe into the background of the subject and in both phases he can present the subject in a favorable or unfavorable light. And since the interviewer-author normally has more material than he can use, he is free to decide what remarks he will include, whether to quote or paraphrase, and even the order in which the comments appear. Obviously, such power over the interview gives the author a chance to make the subject look good or bad.

The interview, then, is one of the most fascinating as well as one of the most popular forms of modern prose. In it the reader comes eye to eye with people of all levels, from the wealthy to the indigent, from the famous to the unknown, and from the learned to the unlearned. It is therefore a form of modern prose which you should know how to read as well as how to write.

Interview with Rod McKuen

HARVEY ARONSON

December chills the city and a raw wind rides the day, hurrying past the hunched-up doormen of Central Park South and hustling through the gaunt, gray frames of the trees across the street. Somber, cold, winter-struck. A perfect setting for a poet. Even a best-selling poet. Enter Rod McKuen, bard of loneliness.

He sweeps into the Hampshire House from the wind-ridden street in a sheepherder coat, white shirt, filmy ascot, cuffless black slacks and blue sneakers. He has the moody look of a poet but he moves briskly; there is also the confident air of an incorporated millionaire. He's Rod McKuen, an American anomaly—"The most unforgivable thing in the world is to be a best-selling poet," he says, and he has a point. It's eminently acceptable to be a filthy rich gadgeteer, but we expect our poets to be at least threadbare. Whereas, Rod McKuen—35-year-old, California-born loner who has had less than five years of formal schooling and has been a cowhand, cookie-puncher, lumberjack, shoe salesman, disc jockey and beachball-movie actor—is a singer, a composer, a screenwriter and, as surely as love alliterates with lonely, the country's top-selling poet. This year his creativity will earn him more than $2,000,000, and an abundant hunk of it will come from his verse.

"Last week alone, I sold 20,000 books," he says as he folds and unfolds in an armchair in his Hampshire House suite, sometime squatting, sometimes sitting. He is tall and slim, with yellow hair combed straight back over a pitted, blue-eyed, full-lipped, sharp-nosed face. He is as comfortable as an old sneaker or one of his new ones, and he has every reason to be. He has written three books of poetry, all published by

---

Literary Cavalcade, Teacher Edition, April, 1969. Reprinted with permission from Newsday, Inc.

Random House—*Stanyan Street and Other Sorrows, Listen to the Warm,* and *Lonesome Cities,* and a brand-new hardcover songbook entitled *The World of Rod McKuen,* and the four volumes have accounted for more than 1,000,000 sales. The statistic, as *Newsweek* expresses it, "places him in sheer volume among the immortals of the English language," and so who cares if *Time* magazine has called his work "banal". . . .

McKuen's own train-whistle-in-the-night style of poetry may leave him open to criticism as some sort of folk genre Edgar Guest, but nobody can accuse him of being difficult to understand. His themes are constant. Love, loneliness and man's ability to communicate with his fellowman. Memories of bittersweet love affairs and solitary rooms and sad cities. And all of it served up with unabashed sentimentality. One of his poem-songs is titled "I'm Strong but I Like Roses," and that gives you the idea. His stops are always out; you might have to dig a little for meter, but one thing you don't have to search for in McKuen's work is hidden meaning. He hits you smack dab in the viscera. Glomp! "I'm strong but I like roses/ and if a bird should come/I'll keep him/till his singin's all done."

There are roses in a vase at the end of the room, but the window faces another building and there are no birds in sight in the storm-darkened day as McKuen quotes one of his lines. "I said once that 'love at best is giving what you need to get.' I think it is lonely in this country. The basic problem relates to families; kids can no longer trust their families. So the kids are in the streets to talk to themselves. Or, it's a shame that in a city the size of New York, we've got only three major papers. It's because of TV talk shows. And radio talk shows. When someone calls up some guy on the radio . . . well, they're just trying to get close to some bodiless voice in the night."

"In the end/" he writes in one of his poems, "the songs I sing/ are of my own invention./ They mirror what has happened to me/ since I was abandoned by my father/ and by love." And so the question is what's doin' with Rod McKuen? He has a 40-room house in Beverly Hills and a couple of acres, and he keeps two sheep dogs, seven cats, a raccoon, a goat and two horses. ("I'm bananas about animals," he says. "That's one thing I'm gonna do with my money, I'm gonna build an animal hospital in California where people can get medical care for animals at decent prices.") But he's a bachelor and there's no family. So what about him, isn't he lonely, too?

"I'm a loner," he says, "there's a difference. I choose to be alone. I get more work done. I have a lot to do to make myself a compatible human being before I can have a wife and a family. I work 18 hours a day. It's difficult to find a woman who'll put up with that, a girl who'll settle for second place in your life. Look, I have a child in France, born out of wedlock, who I gave my name to. He's 7 now. Do I see him? Do I! Several times a year. I want him to grow up with my name. I want him to understand there is nothing wrong about being a bastard child, because those things happen. I want him to have a last name, to know who he is. Yeah, part of it is my own father. (McKuen's father left his mother before Rod was born.) Whenever I used to go to a new city, I'd look in the phone book for a name spelled the same as mine. I wanted to find him. He may have a guilty conscience. I just want him to realize that everything turned out okay."

"Okay," of course, is taking poetic license with understatement. Four years ago, McKuen didn't drive because he couldn't afford a car. Now he has two Mercedeses, including a big 1967 job that he bought by walking into a dealer's office and writing a check for $7,000. He has an eight-track stereo system in his house and a four-track and an eight-track setup in a car. He gets about 1,000 fan letters a week from admirers of all ages. He has written more than 900 songs that have been cut on more than 40,000,000 records by such artists an Andy Williams,

Glenn Yarbrough, Gilbert Becaud and Louis Armstrong. He has given a one-man concert in Lincoln Center, he has written a 22-minute "Concerto for Four Harpsichords," and he has turned down a $100,000 guarantee for permission to put his face on sweatshirts. It's not half bad for a dropout. . . .

"A formal education probably would have hindered me because I wouldn't have gotten out and found out what life is all about," he says. Before he was out of his teens he held a variety of jobs, including one as a disc jockey at a San Francisco radio station. At 20, he was drafted into the Army and sent to Tokyo, where he wrote psychological warfare scripts and sang rock 'n roll on the Ginza by night. After his discharge in 1955, he returned to San Francisco, where Phyllis Diller, who had known him at the radio station, got him an audition at the Purple Onion. The result was Rod McKuen, folk singer. . . .

Words, music—and he scored with a crescendo. "I'm a mosaic of what I am," he says as he broods on success in his third-floor suite. "I never wanted to be a writer. I just wrote out of desperation because I couldn't find the kind of songs I wanted to sing for myself . . . Poetry is anything that can communicate between two people for a small period of time. Like if you're walking down the street and someone you'll never meet again smiles at you and makes you feel different. Or poetry can be a piece of music. I think of myself as one man trying to communicate. I never want to confine myself to one thing. It's always a problem; people want to put you in slots." . . .

He stops for a moment, flipping cards in a mental filing cabinet, and he comes up with another sure symbol of success—the magic name of the man who took the photograph on the book jacket of *Lonesome Cities*. "Frank Sinatra is doing an album of my songs. Sixteen songs. I got a 20-piece orchestra to play them for Frank in Las Vegas. It was a $20,000 demonstration. Then I spent the Fourth of July weekend with Frank; we were guests of Bennett Cerf at his house in Mt. Kisco, N.Y. We all went on a picnic on Frank's boat, which is like a battleship. Frank took pictures the whole weekend; he had a camera that looked like a cannon. The book jacket? It was one of his ways of saying thanks. He's a nice guy. He's an intense family man, you know. He was always calling the kids. Frank Jr. and Nancy and Tina, they were all in different places." . . .

The conversation ranges. McKuen describes his daily schedule when he's at home. "Normally, I get up at 7 AM. I have coffee, and I start thinking about what I'm gonna do. I start placing calls. I break down the day as to what I'm gonna do. I set aside a certain time to compose, a certain time to write. I take a drive in the morning. I usually drive to the beach, I go 125 miles per hour. I love mechanical things; I owned an electric toothbrush when I couldn't afford one. I have a mike set up in the car, so I can talk or sing ideas into the tape recorder . . . I have a great thing for skin-diving. I like anything that has to do with nature. Or I run on the beach with the dogs. Sometimes, I take them for a long run with a horse.

"I have an office in Sunset Strip," he says, "six people full time and seven part time . . . The most important human being in my life is Ed Habib. He's the best friend I've got. I can't get on and off a plane without him. You know, my mind is always on a project."

What's his definition of success? "I equate success with how well I sleep at night. If I do what I set out to do without having damaged another person in the process, I can sleep well at night."

Then lunch comes. There are four people in the room, and McKuen, who dotes on room service, has ordered for them—four club sandwiches, milk, Cokes, coffee, ice cream and chocolate syrup. He grins at the check. "I can remember when four club sandwiches didn't cost $14," he says.

And he can also remember when he couldn't have afforded it. He wasn't always a best-selling poet.

Questions

1. Explain why the descriptive opening of this interview is effective.
2. Would you say that the author is friendly to the subject, unfriendly, or neutral? Support your claim by references to the interview.
3. Why does the writer call McKuen an anomaly? Do you agree with this observation?
4. The writer occasionally uses metaphors to make his point. What do you think he means by calling McKuen's work a "train-whistle-in-the-night style of poetry" or by saying that McKuen's "stops are always out"?
5. Explain the "tie-back" device used in the closing line.

Candid Dope Addict Tells It Like It Was

New York City—(NEA)—There are, officials say, 100,000 drug addicts in this town. Yvonne Lane is one of them. Or was, she says.

She is 28, Negro, attractive.

She is enrolled in a nine-month "rehabilitation" program at Baird School, a privately operated home for women addicts in lower Manhattan. She has fared well. Her counselors say she's talented, vocal, intelligent, ambitious.

She is sitting on a couch. A half-dozen other addicts are in the room. There is a psychiatrist listening. They are in "group therapy"—a free-wheeling, candid dialogue about what makes each of them tick.

Yvonne Lane is the most candid of them all.

"My mother," she says, "always did her best to grow me up straight. Like she always punished me for doing wrong, you know. Like when I didn't move fast enough, that was wrong. And when I said 'huh' that was wrong. And so she'd try to set me straight, you know, by kicking the hell out of me."

Yvonne was raised in Harlem. She doesn't remember a father. Her mother never said what happened to him. Her mother never said much of anything. All Yvonne remembers her mother talking about was religion. "Go tell it to God," she'd say when Yvonne had a problem. "Go tell it to God."

Yvonne ran away for the first time at age six. She says she went a few streets away and, when it got late, she knocked on a door and told the people her house had burned down, her parents were killed and she was all alone.

The police dragged her back a few days later. Her mother "kicked hell out of me again." A few weeks later Yvonne Lane ran away again.

There began a cycle of beatings, escapes and more beatings. Once, at age nine, the girl was placed under psychiatric treatment

---

The Record (Cedar Falls, Iowa), January 18, 1969. Reprinted by permission of Newspaper Enterprise Association (or NEA).

for a year. It solved nothing. The beating-escape cycle was renewed and by the time Yvonne reached her 13th birthday she had left home more than 100 times.

Finally, she ran off for good. She met a man and stayed with him. Then, she says, "I started to hustle." At first there were only a few men a night, then more and more. She worked New York, New Jersey, Long Island, "any place."

"I don't remember how the drugs started," she says. "I think I just wanted to get high. After that, I found I couldn't hustle unless I was high. I found I couldn't get high unless I hustled to pay for the stuff."

She was 15 years old.

At first it was only marijuana. A light-headedness.

Then it was "skin popping" heroin and cocaine with the needle. Euphoria. At last, as her resistance built up, she was forced to "mainline"—shoot it directly into her blood stream.

At her peak she was using 10 packets of powder a day—$5 a packet, $50 in all. It put her in a continual state of escape. The prostitution continued. She had two sons along the way. She spent four years in jail.

"It was bad, man, you know? Like I was nearly dead. Waking up every day in a different bed, reaching for the first shot. Jesus, it was bad."

Early, Yvonne Lane volunteered for the Baird House treatment, a rehabilitation program which offers vocational, avocational and mental training to addicted women. She says she's been "reborn."

So she sits in the group therapy discussion and bounces up and down as she talks. She uses four-letter words passionately. But she makes sense:

"Like, I got two illegitimate kids, right? Well, I love them as much as anybody could. They're both boys. O.K.? So, some day they're gonna maybe decide that they want to start smoking reefers (marijuana).

"All right, I just ain't gonna say no, period, like my mother did me. I ain't gonna tell them to "Go tell it to God!" I'm gonna sit down with them, I'm gonna try to understand, I'm gonna communicate.

"The goddam world's filled with people who don't communicate. It's insane. Man, you gotta feel for your kids' problems, you gotta help them out. They gotta feel like they can come to you and get some answers. And if they can't do that then, man, you don't deserve to have kids at all."

The therapy class continues, the other girls chatter on. But Yvonne Lane sags back onto her couch. She's finished. She's said enough. She's convinced the most important listener in the room—herself.

Questions

1. Show how the writer works in the who, what, where, when, and why details early in the interview.
2. Discuss the use of narration in the account.
3. Use specific examples to show how Yvonne's language adds realism to the interview.
4. The writer describes the group therapy session as "a free-wheeling, candid dialogue about what makes them tick." What makes Yvonne tick?
5. Is the closing effective? Explain.

Broadway Producer Suggests Baseball Adopt a Let-Me-Entertain-You Attitude

MURRAY CHASS

David Merrick, Broadway's most successful producer, has attended innumerable opening nights. But on this particular occasion, it was Opening Day, and the site was not the Shubert Theater or the St. James, but Yankee Stadium.

"I was sitting with Mike Burke," Merrick relates. "I looked at this bunch of players the Yankees have, and I suggested to Mike that nude ballplayers was the only thing that could save the Yankees.

"It certainly would increase Ladies' Day attendance."

The producer, of course, was joking (after all, he hasn't even joined the theater of the naked). But he is serious when he says baseball needs rejuvenation—and he offers some concrete proposals to accomplish it.

On the field, says Merrick, baseball should adopt the two-platoon system and unlimited substitution. Off the field, it needs lots of color and atmosphere.

Merrick professes no expertise on the game—"My only connection is that I'm a fan, and a friend of Mike Burke"—but he obviously is an expert showman.

Producer Scores With Hits

He consistently has a string of hits on Broadway, with his current streak numbering four—"Hello, Dolly"; "Promises, Promises"; "Play It Again, Sam," and "Forty Carats."

"There's not enough showmanship in baseball. It is show business, isn't it? It's entertainment," Merrick said last week in Washington, where he participated in the festivities surrounding the All-Star Game and baseball's 100th anniversary celebration.

"I don't think baseball is dead by any means. But it needs things. In the theater, we're always thinking of the audience. When we put the show together, when we cast it, when we rehearse it, we're thinking of the audience.

"But in baseball they're unmindful of the audience. I find it appalling that they forget about the fans. You almost think they should build a fence around the diamond and play with no spectators. They've forogtten it's entertainment."

That's where Merrick's ideas of two platoons and unlimited substitution take center stage.

"I think pro football was saved by the platoon system," he said, sipping a glass of diet soda in a hotel lounge. "It sounds inconceivable for baseball, but why not an offensive team and a defensive team?

"I suppose a larger payroll is one thing against it, but it would add something to the game. And what's wrong with unlimited substitution?

"I like the idea of having a pinch-hitter for the pitcher, one of the things they tried this spring. The notion of the pitcher walking up there most of the time and swinging futilely at three pitches is preposterous. It's a waste of time.

The New York Times, July 27, 1969. © 1969 by The New York Times Company. Reprinted by permission.

"I don't think either of these ideas would detract from the star image. In fact, they would enhance it. The stars are never the defensive players. They're the hitters and pitchers."

Suspense Vital to Game

In fact, being able to manipulate the players according to the situation, Merrick believes, would add to what he calls the suspense of the game.

"Suspense is one thing baseball has over the theater," he said. "In the theater the audience usually knows the end of the story. It's a better show if we can keep the audience in suspense. That's baseball—you don't know the end. And anything that helps build suspense to the end helps."

At the same time baseball could be helping itself on the field, the producer feels, it could enhance itself in the color that surrounds the game.

It's no surprise that Merrick is a longtime admirer of Bill Veeck, the man of many gimmicks who was frowned upon by his fellow owners when he was in baseball.

Merrick himself has never shied away from a good promotional gimmick. There was the time, for example, when he fixed up a taxi and made it appear that it was being driven on the streets of New York by a chimpanzee.

Then there was the statue of a nude belly dancer that he sneaked into Central Park at night and had old ladies complaining about in the morning.

There are, however, very few baseball owners who would tolerate chimps and nudes.

"They really put down these fellows, like Charles Finley, who try to do things," he said. "And Burke has had his problems. Anything new is rejected. The owners generally are very stodgy.

"The biggest inconsistency is Walter O'Malley, who strikes me as being the most conservative owner of all—and he's out in the show business capital."

As far as show business on the baseball diamond is concerned, Merrick feels the Mets easily do a better job than the Yankees.

I'm more inclined to the Mets because I think there's more going on out there," said Merrick, a former member of the St. Louis Cardinal Knothole Gang.

"The people [Mets fans] always made a picnic out of it with the food and the banners and everything. It didn't matter whether they won or lost. There was always a show going on.

"Their problem was how to give the people a show without a thing going on out on the field, and up to this year they had done that. There also was a good deal of suspense with the Mets. They always could blow a big lead in the ninth inning."

Merrick is also fond of Casey Stengel, who he says was the key factor behind the Mets' success.

For that reason, Merrick was thrilled that he was selected to make the presentation to Stengel as the greatest living manager at the pre-All-Star Game dinner last Monday night.

As Stengel walked to the microphone to say a few hundred jumbled words of acceptance, Merrick called him "the greatest actor in 100 years of baseball."

"Stengel's a rich showman," the producer said. "When you think about it, was he the greatest living manager or the greatest living actor?

Game Will Not Strike Out

Despite his ideas on what baseball needs, Merrick doesn't envision a calamitous end for the game.

"I had been thinking, along with others," he said, "that baseball has been waning the past few years, but I've changed my mind. The attendance around the country is rather good. Give the people anything like a halfway winning team and they'll turn out.

"There's something else. I had to get gifts for the sons of some friends of mine and I inquired about what they would like. These are 6 and 7 year old boys, and I found out they're all baseball fans.

"I thought young kids were football fans, but they don't really know football. They follow baseball. So I had to go out and buy them baseball uniforms, electronic games and things like that."

Merrick displayed his own affection for baseball at the centennial dinner when, before presenting the award to Stengel, he said:

"I was a judge at the Miss Universe contest last Saturday night. I don't want you to think there's anything wrong with me, but I'm enjoying this more."

Questions

1. Analyze the effectiveness of the lead paragraphs in the interview and state the main point.
2. Why did the interviewer include the information in the seventh paragraph?
3. Explain Merrick's proposals—the two platoons, unlimited substitution, and off the field promotion.
4. Considering the fact that Merrick is a broadway producer and not a sports writer, how convincing are his suggestions on rejuvenating baseball?
5. Because of the interesting content of this piece, it is easy to overlook the contribution made by the interviewer. Indicate the skills which were needed to write this account.

Trip to Moon Means Little to L.A. Skid Row Derelicts

Los Angeles (AP)—Apollo 11 is streaking through the sea of space to land men on the moon—but it means little to many of the men on Skid Row.

They dream of other things—a 25-cent bed for the night, a handout, a glass of forgetfulness.

"I get the papers out of the trash and read all about them astronauts," says Happy Dan, shaking his shoulder-length white mane.

"Ain't No Air"

"But I don't know what good it is goin' to the moon. You can't even grow anything there. There ain't no air."

It was night in the asphalt jungle. Somewhere in space, a tiny space ship was carrying three men to the moon's Sea of Tranquility.

"Why, the moon was put up there as a light," says Charley, the moonlight skipping over his shaggy beard.

Waterloo Daily Courier, July 17, 1969. Reprinted by permission of the Associated Press.

"Gotta admire them guys, though. They really amounted to somethin' educated and all.

"Look at me. I'm a bum an' I won't never be nothin' but a bum," he added.

Mooch Quarters

A group of men stood outside Union Rescue Mission, trying to mooch a quarter to pay for a bed for the night.

"Might be somethin' to go to the moon," one hollow-cheeked panhandler said, looking skyward. "But I don't see anything to it. They should use the money to keep people workin'."

"G'wan, you bum," interrupted another. "Bums don't like to work."

Drink "Smoke"

Down on the corner, two men were sitting against a wall, passing around some "smoke" —wood alcohol mixed with a soft drink.

"I sure wish I had some of that money they're spendin' to go to the moon," he said slowly. "I wish I had my own bed. I got beat up last night. I betcha I wouldn't get beat up if I had my own bed. All I'd need is about a hundred bucks."

A man in soiled khaki pants wearing work shoes without socks said: "Godspeed to them astronaut boys."

Questions

1. How do you think the writer thought of the idea for this interview?
2. Comment on the word choice and the use of contrast in the fifth paragraph.
3. Given multiple interviews, how did the writer achieve unity in this piece?
4. Discuss the extent to which the responses throw light on the lives of derelicts.
5. Did the interviewer save an appropriate quotation for his closing?

Interview with Julian Bond

TOM TIEDE

Atlanta, Ga. (NEA)—The Georgia House of Representatives convenes promptly in the morning at 10. Julian Bond, the member from the 111th District, shows up just before lunch.

Last night he was in Birmingham, making a speech. Or was it Boston? Anyway, his plane was late. Or did his car break down? In any event, as he explains it, removing his coat, he was lucky to make it at all.

The Record (Cedar Falls, Iowa), April 12, 1969. Reprinted by permission of Newspaper Enterprise Association (or NEA).

He looks around. He borrows a match, lights a cigarette and sits down at desk No. 77, appropriately at the left of the hall.

"Hi, Julian."

A handshake.

"You're late again, baby."

The House of Representatives is just reaching full steam. There are 195 legislators in the huge, ornate chamber. Some are reading newspapers. Some are slapping each other's backs. One distinguished gentleman is picking his ear with his finger. Another is almost asleep.

Up front, a pudgy legislator has the floor. He is trying to convince his colleagues that his bill (to put protective eyeglasses on all motorcycle riders) is the most important piece of legislation since the brown thrasher was made the state bird.

Few are listening. "Motorcycles," somebody grumps, "hell's bells." A gavel knocks for attention. "Say," a friend asks Julian Bond, "you know how to tell a happy motorcycle rider?" The friend deadpans, "from the bugs on his teeth."

Bond smiles, fleetingly. His own teeth are imperfections in his coffee-and-cream face. They are crooked and gapped, and he hides them with quick smirks.

The smirks are well known in Georgia, and the nation as well. Bond is one of the most familiar Negro activists of the day. Also one of the most appealing. So much so that some people are convinced the 29-year-old "moderate militant" could one day be the first Negro president.

Bond himself shrugs at the prediction. "I'd like to be a congressman," he says, "but president? I won't even be old enough until 1976.

"Let's see. 1976. Two hundred years after the nation's birth. Wouldn't it be something," Bond wonders, "if a Negro could. . ."

But never mind.

Desk Cluttered

Julian Bond's desk is cluttered with the business of the day. Mail (he likes to sniff the perfumed letters), notes from waiting visitors (labor lobbyist, school children) and the crisply mimeographed copies of all pending legislation.

Bond extracts a large photograph. "How 'bout this?" he chirps. It's a picture of Gov. Lester Maddox. "Wow."

Bond studies the photo with slight enthusiasm. He indicates he's proud, in a way, to receive it. And lucky, too. The first two times he was elected to his office (1964 and '65) he was refused a seat because of his "uppity and unpatriotic" opposition to the Vietnam war. Then, the United States Supreme Court insisted he be seated, and he became a national celebrity.

"It's progress," says Bond.

As an elected official, Bond's progress has not yet made anyone forget Abe Lincoln. He has had one bill passed, HB521, a measure designed to protect tenants in run down apartment buildings. It's not earthshaking, but shaking the earth is not Bond's bag.

Believes in Change

Bond's belief is that things will change one day. The change, however, will not come by separating and feuding, but by full-scale allied co-operation.

His idea, then, is to be one of the allies:

"Look, I used to think all politicians were fools, too. I used to believe the legislature in Georgia was made up of a bunch of hateful goons. But now, being in it, I've changed some opinions.

"A politician doesn't have to be bad. He doesn't have to be stuck under a Lyndon Johnson's thumb. If he wants, he can work on his own, even within the established procedure, to get things done.

"I know this. I've seen it happen."

This kind of talk, Bond admits, seldom sets well with the hundreds of organizations currently soliciting his liberal (give 'em hell) speeches (at $500 an appearance, plus expenses).

Like, when he talks to student groups. He tells them he sympathizes with many student wants. But he draws the line on student demands for professional and executive power.

"I'm the son of a college educator," he explains (his father is Dr. Horace Mann Bond, now a dean at Atlanta University; Julian himself has no college degree). "So I'm not conditioned to believe anyone can benefit if students are allowed to set up their own standards."

Bond pauses as if on stage.

"About now," he says, "student audiences always begin to hiss."

In the main, however, Julian Bond is not often hooted by his audiences. They're comprised of too many admirers. Worshiping kids who've seen him on TV; sophisticated adults who are attracted by his compromise; even some conservatives who embrace him as a Black Panther alternative. Many of them like Bond because, though he's angry, he's not antagonistic.

Thus, he profits as the middling militant. He will not condemn black extremism ("Rap Brown is a good friend"); he often socks it to "Whitey"; but it's never his style to shake his fist at the world.

Cool Style

Instead, Bond's style is cool—standoffish, dignified, unemotional. He is neither intellectual nor stodgy. He is ambitious but not scrambly, serious but not grim. He apparently feels it's better to fight a long time in small battles than die quickly in a large war.

In sum, he seems to be something for everyone.

"Actually," he says, as he readies to depart for still another speech (Nashville this time), "I'm not exactly sure what I am. I think black is beautiful and I'm convinced Negroes are worse off now than ever before. But I'm also part of the system. And when anybody asks me why, all I can say is it's the only system we have."

Southern Progress

He says he measures his political progress in less dramatic ways: "If a Negro's garbage is piled up, if he has a bad street or if he needs a sidewalk repaired, he calls on me and I'll get it fixed. And when you think about it, that's a hell of a lot of progress in the South."

Bond says he has also had progress in organizing the other 11 black Georgia House members. Before, they were individualists; Now, says Bond, whenever possible they group for the common good.

And that, he adds, is black power at its best.

Bond sags back in his chair. Pages rush about on the House floor. Ears are being bent in every corner. A microphone is malfunctioning. Members of a high school band are introduced in the gallery. The voice from the podium is lost in the din.

Bond shakes his head.

"I really should try to get here on time," he says. He lights up another cigarette. "But there's one thing about being late in the legislature (the boyish smirk returns)—I never seem to miss a hell of a lot."

Too Well-Mannered

On the surface of it, Julian Bond is a rather odd, even pathetic rebel. He's too quiet, too well-mannered, too objective and reasonable.

He does not believe in rioting; he refuses to take part in character slander; he has little sympathy with anarchism or separation.

Rather, he can only be described as part of the system. His hair is short, his clothing is Ivy League (blue blazers and buttondowns); he is married, a parent, a homeowner and a taxpayer.

With all of this, though, Julian Bond remains the darling of the New Left. They forgive him his weaknesses (such as his avoidance of all violence) and longingly look on him as a kind of black Jack Kennedy.

For his part, the babyfaced Negro accepts the adulation. He may be quiet, but he has ego and ambition. He wants his following to grow and grow.

The More To Help

"I'm getting ready for tomorrow, whatever it brings," he says. "I'm working to get a base of power. I want to go on up; I'd like to run for Congress. Because the higher I get, the more I can help my people."

Sitting at a secretarial desk in a building adjacent to the Georgia State Capitol (he has no office), Bond admits he has liberal shortcomings, fears many young people "have already passed me by," but insists his brand of measured militancy is the surest way to a better next year.

He picks up a newspaper to make his point.

"Look here," he says, reading the advertisements. "Negroes have been rioting for some time now and I don't see many changes in this paper. The girls smoking the cigarettes are still white. The baby photographs are still white. The people shown in the new automobiles are still white.

"Well, here's something. One blackface in an ad. He's a female impersonator. That's not a hell of a big improvement, however."

Questions

1. Do you think the author approves of Julian Bond? Support your point of view by citing relevant details in the article.
2. What does the brief picture of the Georgia legislature add to the interview?
3. For the focus of this interview do we have enough material on Bond's background?
4. Find the descriptive details of Bond's appearance which are scattered throughout the interview. Why didn't the author give them to us in one place?
5. What makes the author call Bond a "measured" or "moderate" militant?

Why He Flunked

CAROLE MARTIN

Trenton, N.J. (AP)—"At first you don't realize you are going to fail. You sit in class while the teacher is explaining things and you just don't understand what she is talking about."

This is the way an unidentified ninth grade boy recited his academic problems to educators studying the causes of pupil failure at the high school level.

Ashamed To Ask

His assessment of what led to his failure is contained in the study team's report just issued by the New Jersey department of education.

"You ask a question or two and the teacher gives you the answers, but you still don't understand," the boy told the interviewers.

The Cedar Rapids Gazette, October 15, 1967. Reprinted by permission.

"So you think you will find out from some of your friends what it's all about because you feel kind of ashamed to keep asking questions; it makes you feel like you're dumb," he continued.

The youth said he thought there should be a time at school when "you could get together with the other kids in your class and talk about the things you would be afraid or ashamed to ask the teacher."

He told of the first big test he failed:

"I just sat in my seat feeling worse and worse. I tried to cover my paper so that the teacher wouldn't see how little I had written. I remember writing answers to questions I made up myself, because I was afraid to hand in an empty test paper.

Sick Feeling

"For the next few days I would get sick to my stomach every morning thinking about that class, and by the time I got to the class I was like jelly inside.

"I got down in my seat and shifted my position so that the teacher could see as little of me as possible. I wouldn't say anything in class to anyone. Then one day she gave back the test papers. She placed mine face down on the desk.

"Without looking at it, I folded it and put it in my pocket. As we were leaving the class, the kids were asking each other, 'What did you get?' I just said 'O.K.'

"I felt so upset I couldn't go to my next class right away. I went to the boys' room. I went into the john and took the paper out of my pocket to look at it. It didn't have a mark. She had written in red pencil: 'See me after class.' "

"Waste Time"

The teacher arranged to help him and some others after school but when the boy missed several days of school after that, he said she became angry and told him she wasn't going to waste her time with him anymore.

After that, the boy said, he stopped doing his homework.

"In class, I was hoping that we would get on to something new that I would understand better, but it didn't work out that way.

"Occasionally I would cut the class when I knew we were going to have a test or when I just couldn't face the idea of being there like a sitting duck waiting to be shot down.

"By April my parents had accepted the idea that I was going to fail and they couldn't do anything about it," the boy said.

Questions

1. What do you learn about academic failure, from this boy's own words, that you might not get from a second-hand report of his ideas?
2. Can you recall your own anxieties about grades that were similar to this boy's fears?
3. Would this interview be improved if you had more on the boy's background, appearance, and interests?
4. Which parts of the story were most interesting to you?

Sports of Times—Interview with Roosevelt Grier

ARTHUR DALEY

New York—That mountain of amiability, Roosevelt Grier, hove into view, looking slightly larger than life. At 290 pounds and six-feet-five he has to be the biggest guitar-strumming folk-singer in the entertainment business. He bubbles over with such good nature that it's difficult to reconcile the fact that he once was a defensive tackle of such ferocity that he regularly made the all-pro team for the New York Giants and later for the Los Angeles Rams.

Rosey's skills as an entertainer were on public display when he appeared on television as a member of Bob Hope's troupe that toured Vietnam. He has cut a record for Bell Records with two engaging tunes, "Bad News" and "Ring Around the World." He just completed a movie in Mexico, "Jaquin Murietta." It stars Ricardo Montalban.

"The part I play," said Rosey, trying to repress a laugh but not succeeding, "is that of a colored man. How do you like that for casting?" I'm on the borderline between being a good guy and a bad guy until the hero straightens me out. He's a sort of Robin Hood.

"It was a fun thing and I learned a lot about myself. I guess I'll always be learning. One lesson was taught me by a little Mexican girl. She came on the set one day, selling tortillas. I asked her what she'd do if I bought them all. She told the interpreter that she'd give them to her friends. So I bought all she had.

"Then I noticed that she was limping from a cut that had become infected and I took her to our doctor. He had no anesthesia and said it would be very painful if he were to clean the wound. 'I won't cry,' she said. I held her hand and she didn't cry. The next day she came back with her father and mother. They had a bucket of chicken that I knew they couldn't afford to give me. That's how poor they were. So I gave the chicken to another family that had no food at all.

"I never saw poverty like the poverty there. It made me think how much better off we are in the United States and what a wonderful country this really is. I know it's far from perfect but if people would search deeply enough within themselves we can live in harmony.

"John F. Kennedy said it best when he said we should not see what our country can do for us but what we can do for our country. Each should try to do a little more. We can't survive as we are. I'm no militant. I'm a human being, interested in white, black, blue, green or whatever. I'm in favor of brotherly love. A lot of militants got mad because I aligned myself with the Kennedys but they stood for what I stand for. Bobby Kennedy was a tremendous man. If you don't mind, I won't say any more about him."

Rosey, along with Rafer Johnson, apprehended and disarmed Bobby Kennedy's accused assassin. Since he will testify at the trial of Sirhan Sirhan, his reluctance was understandable.

"I thought the end of the world had come," said Rosey skillfully reversing his field, "when the Giants traded me to the Rams in 1963. But it was the best break I ever could

---

The Record, January 21, 1969. © 1969 by The New York Times Company. Reprinted by permission.

have had. The whole world of show business opened up to me and I've been in movies, television and everything else. At the age of 36 and out of football for two years I have a whole new career in front of me."

Rosey delighted the servicemen in Vietnam.

"It was the experience of a lifetime," said Rosey of his trip. "And Bob Hope! What a man! What a man! I had insisted on going out with a jeep patrol. I was a little nervous. But I had to go."

Quite a man also is Rosey Grier. And a rather remarkable human being, too.

Questions

1. What is the main personality trait that the author calls attention to? Do Grier's comments about the little Mexican girl serve to illustrate this quality?
2. Why does the author mention Grier's records and his movie in the opening paragraph?
3. Would Grier's celebrity as a football hero make his comments on black militants more persuasive?
4. Would you agree that the closing is effective?

Suggested Writing Assignments

1. Interview an unusual or interesting person in your locality and then write up your story. Although you may want to work out some questions in advance, do not hesitate to follow an interesting slant if one appears during the interview. Be sure to answer the basic questions: who, what, where, when, why?
2. Using any three of the text selections, write a paper in which you try to pin down some of the main characteristics of an effective interview. Illustrate your points with concrete examples drawn from the samples in the text.
3. Compose a paper on how to conduct an interview. Include these points: how the interviewee might be approached, the kinds of questions which should and should not be asked, and how to take notes. For ideas, reread the text discussion and conduct some interviews of your own.
4. Provide an analysis of an interview taken from a current magazine or newspaper—perhaps an item which you have included in your scrapbook of clippings.

8

The Personality Sketch

A personality sketch, like an interview, may contain what the subject says, but it must have more.

A personality sketch should give us a fuller account than the interview, including something of the subject's background. The sketch may, for instance, reveal such things as the subject's vocation, his avocation, his domestic life, his childhood, and his education. The personality sketch of a famous movie actor might start by referring to his latest and best-known film, and then go on to tell us about his life on the family farm in Indiana, his own immediate family, his zest for duck hunting, or his devotion to professional football. Or, a personality sketch of a new student at a university might start with the observation that she may look like any other member of the freshman class, but go on to point out that she is a professional dancer who has devoted herself to grueling hours of training.

In all such details about a subject the author tries to capture the precise and relatively unknown qualities which make the individual unique. The successful author of a personality sketch, then, may try to bring out his subject's deepest values by exploring his attitudes toward love, religion, or his work. A sketch of a politician, for instance, might emphasize that the man is a devout Catholic, a lover of animals, and devoted to a political career.

While an interviewer can get all the material he needs from one or two meetings with a subject, the author of a personality sketch will have to investigate further—in fact, he *must* look into all available sources. He should get information from the subject's associates, friends, family, and even his enemies. This last can give spice to either a laudatory sketch or an unfavorable one. For example, the student dancer may seem quite conceited and yet, an author might demonstrate that she is truly humble.

Just how deeply a writer can go into a particular personality depends on the time he has available for research and the length of the projected piece, but even a relatively short sketch should give us both foreground and background. A personality sketch is, indeed, a brief biography. A book-length study of General Eisenhower, for instance, will give us full details on both the General's military and political life, while a personality sketch will give us merely a few salient points from his crowded career.

The subject of a personality sketch, like that of an interview, can be either a celebrity or a relatively unknown person whose experiences are interesting. If the subject is well known as a politician or businessman, then the reader will follow the sketch because he knows something of the subject's public life and is curious about his private life.

In the case of a relatively unknown subject, however, readers are attracted merely by the accomplishments. For example, a subject may be a typical airline pilot or a go-go dancer. What is the particular quality of an airline pilot's life or a go-go dancer's life?

Since personality sketches often supply background material for current events, they may open with the subject's most newsworthy feature: the facet which has the widest interest. The sketch of a surgeon who has recently completed a celebrated operation, for example, might start with a dramatic incident from the doctor's best-known operation, and then move on into an account of his training and other surgical experiences. Following this might come a description of the subject, something of his family life, or his comments on the value of his work and the future for his particular branch of medicine.

Thus, it can be seen that a personality sketch is a complex composition. It may employ all the principles of organization relative to narration, to dialogue, and to biography. The arrangement of the various sections may be chronological in one part and logical in another, but all the parts must fit harmoniously together in order to win the reader's attention at the outset and hold it to the end. Needless to say, a good personality sketch demands skill and judgment as well as the ability to dig out relevant data, whether it be obtained by leg work or library research.

Bertrand Russell (1872–1970)

By the time he was in his 50's, Bertrand Russell had revolutionized mathematical logic, written twenty books on topics ranging from geometry to Bolshevism, married twice, gone to jail for his pacifist principles and started a progressive school. For most men it would have been a full life, and time to taper off. Russell, of course, did not retire then—or ever. Over the next half century he wrote at an even more furious pace, churning out some 50 books and thousands of letters to friends such as Albert Einstein.

Newsweek, February 16, 1970. Copyright Newsweek, Inc. February 16, 1970. Reprinted by permission.

He married twice more, the last time at 80, and drank seven double Red Hackle Scotches every day. In 1950, he won the Nobel Prize for Literature, and from then on he devoted himself primarily to organizing worldwide efforts to prevent nuclear war. Mathematician, pundit, man of letters, philosopher and activist, he became a symbol of tireless, sometimes frantic labors on behalf of human survival. Last week, shortly after firing off a condemnation of the current Israeli raids on Egypt, Russell succumbed to uremia, pneumonia and mortality. He was 97 and, as he put it on the obituary he puckishly wrote for himself in 1937, "the last survivor of a dead epoch."

Even as a boy, born into the center of the Victorian intellectual aristocracy, Russell felt like a relic. "From the time of Henry VIII onward," he wrote later, "English history came to me as bound up with the history of my family." Since Bertie's atheist father, suffragette mother and philosopher godfather, John Stuart Mill, all died before he was 5, his grandparents raised him from then on, and further heightened the boy's personal sense of the past. Grandfather John Russell had twice been Prime Minister and had met Napoleon on Elba. He died when Bertie was 6, leaving the boy in the hands of a cultivated but priggish grandmother, her servants and a succession of private tutors until he left for Cambridge University. Of these sheltered years, Russell later recalled, "I had an increasing sense of loneliness, and of despair of ever meeting anyone with whom I could talk. Nature and books and (later) mathematics saved me from complete despondency."

Love

At 11, his brother Frank taught him geometry, in the traditional way, from Euclid. "This was one of the great events of my life," he wrote in his autobiography, "as dazzling as first love. I had not imagined there was anything so delicious in the world. After I had learned the fifth proposition, my brother told me that it was generally considered difficult, but I had found no difficulty whatever. This was the first time it had dawned upon me that I might have some intelligence. From that moment until [Alfred North] Whitehead and I finished 'Principia Mathematica,' when I was 38, mathematics was my chief interest and my chief source of happiness."

Indeed—though Russell in that period also discovered sex, did brilliantly in the brilliant company of John Maynard Keynes and Lytton Strachey at Cambridge and married Alys Pearsall Smith, an American Quaker five years his senior—only symbolic logic seemed to bring real passion into his life. In 1900, after a long search, he found a way to analyze the fundamental notions of mathematics. "The time," in his view, "was one of intellectual intoxication. My sensations resembled those one has after climbing a mountain in the mist, when . . . the country becomes visible for 40 miles in every direction."

For the next decade, his never very ecstatic love for Alys ebbed away, while his work on the "Principia" turned into an ever greater obsession. Ultimately, he believed the strain damaged his mental powers: "I have ever since been definitely less capable of dealing with difficult abstractions than before."

Not yet 40, then, the old, donnish, Victorian Bertrand Russell died away in a sense, giving birth to the Russell everyone knows—the activist apostle of peace and social experiment. World War I had galvanized his pacifism into action. He gave antiwar lectures, abetted conscientious objectors and in the book "Justice in Wartime" compared the belligerents to dogs infuriated by each other's smell. Finally, in 1918, he spent six months in Brixton Prison for libeling the American Army. His writing in the pacifist cause also cost him his post at Cambridge and lost him the affection of many of his friends. On his release, Russell also gave up all but a legally inalienable amount of his inherited income and began to earn his living with his pen and through public lectures.

Wit

Like Voltaire, Russell's strong suits as an intellectual propagandist were wit, fluency and a vast fund of information. Over four decades he managed to popularize Western philosophy, atomic physics, relativity and any number of moral questions. He was almost always provocative and quotable. In an attack on puritanical moralists, for instance, he wrote in 1929: "They have compelled young people to take sex neat, divorced from daily companionship, from a common work and from all psychological intimacy." To combat this, Russell proposed trial marriages for university students. A decade later, this and other advanced theories on sex brought him public disgrace in America.

By 1940, well into his third marriage (having divorced Alys and the promiscuous Dora Black), he was about to accept a teaching appointment at the City College of New York. Local religious groups fomented public feeling against Russell as a sexual monster. And the lawyer for a Mrs. Jean Key of Brooklyn challenged the appointment in court, reviling the philosopher as "lecherous, libidinous, lustful, venerous, erotomaniacal, aphrodisiac, atheistic, narrowminded, untruthful and bereft of moral fiber." The judge agreed and rescinded the appointment. Subsequently, Russell became "taboo throughout the whole of the United States." He found haven with Dr. Albert Barnes, the art collector and millionaire inventor of the antiseptic Argyrol, who hired him to lecture for five years at the Barnes Foundation in Merion, Pa.

Fears

From this wartime vantage, Russell rebounded into the public arena, grown more strident with time and egomaniacal about his political acumen. Among the first to see the dangers of nuclear warfare, he was prompted by his fears to suggest, in late 1948, that the U.S. should force nuclear disarmament on the Soviet Union by threatening immediate war. This stand, curious even for a pacifist who had backed the Allies against Hitler, clouded Russell's reputation till the end of his days.

His sage-like bearing, his Nobel Prize and his Order of Merit (Britain's highest award for personal achievement) offset but could not dispel the shadow of such toplofty and sensationalistic forays into world affairs. During a 1961 prison term he served for civil disobedience in the cause of nuclear disarmament, Russell wrote a message to "all, in whatever country, who are still capable of sane thinking or human feeling" that "Kennedy and Khrushchev, Adenauer and de Gaulle, Macmillan and Gaitskell, are pursuing a common aim: the ending of human life."

Apex

Open letters were one thing, but even fervent foes of the nuclear-arms race wondered at Russell's wisdom in dispatching hortatory telegrams and letters to heads of state, especially during the Cuban missile crisis. His hauteur reached its apex with the Vietnam War Crimes Tribunal of 1967, which Russell called to serve judgment on alleged American atrocities. Had it not aspired to the status of an impartial world court, the tribunal might have borne legitimate polemic witness to reported U.S. war crimes in Vietnam. But its hypocritical claim to judicial authority undermined whatever force it might have had on world opinion. The trial also called into question whether Russell or his Rasputin-like secretary, Ralph Schoenman (whom he publicly repudiated finally only last December), was master in Russell's house.

In the end, too great a gift for abstract thought and too little patience led Russell astray. Possibly he sensed this himself when he wrote: "I may have thought the road to a world of free and happy human beings shorter than it is proving to be, but I was not wrong in thinking that such a world is possible . . . Impatience, after all, is utterly rational at 97."

Questions

1. What character trait or traits does the author stress which unify this brief sketch?
2. Do these traits show up in Russell's work as pacifist, moralist, and mathematician?
3. In what ways is the author critical of Russell? Do you agree with the charges?
4. Discuss the use of quotations in this sketch and their source.
5. What simple technique does the writer use in ordering the parts of this sketch?

Traveling Tony Seeks Solutions

"If you stay in one country for more than one year, you begin to get stale," says Tony Robinson, 27 years old and a world traveler. "And, because I don't want to get stale, I move around."

The way Tony moves is unique, for it is by any method most convenient at the moment, ranging from hitching rides in American cars to animal-drawn carts in Mexico to canoes and dugouts in Central America. But it is, he says, the cheapest way to go.

Visiting Beatons

Born and raised in England near Oxford, Tony has been capitulating to his restlessness for the past several years and doubts that he will ever completely overcome it even should he so desire. Presently, he's been spending a week at the home of Mr. and Mrs. Jack Beaton at 1241 Lyon St.

"His grandmother, a distant relative of ours, visited us several years ago," Mrs. Beaton explains. "Recently, we received a letter from her informing us that her grandson might be in the area soon. On April 4, completely unexpected, Tony called and we went and picked him up."

Never Plans Tomorrow

"I was passing through on my way to the West Coast from the East Coast," the affable Briton says, "and gave them a call. But I never plan tomorrow, so I can't say how long I'll remain here."

After having graduated from college in England at the age of 20, Tony gave in to his free spirit and journeyed around Europe. He emigrated to Canada three years ago. For a time he worked as an architect.

"But two years at the same job was too

Waterloo Daily Courier, April 13, 1969. Reprinted by permission.

much," he reveals. "I had to travel." Then, his odyssey began . . . and today it continues; perhaps, he admits, never to end.

'Moving Experience'

"I've seen so much, and met so many people. When people who have 15 or 20 children and absolutely no wealth invite you into their home, in Central America countries, to share bedding facilities and what little food they have, it's a moving experience."

Tony confesses that he has enjoyed his travel through Mexico and the countries between there and South America the most. He has, he claims, met with men who have murdered and been indirectly responsible for major governmental upheavals in these lands.

Expects Revolution

"Guatemala will rebel within the next two years," he says, obviously concerned. "It is strange to walk through that country, where men carry machine guns on the streets. They (machine gunners) are on rooftops and every street corner, always watching.

"In El Salvador, 14 families own 98 per cent of the land. So, when we (the capitalist countries) support their country, we support those 14 families and ignore the peasants who make up the true country. The rich become richer," he says somewhat forlornly, "and the poor poorer."

Peace Corps Failing?

Tony has lived amongst the natives and has also seen and talked with many Peace Corps workers. He has respect for the latter, but feels they are not doing a great deal of good, even though he thinks they are striving to do so.

"Peace corps workers are so upset by the conditions they find that they feel helpless. They come home, then, and are depressed; they don't know what to do."

Does Tony?

"I'm just trying to find a niche for myself," he says. "I want to help, but . . ." He shrugs his shoulders, and then, after a pause continues. "Nobody realizes what a terrible mess all of this is," he says, running his hand over a map of Central America.

"The more I travel, the more I realize how poor these countries are. It is very sad . . I think there is a duty for people to try and do something."

What Tony is trying to do is understand the problem and then to cope with it someday, somehow.

"Maybe I'll return to England or Canada and teach school," he says. "Or maybe I'll just lecture; I don't know yet for sure. But I know that I'll know more about peoples and cultures, and I'll be able to teach a greater understanding because of my travels."

Though he admits to having known fear from time to time in his journeys, it's not a fright of unknown places or hostile people. It is, Tony states, a fear of coming to grips with yourself. Traveling alone, hitchhiking across the United States, Canada, and deep into the jungles of southern Mexico, he has had an opportunity to face himself.

"The only scary thing is being by yourself—but if you know yourself, you're all right."

Americans Friendlier

Little that he has experienced in the United States has surprised him, other than that the people he has met have been friendlier than he thought Americans would be.

"Sometimes you have to force people everywhere to be friendly," he states, "by being overly friendly yourself. Once you start telling people where you're from and what you're doing, they seem to become interested and much friendlier, though."

Carrying only a hammock and the basic necessities, he has slept wherever he could find a spot, and washed himself and his clothes when possible.

Washing Lesson

"One time I was scrubbing my clothes in a river in Central America, with an Indian woman right next to me. All of a sudden she grabbed my shirt, elbowed me aside and instructed me to watch her as she did my shirt."

He has travelled as cheaply as possible, some days covering hundreds of miles and never spending a penny for food or transportation.

"You can do it if you want to," he says emphatically. "I came across a fellow in the jungles of Costa Rica who had been doing this thing for 16 years. Just knocking about. I was talking to him, and then he just turned and left and went back into the jungle, with only his machete. I couldn't do that," he says with conviction.

What he can do, however, and will do, is search for a meaning in his travels, to learn what he can. And then, maybe, Tony Robinson will be content.

Questions

1. Indicate the nature of the background details.
2. Is the point of this sketch merely the fact that Tony likes to travel?
3. Over half of the detail in the article consists of quotation. Which of Tony's statements do you believe give us the greatest insight into his personality?
4. Identify the two anecdotes which appear in the closing section of the sketch and speculate as to why the writer waited until that point to use them.
5. One student critic observed that the final paragraph provided by the writer is abrupt and overly brief. What do you think?

W. Somerset Maugham (1874–1965)

Years ago, when William Somerset Maugham was a young man of 64, he turned his thoughts to a subject of considerable importance to him: a fitting end to his own story. "Having held a certain place in the world for a long time," Maugham wrote in *The Summing Up,* "I am content that others soon should occupy it. When nothing can be added without spoiling the design the artist leaves it."

But the end was too long in coming: 27 years. The design was spoiled and it sorely strained the patience of the man who was dedicated to the idea that a well-constructed narrative should draw to a swift and orderly close. At his seaside villa on Cap Ferrat, going deaf and blind, Maugham complained bitterly at the way time's slow hand was writing his last chapter. "I am sick of this way of life," he said. "I want to die." Earlier

---

Time, December 24, 1965. © 1965 Time, Inc. Reprinted by permission.

this month, he sank into a coma following a stroke. The 91-year-old heart beat six days longer in a hospital outside Nice. And then last week it stopped.

His death committed to posterity the work of one of the most productive, most popular, most successful and most versatile authors of the century. This year alone, some 2,000,000 copies of his books will be added to the 80 million already in print. *The Razor's Edge* has sold more than 5,000,000 copies since its appearance in 1944. *Of Human Bondage*, published in 1915 when Maugham was 41, has entered literature courses and has been adapted three times to film. At least two Maugham characters—Mildred Rogers in *Bondage* and Sadie Thompson in *Rain*—belong to that distinctive fictional company that the world will not forget.

Characters in Action

Rich beyond most writers' dreams, Maugham became a kind of semipublic personage, a figure of Edwardian origin and habits, projecting an Edwardian image on modern scenes. He looked like a character from one of his own novels: heavily lined patrician features, thin lips turned down at the corners, hooded eyes. Traveling the world in search of stories, he napped after lunch wherever he happened to be—aboard a tramp ship plowing the South Seas, in a Burmese hut or an outrigger canoe. Churchill, Wells, Cocteau, the Duke and Duchess of Windsor, the Kings of Sweden and Siam called on him at Villa Mauresque, his Moorish retreat on the Riviera where, working never more and never less than four hours a morning, he set down most of his books.

Though he got away from common men as soon as he could and avoided them when possible, it was from common men that his invention took flight. "The great man is too often all of a piece; it is the little man that is a bundle of contradictory elements," he once said. His boast was that "I could not spend an hour in anyone's company without getting the material to write at least a readable story about him."

For this, he was often described as a mere storyteller. Today, after Joyce and Freud, "storyteller" is somehow considered a term of denigration, and critics may reasonably question the depth of Maugham's insights. But he was able to do supremely well what storytellers are supposed to do—to dramatize character by putting that character into action, a specific action that displays in kinetic terms his or her faults and virtues.

Measles and Rain

Maugham cites his own example. He once met a dull couple at a dull dinner. The man had been a civil servant in Asia, and the only memorable thing about him was that he was a onetime drunk, taking a bottle to bed with him every night and finishing it before morning. His wife seemed a drab mediocrity, but she had cured her husband of drink. Out of this, Maugham contrived a superb story (*Before the Party*), which begins in a prim country dwelling, turns into a confession by the fat widow that she had slashed her backsliding husband to death with a parang one hot afternoon in Borneo. After the confession, they all go to the vicar's garden party.

Well, how many wives married to drunkards have not had the same impulse? And gone on to parties? Or take the case of *Rain*. Maugham saw a prostitute hurry aboard his Tahiti-bound boat. A missionary and his wife were also aboard, and on arrival in Pago Pago, the group was thrown into quarantine because of a measles epidemic. Maugham added a tropical rain season to the measles, and made the confrontation of missionary and whore into a classic contest between righteousness and sin. What man (or clergyman) has not felt the visceral taint of the sensual in his ostensibly selfless concern for a pretty sinner's soul?

Maugham was by nature, and by his own admission, cold and withdrawn. "There are very few people who know anything about me. And even they do not know as much as they imagine." He was a watcher, not a participant.

But if he was cold, it was because he was unwarmed. At ten, he was an orphan in a strange land. His father had been solicitor to the British embassy in Paris. His mother, afflicted with chronic tuberculosis, had had children at regular intervals on doctors' advice—pregnancy was thought to be good for tuberculosis in those days—and eight years after Somerset's birth she died. His father died soon thereafter. The boy was shipped off to England to become the unwanted ward of an uncle.

Shy, afflicted with a humiliating stammer, the young Maugham recoiled in misery from the hostile new environment. At the vicarage, his uncle pumped him so full of religion that Maugham ultimately rejected God; he remained a nonbeliever all his life. At King's School in Canterbury, classmates and even the headmaster mocked his speech impediment. These unhappy transplanted years were later to appear in *Of Human Bondage*, the most intensely autobiographical of his novels. Even years later, he was unable to read it without tears.

The writer in Maugham emerged at medical school in London, where before getting his degree he waded systematically, if surreptitiously, through the classics and published his first novel, *Liza of Lambeth*, in 1897. Maugham was 23, *Liza* was only a modest success, but on the strength of it, he abandoned medicine for good.

Within eleven years he had scored his stunning triumph on the London stage. The theater gave him just what he had hoped to get from it: money and fame. Both became fixtures of his life. When critics accused him of writing for mere profit, he countered by saying: "I've found out that money was like a sixth sense without which you could not make the most of the other five."

Spareness and Clarity

Sudden success can overwhelm a budding talent. But to Maugham, it only brought the exhilarating privilege of doing exactly as he pleased, which was to master his craft: "The books I wrote during the first ten years were the exercises by which I sought to learn my business. Writing is a wholetime job. No professional writer can afford only to write when he feels like it." He worked stubbornly at refining and paring down his style, inflicting on himself tedious hours of discipline. The result was a style so spare, so clear of the extraneous adjective or the decorative phrase that it almost escapes notice. But no major writer has been more ruthlessly candid, or more humble, about his own abilities. Despite the pains he had taken, he once confessed: "The fact remains that the four greatest novelists the world has even known —Balzac, Dickens, Tolstoi and Dostoevski —wrote their respective languages very badly. It proves that if you can tell stories, create characters, devise incidents, and have sincerity and passion, it doesn't matter a damn how you write."

As for his own literary rank, Maugham himself had no doubts about where he belonged—"in the very front row of the second-raters." That is not as modest a ranking as it might seem. Maugham himself put Stendhal, Voltaire and A. E. Housman there. "I think that one or two of my comedies will be remembered for a time and a few of my best short stories will find their way into anthologies," he told a visitor in 1944. "This is not much, I'll admit, but it is better than nothing."

Questions

1. Comment on the effectiveness of the opening as it is developed in the first three paragraphs.
2. Where do the biographic details appear?
3. The writer of this piece used quotations sparingly but effectively, often as a means of illustrating one of his observations about Maugham. Find an example of this technique.
4. Would you describe the language level of this sketch as being formal? In answering this question, you may want to refer to the section on language in Chapter I.
5. Does a picture of Maugham as writer and man emerge from this character sketch?

Good-by to Shamrock

FREDERIC A. BIRMINGHAM

He was a miniature white poodle and his registered name was Snowdrift Highstepper of Greenglade. But we called him Shamrock because he was born on St. Patrick's Day. True to his name, he was blithe and gay, and he graced wherever he visited simply by being there.

Yesterday was his last. It was I who had to give the order for his execution, and afterward I buried him. Those who have their own Shamrocks will understand why I am not ashamed of my tears and why I have been driving my car very badly, now that he is gone. I think I see Shamrock behind every tree. Last night when I found a rubber band on the floor of my study I picked it up with great relief, at the thought of discovering it before Shamrock found it and accepted the challenge of perpetual gnawing. Until I remembered.

Shamrock had been destined for high glory in the show-ring by his forebears. But after he had had a few puppy triumphs, he slipped out of the house one day and was run over by a delivery truck. Our veterinarian found that Shamrock had numerous compound fractures in the rear of his body, and he was twisted and torn in a dozen other ways. After a long operation the doctor shook his head. I looked at Shamrock's battered body and said that I would like to try and keep him alive, even though the doctor warned me Shamrock had probably lost the use of his hind legs and that his tail would never wag again.

Yet yesterday, when Shamrock died, he was 12 years old, and even at the last, the stub of a pompon on his stern wagged once again so furiously as to justify his third name of Old Propeller Tail.

Reprinted with permission of the publisher and Frederic A. Birmingham from the December 1968 *Reader's Digest*. Copyright 1968 by The Reader's Digest Assn., Inc.

In the first months after his operation he could only pull himself along the ground a little at a time by his front paws. It seemed impossible that he could ever make it. But he did, thanks to the lion's heart in him. I would set him on the steep hill up among the small pines, and free his splinted, bandaged hind legs a little as I faced him downhill. After a while he learned how to move them to keep his balance. Then he began to walk on level ground, too. Finally I could walk uphill slowly with Shamrock laboring after me. In the end, he ran like a breeze again.

Some might call it a triumph of medical science. But I know that it was actually a triumph of the will to live.

Shamrock was gentle in manner, an aristocrat who ate his food as cleanly and daintily as any duchess. He had only one dog fight, but in his own eyes it was victory enough for a lifetime. A rather nasty customer of a collie was chewing up a beagle in front of our house one day, so I went out to break it up. I caught the collie by the scruff of his neck and lifted him off the beagle. Shamrock saw his big chance to come to the aid of his master—ostensibly—and hurried over and got hold of the collie's tail in his teeth.

Until then I had the big dog fairly well under control. But when Shamrock attacked, the collie flung his head around and got my left forearm in his mouth. Soon I was at the doctor's having my wound treated. I have a white scar there to this day. But Shammy had saved me, to hear *him* tell it, and there we let the matter lie.

Shamrock had the clear and beautiful eyes of the thoroughbred. When you looked deep into them there were flickers of tiny flames coming from somewhere inside. He was not thinking of borrowing a small sum of money from you. He did not want to talk about what a devil he is with the women. His subject for discussion was You, every time and always. Even after an absence of only a few moments, he greeted me as if I had been away for years.

In middle age, Shamrock began to wane a little, and I thought I saw That Look come back to the veterinarian's face. By now Shamrock had survived another serious operation, and one hind leg was off-and-on gimpy. He would be running at full speed and it would throw right out of whack, and down he would go.

But then Shamrock suddenly found his true heaven. One year we took a country place in the mountains. It was close to a primeval gorge where the pine trees stand as tall as the masts of clipper ships, where a stream tumbles for a couple of miles over rocks until it grows into a roaring waterfall, and where the ground is springy from centuries of pine needles falling like rain in the nights. There are deer there and bear cubs in the apple trees. Something in the primitive place was balm to Shamrock's soul. He waked me at six every morning, nose nudging urgently and eyes fixed on mine to catch the grand opening, to take him for his walk by the waterfall. I remember him drinking at its edge, then raising his eyes to mine in holy joy.

We took him to the gorge as often as we could, summer and winter. It gave him additional years of life, I think. But still, he was cold at night. He could not jump up on my bed for fear of a fall in the dark with his bad legs. So he slept underneath, wearing one of my polo shirts as a nightgown. The short sleeves made perfect trousers for him.

The end came suddenly.

My wife and I were away for a couple of months on business, and we put Shamrock in a kennel where they knew and loved him and he had the run of the place. But when I went back there yesterday, Shamrock's fires were dim. He could not hear. His eyes were almost sightless. His legs wavered under him. He didn't even know me—until I put my hands around his beat-up little body. Cancer was burning up his insides.

Then he stood up on those hind legs for a last time, put his front paws on my leg, and turned his blank eyes up to where he remembered my face would be. The kennel man looked at me and asked the question dumbly he could not bear to put into words. I nodded.

That afternoon I drove Shamrock's body back to the gorge in the hills and buried him there. The bear cubs will tell the others that the little white lion has come home at last.

And when winter comes, the deer will step high in the snowdrifts in the green glade, over the place where lies my little friend, the one I can never forget.

Questions

1. In the opening paragraph the writer tells us that his dog was "blithe and gay, and he graced wherever he went simply by being there." Does this statement do justice to Shamrock's personality, as it is revealed in the sketch?
2. Because of the excellence of the writer's style, it is easy to miss the underlying structure of this piece. Block out the topic headings which give direction and purpose.
3. Discuss one or two examples to show the writer's skill in handling physical description.
4. One of the marks of a professional writer is his ability to put a great deal of thought into a few words. In this piece, some examples are "I thought I saw That Look come back" and "raising his eyes to mine in holy joy." Discuss these and other instances of the author's ability to say a lot in a little.
5. Analyze the last two paragraphs. What specific elements do you find which account for the appeal of the closing?

Closeup of a Hippie: Long Hair, Short Skirt, Sad Eyes

Milwaukee, Wisc. (AP)—She wears her hair long and her skirts short and her eyes are wise, sad, glazed but still innocent.

She is a seeker after simplicity but her life is an endless complication. Her creed is to hurt no one but herself. Life, she says, is pain; and suicide she accepts as an option for later, but not now.

There is too much life yet to be tasted; too many experiments yet to be tried; too much pain to sift for meaning.

Her name, not her real name, is Ursala.

Girls who resemble her are returning to campuses all across the nation this month. They are part of a growing army of the alienated.

The Oelwein Daily Register, September 20, 1967. Reprinted by permission of the Associated Press.

Ursala spent her summer in Canada. She thought it would be cool to spend time observing the profusion of symbols of the mechanized, computerized society she can't abide.

Boredom set in and sent her to Mexico.

She could have gone to London or Athens or Paris. That will come later. Her life is a conscious pursuit of the individual self but her style falls into a shared pattern of pot, promiscuity and petty crime. She is stamped a hippie and judged. Dropping out of one society, she drops into another.

Ursala is tall, rawboned and nearly beautiful. In her freshman year in college, she had started out to be a psychiatrist. She began sleeping with a graduate student. He moved on. She began sleeping around. She still considers herself innocent but adds with a touch of sadness, "I find myself constantly redefining what I mean by innocence."

The daughter of professional people, Ursala's intelligence quotient is in the 150s. She was a leading student in her high school class. She was active in school clubs. She liked science. She liked drama.

But in college something happened. "I became aware. I became open. I began to search for myself," she said.

Ursala's parents were of little help to her even before college. Her home life was painful. Her mother had lovers. Her father had mistresses. Eventually, they had a divorce. Ursala doesn't blame them. She doesn't pity herself. She says she accepts, she understands, she forgives. Her anger is reserved for less personal things—the war in Vietnam, racial hatred.

God or the traditional idea of God is irrelevant to her. "The solace to be plucked from a cold and barren universe is love and love alone," she said as a freshman. She is now a junior and she has collected her material. But the energy for the long novel isn't there. So she writes poetry, love poetry, but talks with contempt of her lovers.

At a party, she danced in bare feet and wore flowers in her hair. The windows were open, but the smell of pot was there.

Her friends sat on the floor and devoured watermelon as if it were the source of life.

Ursala danced and danced, and her loneliness was utter.

Questions

1. The title of the sketch promises a "closeup" of a hippie. Does the writer succeed? Base your answer on concrete illustrations.
2. Is this a sketch of an individual person or of a general type? In answering this question you may find it useful to compare Ursula with Tony Robinson in one of the preceding sketches.
3. Are the opening and closing paragraphs tied together in any way?
4. Identify the name of the device which the author uses in the following lines: "a seeker after simplicity" and "pot, promiscuity, and petty crime."
5. Few readers will deny the impact of this piece. The question is: how does the writer achieve such a powerful effect in a scant 600-word treatment?

Finds Joy in Hauling Kids

Onawa, Ia.—Dooley Carritt has probably broken up more fights, dried more tears, and watched more children grow up than anybody else in Onawa.

And Dooley has done almost all of it while traveling down the highways and back roads of Monona County at the wheel of a big yellow school bus.

Dooley, 66, a driver for the West Monona Community School District here, has driven school buses for the last 35 years. He started hauling children to school in a horse-drawn buggy as a way of making a buck during the Depression.

Since then he figures he's driven about 250,000 miles, with as many as 500 children a day, laughing, shouting and squirming in their seats behind him.

Strenuous Service

His years of driving a bus filled with energetic kids have left him with a face as wrinkled as an old baseball glove, salt-and-pepper gray hair and a wry twinkle in his pale blue eyes.

Although Dooley has probably driven longer than any other active school bus driver in Iowa, and has never had a serious accident, he's proudest of the rapport he's enjoyed over the years with his thousands of passengers.

"Kids are about the most wonderful people we have," he smiles, "and they haven't changed a damn bit in 35 years, not a bit. If anything, they've improved."

Dooley lists a set of steady nerves as the most important requisite of a school bus driver. After that comes patience, a sense of humor and a liking for kids.

He says he's disciplined bullies, bolstered the egos of introverts, given a sympathetic ear to troubled kids, and helped slow students with their homework while driving his bus.

Friend in Need

He's watched romances bloom in his rear-view mirror, and has called youngsters aside for special attention when it was apparent they were having problems and needed help.

As a result, Dooley is known by more kids than any other man in town. They send him cards and letters at Christmas and on his birthday, even after they've gone on to college or into the service.

Due to retire next month, Dooley says the most rewarding aspect of his 35 years as a school bus driver is that he "helped some kids become good citizens."

"You keep a kid or two out of trouble," he says, "and you ain't done too bad."

Dooley Carritt obviously ain't done too bad.

The Des Moines Register, May 11, 1969. Reprinted by permission of The Des Moines Register and Tribune.

Questions

1. What do paragraphs one and two provide as contrasted with paragraphs three and four?

2. Quote one or two of the Dooley Carritt's observations about kids which you found most interesting.
3. What was the probable occasion for this piece?
4. Would you agree that the last line could be omitted?

Suggested Writing Assignments

1. The examples in the text include sketches of a young wanderer, a hippie, a novelist, a bus driver, a philosopher, and a dog. Do you know anyone whose accomplishments, habits, oddities, or other characteristics would make him a good subject for a personality sketch?

After you have selected a subject, remember to begin by prewriting your thoughts. It is by this means that you can determine the specific trait or traits which will serve as the basis of your paper. Also, listing ideas under your topic will uncover strong opening and closing possibilities. If conditions permit, by all means interview your subject. The text selections make it very clear that quotation provides excellent supporting material.

2. Choose what, in your opinion, is the most effective personality sketch from the six examples given in the text. In defending your choice, contrast it with those pieces which you would rank second and perhaps third. Look at the writer's selection of thesis, the opening and closing paragraphs, the supporting detail, the language, and other elements which account for the appeal of the writing as you see it.

3. Analyze a personality sketch from a magazine or newspaper which is not included in the text. You might want to take something from your own collection of clippings. Your first task will be to find a good sketch, one which gives the reader a real insight into the subject. Your next step will be to determine the various aspects to be discussed—for example, the dominant trait or thesis, the effectiveness of the lead paragraph, the kinds of detail used, the word choice, audience, and so on.

9

The Review

Reviews may be described as brief, evaluative accounts of books, music, films, plays, or art exhibits. In fact, the subject of a review, the thing examined and judged, may be anything: a TV show, a new car, new clothes, or a World's Fair.

Of course everyone experiences new things and, inevitably, has opinions about them, but the reviewer differs, because he must organize his ideas and put them into words. His written account tells us both *what he experienced* and *what he thought about it*.

Reviews are as ubiquitous and diverse as any modern prose. They appear almost everywhere, in any sort of magazine or newspaper, and their style ranges from the solemn sentences one finds in scholarly journals to the breezy language of weekly news magazines. The following titles, taken from current newspapers and periodicals, will suggest some of the possibilities: "The Beatles Do It Again," a review of a new record album; "The Shape of Tomorrow," a review of the Miss America Pageant; "The Fury of a Hebrew Prophet," a review of a new Norman Mailer book; "Age Doesn't Dim the Masters," a review of an exhibit of classical paintings; "Character with Voice," a review of an opera; "Between Pathos and Horror," a review of the film, *The Boston Strangler*; "Dance Peak in the Rockies," a review of modern dance at the University of Utah; "Gut Theater," a review of a new play titled, *The People vs. Ranchman*; and "Jazz Expo 68," a review of a recent London Jazz Festival.

As far as the length of reviews is concerned, here again there is remarkable range. One review may contain no more than a hundred words; another will run to thousands. In general, however, reviews are relatively short because the modern reader does not have time to study long, critical analyses.

No matter what the length of the review, they are often controversial. Sometimes the author himself will enter into a developing controversy and reply to a negative review; sometimes reviewers fight with each other, in a kind of critical, civil war. Taken as a whole, reviews occasion a quiet and rather constant conflict, and the very liveliness of these disputes helps to make reviews some of the most spirited prose in our mass media.

But who are the reviewers? Are they really experts? Should the public bow to their opinion? Suppose we disagree with a reviewer; should we shake off his opinion and cling to our own?

Some reviewers are, indeed, experts and we should pay close attention to what they write. The more affluent newspapers and magazines employ persons who do nothing but review films, plays, or the dance. Indeed the more elegant the media, the more they are apt to employ persons who write well and who have a proper background for judgments. Such reviews deserve our respect. But not all reviews are written by experts. Many are written by amateurs. The reviews in your local paper, for instance, may be written by a lady next door who penned a critique of the Christmas cantata or the local play.

We can see, then, that some reviewers have considerable training and others do not. But expert or not, judgments are not absolute. Equally reasonable people, who are equally well informed, may still disagree about the worth of a movie or a TV show. Judgment is a matter of taste, and on such issues, there may be eternal dispute.

Reviewers are necessarily engaged in the art of persuasion, because they evaluate and they want us to agree with their judgments or at least respect them. It is true that some reviewers may play down their judicial aspect. Occasionally, they will spend their words describing the experience and perhaps merely imply with a hint or two, what they think of the subject.

But other reviewers will not soften the judgment. They are open about their ideas, aggressively judicial, boldly pushing on into overt pronouncements. For instance, some urge us to buy the book or see the new play. Since such reviews have great advertising value, they are closely scanned by those who want to buy.

If a reviewer does declare a subject good or bad, in such an open way, he usually goes right on to try to convince us that his judgment is correct by citing specific illustrations to support his opinion. If, for example, a reviewer thinks that the movie, *The Graduate*, is an admirable film because it attacks adult, middle-class values, then he may argue that Benjamin, the young hero, is smothered by his parents' vacuity and the stifling adult world around him. He may claim that Mrs. Robinson's illicit interest in Benjamin is an exhibit of her restlessness, ruthlessness, and aimlessness.

On the other hand, another reviewer may attack the film for the reason that the hero himself is a rudderless, mindless boy, moving into a senseless affair with a middle-class comedian like Mrs. Robinson. Such a hostile reviewer may go on to argue that the major fault lies in the conception of the chief character himself, Benjamin: that he is an unbelievable, an improbable young man. This reviewer may point out that Benjamin is impossibly naive in his relationship with the mother and impossibly romantic in his relationship with the daughter.

If we look, finally, at the other side of reviews, the informative side, we can see at once that it would be difficult to judge something without also telling the audience about it. Certainly, in casual conversations, we can sometimes get away with saying that a book "is great" or "lousy," but if we write a review, then we are obliged to explain "why." When a reviewer gets into the "why" part of his remarks, he cannot help but inform.

If we read a review of the latest record album, for instance, we may learn a number of things that we might not discover from the album itself. We might find out exactly what instruments were used, who played them, how the recording was made, and how the music relates to other compositions by the same group or by similar groups.

Or, in a book review, we may learn something about the nature of the work and, ordinarily, a great deal more. If it is a study of our country's policy in Viet Nam, for instance, we can discover what the author thinks of that policy as well as what the reviewer thinks of it.

In all these ways reviews can be informative and persuasive. While the balance between these two aspects changes from one review to the next, still the twofold aim is ordinarily achieved. We read reviews for that very reason.

The Family: Dr. Spock of the Emotions

With irrational finality, your child insists that his soup is too salty, his homework too hard. What should a parent do? Easy, answers Psychologist Haim Ginott. Just keep cool and coo something sympathetic, like "Oh, it's too salty for you. I wish we had something else," and "Yes, you *do* have a lot of homework." Chances are the child will eat the soup after all and resolutely go off to study.

As a growing band of grateful parents are willing to testify, Ginott's strategy of sympathy seems to work. The secret is that it encourages parents to show respect for a child's feelings without compromising their own standards, and strikes a balance between strictness and permissiveness. Parents should draw the line between "acceptance and approval," Ginott says. "A physician does not reject a patient because he bleeds; a parent can tolerate unlikable behavior without sanctioning it."

None of this theorizing is terribly original, but thanks to a shrewd talent for translating well-known psychological principles into jargon-free "childrenese," the Israeli-born Ginott has gained a national reputation as a kind of Dr. Spock of the emotions. First published in 1965, his *Between Parent and Child* has been translated into 13 languages and has sold an estimated 1.5 million copies. Ginott is now a resident expert on the *Today* show, writes a monthly column for *McCall's* and frequently lectures around the country. A new book, *Between Parent and Teenager,* repeats the principles in Ginott's first volume almost word for word and applies them to adolescents. It has already become a bestseller in the three weeks since it was published.

Ginott's basic point is that mature parents can easily increase their sensitivity to their children, becoming demi-psychologists who seek out the source of a child's behavior rather than concentrate on its surface expression. With a little common sense, he insists, children of any age can be intelligently decoded. When they refuse to cooper-

---

Time, May 30, 1969. © 1969 Time, Inc. Reprinted by permission.

ate with a mother getting ready for the evening, she should be alert for more than ordinary balkiness and attempt to sympathize with whatever is bothering them. One kindly mother in that situation, Ginott reports, calmed her kids by saying: "I bet you all wish you could come to the theater with Daddy and me"—even though the line might seem capable of provoking some teenagers into paroxysms of fury.

Ginott also urges parents to realize how easily their children read many levels into the most innocent remarks. Don't tell a cooperative child, "You are always so good —you are an angel," he warns; a child knows he is not always perfect, and is likely to feel anxiety under "an obligation to live up to the impossible."

In anger, specifics are most important. Parents should avoid sweeping, satiric barbs like "With that handwriting you won't even be able to cash unemployment checks." Ginott advises them to express their "anger without insult," and describe the offense candidly and explicitly: "When I see cards, soda bottles and potato chips scattered all over the floor, it makes me feel unpleasant. It actually makes me angry." When the point is made clearly enough, most children will calmly decide to repair the damage without hurt feelings. "Our anger has a purpose: it shows our concern," Ginott writes. "Failure to get angry at certain moments indicates indifference, not love. Teenagers can benefit from anger that says 'There are limits.' "

To some parents, Ginott may seem excessively tolerant of misbehavior. About some aspects of adolescent life his new book reveals him as tartly old-fashioned. He abhors early dating, for example. "The ones who enjoy such spectacles as paired parties for twelve-year-olds, padded bras for eleven-year-olds, and going steady for an ever younger age are adults to whom the clumsiness of children looks cute." He is against marijuana, at least until harsh legal penalties are relaxed, and urges parents to suggest moderate alternatives when teenage behavior is likely to hurt others. He approvingly quotes a father who told his son: "If you feel high, ask your date to drive or call a cab. We can get your car back in the morning." Ginott does not flatly condemn premarital intercourse, but simply pleads that parents provide their children with some sense of the psychology of sexual awakening as well as the basic biological facts. Children who ask their parents for contraceptives should be turned down, he insists, since the teen-ager is showing "a lack of readiness for adulthood. An adult makes his own decisions and accepts the consequences."

Parent Development.
Although he is deeply hostile to questions about his personal life and refuses to say whether he is married and has children, Ginott's "empathy first" approach stems from solid clinical experience. He has spent nearly 20 years doing therapeutic work with parents and children, and teaches part-time at Adelphi and New York universities. In front of children and parents alike he is known for pulling out a harmonica and zipping through Hebrew folk songs; he has the stand-up comic's uncanny ability to mimic revealing snips of parent-child dialogue. He is at home quoting both Tolstoy and Bob Dylan, and can rattle off 58 slang terms for drugs. Says the *Today* show's Barbara Walters, who plans to begin applying Ginottisms to her own eleven-month-old daughter as soon as she is old enough to talk: "There's nobody else who can put together his combination of psychology, common sense, and Harry Golden *gemütlich* wit."

Other child-guidance experts find Ginott's suggestions sound enough and admire his direct, down-to-earth style. But they also point out that a parent confidently playing instant psychologist who misinterprets his child's action may end up doing more harm than good, and that childrenese presupposes well-balanced, emotionally healthy parents and is not likely to be much use in deeply troubled families. "He is a significant contributor not to the field of child development but to parent development," says Los Angeles Psychiatrist Saul Brown. But Ginott's techniques are not limited to the home. When he began sympathizing with the difficulties auto mechanics faced in repairing his car, Ginott reports, he got superior service.

Questions

1. Why did the reviewer wait until the third paragraph to mention Ginott's new book, *Between Parent and Teenager*?
2. According to the writer, what do Ginott's two books have in common?
3. Where does the reviewer introduce the who, what, where, and when information?
4. Does the reviewer offer only generalizations about Ginott's new book or does he quote specific examples? Illustrate.
5. How persuasive was the reviewer's endorsement? Would you like to read the book?

Pianists: Rescued from Limbo

As they watched Pianist Alexis Weissenberg play Chopin with the New York Philharmonic, the audience at Manhattan's Lincoln Center last week could easily have felt a twinge of memory. Weissenberg bore a strong resemblance to a younger pianist named Sigi Weissenberg, who had made his U.S. debut playing Chopin with the New York Philharmonic 20 years earlier. Alexis even had some of Sigi's pianistic traits—triphammer virtuosity, brilliant tone, a briskly commanding approach to a score—but they were tempered with subtler shading and a surer sense of structure.

A puzzling case, young Sigi. He was one of those comets in the musical sky that turn out to be meteors, burning out and falling below the horizon. Born in Sofia, he studied under Bulgaria's foremost composer, Pantcho Vladigerov, and made his way to Manhattan's Juilliard School by way of Turkey and Israel. In 1948 he won the prestigious Leventritt award. His career was launched in a blaze of critical superlatives. But over the years, instead of flourishing on the concert circuit, he faded. In 1957 he disappeared from it.

Whatever became of Sigi? Alexis knows. He *is* Sigi—now a seasoned 39, sadder but wiser, a vigorous survivor of a career gone sour, a revenant from the limbo of semi-retirement.

Free and Faithful

Alexis Sigismund Weissenberg realizes now that his problem was not the critics who switched from cooing to carping. Nor was it the managers who booked him into

Time, December 20, 1968. © 1968 Time, Inc. Reprinted by permission.

that deadly round of whistle-stop tours called Community Concerts. His problem was the quandary of every young performer: "He must perform early for an audience to develop his personality. On the other hand, the inner gifts need development privately. If these are developed in front of the public, many things are exaggerated, experimental, uncertain."

Weisssenberg's way out of this quandary was to take a sabbatical. Freed from financial worries by an inherited income, he moved to France, determined to "read more, live more, and rethink everything." His playing became "freer," he says. "I mean free in the sense that you are absolutely at one with yourself, and whatever you do is faithful to a single intuitive interpretation, whereas at earlier stages we are all so influenced by different interpreters that our playing is a patchwork."

As time passed, Weissenberg's sabbatical threatened to stretch on indefinitely. Then, in 1966, Conductor Herbert von Karajan re-established him in Europe overnight by choosing him to open the season with the Berlin Philharmonic. Last year the comeback was completed in the U.S. when Weissenberg dashed off an exhilarating version of Rachmaninoff's *Piano Concerto No. 3* with the New York Philharmonic. As his performance of Chopin's *Concerto No. 2* last week showed, his playing nowadays bristles with the strength of a new maturity.

No Seasickness

The interpretation reflected Weissenberg's desire to "take Chopin out of the salon, make him not old-maidish but masculine." In making the piece surge ahead with a calculated tensile force and precise gradations of color, he sacrificed some of the spontaneity and relaxation that Chopin's score invites. Weissenberg shrugs off the criticism that he is "an ice-cold interpreter, even an IBM machine," arguing that his emotionally objective approach is much sounder than that of pianists "who would nearly vomit on the keyboard to show that they are so sentimental and inspired. They have a sort of seasickness on stage."

In short, Weissenberg is playing exactly the way he wants to play, and he is "convinced that it is better than it was before." Others agree. Two record companies have signed him on to make a total of 20 albums in the next two years. He has solid bookings through 1970, including a tour of the Soviet Union and Japan. In fact, he is busy enough to start thinking ahead about the next sabbatical. That one, however, will not last ten years.

Questions

1. Explain the technique used by the writer in the opening paragraph to create interest in his subject.
2. Was the pianist given a good or a bad review?
3. Phrases such as "trip-hammer virtuosity" and "a blaze of critical superlatives" reveal the aptness of the writer's choice of words. Find other examples.
4. Illustrate the effective use of quotation in the account.
5. Explain how the use of the word "sabbatical" in the closing lines strengthens the unity of the review.

Angry Young Hamlet

RAYMOND A. SOKOLOV

It has been said and said again that Shakespeare, traditionally performed, is irrelevant to a modern audience. And at least since the old Mercury Theater's modern-dress "Julius Caesar" of 1937, directors have been trying to update, undress or politicize the Bard, mostly without accomplishing much of value for him or themselves. Setting "Much Ado About Nothing" in Texas, as was done some years back, was an arbitrary and frivolous gesture that ultimately distracted from the play rather than increasing its power. On the other hand, and this is probably even truer in America than England, the gorgeous, deodorized, upper-class British accent that Shakespeare has been stuck with since the nineteenth century really is a life-destroying style. At its worst, it turns drama into elocution. At its best, as done by Sir John Gielgud or Sir Laurence Olivier, it is elegant and melodious, but so obviously put on and super-refined that it requires a special suspension of disbelief from the audience in order to work.

But junking the accent and the romantic manner has most often left nothing but a kind of slack informality that unhinges the poetry. How, then, if at all, *can* Shakespeare be acted successfully today?

Illusionless

Nicol Williamson has found a way. Star of the Tony Richardson production of "Hamlet" just over from London after a smash season, he revolutionizes the most oft-played role in the dramatic repertory, transforming the "melancholy Dane" from the brooding, wayward matinee idol of yore into a tense but finally confident, sardonic, unromantic, illusionless, tragic, common sort of bloke.

He enters the almost totally bare stage bearded, wearing shabby black and speaking in precise, sometimes rasping, nasal tones. His accent is broadly provincial, right out of England's Midlands. At first this seems like a stunt, but Williamson doesn't use the accent just to twit the Gielgud school. It's a device that liberates him from all the fancy echoes of previous performances and lets him get on with speaking the lines at if they actually meant something. The metrical soul of the verse remains as the hidden backbone it should be, but the effect is as natural-sounding as Chekhov.

And yet, the play has not been modernized, politically or historically. The Midlands accent does not democratize Hamlet so much as it universalizes him. The costumes are modified Tudor. And the spectral set, whether inky black and transected with spots or dazzling bright with incense-like smoke, is an abstract world, Denmark in name alone.

By cutting Shakespeare's last scene, in which the Norwegian Fortinbras enters from the outside world and brings politics and reality to Elsinore, Richardson has made his "Hamlet" even more divorced from specifics of time and place. Elsinore becomes a limbo of doom. And Williamson's Hamlet, stripped of the fake psychology (which can now be seen as the romantic posturing it always was) emerges starker and bolder than the indecisive stripling too well known from earlier renditions.

Newsweek, May 12, 1969. Copyright Newsweek, Inc., May 12, 1969. Reprinted by permission.

Williamson starts slowly and accelerates as his plan forms. By the bloody end, the pace he sets has spread through the cast. Frenzy is everywhere, foils flash expertly and the usually grotesque pile-up of bodies about Ophelia's grave for once is the logical finish to a steadily quickening *danse macabre.*

Splendid

In all of this, Williamson is the undeniable star, but the rest of the cast follows his lead splendidly, though definitely from the background. Mark Dignam's Polonius is high comedy at its highest. Francesca Annis is a subdued Ophelia, but Ophelia nonetheless, her bosom heaving palely, her reed-clear voice piercing the heart and her legs shimmering ghostlike through the diaphanous folds of a white death gown.

If spectacular diction and pacing are the twin virtues of this "Hamlet" they are also, in a minor way, its only weaknesses. Some lines are spoken a bit too trippingly on the tongue and whiz by like phrases in a foreign language. The accent, too, makes some things hard to catch, at least for an American ear. But even with a few dropped lines, this is the event of the year on Broadway, and possibly the start of a new era for Shakespeare. Hamlet lives.

Questions

1. Sum up the elaborate background detail provided in the opening paragraphs.
2. How does the reviewer support his belief that "Nicol Williamson has found a way"?
3. Was the reviewer justified in giving only one paragraph of discussion to the other members of the cast?
4. In the final paragraph the writer mentions the weakness of the play. Does he end on a negative note?

New Musicals: A Guide to Modcom

Hair begat *Salvation,* and this new musical is an aesthetically retarded child. However, *Salvation* is instructive because it epitomizes a specific kind of phoniness that began with *Hair* and surfaced again in *Promenade* and the Living Theater. What knits these shows together is something that might be called Modcom.

Modcom is the commercial exploitation of modernity without regard for dramatic art. Modcom peddles the youth cult as a product. It is replete with cynical counterfeits of innocence, freedom and dissent. Enough evidence has now accumulated about how to put together a Modcom show. The rules:

Be plotless

It saves time. Nothing is quite so easy as not to write a book for a show. If plot insists on cropping up, be opaque. A story line that

---

Time, October 3, 1969. © 1969 Time, Inc. Reprinted by permission.

cannot be followed may not be exposed for the meaningless rot that it is. Always assume that the audience has the attention span of an agitated grasshopper.

Be lavish with four-letter words

This is the largesse of an impoverished mind. It is a hair transplant on a would-be manly chest.

Beslime the U.S.

Find some degrading way to display the flag. State the President is an idiotic monster of corruption. Repeat the Modcom pledge of disallegiance: this is a Government of the hypocrites, by the hypocrites, for the hypocrites.

Mock religion

This should preferably be the Catholic religion, since it is distinctly more theatrical, and not terribly retaliatory these days. Avoid knocking Judaism. After all, the bulk of New York theatergoers are Jewish, and if unduly nettled they might complain to B'nai B'rith. Protestants, like other apathetic majorities, may be ravaged at will. Having established a reputation for being fearlessly irreverent, make sure that the cast chants a few Hare Krishnas before the evening is over so that the audience will know that the show is profoundly rooted in the mystical spirituality of the East.

Drug taking is a must

A Modcom producer ought never to forget that it is good box office to proffer simulated wickedness as an act of liberation. That is what is known as a low high. Many a boy's only contact with opium was Dr. Fu Manchu, and the closest that many a playgoer gets to a whiff of pot is Modcom.

Be blatant about sex

Nudity is optional, but crudity is mandatory. Sex may be fun, but Modcom insists that its main purpose is to end the war in Viet Nam and provide a physically acceptable substitute for violence. Parting his beard for the press the other day, Beatle John Lennon put it this way: "All you've got to do to prove your manhood is lay a woman." Group grope is very much in vogue and the choreographer who can animate a stageful of writhing, slithering, intertwined bodies stands a good chance of winning this season's Laocoön Award.

Deafen the audience

Cudgel it severely about the ears with a blunt amplifying instrument. A hard-rock Modcom musical gives a theatergoer an acoustic third degree. His eardrums are refunded on the sidewalk. However, the test of a good musical score remains unvarying: not whether one can hum the songs but whether one can tell them apart. *Hair* has a beguilingly individuated score; *Salvation* does not.

Mingle with the audience

This takes a little effort, but it is well worth the time wasted. With no plot, the playgoer might get bored. This way he cranes his neck every which way and wonders if he is going to be kissed, prodded, or punched. It's a good way to smell an actor, too, and the odor isn't always as appealing as ham.

Excoriate Viet Nam

Even hawks, let alone parrots, have learned to deplore Viet Nam by now, so this particular arsenal of invective doesn't stir up a Modcom audience as visibly as it once did. Time was when playgoers would weep on their armrests at the old "We won't go" non-fight pep talk.

Apart from its manifold defects, *Salvation,* like all Modcom products, trades on the residual puritanism behind its ostensibly anti-puritan outlook. A people at ease with sexuality, and casually and thoroughly iconoclastic, would not pay good money to see an inept affirmation of a puerile paganism.

Questions

1. Did the reviewer like *Salvation*?
2. Define "modcom" and indicate some of its characteristics.
3. Instead of dealing directly with *Salvation,* the reviewer spent most of his time setting forth the rules for writing a modcom musical. Was this an effective device?
4. Illustrate the writer's use of humor and satire.
5. Did the writer make a wise choice in closing his review with some specific references to the new musical? Explain.

The Bill Cosby Show

CLEVELAND AMORY

Casual is the word for Cosby. He acts as if he weren't acting, as if he were just a friend of yours. The camera just happened to be photographing. And his whole show is written as if it weren't written at all, but actually did happen. At its best, it works beautifully —a kind of vignette which is not only a real slice of life, and the way life really is but also a welcome relief from all the carefully carpentered half hours which have just about as much relation to reality as their ridiculous laugh tracks do to what's funny.

On the other hand, once in a while it doesn't quite come off—and, unfortunately, one of these was the episode the producers picked for their first. In this, you'll recall, physical-education instructor Chet Kincaid (Mr. Cosby) is out jogging and answers a public phone and, trying to be helpful, gets himself involved with everything from a domestic squabble to the police.

The second episode was better—Kincaid needed a night's sleep and was kept awake by a noisy dog—but it was still on the thin side. By the third episode, however, the show began demonstrating—still in its individual, understated, off-hand way—its real potential. Here Kincaid, faced with getting his basketball team ready for its first game, is accused of prejudice against 5-feet-1 Joey (Gregory Gordon). "I'm not prejudiced," he protests to counselor Marsha Patterson (Joyce Bulifant), "some of my best friends are short." "You pre-judge," she answers, "and that's prejudice." "I have nothing against little people," he persists. "Yet," she pursues, "the only way you could describe him a few minutes ago was that he was a little guy."

This episode was not only full of meaning—Mr. Cosby gets a message across but doesn't hit you over the head with it—but was also full of wonderful little touches. "See you here tomorrow at 3:30," he tells his team. "And no smoking or drinking or carrying on like grown-ups." It also demonstrated Mr. Cosby's amazing versatility— from tossing in baskets to throwing away lines that most comedians would dine out on.

TV Guide, November 8, 1969. Reprinted from *TV Guide* with permission from Triangle Publications. Copyright © 1969 by Triangle Publications, Inc.

The fourth episode, too, was full of these touches—and particularly touching ones too, since in this episode, entitled "A Girl Called Punkin," Kincaid was faced with the problem of a withdrawn girl child (Arlyce Baker) coming over to his bachelor quarters, unannounced, to spend the night with him.

By the fifth episode, we were won over for good. In this, Kincaid and the hefty Miss Fiske (Alice Nunn) undertook to chaperone the school dance. From start to finish it was a small riot. It started with Kincaid Indian-wrestling with Miss Fiske, went on to looking in a boy's mouth for the boy's lost bite plate—with Kincaid making bite faces too—then on to Kincaid having to pick up his date in a garbage truck, and finally ending with Kincaid sedately fox-trotting with his date surrounded by a swirling, swinging, twisting mass of teen-agers. All in all, we give this show a B-plus for originality and a straight A for effortlessness.

Questions

1. Block out the parts of this review. What does the writer do in each of the five paragraphs?
2. Was the reviewer justified in holding back his overall opinion of the Cosby show until the last paragraph?
3. The reviewer provided very few illustrations in describing the first episode and a great many for the second. Why the difference?
4. Discuss the effectiveness of the word choice in the closing line.

Movies

MICHAEL V. KORDA

I recently met one of my fellow film critics at a party, who asked me, "Have you done your sex-and-nudity piece yet?" For a moment I thought he might be mistakenly crediting me with some funny party trick which he hoped to see me perform or perhaps hoped to avoid seeing by leaving early. Then I realized that he was talking of professional matters, and I confessed ashamedly that I had not written such a piece—I hadn't even been *thinking* about sex-and-nudity very much, except in the normal, personal way. However, I determined to expose myself to the New Freedom at the earliest possible opportunity.

Thus, I found myself standing in line one gloriously sunny afternoon to see *I Am Curious (Yellow)*, surrounded by quietly expectant young soldiers and sheepish elderly couples nervously clutching each other's hands at the prospect of two hours of unbridled Swedish libido. There were no non-military young people, which I took (rightly) to be a bad sign. Hopefully, they were out in the park or at home, doing whatever was to be seen in *I Am Curious (Yellow)*.

Reprinted from *Glamour*, October, 1969. Copyright © 1969 by The Condé Nast Publications Inc., and reprinted by their permission.

In my case, overreaching as usual, I had decided to see Kenneth Tynan's new (and sensational) review, *Oh! Calcutta!*, that same evening, partly because I wanted to see the difference between nudity and sexual activity on stage and on screen, partly because I wanted to test the effect of all the erotica on this *homme de sensualité moyenne*. As it turned out, from the sensual-pleasure point of view it was a wasted day, with the exception of a chocolate-fudge Good Humor that I ate while walking up Fifth Avenue.

I Am Curious (Yellow) is already a phenomenon—at this writing, over 250,000 New Yorkers have seen it (God knows how many people more beyond the city limits) and both its content and the fact that the U.S. Supreme Court allowed it to be released have made it something of a landmark in film history. . . .

The first thing that has to be said about *I Am Curious (Yellow)* is that its reputation for sexual frankness has obscured the fact that it is basically a tedious and naïve piece of Swedish Left Socialist ideology. The general impression it gives is that of an attempt to imitate Godard, but without Godard's intelligence and visual sense. Like Godard, Vilgot Sjöman, the director of *I Am Curious (Yellow)*, is addicted to rapid cuts, to the Brechtian "breaking up of reality" and to constant editorializing. The difference lies in the quality of mind: Godard is a brilliant and analytic film-maker; Sjöman, by comparison, reminds me of an earnest high school valedictorian who has just been given a Kodak Super-8 camera and a copy of *Great Ideas Today*. He is portentous, heavy-handed, crashingly obvious and totally humorless.

The political parts of the film are simple-minded and uninspired: shots of Martin Luther King, some documentary footage of Yevtushenko reciting poetry, a poorly thought-out fantasy about nonviolence as a way of life in Sweden, some old-fashioned Socialist realism. . . .

The sexual scenes don't seem to me to have much to do with the rest of the film.

They *don't* indicate that sexual freedom is part of the new society, since the heroine's lover already has a child by another woman, makes the heroine miserably unhappy in a perfectly conventional way and ends by giving her a bad case of scabies. It's possible that there is a subliminal message *against* sexual freedom, now that I think of it, judging by what happens to the people involved in the film, but I'd have to see the movie again to decide about that and *my* curiosity has its limits.

As for the spectacle of two people making love on screen, it is neither exciting nor shocking. . . . Possibly I'm simply put off by all that healthy Swedish athleticism, but the whole thing reminds me of the kind of nudist magazine of which Germans are so fond, as if there were some kind of Nordic compulsion to associate sexual activity with health, fresh air and idealism—in short to make a serious matter of what ought to be a pleasure.

I can think of a good many movies which . . . were far more sexually interesting. If a director is going to convey sexuality, he must do more than simply show the audience what they can see in any Turkish bath.

Strictly speaking, *Oh! Calcutta!* shouldn't be part of this review at all, since it's a play, but the point is that it makes far more sense than *I Am Curious (Yellow)*. It is a series of comic sketches, most of them concerned with sex, and what makes it famous is that the actors strip naked right at the beginning (they then have to put their clothes back on for certain scenes, but through part of the evening they wear nothing). As it happens, what doesn't work in *I Am Curious (Yellow)* works very well in *Oh! Calcutta!*, partly because real live human bodies are more pleasant to look at than photographs, partly because one soon ceases to notice that the actors are naked. The subject matter of *Oh! Calcutta!* demands that the actors go naked, and it seems natural for them to do so *when* their material is good. When it isn't, you notice the cast is stripped.

What really sets *Oh! Calcutta!* apart from

I Am Curious (Yellow) is that the people involved have talent and bring to the problems of showing sexual activity on stage a certain sense of humor and style, rather than treating it like just another Scandinavian field sport. There is a marvelous sketch on wife-swapping (as The Other Couple arrives, the young wife, breathlessly readying her house for the orgy, shouts to her husband: "They're here, for God's sake put the Fritos in the lazy Susan!"); there is a very funny parody on *Fanny Hill*; an excellent sketch of a young Southern boy talking to his pa about sex . . . and a very interesting piece of modern dance which makes one wonder why any ballet dancer should bother wearing tights—the tights seem, on reflection, far more obscene than the sight of two people dancing naked in *Oh! Calcutta!*

In short, *Oh! Calcutta!*, while certainly not perfect, has a point of view, some charm and a good deal of humor, which is far more interesting than the ponderous newsreel photography in *I Am Curious (Yellow)* and perhaps an indication of the way these things ought to be done. . . .

Questions

1. Why does this movie reviewer bring a play, *Oh! Calcutta!*, into his discussion of the film, *I Am Curious (Yellow)*?
2. Indicate the specific criticisms which the reviewer directs at *I Am Curious (Yellow)*.
3. What is the chief difference he sees between the nudity in the play and in the film?
4. What does the phrase "New Freedom" refer to in the opening paragraph? Why is it capitalized? To what extent does the writer endorse it, as indicated by his closing remarks?

Suggested Writing Assignments

1. Write your own review of a current film, play, television show, recital, or exhibit. Study the text examples to find ways to organize and develop your material.
2. Compare and contrast any two of the reviews given in the text. Your discussion might include the elements of form, slant, illustrative detail, humor, satire, and other matters which pertain to language.
3. Find a review of a current motion picture or television show with which you disagree. Then write up your own review in which you support the other side. Hand in both write-ups so that the reader can appreciate the difference of opinion.
4. Compose a paper in which you explain some of the do's and don'ts of writing an effective review. You might want to restrict your discussion to a particular subject matter, such as motion pictures or records. Remember to support your statements with examples and illustrations from published reviews.

10

The Column

Most of us follow a column or two in our favorite newspaper or magazine, perhaps a sports column or one for the lovelorn, but we may still not be aware of just how many forms this example of modern prose can take. Consider, for instance, that there are columns, both local and national, on cooking, decorating, health, investing, education, raising children, reading horoscopes, psychology, science, drama, movies, television, politics, sports, public opinion, military strategy, books, music, cars, manners, men's and women's fashion, gardening, sailing, pets, and society. And that is not an exhaustive list; it only suggests the range.

One of the reasons for the popularity of the column is that it is a welcome relief from the impersonality of our relatively objective prose. Most of the articles we see, especially news articles, are written by professional writers and sent on, unsigned, to other publications through such national wire services as The Associated Press or The United Press. Even editorials do not necessarily represent an individual's reaction, but rather the views of a collective "we."

In contrast to this pervasive anonymity there are the columnists who "voice their own opinions," who "speak their minds." One columnist, for instance, even titles his piece, *Strictly Personal*. He says what he thinks on such diverse subjects as teachers, authors, and politicians.

Literally, anyone may become a columnist. Among nationally syndicated writers there are professional authors, like Art Buchwald or Sydney J. Harris, who became nation-wide columnists and others, like Hubert Humphrey or Roy Wilkins, who achieved fame in quite different areas.

Some syndicated columns, quite specialized in character, ordinarily dwell on one subject, like Abbey on love, Heloise on household hints, Goren on bridge, or Dr. Brandstadt on medicine. But others are less focused. They may explore all kinds of subjects, from aesthetics to atheism, indeed anything that may catch a reader's fancy. Among these less specialized columns are those by Bob Considine and Hal Boyle.

Since columns necessarily cater to human interests, there are columns on any subject, but, however various, most of them fall into one of three categories: humorous columns, like Art Buchwald's and Russell Baker's; advice columns, like Dorothy Ricker's *Tips for Teens*; and finally those more reflective and more informative pieces which give a topic (or a situation) and then explain and analyze it. Among this last group of columnists are the popular political columns by Jack Anderson, Carl Rowan, Evans and Novak, Josef Kraft and a new team of columnists, Mankiewicz and Braden.

And in almost every town there are popular local columnists. These writers also have their small yet devoted following and their work is similar to the syndicated columns. Naturally, these local columns feature local people and issues. The local society column, for one instance, will ordinarily contain as many names as possible and the local humorist, for his part, will find incongruities on his main street or on the local campus.

There is, to be sure, no uniformity of style or tone in columns. The rule is variety, because individual columnists and their audiences determine not only the subject, but also the way it is treated. Anderson, for example, has a rather formal approach with well-developed paragraphs, a clear beginning, middle, and an end to the piece. Earl Wilson, on the other hand, who writes about people in show business, skips easily from one subject to another with usually no more than a sentence devoted to each person. There is in his column nothing of the development of ideas that one finds in "Washington Merry-Go-Round."

Thus, in our mass society, the individuality of a few outgoing, articulate, and gifted writers has an outlet in both local and mass-produced columns. If many of our editorials have become bland, noncontroversial pieces, it may be because there are too few strongminded columnists to fill the need for responsible controversy, and if we seem to encourage a bold individuality, it may be because we have so little left.

What's the Real Mr. Nixon Like?

JAMES RESTON

Washington—The most interesting reaction to the recent state and city elections in the United States was the President's.

For the pundits and new governors and mayors can be wrong and even silly without doing too much harm, but the President's conclusions influence all the policies and priorities both at home and abroad.

He obviously took these elections seriously. He planned his defense of Vietnam

---

The Record, (Cedar Falls, Iowa), November 12, 1969. © 1969 by The New York Times Company. Reprinted by permission.

speech on election eve. He wrote it himself and aimed it against the antiwar extremists —as if they represented all the people who were against the war. He went into Virginia and New Jersey in support of the Republican candidates for Governor in those states, and when they won, he acted, not like a President, but like a chairman of the Republican National Committee.

This was a switch.

Nixon has not been a very partisan President. His appointments, outside the Supreme Court, have been comparatively non political. His policies have not followed the traditional conservative Republican line. He has avoided public press conferences and rejected private conversations with White House correspondents and columnists.

In fact, the main thrust of his Presidency until recently has been nonpartisan, objective and private. But in this election, he suddenly changed all this. He intervened in Virginia and New Jersey, appealed on election eve against his Vietnam critics, and exploited the results of the election as if he were once more back in the old days when he was the spear of the Republican political party.

The morning after the vote, by pre-arrangement with NBC he went on the Today show. At noon of the same day, he had the victorious Republican Governors in the Virginia and New Jersey races to the White House for lunch.

He called in the reporters and photographers to see all the telegrams and letters that supported his Vietnam speech, and interpreted all this as majority support for his Vietnam policies.

This, of course, is standard old-fashioned political tactics. He talked about the elections that seemed to support his policies in Vietnam and ignored the elections like the one in New York, that went against his Vietnam policy.

Any Republican or Democratic county chairman would have done the same, but in a President who had previously avoided publicity and partisan politics, this raised some fundamental questions.

Does he really believe, as he seemed to be saying, that his Vietnam speech and the elections prove that the majority of the American people support him on Vietnam? And if they do support him, do they support his determination to get out of Vietnam or his determination to stay there until the Saigon regime can defend that peninsula? After all, he said both things in his election-eve speech, and it is not clear either what he meant or what the pro-Nixon letter-writers were supporting.

The critical question, therefore, is how Nixon interprets the letters and the Republican victories in Virginia and New Jersey.

He was in trouble with the antiwar factions in the Congress, the press, and the universities a month ago, but since the elections, he seems to be persuading himself that he is now in control of the situation and can go on fighting the war as before. This is not a new situation with Presidents: their capacity over the generations for self-deception is almost unlimited.

This, of course, is precisely what President Johnson did.

He convinced himself that the optimistic military reports from the Joint Chiefs of Staff and the embassy and military commands in Saigon were right. He listened to the people who told him the opposition to the war came only from the extremists and that the "silent majority" was with him, and every Democratic victory at the polls reassured him that his hopes were realities.

The interesting question now is whether Nixon is going through the same process. He has been withdrawing his troops but withdrawing them slowly and hoping for a break and telling himself that support at home might convince the enemy to accept a compromise peace.

Thus, when the letters and telegrams came into the White House supporting his speech, he called in the press and said these letters of support could be more important than all the diplomatic and military tactics in ending the war, for this, he assumed, would persuade the enemy that the American people were united behind his policy.

This made the headlines and no doubt, persuaded many politicians, but it had some other consequences. It troubled his own colleagues in the State Department and even in the White House, who know the enemy is not going to be convinced by this kind of political propaganda, and it troubled the White House reporters, who had been told about Nixon's sincerity but were now forced to watch merely the impression of sincerity on the Today show.

The result is that the really important men reporting on the Presidency—not the columnists but the reporters and White House correspondents—are now wondering about the President after his Vietnam speech and his partisan reaction to the elections.

He invited them to believe that he would not be like Johnson, that he would be open and candid. But his approach and reaction to the election have not been open and candid but personal and partisan.

Like Johnson, he has dealt with the politics of his problem but not with the problem of Vietnam.

Senator Kennedy's Impossible Question

JAMES RESTON

Edgartown, Mass., *July 26*—The question Senator Edward Kennedy has put to the people of Massachusetts—should he resign from the United States Senate?—is really unfair. They have only his own account of the tragedy, and if they accept it as true, the question of resignation should not arise.

His testimony is simply that he misjudged a turning on a dangerous bridge and plunged into the water, killing a young woman whom he tried at great peril to his own life to save.

The Senator's Report

He said in his report to the people that he was not "driving under the influence of liquor." "There is no truth, no truth whatever, to the widely circulated suspicions of immoral conduct." Only "reasons of health" prevented his wife from being with him on this tragic night. Therefore, the one and only issue, as he and the courts see it, is his failure to report the accident during a period of severe personal shock; and he has pleaded guilty to this charge.

Why then the talk of resignation? He says, quite rightly, that on questions of conscience, "each man must decide for himself what course to follow." But there is nothing in his account that raises any question except the question of the delay in reporting the accident.

Indeed, his television account of the event is a kind of tragic "profile in courage." What he has really asked the people of Massachusetts is whether they want to kick a man when he is down, and clearly they are not going to do that to this doom-ridden and battered family.

The New York Times, July 27, 1969. © 1969 by The New York Times Company. Reprinted by permission.

The Question of Belief

The trouble is that even many of his own supporters in this center of the controversy are not satisfied with the record or the procedure in the case. Nobody but the Kennedy haters want to add to the tortures of unhappiness in this family, but serious doubts remain even among those who would prefer to drop the whole question rather than perpetuate the grief.

"A man does what he must," Senator Kennedy said in his television account, "in spite of personal consequences, in spite of obstacles and dangers and pressures, and that is the basis of all morality."

The Persistent Doubts

But most men don't meet this ideal and one wonders why the Senator raised it in these awkward circumstances. For the hard facts are that he ducked the main questions, evaded the press, pleaded guilty to the charge of not reporting the accident on time, which avoided cross-examination in the court. And in these circumstances—with all witnesses to the evening's proceedings gone from the island and silenced, and all questions to the Senator barred in court—it is not clear why he and his counselors should raise the moral issue and appeal to the voters who have no means of questioning the cast of characters.

So doubt remains, and probably the real question is not whether the voters of Massachusetts can live with the Senator's account of the tragedy, but whether he can.

He has gone through a ghastly experience —not only on this island recently, but ever since the murder of his two brothers. It may be that the pressures of the last year, when he became the proxy father to his brother Robert's children, the Democratic whip of the Senate and the leader and symbol of the Kennedy clan and its ambitions, were too much for him. But to end the Kennedy story on this tragic note, to ask for an impossible referendum on unknown facts by the people of Massachusetts is ridiculous.

The chances are that this spectacular and tragic accident has startled him out of his rather casual ways and made him choose between his impulses and his responsibilities and family ambitions. But that is for him to decide. The voters of Massachusetts will live with his troubles. The question is whether he can do the same.

Questions

1. If these samples are typical of Reston's columns, what would you say is his special concern?
2. Is Reston critical of both Nixon and Kennedy? Illustrate.
3. How does Reston support his claim that Kennedy's asking the people of Massachusetts whether he should resign is both "unfair" and "ridiculous"?
4. Why does Reston speculate that it will be difficult for Kennedy to live with his own account of the tragedy?
5. Is the closing of Reston's column on Nixon an effective one? Could it just as well serve as an opening?
6. One of Reston's strong points as a columnist is that, although you may disagree with his opinions, you are seldom in doubt about what his opinions are. Justify this statement on the basis of the two selections.

Public Nudity Can Mean a Variety of Things

JOYCE BROTHERS

New York, N.Y.—Not too long ago, anybody who felt moved to strip in front of strangers could be readily categorized as either a burlesque queen or an exhibitionist.

Of course, nudist camps have been around for many years, but nudists have managed to stay out of the public eye preferring seclusion.

Today, actors and actresses strip for the stage and screen in the name of art. Members of encounter groups involved in psychological "sensitivity training" sessions remove their clothing with the aim of increased self-awareness. And a small, but uninhibited number of politically-minded activists throw off their clothing as an act of social protest.

Psychologically, clothing can be understood as arising from two conflicting human impulses towards exhibitionism and modesty. Naturally, clothes have a very practical and functional purpose as well, and even an ardent nudist will wear sunglasses or shoes if the occasion warrants.

In a society in which people wear clothing most of the time, temporary nudity has a definite shock value.

The privilege of seeing another adult nude is generally restricted to members of the same sex, physicians, and spouses.

It is the impulse toward exhibitionism, paradoxically, that causes us to cover our bodies with make-up, clothing and jewelry. For, while clothing serves the modest function of covering up parts of our body we regard as most private, it also calls attention to our body by stimulating curiosity about that which is covered.

Then why the inclination to take off clothing or to reveal the body underneath in the "see-through" look?

Dr. Ernest Crawley suggests society alternates between attention focused on the body and attention focused on the extensions of the body—that is, clothing.

Culturally, we seem to be moving back towards a focus on the body itself. Social critic Marshall McLuhan has also observed that the current emphasis is on the tactile-auditory stimulation as opposed to visual, describing nudity as not so much a visual as a sculptural and tactile experience.

One factor determining the effect and significance of nudity is whether or not the complete group is naked. Nudity serves to remove artificial symbols of status. Deprive a king of his crown and robes and he loses his uniqueness.

Besides the health benefits, practicing nudists believe nudity helps people relate to each other in a more natural and uninhibited way.

In encounter groups, psychologist Paul Bindrim explains, the hope is that by shedding their clothing, the members of the groups will also be able to shed some of their emotional inhibitions. Of course, nudity is only one of a number of techniques sometimes used in sensitivity-training groups.

The importance of group trust and communal spirit was emphasized in the preparation for actors and actresses for nude performances in the production "Oh! Calcutta!" It took some time before the group developed confidence enough to feel comfortable with each other without clothing.

But the addition of clothed spectators

The Des Moines Register, August 25, 1969. Reprinted by permission of the North American Newspaper Alliance.

necessarily changes the meaning of nudity. Visitors to nudist camps must follow the example of camp members, but an audience in a theater is able to observe without disrobing.

While it is argued the actors and actresses are not really exposing themselves, only the characters they play, and are therefore not demeaned by their nakedness, some observers feel this distinction is specious.

Of course, the performers are nude presumably because they want to be. Enforced nudity, on the other hand, is a historical means of punishing or ridiculing those society wishes to condemn.

Forcing the individual to be naked while spectators remain clothed is one of the most humiliating of human punishments.

Psychiatrist Alexander Lowen feels it is important to distinguish between prudery and modesty. Prudery is a shame of the body while modesty is a respect for privacy and individuality.

While in some instances nudity can be an important catalyst for breaking down barriers between people, this impulse to exposure can be overdone, with the effect that the dignity and integrity of the person is violated.

The Importance of Father-Daughter Relationship

JOYCE BROTHERS

Fathers today no longer feel obligated to play the role of the stern authoritarian with their children.

They give baths, change diapers, and tell bedtime stories as well as doing such traditionally fatherly things as tossing their offspring in the air. And they are less restrained about showing affection for their children.

The importance of a positive relationship with both parents for the child's development is realized by modern parents. We often hear the term "father figure" bandied about. But most often it is concern over the father-son relationship that prompts the discussion. What about the girl and her need for a "father figure?"

There is a strong preference for sons in our culture: A woman hopes to be able to present her husband with a male child, to provide him with the legacy of a male heir.

How, then, does a father feel towards his daughter?

Too often the father-daughter relationship is described only in sentimental terms of "daddy's little girl" in which the girl is idealized as a perfect bit of femininity without recognition of her uniqueness as a person and individual.

Admittedly, the young father may at first be taken aback by his infant child, regardless of sex, but if it is a boy, he can eventually feel comfortable with him, treating him as an extension of himself.

A girl, on the other hand, may confound him with her femininity, especially if he has always had difficulty in understanding and relating to women. He feels uncomfortable in the realm of tea parties and dolls and may

---

The Des Moines Register, June 12, 1969. Reprinted by permission of the North American Newspaper Alliance.

tacitly decide to leave his daughter's rearing to her mother.

The father plays a crucial role in his daughter's development. His presence and affection for her allow her to develop trust in men and to feel that she is an individual, distinct from her mother, who is worthy of love and attention.

If the father is too rejecting or too seductive, her self-concept and sexual identity may be damaged.

Ideally, the father reacts to the femininity in his daughter from the very beginning, demonstrating his acceptance of her as a female and his child.

What we call femininity is as much determined by parental attitudes and responses as by biology and physiology.

If the young girl's parents unconsciously reject her sex, having longed for a boy, they may cause considerable psychic damage by unwittingly expecting her to serve as a male substitute.

One study tested the differential reactions of parents to a child's voice. When fathers were led to believe that the child speaking was a girl, they were more tolerant of dependency and aggressiveness than when they believed it to be a boy.

Another survey found that in regard to scholastic aptitude, girls tended to be more adversely affected than boys by the absence of the father from the home.

For, even though a father may feel dolls and tea parties are beyond his ken, it is evident that little girls need to share in their father's masculine world, as well as that of their mother for their fullest development.

Children of both sexes in early adolescence tend to regard the father as the model of courage, strength and honesty. The father provides the child, male or female, with a sense of the importance of the world beyond the home.

The daughter's adolescence may stir up conflicts within the father, who is unsettled by his daughter's budding sexuality. If he has recognized her femininity from the beginning, he will have less trouble in accepting her growth into mature womanhood and association with boys her age.

But for some fathers, unconscious sexual attraction to their daughters may create considerable turmoil within and affect the daughter.

Psychiatrist A. M. Chapman describes one type of these fathers who respond by acting as if "all boys are lechers." They become watchdogs over their daughters, tyrannically supervising the girl's contacts with boys and suspecting the most innocent 15-year-old males of being potential sex fiends.

Sadly, daughters often attempt to escape from such fathers by rushing into premature marriages.

Psychiatrist Eric Berne notes another pattern in response to anxiety about the daughter's sexuality. In this method, the father avoids threatening intimacy with his daughter, and the daughter reciprocates, by engaging in constant battle.

But ironically enough, it is the independence of the daughter that may upset the father the most. The joke that the father of the bride is the saddest man at a wedding only because he is paying for it all hints at the real emotional loss a father feels. For in our culture, it is the bride, not the bridegroom, who is "given away," also giving up her family name. The replacement of the father by the husband as the primary protector and masculine object is dramatically portrayed in many wedding rituals, as the father steps away from his daughter.

Questions

1. Are Dr. Brothers' columns addressed to the general reader or to an audience with a special interest in psychology? Explain.
2. Illustrate the similarities in the two columns in regard to the lead paragraphs, word choice, and the use of authorities.
3. Dr. Brothers claims that sons are more important than daughters in our society. Do you think she is correct on this point? What support does she offer for the observation? If you differ with her, what sort of evidence would support your assertion?
4. Why is it important, according to Dr. Brothers, for daughters to share in their father's masculine world?
5. Dr. Brothers says that public nudity may be damaging under some circumstances and not under others. Explain this seeming contradiction.
6. Nudity and father-daughter relationships are difficult subjects to analyze, particularly in a brief column. Do you believe that Dr. Brothers has handled them effectively?

A Good Reason To Use Slang

SYDNEY J. HARRIS

Chicago, Ill.—Hardly a month passes that I don't receive a letter from some English teacher, wanting to know what I think about using slang. In most cases, these teachers would like me to buttress their resistance to the use of slang expressions by their pupils.

I can't oblige them. My attitude toward slang is the same as my attitude toward any other kind of speech: one should use the most fitting word for the subject and the occasion, and if a slang phrase happens to fit best, it should be used.

There are three principal reasons for using slang, and only one of them is legitimate. The first reason is mental laziness: it is often easier to use a slang word, as a kind of verbal shorthand, than to use another and more precisely descriptive word.

Use It If
It Fits

The second reason is snobbishness: the desire to seem *au courant*, to be with it in terms of the latest phrases, to show that you are not musty and dusty and dated. (But, ironically, nothing dates faster than most slang, and by the time a phrase receives wide currency, it is already *passe* with the real in-group.)

The third reason, which I mentioned

The Des Moines Register, November 30, 1968. Reprinted by permission of Sydney J. Harris and Publishers-Hall Syndicate.

above, is the only good one that justifies slang: if the word or expression fits a need that is not met by any other word in standard English.

Of course, this is precisely the test by which words either die out or pass into the permanent body of language. Hundreds, and even thousands, of words that began as slang found their way into the dictionaries because they filled a real verbal need.

"Mob," for instance, was attacked by lexicographers as a cheap adaptation of the Latin phrase, "mobile vulgum." But the English language needed a word like "mob," and quite sensibly adopted it and made it respectable.

Chief Offense: Faddishness

It may surprise many to learn that "weekend" was a slang word and is only about 100 years old. People used to say "Friday-to-Monday," which was a clumsy mouthful; and "weekend," at first sneered at by purists, is now a word not only of English, but of worldwide, usage. Yet its origin was disparaged by English teachers of the mid-nineteenth century.

The chief offense of slang is its faddishness. Most slang is not more accurate, more colorful or more freighted with connotations than standard English, but simply more "current." When it is used just for fashion, it debases language more than augmenting it.

America, Britain Divided by Language

SYDNEY J. HARRIS

I FORGET whether it was Wilde or Shaw —it was certainly some wickedly witty Irishman—who remarked that "England and America are two nations divided by a common language."

Whoever it was, I thought of him when my British sports car developed a slight stutter last week, and I leafed through the "Maintenance" section of the Owner's Book provided by the manufacturer, which again reminded me of the great disparity of names for ordinary parts of a car.

Of course, as everyone knows, our hood is the British "bonnet" and our gas is the British "petrol." But even a windshield is called a "windscreen," a trunk compartment is called a "boot," fenders are called "wings," bumpers are called "buffers," and a monkey-wrench is known as a "spanner."

Go Own Way

Though Britons complain that the English language is becoming "Americanized," there seems to be little growing together of the two branches, except for slang words and vulgarisms. In the field of ordinary vocabulary, each nation goes its own way, and no linguistic Common Market has yet risen, nor seems even to be on the horizon.

Their janitors remain "porters," their workmen remain "navvies," their newspapermen remain "pressmen," their saleswomen remain "shop assistants," their street-cleaners remain "crossing sweepers."

Likewise, our saloons are "public houses," our orchestra seats are "stalls," our mantelpieces are "chimney pieces," our letter boxes are "pillar boxes," our legal holidays are "bank holidays," our long-distance calls are

---

Waterloo Daily Courier, August 18, 1969. Reprinted by permission of Sydney J. Harris and Publishers-Hall Syndicate.

"trunk calls," our road beds are "permanent ways," our soft drinks are "minerals," our round-trip tickets are "returns."

The most ordinary objects in every-day use have somehow divided their nomenclature across the ocean. An ash can is a "dustbin," a billboard is a "hoarding," a clipping is a "cutting," a can is a "tin," an elevator is a "lift," a subway is a "tube," a sweater is a "jersey," an undershirt is a "vest" (what we call a "vest" is a "waistcoat" there), a shoe shine is a "boot polish," a trolley is a "tramcar," a filing cabinet is a "nest of drawers," a cracker is a "biscuit," a piece of candy is a "sweet," and a freight-car is a "goods-wagon."

Abstractions, Too

Not only objects, but even abstractions, have gone their separate ways. An editorial is a "leader," the installment plan is the "hire-purchase plan," quotation marks are "inverted commas," a ticket-office is a "booking-office," internal revenue is "inland revenue," receipts are "takings," taxes are "rates" (and taxpayers, of course, are "ratepayers"), the game of checkers is "draughts," and bids are "tenders."

Those who still dream of a universal language, artificial or not, fail to reckon with the stubborn fact that even the same church is called by different names—Methodist here, and Wesleyan over there.

Questions

1. What are the similarities in the organization of the two columns and in the author's attitude toward language?
2. What is the function of the first two paragraphs in "A Good Reason"?
3. Explain how the following statement helps to give structure to the column: "There are three principal reasons for using slang and only one of them is legitimate."
4. Harris uses the term "purists" when he mentions that they once opposed the word "week-end." What general attitude would purists have toward slang expressions? In what way is Harris different from the purists on the use of slang?
5. How does Harris classify the various terms he uses to illustrate his point in the column on America and Britain?
6. According to Harris, why do some slang expressions become a permanent part of the language? Can you think of slang words which have become respectable?

Is Apartment Living Right for Graduate?

ABIGAIL VAN BUREN

DEAR ABBY: My husband and I are going 'round and 'round because our 17-year-old daughter has said that after she graduates from high school she wants to get a job and move into an apartment with another girl.

My husband hits the ceiling whenever she mentions it. He thinks that girls want to live alone so they can entertain boyfriends without parental supervision, stay up until all hours, and go wild in general.

I don't feel that way. I think our daughter has good sense, good moral values, and her choice of friends has always been to her credit. I think parents can teach their children only so much. The rest they have to learn by standing on their own two feet.

How do you feel about this, Abby?

MOTHER IN THE MIDDLE

DEAR MOTHER: I think you are right. By the time a girl graduates from high school, the twig is bent the way it will grow, and from the sound of your letter, I would say your daughter will not disappoint you.

Waterloo Daily Courier, July 11, 1969. Reprinted through the courtesy of the Chicago Tribune-New York News Syndicate.

Readers Come to Aid of 41-Year-Old Virgin

ABIGAIL VAN BUREN

DEAR ABBY: Please tell "WAITING"—the 41-year-old virgin, to keep waiting. A woman's virginity is still the greatest gift she can offer a man in marriage. Even tho a man makes excuses for himself, he still prefers a virgin for a wife. Please don't conclude from my signature that I know nothing about life. I was in the business world for over 30 years before I became a priest.

Respectfully,
SAN DIEGO PRIEST

DEAR ABBY: For "WAITING": Lady, you are to be commended. Don't let a clod sell you. If he says, if you don't give him what he wants, he will go elsewhere—let him. He will be doing you a big favor.

R. B., OKLAHOMA CITY

DEAR ABBY: Why all the emphasis on virginity? A man who insists that he be the "one and only" probably does so because he doesn't want the woman he marries to be

---

Waterloo Daily Courier, March 31, 1969. Reprinted through the courtesy of the Chicago Tribune-New York News Syndicate.

able to make comparisons and find him lacking. Me? I don't have that problem.

A MAN NAMED "MANN"

DEAR ABBY: I am a U.S. serviceman with 18 years' service and three overseas tours of duty, and all that time I had no sexual experience. I've taken tremendous ridicule. It hasn't always been easy. I married a wonderful girl who believes as I, and I cannot begin to express the closeness, trust and warmth of feeling it has brought to our lives. We've been married 16 years and have six fine children, and we're still "in love."

OLD SARGE
Vandenberg AFB, Calif.

DEAR ABBY: In reply to "WAITING," who claims she's been on her own since 17, lived abroad, is romantic, sensitive, and not ugly. She has got to be kidding! I'm all for purity, but at age 41, what kind of a "prize" does she think she's going to give a man?

No man, for example, is going to ask a Chinese girl, whose feet have been bound since infancy, to go on a hike with him. She'd be lucky to be able to walk around the block. And marriage is a long hike.

COMPASSIONATE in L. A.

DEAR ABBY: Please forward to "WAITING": My advice to you is to go out in the country, buy a little farm, and start raising chickens. One rooster and a half dozen hens will do. Feed them yourself and keep your eyes open. You'll notice that the hens always run away from the rooster, but they never run so far or so fast that they avoid getting caught. Try it. You'll be glad you did. With love.

AN OLD ROOSTER

DEAR ABBY: This is for "WAITING": I was all for your clinging to your virginity —until I read your age. Come on now, at 41, what are you waiting for? There is a happy middle ground between waiting and swinging, and it's called "discretion."

DISCREET IN N. Y.

DEAR ABBY: If at age 25, an attractive, normal, fun-loving woman surrenders her virtue without marriage, I wouldn't think less of her. It's nice to marry a virgin, but I think it's more important how a woman conducts herself AFTER marriage than before. I married a virgin who didn't confine herself to me afterwards. That is why I am—

"SINGLE AGAIN" IN TULSA

DEAR ABBY: By what law of nature, morals, or divine sanction must a woman love only one man while we men may love as many women as our hearts desire, and without reproof of anyone's conscience—including our own?

If, indeed, the most precious gift a woman may bring to a man in marriage is her body, untouched, my first concern would be for the man. For surely there are better recommendations for marriage than never having loved.

HAPPILY MARRIED IN ITALY

Lousy Housekeeper Wakes Up

ABIGAIL VAN BUREN

DEAR ABBY: I was one of those sloppy housekeepers who never seemed to get her housework done. I could sit for hours, daydreaming, and when my husband came home from work, the house looked about the same as when he left, or worse!

Gary never complained, so for four years we lived in a pigpen, whether I was working or not.

Finally I became pregnant, and when the day came for me to go to the hospital I left behind dirty dishes from three days, an oven full of dirty pots and pans which had been "hidden" there for weeks, and soiled clothing piled high to the ceiling right next to my new washer-dryer.

This is only a partial description, but it will give you an idea of what a lousy housekeeper I was.

I realize this is long, Abby, but I'm sure it describes many homes from Boston to San Francisco, and I want to be sure these lazy women recognize themselves.

Well, I am sending you a copy of the letter my mother wrote to me while she stayed at my house when I was in the hospital. Perhaps if you print it, it will wake up some other lazy wives. It sure did wake me up. And though it's been two years, her letter has been read and re-read and cherished. I am still so ashamed of my old habits, I've changed the names, so feel free to print it as it is.

"Dear Lisa,

Just a note between us girls. I am cleaning your house today so you won't have so much to do when you come home.

Now you're probably saying, "Gee, that's sure nice of you Mom, I didn't ask you to." Well, the truth of it is, you didn't. But I wanted to, and it sure needed it. But that is all in the past. Let's look at the future.

You are now a mother, and it's time you became a housekeeper, so get busy! If Gary made you a living the way you keep house, you would starve to death. He does his job well, and you should start doing your job, too. Okay?

If you're tired, talk to your doctor. If you're too lazy, talk to yourself.

You may say, "Mom, you have no right to say this!" I say, "Oh, yes, I have. It's a mother's right."

Your house is spotless now. Keep it that way! And when you get over being mad, make a pot of coffee and invite me over.

All my love,
MOM"

Waterloo Daily Courier, October 26, 1969. Reprinted through the courtesy of the Chicago Tribune-New York News Syndicate.

Says Tango With 'Pill' Beats 'Rockabye Baby'

ABIGAIL VAN BUREN

DEAR ABBY: My daughter is engaged to be married in November. Well, last week, while looking for bobby pins in her dresser drawer, I came across some little pink pills in a queer-looking pill box. When I asked her what they were, she said, "Birth control pills. You know I'm supposed to take them 3 months before the wedding." (I know she had taken one that day because there was one less than the day before.)

My question is this: "Why is she taking them now when the marriage isn't until November?

I would throw her fiance right out on his ear but I'm afraid she'd go with him, and it would break my heart as I love my daughter very much. Every time I look at her fiance now I get a terrible feeling of hatred. How in the world can I help plan a wedding in November feeling the way I do about him?

DISAPPOINTED MOM

DEAR MOM: You had better get over your feeling of "hatred." It takes two to tango, and while I do not condone this type dance step before the wedding march, it beats the "Rockabye Baby" waltz.

Waterloo Daily Courier, May 27, 1969. Reprinted through the courtesy of the Chicago Tribune-New York News Syndicate.

Questions

1. Indicate the characteristics which would enable you to recognize Abby's column if you came upon it in a newspaper.
2. What use does Abby make of proverbs in answering the question about a high school graduate getting an apartment?
3. Why did Abby choose to let her readers reply to the question posed by the 41-year-old virgin? Which of the answers do you believe is the most effectively written?
4. In the column on the poor housekeeper, comment on the level of the language and the writer's use of a personal letter.
5. To appreciate Abby's lively style, write a straight version of her answer in the column about birth control pills. In your rewrite omit references to dancing and music and simply state her answer flatly in two lines.

Self-Defeating Black Violence

ROY WILKINS, EXECUTIVE DIRECTOR, NAACP

New York, N.Y.—The future of the American Negro population may be threatened more from activities within black ranks —and especially within black students ranks —than by any act of the white majority. This hampering may come not, as the doom forecasters predict, from white backlash, but from the immature and parochial stance of the vociferous black minority element.

Negro homes and businesses have been burned along with white-owned stores in the heart of Negro neighborhoods. In one New York City neighborhood one Negro-owned drugstore had to close because of repeated robberies, and another, white-owned, was finally burned down. Today, black families there must walk blocks to reach a drugstore. Who is being hurt?

Reform
Long Overdue

Now the senseless fires are being brought to college campuses. Much of the general reform being demanded is valid and long overdue. Many reforms which affect black students, textbooks and curricula, are justified.

The real and lasting damage is in the crippling of the future of black people. Colleges are for learning. If students spend their time in boycotts, in occupying administrative offices, in scrounging weapons and in campus pitched battles, they are frittering away learning time that may determine the status of their race in years to come.

In the midst of the campus disturbances came news of the oil-rich future of Nigeria, which may be among the 10 top oil-producing nations of the world by 1975. Its revenues from oil may be $800 million a year. Can any black adult who spent his college years in burning and fighting direct the handling of $800 million of oil revenue? Of course not. The men who guide a people and a government will be those who spent their time in college libraries and laboratories, not in burning them down.

Apathy
Shaken

Who will pilot governments, handle sensitive currency crises, negotiate tariffs and direct air, land and sea commerce—the black rah-rah boys, counseling and practicing violence, or the students who use colleges and business seminars to acquire the knowledge to manage their destinies?

By now, apathy has been shaken. The present danger is that emotional excesses may harden into racial polarization. Let whites react with reason and understanding, in programs of accelerated correction. Let blacks react with a renunciation of the black racist frills, but with no compromise on the basic changes—and, above all, with determination to secure the knowledge and skills that will be needed, whether the future world is white, black, yellow or speckled.

Des Moines Register, May 22, 1969. Reprinted by permission of The Register and Tribune Syndicate.

Dangerous Propaganda

ROY WILKINS, EXECUTIVE DIRECTOR, NAACP

The long campaign is over and the next mayor of New York City has been elected. But in Harlem were uncovered tactics that could threaten any free society, whatever its color.

Some spokesmen urged Negroes not to vote. It was said they ought to use the ballot boycott as a protest. Another part of this propaganda was that Blacks should cut themselves off from white society and all its ways, including voting, to demonstrate the independence of Black people.

This reasoning is not only nonsense, but, considering the vulnerable position of Negro Americans, straight suicide. The vote may not be all-powerful, but it is the only channel through which the ordinary citizen can express himself. He can defeat bond issues calling for additional taxes. He can elect officeholders whose policies will affect his livelihood, the welfare of his family and the education of his children. Smart groups use the vote.

The call to by-pass the ballot box is a call to sulk in a corner and to permit others to share the black man's future. There may be dark days in a defeat, but there cannot be disgrace unless a people deliberately follow a course that leads to disgraceful defeat. If the Black citizens of Los Angeles had abdicated in the Yorty-Bradley contest there would not have been the development of a healthy respect for the minority population.

The slowing down of progress on minority problems is given impetus by the "don't vote" campaign. Mayor John V. Lindsay lost the New York City primary election. In Washington the atmosphere is cool and correct and there is a chipping away at minority gains. The excuse of the course-plotters is: "They (the Negroes) did not vote for us so we do not owe them anything."

Throat-Cutting

No, the advice to a minority not to vote in any country that has anything approaching free elections is throat-cutting advice. One may not gain—in one election—all that one should gain, but one is not left stuttering and helpless. In addition, voting gives a validity to protests that no amount of threatening by non-voters will give. There are rumors that the Black New York City precincts are badly under-registered and that a black bark, therefore, is just a cover-up for a tiny bite.

Then there was the threat that the mayoralty candidates who did not appear at a certain rally would be barred from further campaigning in the streets of Harlem. According to this arrogance, Harlem is not a part of New York City; Harlem is not an area where 300,000 people live. Only one candidate appeared and he was drowned out by hecklers.

Coupled with this threat was the deliberate refusal of small groups armed with electric bullhorns to permit candidates to speak. If these people had their way there would be no free speech in a Black community. Today it would be a candidate; tomorrow it would

---

New York *Amsterdam News*, November 8, 1969. Reprinted by permission of the New York *Amsterdam News*.

be anyone who disagrees with the group. Free speech goes out the window and gags come in the door.

With the non-thinkers in charge, a free society—the only one in which a minority has a chance—departs. The Harlem Hecklers could easily become the Harlem dungeon diggers.

Questions

1. As a black writer, is Wilkins speaking only to black readers?
2. Are these columns clearly structured? To answer this question, identify the specific thesis and the supporting material in each piece.
3. Since Wilkins writes a regular column, one might expect to find some similarity in his subject matter, general approach, and style. Are any of these similarities present in the two samples of his writing?
4. Which of the columns contains the more appealing lead?
5. How does Wilkins use statistics to advance his argument in the column, "Self-Defeating Black Violence"?
6. In the same column, discuss the effective use of the "rhetorical question."
7. Is Wilkins aware of the need for strong closing lines? Base your answer on concrete illustrations.

Remember the Traditional Look, Too

MARY BRYSON

Your Decorating

There's so much excitement in home decorating circles about space-age furniture, that the fine traditional designs being introduced by many companies are likely to be overlooked.

Several firms have added to their traditional collections this year, with the big surge in the Mediterranean, especially Spanish, groups. However, there also will be handsome seventeenth and eighteenth century English and French designs in the stores this spring.

One company, for example, has added more than 25 items, including poster and chairback beds, five different chests and a dining group, to its American Restoration collection.

* * *

The grandfather clock, something that was in danger of being abandoned by furniture

---

The Des Moines Register, February 1, 1969. Reprinted by permission of The Des Moines Register and Tribune.

makers 10 years ago, was a prop in many of the showrooms at the recent winter furniture markets.

"People like the solid dignity of a big clock. When we stopped producing them, customers had them custom made by cabinet-makers, so we decided to get back in the act," one furniture company executive explains.

His company introduced, in addition to traditional clocks, three modern grandfather clocks, one in walnut, another in rosewood, stainless steel and marble, and a third with a burl front and walnut sides.

Your House

A new heating-cooling system will utilize body heat, even when the bodies are in absentia.

The warm bodies being used for the first experimental models are college students on the Johnstown, Pa., campus of the University of Pittsburgh.

Students sitting in air-conditioned classrooms there will be heating their own dormitory rooms through the world's first climate control system based on reclaimed body heat. Excess heat from students and from lights and cooking in the kitchens is being collected at a central plant during the winter and redistributed through underground pipes to heat six new dormitories.

Despite temperatures of 10 below zero, the heat reclaimer is working, according to officials of Carrier Corp., the manufacturer.

In summer, the system will draw off the heat and "throw it away." On a giant scale, the reclaimer is something like the electric heat pump used in many homes.

Your Garden

The roses that are introduced commercially each year don't get selected in a hit-or-miss way. Each one represents an enormous investment of time, thought and human labor.

One nursery, for example, tests 600 to 800 new varieties each year, and selects less than one per cent of those it tests for introduction. This year, the company has selected only five roses.

All the roses it receives to test may represent a quarter of a million seedlings from hybridizers throughout the world, who have done preliminary weeding and pre-selecting before sending in their favorites.

Your Kitchen

Now that swinging refrigerator door won't have to swing open so often. You can get your ice cubes or a cold drink without opening the door.

General Electric is making a new refrigerator with a handy dispenser on the door. It automatically delivers ice cubes or chilled water at a touch. You merely press your glass or ice container against a cradle to trigger the action. One outlet is for ice, the other for water, and the outlets can be used separately or at the same time.

There's even a little light above the dispenser so you can get a drink of water in the dark.

The dispenser is supplied by an automatic icemaker and stores up to 260 cubes, and a single connection to the household cold water system will supply fresh water to both the icemaker and the reservoir.

Mirror, Mirror On The Wall—Wow!

MARY BRYSON

Your Decorating

Color has invaded the world of mirrors. The old-fashioned looking glass is now designed for looking at as well as in.

Frames of gold, gold with white, gold with brown, bronze or wood tones have always been the favorites—and they still are. But there also are dozens of new mirrors framed in shades of red, green or mustard yellow. Usually the colors are toned down to give an antique look.

In shape, too, mirrors are changing, though the round and rectangular ones still have the lion's share of the market. There is a variety of new shield shapes which seem appropriate with Mediterranean and Spanish decorative themes.

Your Garden

Don't let your evergreens go into the winter thirsty. That's the advice of landscape architects who recommend several thorough soaking of all trees and shrubs, but especially of evergreens.

Deciduous trees lose moisture as water vapor is passed out into the atmosphere from the leaves, one expert explains. Even after the leaves fall, some loss of water takes place through the branches and twigs.

Evergreens lose their vapor through the pores, which stay closed when the weather is cold. If mild weather develops during the winter, however, the evergreens open their pores in the warm air and may lose water, gradually drying out their tissues. Winter winds also tend to desiccate the trees and in extreme cases so much water is lost the trees die.

Regular watering of trees and shrubs in the next two months will help combat the hazards of excessive winter drying, say the experts.

Your Housework

You may be shocked when you check the electrical cords in your home for defects. One homeowner was dismayed when he discovered the insulation on an extension cord he was using for his room air conditioner had almost melted away.

Frayed or cracked insulation and loose connections on lamps, appliances and extension cords can go unnoticed unless the cords are checked often, as usually cords are tucked out of sight behind furniture.

Never attempt to repair a frayed cord by taping over bad insulation, say electricians, and don't make the mistake of running cords under rugs. If there is no electrical outlet nearby, have one installed where you need it.

The Des Moines Register, September 27, 1969. Reprinted by permission of The Des Moines Register and Tribune.

Questions

1. Why does the writer employ subheadings?
2. Who is the intended audience?
3. Find two examples in the first column which illustrate the writer's ability to set forth clear explanations in a few words.
4. In the second column, what do the expressions "That's the advice of landscape artists," "one expert explains," and "say electricians" tell us about the writing of these pieces?
5. Provide three examples of the use of concrete details in the second column.
6. What are some of the distinguishing features which would enable you to identify this column?

Suggested Writing Assignments

1. Write two columns of your own based on a subject taken from your own experiences. Make sure the columns are alike in style and general topic. For ideas, consider your hobbies, recreational activities, work experience, and other special skills and knowledge.
2. Write a column in the style of any one of the columnists illustrated here. First study the technique carefully and then see if you can imitate it.
3. Analyze two examples of the writing of a columnist not included in the text. In your discussion, try to pinpoint the characteristics which make the column a distinctive feature of the newspaper or magazine in which it appears.
4. Compare and contrast any two of the columnists in the text. Focus on topic, audience, and language.

11

The Argumentative Article

At this point we want to take a look at that form of modern prose which is distinctly persuasive—the argumentative article. Simply stated, any article can be said to be argumentative if the writer takes a stand on a controversial issue. The subject matter of argumentative pieces is, of course, endless, ranging from abortion, the use of drugs, and admitting Red China to the U. N., to pay television, crash diets, and the rule about ending a sentence with a preposition. On a single page of a local newspaper the following controversial topics were discussed: increasing city taxes, changing the curfew hours, lowering the voting age, hiring two additional patrolmen, and eliminating fishing licenses for persons 65 years of age.

Needless to say, the tone and language of the argumentative article depend on the topic and the audience. Thus, if a writer were presenting arguments against euthanasia, he would choose his language carefully in order to convey a tone of dignity appropriate to the topic. If he were writing a humorous defense of mini skirts, he would employ the slang, idioms, and anecdotes characteristic of the informal style.

But how is an argument put together? How do professional writers build a case? Boiling the process down to the essentials, we can say that in the introduction of the article, the writer states his position or thesis in regard to the controversial issue, provides supporting evidence in the body (logical reasons, facts, statements from authorities), and in the closing summarizes, draws a conclusion on the basis of the evidence presented, or perhaps advances his strongest point.

As an example, consider Jeri Engh's article, "The Case for Year-Round Schools" (Saturday Review, September 17, 1966). In the opening paragraphs the author states that he is opposed to the nine-month school year because it lacks the advantages to be found in the "year-round operation of elementary and secondary school, with students attending three out of four quarters on a rotating basis. . . ." He supports his contention with a number of arguments: a) existing student capacity would increase by one-third, b) construction needs could be cut, c) the holding power on potential high school dropouts would be strengthened (a Newark school on the four-quarter system from 1912 to 1931 graduated 22 percent more students than their nine-month counterparts), and, d) the explosive situation of graduating millions of school children at the same time would be eliminated. The writer closes by concluding that while year-round operation is not a cure-all, economic pressure plus clear educational advantages will produce increasing interest in the changeover.

Although the simple sequence of stating one's contention, giving supporting evidence for it, and closing it provides a useful overview, the argumentative article is usually a bit more complicated. For instance, in the foregoing piece on year-round schools, the author does more in the introduction than merely state his thesis. He also provides effective background details by pointing out that whereas the nine-month school year fits the needs of the agrarian economy of fifty years ago, it does not work in the modern context. And in addition to setting forth supporting arguments in the body, he also acknowledges and answers several objections to his case. For example, he refutes the objection that teachers need the summer for recuperation by showing that when the Rochester, Minnesota, schools offered their teachers a choice, 91 percent rejected the traditional summer vacation and chose the year-round contract because it provided professional prestige and pay.

As to strategies in building the argumentative article, there are a number of choices. Aside from the simple technique of providing supporting arguments and/or answering opposing arguments, the writer may choose to begin by granting certain objections to his case, and then turn the tables by presenting a very strong point in defense of his own position. One article writer employed this strategy in making a case against capital punishment. Having conceded that there was some truth in the arguments that life imprisonment might be more inhumane than death and that the death penalty would serve as a strong deterrent, he contended that capital punishment was still wrong for the single reason that a man might be put to death in error. Judges and juries make mistakes; the records show that innocent men have been executed; and for this reason alone capital punishment must be abolished.

Another very common strategy is based on the pattern of problem-solution. After establishing the fact that a problem exists, the writer introduces a plan or a solution to the problem. Milton Friedman's piece, "Up in the Air," (Newsweek, July 28, 1969) affords a good example of this approach. The problem concerns the fact that the plane in which Friedman was a passenger "had crossed the Atlantic in six hours but had now been circling Kennedy for an hour, stacked up awaiting permission to land." The writer goes on to show that, in addition to wasting the passengers' time, these routine delays cost airlines thousands of dollars an hour in fuel and salaries paid to skilled crews. What is the solution? How can airlines throughout the nation eliminate these costly delays? According to Friedman, the answer is simple: put the airports, which are presently financed and operated by the government, into the hands of private enterprise. Since all other activities relative to air travel are handled successfully by competitive businesses (building, fueling, and flying the planes), the author believes that the problem of airport congestion can be solved by the same means.

Frequently, the evidence found in the argumentative article takes the form of an extended example. Instead of producing arguments and solutions as such, the writer may relate an incident or personal experience to support his thesis. Consider the familiar charge of snobbery and elitism in Greek letter organizations. Two strategies are open to the writer on this topic. He could make his case in defense of fraternities by presenting a series of formal arguments designed to show that not all of these organizations are cliquish and prejudiced, or he could relate his own personal experiences on campus with a given fraternity— how and why he joined, the goals of the fraternity, the friendships he has cultivated—as a means of showing the good side of fraternity life. Note that the techniques of using arguments and personal experience are basically the same: each involves evidence given in support of a thesis. It is only the slant or strategy which distinguishes them.

Now that we have examined the various issues, kinds of evidence, and strategies involved in persuasive writing, we must not fail to observe the nontechnical nature of the argumentative article. Since the modern reader has neither the time nor the inclination to peruse lengthy treatments of current issues, it follows that professional writers clear out many of the technicalities found in scholarly argument. Quotations are brief and are documented within the article or in summary form at the end, statistics and other facts are condensed to the essentials, and references to the qualifications of authorities are touched on incidentally or taken for granted.

From this brief discussion it should be obvious that the argumentative article is designed to give the reader food for thought on a controversial topic, not incontestible proof.

The Case for a Volunteer Army

The concept of a volunteer armed force for the U.S. is one of the few national propositions that have scarcely a single enemy. President-elect Richard Nixon is strongly for it. The Department of Defense holds that "reliance upon volunteers is clearly in the interest of the armed forces." Such conservatives as Barry Goldwater and William Buckley back the idea, and so do many liberals, including James Farmer and David Dellinger. Young men under the shadow of the draft want it, and so do their parents. Most of American tradition from the Founding Fathers on down is in favor, as were the untold millions of immigrants who came to America to avoid forced service in the conscript armies of czars and kaisers.

A volunteer armed force would seem to have something for everybody. For the Pentagon, it would provide a careerist body of men staying in the ranks long enough to learn their jobs and do them well; as it is,

---

Condensed from *Time*, January 10, 1969. © 1969 Time, Inc. Reprinted by permission.

93% of drafted soldiers leave the service when their two-year tour of duty ends. For constitutionalists, a volunteer army would affirm the principle that free men should not be forced into voluntary servitude in violation of the 13th Amendment. For philosophers, it would restore freedom of choice; if a man wants to be a soldier, he can do so, and if not, he does not have to. The idea also appeals to all those who have become increasingly aware that the draft weighs unfairly upon the poor and the black, the dropout and the kid who does not get to college.

For all this rare unanimity of opinion, however, it seems hardly likely that the U.S. will soon achieve what Nixon has promised to build toward: "an all-volunteer armed force." A main reason for this is that the Pentagon's basic support for the idea of a volunteer army is heavily qualified by worries that it will not work—while the draft has now delivered the bodies without fail for two decades.

Worries in the Pentagon

Burned into military memories is the hasty dismantlement of the U.S. armed forces after World War II, when the nation returned to its traditional military stance: a small number of voluntary regulars, backed up by reserves and the National Guard. The Army managed to attract 300,000 volunteers, of whom West Point's Colonel Samuel H. Hays wrote: "In an infantry battalion during that period one might find only two or three high school graduates in nearly a thousand men. Technical proficiency was not at a high level; delinquency and court-martial rates were." Getting choosier, the Army raised qualifying scores on aptitude tests from 59 to 70, 80, and finally 90. Simultaneously, it limited recruits to men without dependents and those willing to sign up for a three-year hitch. When the Berlin blockade and the Communist seizure of Czechoslovakia took place in 1948, the Pentagon complained that it was far under strength and that relying on volunteers had failed. Congress was told that the draft was needed to get manpower and show U.S. determination to check Communist aggression. The clumsily titled Universal Military Training and Service Act was passed. After that, proposals for returning to a volunteer army were not heard for years.

The military arguments against the volunteer army nowadays derive from new judgments about the size of the forces needed, the cost, and the necessity of flexibility. Certainly nothing but a draft could have supplied the 2,800,000 doughboys of World War I or the 10 million G.I.'s of World War II, and the Pentagon's estimate of its current needs runs to similar magnitudes: 3,454,160 of the present moment, and 2,700,000 when peace returns. To raise the Viet Nam-inflated forces, the Department of Defense has relied on the draft to bring in about one-third of new troops and on the scare power of the draft to induce thousands of others to "volunteer." The draftees go to the Army, mostly to the infantry; the glamorous Air Force never has to draft anyone, and the Navy and Marines only rarely.

The Defense Department's study of the practicability of a volunteer army, made five years ago, proved to the department's satisfaction that it still would not work. Even allowing for growth in military age population, DOD found that it could not expect to get more than 2,000,000 men, at least 700,000 short of pre-Viet Nam needs. As for the possibilities of increasing incentives, the Pentagon concluded that "pay alone is a less potent factor than might be expected" and that fringe benefits have small appeal for young men not deeply conscious of the value of medical care or retirement pay. On the other hand, Richard Nixon holds to the old American idea that it should be possible to devise incentives—pay among them—that will draw men into service. . . .

Phantom Fears

Civilian reservations about volunteer armed forces also focus on some fears that tend to dissolve upon examination. Some critics have raised the specter of well-paid careerists becoming either mercenaries or a "state within a state." Nixon, for one, dismisses the mercenary argument as nonsense. The U.S. already pays soldiers a salary. Why should a rise in pay—which for an enlisted man might go from the present $2,900 a year to as much as $7,300—turn Americans into mercenaries? Said Nixon: "We're talking about the same kind of citizen armed force America has had ever since it began, excepting only in the period when we have relied on the draft." The Pentagon itself rejects the Wehrmacht-type army, in which men spend all their professional lives in service.

Nixon has also addressed himself to the possibility that a careerist army might become a seedbed for future military coups. That danger is probably inherent in any military force, but, as the President-elect points out, a coup would necessarily come from "the top officer ranks, not from the enlisted ranks, and we already have a career-officer corps. It is hard to see how replacing draftees with volunteers would make officers more influential." Nixon might have added that conscript armies have seldom proved any barrier to military coups. Greece's army is made up of conscripts, but in last year's revolution they remained loyal to their officers, not to their King.

Might not the volunteer army become disproportionately black, perhaps a sort of internal Negro Foreign Legion? Labor Leader Gus Tyler is one who holds that view; he says that a volunteer army would be "low-income and, ultimately, overwhelmingly Negro. These victims of our social order 'prefer' the uniform because of socio-economic compulsions—for the three square meals a day, for the relative egalitarianism of the barracks or the fox-hole, for the chance to be promoted." Conceivably, Negroes could flock to the volunteer forces for both a respectable reason, upward mobility, and a deplorable one, to form a domestic revolutionary force.

As a matter of practice rather than theory, powerful factors would work in a volunteer army toward keeping the proportion of blacks about where it is in the draft army —11%, or roughly the same as the nation as a whole. Pay rises would attract whites as as much as blacks, just as both are drawn into police forces for similar compensation. The educational magnets, which tend to rule out many Negroes as too poorly schooled and leave many whites in college through deferments, would continue to exert their effect. Black Power militancy would work against Negroes' joining the Army. Ronald V. Dellums, a Marine volunteer 13 years ago and now one of two black councilmen in Berkeley, opposes the whole idea of enlistment as a "way for the black people to get up and out of the ghetto existence. If a black man has to become a paid killer in order to take care of himself and his family economically, there must be something very sick about this society." But even if all qualified Negroes were enrolled, the black proportion of the volunteer army could not top 25%. Nixon holds that fear of a black army is fantasy: "It supposes that raising military pay would in some way slow up or stop the flow of white volunteers, even as it stepped up the flow of black volunteers. Most of our volunteers now are white. Better pay and better conditions would obviously make military service more attractive to black and white alike."

One consideration about the volunteer army is that it could eventually become the only orderly way to raise armed forces. The draft, though it will prevail by law at least through 1971, is under growing attack. In the mid-'50s, most military-age men eventually got drafted, and the inequities of exempting the remainder were not flagrant. Now, despite Viet Nam, military draft needs are dropping, partly because in 1966 Secretary of Defense Robert McNamara started a "project 100,-000," which slightly lowered mental and physical standards and drew 70,000 unanticipated volunteers into the forces. Meanwhile, the pool of men in the draftable years is rising, increasingly replenished by the baby boom of the late '40s. Armed forces manpower needs have run at 300,000 a year lately, but they will probably drop to 240,000 this year. On the other hand, the number of men aged 19 to 25 has jumped from 8,000,000 in 1958 to 11.5 million now—and will top 13 million by 1974. The unfairness inherent in the task of arbitrarily determining the few who shall serve and the many who shall be exempt will probably overshadow by far the controversies over college deferments and the morality of the Viet Nam war. In the American conscience, the draft-card burners planted a point: that conscription should be re-examined and not necessarily perpetuated. The blending of war protest with draft protest, plus the ever more apparent inequities of Selective Service, led Richard Nixon to move his proposal for a volunteer army to near the top of his priorities.

Healing Tensions

The position from which to start working for a volunteer army is that, to a large extent, the nation already has one—in the sense that two-thirds of its present troops are enlistees. Neither Nixon nor anyone else visualizes a rapid changeover. The draft will doubtless endure until the war in Viet Nam ends, but it could then be phased out gradually. After that, the draft structure can be kept in stand-by readiness, thinks Nixon, "without leaving 20 million young Americans who will come of age during the next decade in constant uncertainty and apprehension."

If Nixon and his executive staff can move ahead with legislation and the new Secretary of Defense prod and cajole his generals and admirals, the new Administration will go far toward its aim. A volunteer army might help ease racial tensions, perhaps by ending the imbalance that has blacks serving in the front lines at almost three times their proportion in the population and certainly by removing the arbitrariness of the draft that puts them there. The move would also eliminate the need to force men to go to war against their consciences, and end such other distortions as paying soldiers far less than they would get if they were civilians, or forcing other young men into early marriages and profitless studies to avoid the draft. Incentive, substituted for compulsion, could cut waste and motivate pride. Not least, a volunteer army would work substantially toward restoring the national unity so sundered by the present inequalities of the draft.

Questions

1. How does the writer open? Identify the main points in the first three paragraphs.
2. How was the case for a volunteer army affected by the dismantlement of U. S. armed forces after World War II and by the Communist seizure of Czechoslovakia in 1948? Explain each point separately.
3. In paragraph five, how does the author classify the current military arguments against a volunteer army?
4. Show how the writer answers the objections that a volunteer army will consist of mercenaries and blacks.
5. Did the author employ good strategy by dealing first with the historical background and objections to a volunteer army so that he could close with a number of strong supporting arguments? How many of these arguments can you find in the last two paragraphs?

Women Demand Right To Create Own Life

WOMEN'S LIBERATION, WATERLOO-CEDAR FALLS

Before all else we are human beings, women second; and we demand and respect the right of every individual to create his or her own life and to develop fully his or her potential. Our movement finds it necessary to reaffirm these basic rights because they have historically been denied to women.

Women's liberation is not a new movement but a continuation of a revolution that has been waged by women against their oppression from the beginning of time. Male dominance and female subordination have had varied expressions, according to age and culture, but in whatever form, oppression of the female has been universal. For our society and time, the dehumanization of women may be summed up as follows:

"A Sexual Being"

First, woman has traditionally been defined in terms of her relationship to man, not in terms of her Self. Society perpetuates the myth that woman is chiefly a sexual being suited primarily for male gratification, childbearing and motherhood. The female is taught from infancy to play house and dolls, to be nonaggressive and dependent, and to direct all efforts toward securing a husband.

Second, this dependence and passivity has led to her exploitation as a consumer. A woman's conditioned sense of inferiority to man creates deep-seated insecurities. The advertising industry feeds on her insecurities and identity problems by persuading a woman that by buying things—cosmetics, clothes, household furnishings, cleansing agents, and packaged creativity—she can fill the void.

Surplus Labor Force

Third, the woman who pursues a career outside the home or seeks a job out of financial necessity is confronted with another kind of economic exploitation—equally dehumanizing. She serves as part of a surplus labor force which provides the business world with a "steam lever" in maintaining wage ceilings and controlling employee demands. Because of roles prescribed for the woman "in the home," women leave jobs to have babies, and women are not recognized as "breadwinners" in our society. Thus, employers have ready-made rationalizations for paying women lower wages than men for similar work.

The women's liberation movement will continue to resist these patterns of exploitation and oppression. We begin on a local level by meeting together and accepting each other as full, thinking human beings and proceed to redefine ourselves and our role in this society. With resultant group strength we exert pressure and influence for change in areas that are basic to women's freedom. Paramount among these are the issues of birth control and abortion, and the traditional male-female roles as taught in home and school.

Abortion Laws—Unconstitutional

The present abortion laws are a matter of women allowing men, in church and in government, to decide for them what they may do with their own bodies. We view present abortion laws as unconstitutional in their denial of basic rights to both women and

---

Northern Iowan (University of Northern Iowa), October 10, 1969. Reprinted by permission.

their doctors, and shall take group action in support of this view.

Because attitudes of timidity in women and aggressiveness in men are not inherent but learned, group pressure is needed for a whole new orientation to education and curriculum planning in schools and colleges. We call, also, for the abolition of traditional male-female roles in the home and for the establishment of free and equal participation in domestic chores and child care, as well as in career and income activities.

The contention that present male-female roles are "equal but different" is as shoddy as the racist slogan, "separate but equal."

Questions

1. What is the writer's position on the issue?
2. Briefly indicate the three ways in which the "dehumanization of women" has occurred.
3. Identify what you believe to be the most effective of the three arguments.
4. How would you describe the language in this piece?
5. Were objections to the writer's case acknowledged and answered? Why?
6. How convincing is this argumentative article? Base your answer on the evidence, tone, and strategy employed.

The Case for Black Literature

JAMES C. KILGORE

"Not to teach, in the context of American Literature, that literature which treats honestly the humanity of black Americans is to continue to be, to black and white Americans, academically dishonest, humanistically cruel, and psychologically destructive."

Most of those who object to the teaching of black literature do so on aesthetic grounds. They suggest that the black writer does not present a "realistic" view of his society, that his version of America and the world is shameful fantasy, that his art is "slanted by racism and well-meaning sentimentalism."[1] Arguing that a valuable aesthetic experience must be primary to the teaching of literature, they go on to suggest that all black literature is aesthetically inferior. They imply in their art-for-art's-sake thesis that all aesthetically valuable literature, with only a few exceptions, is white.

No one should disagree with the notion

Negro Digest, July, 1969. Copyright July, 1969 by *Negro Digest*. Reprinted by permission of the publisher and James C. Kilgore.

[1] LeRoi Jones, "Black Writing," *Home*, New York: William Morrow & Co., Inc., page 164.

that literature should afford one a valuable aesthetic experience. An elementary test of the aesthetically valuable, however, is concerned with the relative beauty of art. The art that is literature is concerned with the relative beauty of the lives of people: how they stand on top of a Western mountain and die, how they live their short happy lives in search of "success." Of course, there is universality in all human experience, but when teachers present experiences to a class of black and white children, they should present experiences which compliment the humanity and dignity of a black and white class. Surely, no sane teacher will defend presenting literary experiences to any student which implies denial of that student's humanity, his human beauty. Literature should facilitate a person's search through the mirrored past of human experience for reflections of his own life worth, his own humanity. If every image in the "aesthetically valuable" is white and if, in contrast, the only black image presented is one concerning a black child chased by a child-eating tiger, is this not a cruel denial of the child's human beauty and worth? Is it not building a social dynamite which must some day explode in black summer rage?

The demand for the teaching of black literature is a demand for a more human definition of the "aesthetically valuable." It is, more specifically, a demand for a literature that serves the specific human needs and aspirations of black life, black humanity. The literature that is presently called "American Literature" is complimentary to white images. It is, in short, what may be called "white literature." I do not mean to suggest that what is presently called "American Literature" is not good literature. Much of it, however, lacks the basic ingredient of literary integrity and is indeed slanted by racism and well-meaning sentimentalism. Since black life experiences are "normally" different in America from white life experiences, constantly in aesthetic and actual conflict, there is no reason why a clear-thinking teacher should expect one valuable aesthetic experience from honest literature. What is reasonable is that there should be at least two aesthetically valuable experiences. And there should be beauties in between. The solution, it seems to me, lies in the acceptance of all of our American selves—white, yellow, red, black.

Gwendolyn Brooks is a Pulitzer Prize winning poet. Her *In the Mecca* was nominated for a 1969 National Book Award. Her "Beverly Hills, Chicago" is a splended example of poetic excellence: but in spite of awards and nominations, Gwendolyn Brooks, Poet Laureate of Illinois, is edited out of "books of American verse."

The prose of Richard Wright is as clear and clean as that of Ernest Hemingway. The dominant, most admirable image in the fiction of Hemingway is white. "The nigger that cooks" is in the kitchen in Hemingway's fiction, and he seems to want to stay there. The nigger may be in the kitchen in the fiction of Richard Wright, but he does not want to stay there. He does not wish to remain a nigger either. Implied in the fiction of Richard Wright are the hopes and aspirations of black life in America. Implicit in the fiction of this black writer is what the Civil Rights Movement *is*—or *was*—all about. Black students, as I understand them, are saying that if they must read Hemingway's "The Short Happy Life of Francis Macomber," then white students ought to read Richard Wright's "Big Boy Leaves Home"; that if they must read Emily Dickinson's "As imperceptibly as grief," then white students ought to read Gwendolyn Brooks's "Beverly Hills, Chicago."

"To thine own self be true" was the last admonition Polonius gave his son, Laertes, when Laertes left home for school in France. "The proper study of mankind is man," Alexander Pope wrote in his *Essay on Man*. An elementary lesson in modern social problems reveals that thousands of people are institutionalized each year because they do not know themselves. Thousands of lives are lost each year as they are washed down ghetto drains in search of other selves, through drugs, alcohol, LSD. When Laertes left home for school, he had been taught well the ways of other men; but more important than that, he had been taught to *know himself*. If we teach, on the green grounds of "universality," a black child the life experience of a white child, we are saying to that black child that there is no American difference between him and the white child. We may desire that dream to be true. But it is not true today. A white child may go to Mississippi from his home in Cleveland and find that only the weather is different and perhaps, "The people walk and talk a little slower than they do in Cleveland." But a black child, having been taught that there is no American difference between him and the white child, may go to Mississippi and die in the bloated belly of the Mississippi Pearl where Emmitt Till, far from Chicago, floated to a deathly adolescent truth. Black child truth is not the same as white child truth in Mississippi. There is a deadly difference between the two kinds of "childish" truths. Surely most educators would like to equalize the two truths. Recognizing and teaching them may be one way of equalizing them. Meanwhile, however, the child must know the truth of the world he lives in. That truth may not set him free in Mississippi, but it may well save his life.

Those who contend that the black writer cannot—or does not—present a realistic view of society are obviously not black. They do not know the reality of black American experience. Often they do not even sympathize with the needs and aspirations of black humanity. And a writer ought to sympathize. He really ought to empathize. He ought at least to sympathize with the denial of black feminine narcissism, illuminated in *Black Rage:*

The girl who is black has no option in the matter of how much she will change herself. Her blackness is the antithesis of American beauty. . . . She has no real basis of feminine attractiveness on which to build a sound feminine narcissism.[2]

Waring Cuney, in "No Images," described the situation of black womanhood nearly half a century before *Black Rage:*

She does not know
Her beauty,
She thinks her brown body
Has no glory.

What Robert Herrick does for white womanhood in his "To Electra" is denied black womanhood, barred from the classrooms by "traditional" professors who apparently know nothing about human needs and aspirations and their relations to literature.

Of course, there are black writers who have not presented a realistic view of their society. Most of these writers, however, had their brains washed in the stagnant waters of slavery or self-hate. Sometimes, "success" in the white world drove them to copy the stereotypes of their humanity. Phillis Wheatley, an outstanding example of a black woman who was denied feminine worth, most probably hated herself. How else could she write, in her "On Being Brought from Africa to America":

Remember, "Christians," "Negroes," black as "Cain,"
May be refined, and join the angelic train

Looking at Phillis Wheatley's poem through contemporary "Black-Power!" and "emerging"—Africa eyes, one must conclude that Miss Wheatley was ashamed of her native land; ultimately, of herself. But Phillis Wheatley was a slave, and so it is easy to forgive her for her "mask." Jupiter Ham-

---

[2] William H. Grier and Price M. Cobb, *Black Rage,* New York: Bantam Books, 1968, p. 33.

mon, a contemporary of Miss Wheatley, was a slave who was encouraged by his "Kind Master" to write, and it is easy to forgive that "Dutiful Slave."

Paul Laurence Dunbar, in his poem, "We Wear the Mask," suggests that there have been many black lies told to white America:

> We wear the mask that grins and lies,
> It hides our cheeks and shades our eyes,—
> This debt we owe to human guile;
> With torn and bleeding hearts we smile,
> And mouth with myriad subtleties. . . .

Jupiter Hammon and Phillis Wheatley wore "the mask." So have dozens of white American authors worn white puritan masks. But there are black writers who have grown up, who have taken off the mask; there are black writers who have never worn a literary mask. They paid a painful price for their integrity. It is they who can take the slogan, "Black-is-beautiful!" and develop it *lovingly* in all of its American shades. It is they who can most vividly portray the racial glory and dark beauty of black life.

Most white writers in America have not described honestly the human beauty of the black American. Perhaps, these writers are too near, in their imagery, Herrick's "To Electra." Perhaps, unconsciously, they distort the humanity of black life. Perhaps they do so because it is—it certainly *was*—in vogue. It was the literary thing to do. At any rate, they cannot treat the humanity vividly and lovingly—not as vividly and as lovingly as the black writer can. They cannot measure the extent of rejection the black man takes to his "You-can-make-it-if-you-try" brainwashed home. If they have not felt the electric cattle-prod stabbing Afro-American dignity, they cannot measure, not truly, the aesthetic value of black-life dignity because they have not felt the electrocution of it. If they have not been *Black like Me* for one day, they cannot begin to know "the realism" of my Uncle Johnny's 63 "separate but equal" Louisiana sawmill years.

While black students may seem to be saying that "The proper study of black man is black life," I understand them to mean that they want to be told the American truth of themselves. I understand them to mean that *the proper study of any* man is honest life. They know that Jim of *Huckleberry Finn* is a compromise of man in them. They know that *Little Black Sambo* is a "classic" black lie. They know that virtually every story about black life in "American Literature" is a story that presents a questionable humanity. Black life is portrayed as primitive, savage life or saintly, romantic life. Neither is honest, earthly, American life.

The image of the black American in "American Literature" has been, to say the least, dishonest. Black humanity as represented by most white writers has been capsulized, categorized, and dis-integratized. The Happy Slave is a literary hoax; the Tragic Mulatto was tragic because he was a social slave, trapped in the iron grip of "class." The Wretched Freedman was not free, and the Local Color Negro is a romantic "creation," like the Exotic Primitive. If there was ever such a man as the Local Color Negro, he is dead now; if he is not dead, then he has moved to the city. If there was ever such a wretch as a "Wretched Freedman," he lives solely in the territory of American "fiction." The Tragic Mulatto has integrated now, and the Exotic Primitive has lost his exoticism as well as his primeval loveliness in urban ghetto reproduction.

We teach by what we teach as well as by what we do not teach. For too long, aesthetic "reality" in American literature has said that the humanity of black Americans is ridiculous, with Stepin Fetchit; amusing, with Amos and Andy; entertaining, with white, black-faced minstrelsy; and human only in exceptional cases, like *Uncle Tom's Cabin, Up From Slavery, The Jackie Robinson Story,* and *Yes I Can.* What we have said as a nation about and to black humanity is this: *Basically your humanity is questionable. However, if you are fantastic, like Uncle Tom, Booker T. Washington, Jackie Robin-*

son, and Sammie Davis, Jr., we will concede your exceptional ability.

Now those are not kind words to utter to a human being. They are not kind words to speak to any child regardless of the color of his humanity. They are unkind, and they erect a stone wall between the human needs and aspirations of people.

Much of the fault for the "communication" gap between people in America today is due, in part, to three centuries of "classic" lies. And not to teach, in the context of American Literature, that literature which treats honestly the humanity of black Americans is to continue to be, to black and white Americans, academically dishonest, humanistically cruel, and psychologically destructive. Not to teach black literature at all is to continue to build, with scholarly arrogancy, a summer bomb that must explode over the "traditional" September walls of academic paranoia onto the green canvas of American liberty. Thomas Jefferson might have written that "While all men are created equal, literature keeps them equal; literature can build a fortress of human dignity in a child's heart." Thomas Jefferson did not write that, however. He wrote "All men are created equal." It is up to education to write the rest; it is up to education to build the fortress of human dignity in black and white American hearts.

Questions

1. Indicate the objection to the teaching of black literature which is stated in the opening paragraphs. How does the writer answer it?
2. The author says that he "does not mean to suggest that what is presently called American literature is not good literature." What is his criticism of it?
3. Explain the parallel which is set up between the two white and the two black writers.
4. How does the author illustrate the point that "Black child truth is not the same as white child truth in Mississippi"?
5. Which of the two arguments do you believe is the more convincing—the one involving the physical beauty of the black girl, or black writers who "wear masks"?
6. Characterize the level of the language in this piece, and provide two or three examples which illustrate the writer's effective use of words.
7. Was any evidence given in the article to show that the author is black?

A Letter to Chris

MRS. RICHARD PLUMER

DEAR CHRIS,

I am writing you today because your sister Penny has died of cancer. Which, of course, you know. You came home five days before she died, talked to her, joked a little, and believed with us that a miracle would let her live. You suffered through the two days of coma and gasping breath, and conducted yourself manfully during the funeral weekend.

Now you have returned to prep school—away from home, as you were during most of Penny's illogical illness: four long-short months of diminishing life. To have you stay away was our deliberate choice (over which you had no control).

You were only 16 years old. She was 18. You kidded and played "hearts" with her. We saw no good in disrupting your life, keeping you here to wait with us in doctors' offices, tumor clinics, and hospitals. Dad and I would do that.

But now we are racked with misgivings; for there was a gain to be made by your staying home, and we missed it.

You could have been at Penny's side in the hospital, as we were. You could have heard her tell of pain and could have tried to ease it, as we tried. You could have met cancer face to face. Because Penny died of lung cancer as much as of the abdominal cancer that began it all. She learned what lung cancer is all about.

And yet two nights ago, before you returned to school, you kissed me goodnight—and I knew in that instant that you are smoking again. I know you have already forgotten that Penny planned to write a book about cancer. You obviously do not believe that cancer is anything for you to worry about.

As Penny told us both, "I used to be like that. The older folks told me that if I smoked I would get cancer and die. But that didn't bother me because I was not afraid to die. But no one ever told me that I could get cancer and live with it."

Penny was living then. And she had known this vicious invader for three months. She wanted to write and describe it. She wanted very much to write it for kids like you.

Linda was going to illustrate the book . . . short little Linda with the deep brown eyes and the deep affection for your sister. Linda stopped smoking, Chris, but then Linda had an advantage over you in that she visited Penny every day of her fight against cancer. And Linda stopped smoking the day that Penny looked at her—blue eyes meeting brown—and said, "Here I am with something I don't want, and you are trying so hard to get it."

This is what we denied you.

**Sunny World
For 60 Days**

Linda saw Penny's legs and face grow thin, a funny thing to two girls who had always kidded over Pen's pearshaped figure. She saw a bouncy high school senior who was dating, going shopping, lugging books, begin to lose her steam, lie on the sofa, decline dates, and struggle to climb the stairs.

Waterloo Sunday Courier, January 12, 1969. Reprinted by permission of Mrs. Richard Plumer and The Miami Herald.

She endured with Penny the weeks of half-questions and half-answers while we all waited for Penny to get well.

After her initial operation, Pen recovered wonderfully, and for 60 bittersweet days the world was sunny. The program of chemotherapy was begun and the cancer seemed arrested. Three times a week she went to our pediatrician's office for heroic injections of chemicals into her veins.

These monster injections would nauseate her temporarily—but she always bounced back for more fun and action. She dated. She went skin-diving. She listened to Simon and Garfunkel. She even held a job at a Dadeland store to earn extra money for college clothes.

There came a day, however, when she realized she must resign and did so tearfully. Yet, her last night on the job, she tucked evening clothes into her yellow car, changed quickly, and had Elliott pick her up at the store so they could hurry to a debutante dance for two friends.

But nausea and weakness cut her down. Next she started swelling with fluid, growing bigger, and bigger, until she cried out on the sofa one day, "Mama, do something—or I'm going to pop!" A telephone explanation brought our surgeon-friend to the hospital where he used a syringe to tap off much of the fluid. And she went home more comfortable.

Penny was a remarkable patient all the way—cheerful and always optimistic. No matter how painful it was, she did as she was told . . . she wanted so desperately to get well.

Not too long after that emergency treatment, we made what was to be our last car ride together, although we did not know it at the time. A consultation of specialists here and in Boston had determined to try a two-weeks' series of chemical injections, after which she was to go home for a month, and then return for another two weeks of treatment.

When she learned of this, Penny realized for the first time that her entry into Middlebury College would be delayed by her battle to get well. But she was philosophical about it and was game to fight cancer until she won—a whole year if necessary—to get her chance to be a freshman.

At the hospital Penny was initiated into an around-the-clock system of injecting chemicals and what they called "pediatric maintenance" into her veins. Feeding of chemicals into the veins to stop the cancer; feeding of fluids to overcome the vomiting that the chemicals caused; feeding of human albumin to replace the protein being lost in fluid buildup; feeding of penicillin to prevent infections.

Something always being fed into Penny's veins.

**Dreams Ended
In Nightmares**

After many hours of this the needle would become dislodged. The skin would swell with yellowed puffiness as the fluid seeped into the wrong area. And the needle would be pulled out and reinserted.

This is a technique that separates an experienced doctor or nurse from a less experienced one. But even the good ones have trouble when the veins have been used up and the arms are bruised purple with blotches and swollen from dislodged needles. Human albumin is a thick, viscous protein substance like egg white which drips in slowly and often clogs the needle until the needle must be changed.

Penny and Linda learned to hate the coming of the albumin twice a day.

For hours the two of them played gin rummy and talked and pretended that Penny would get well. Often Linda would just sit by the bed while Penny slept. When she awakened, Linda would rub her back with baby lotion, and try to rub, rub, rub away the lung cancer deep inside by her tender hand pressure, accompanied by prayer.

Later came days when Linda could not talk to Penny at all—for Pen was dopey with sedation to ease the pain. Linda would just wait by the bed, and Penny would moan and make senseless remarks in her sleep, as the drugs seemed to cause dreams which ended in nightmares.

Suddenly she would jump and cry out, awakening herself. Then she would tell about her "trip" to Linda . . . and talk . . . until she found it necessary to ask for another pain injection. These could only be given every four hours and sometimes she wanted them sooner and had to wait.

Most of Penny's pain was caused by the fluid which accompanied the cancer in her lungs, shutting down her supply of air, until she would say, "Doctor, I just can't breathe. Can't you do something to let me breathe?"

So they did what they could do. Our good, kind pediatric surgeon, who loved Penny for her smiling courage, as she loved him for his humor and gentle hands, inserted a long-needle syringe between her ribs and slowly sucked out syringe after syringe of orange pulpy fluid, full of protein and other life-giving qualities. He did not withdraw it too quickly lest he put her in shock. Later a tube or catheter was taped into an opening he made in her abdomen. And from this he released another two quarts of the same thick fluid into a brown gallon bottle he placed under the bed.

By this time a radioactive substance (P-32) had been flown from New York and inserted into Penny's lung cavity in an attempt to stop the wildfire cancerous growth. Great care had to be taken of all fluids which came out of her body after that, as the fluids, too, were radioactive. And one of our nurses quit the case out of fear of the radioactivity.

Tethered as she was to tubes and bottles, it was hard for Penny to find a position in bed in which she was comfortable.

"Mama, what am I doing wrong?" she asked me one day. "Why don't I get well?" But there was no answer. Nothing she did was wrong and nothing the doctors knew to do seemed to be right. The cancer worked daily and fast.

Yet Penny received every medical attention it is known to give. Each x-ray showed, progressively, a larger mass in both lung and abdomen. Finally it reached the liver and her eyes became yellowed. As the cancer spread we learned the term that the doctors had not called by its medical name at the beginning.

Metastasis.

This means that the cancer has jumped the boundary of a self-contained tumor and is spreading out of control, attaching itself to other organs.

**The Book Was
Never Written**

Every day our doctors evaluated, analyzed, researched, battled the agonizing mystery of cancer. Never doubt, Chris, our admiration and gratitude for the magnificent team of doctors and nurses, both in Miami and at the Jimmy Fund in Boston. They were many—these intelligent men and women, always honest with us, always kind, always hoping for a miraculous remission from a disease for which they have no cure. Our battle was their battle, our girl was their girl, and they fought like tigers for her life.

When we entered the hospital where you last visited Penny, we did not know she had only three weeks to live. In these weeks she knew cancer intimately but it left her too weak to write her story, the book she wanted to dedicate to you and your brother. She intended it, also, for others like you who flirt with smoking, and who think it is all right to smoke.

Penny died of cancer in lung, liver and abdomen—a spreading, choking foe that would not give in to medicine or prayer.

During these miserable days as she grew worse and worse, Dad and I asked so many knowledgeable doctors the same question, WHY? Why should Penny have cancer?

One white-smocked tumor specialist spoke

for them all. "It is so terribly difficult because there are hundreds of different types of cancer. And we do not know what triggers their growth. So far we only know the direct cause of two of them. And one of these, people will not believe."

Won't you believe, Chris? Penny had something she did not want, but she wanted you to know what it could do to you.

Won't you listen to her?

—MOTHER

Questions

1. Explain how the writer used an extended narration of a personal experience in the form of a letter to make her case against smoking.
2. Would the article have been more, or less, convincing if the writer had employed the conventional technique of setting up a series of formal arguments against smoking?
3. Provide examples to illustrate the writer's effective word choice, use of quotation, and handling of technical medical points.
4. How does the reference to Chris in the seventh from the last paragraph ("Never doubt, Chris . . .") contribute to the unity of the article?
5. The final test of an argumentative article is the extent to which it persuades the reader. Were you persuaded?

Still Playing It Dumb?

LAURA CUNNINGHAM

When Marilyn Monroe confided, "I keep my undies in the refrigerator in hot weather," she epitomized the brainless sexpot of her time. Nothing tantalized a man more than large breasts and a tiny brain. Intelligent girls were stereotyped as frigid. The lower the I.Q., the higher the Sex Q. By this scale, cretins must have been irresistible in 1950.

There is nothing appealing about stupidity in 1969. The girl who plays dumb today is as out of style as a padded bra. Yet I know many girls who persist in hiding their brains. These girls all regard their intelligence as a defect. "Smart girls scare men off," they claim. So they fake stupidity to make men feel smarter. They believe the male ego withers when confronted by a girl with a master's degree.

These pseudosimpletons still cling to this fallacy because ten years ago their misconceptions were true. Before premarital sex became more or less (more!) acceptable, men preferred dumb girls for one, subconscious reason. They were titillated when a girl behaved brainlessly because they assumed it would be easy to seduce her. There's Marilyn

---

Cosmopolitan, August, 1969. Reprinted by permission of Laura Cunningham.

again, caught in a clinch, cooing—"Oooh, what are you doing to me?" Because sex was forbidden, men sought girls too dumb to know sex was something they shouldn't do. Stupidity was sexy because it implied little-girl naïveté.

Okay, we had a sexual revolution, remember? Most girls have become partisans. Armed with a pill, we don't have to be dumb nowadays to make love. The result is that hardly anyone is sex-starved anymore. No man is so frustrated that he has to take his chances on seducing Miss Bibbitty Boo. Today men look for more than a "yes" from a girl. Since sex is free, the double-standard "John" outlook, that a woman is a plaything, not a person, has been discarded by all but the most militant middle-aged conventioneers.

If you want an attractive, intelligent man, act as smart as you are. He wants a girl who can understand his interests and ambitions. The competition is tough. If you don't know what he's saying, you'll bore him into the arms of a more perceptive girl. You can no longer flatter a man by pretending to be stupid. You can only insult him and *hurt* his ego. Today a man chooses a girl, later a wife, to be the *best* possible extension of himself. She reflects his position in life—socially, intellectually. Therefore, a man wants to present the most dazzling, *accomplished* girl he can find.

If you've been acting dumb, you've probably run through your act in these arenas: at work (so you won't be considered a threat to male co-workers), on dates (to let a man feel oh so important), in bed (to make him feel more experienced), and at parties (to let everyone know what a gay, silly time you're having).

And all you've probably accomplished is a guarantee that you'll never get ahead on your job (you *convinced* the men at work you're no threat). And you'll bore your date (he'd rather *discuss*, than have to patiently explain the obvious). In bed, you've actually made yourself less exciting (he already *knows* he's experienced). And at parties, you may have scared off some bright young men (who didn't want you to guess their zodiac signs when they were in the middle of a political debate).

Now, wouldn't it be better to have played it smart? "You bet your sweet Bippy!"

Questions

1. Show how contrast is used in the opening paragraphs to introduce the issue.
2. According to the writer, what effect did birth control pills have on the old view that "stupidity is sexy"?
3. What evidence is given for the statement that nowadays a man wants an intelligent girl?
4. By means of specific references, show that this piece is an excellent example of informal prose.
5. A controversial issue is one which has two sides. Do any arguments occur to you in support of the other side of this issue?

He Can't Purchase Fireworks But Can Easily Buy Dynamite

TOM TIEDE

Let's assume for a few moments' reading that I am an irrational madman. An anarchist. A revolutionary. Or a man with a sick grudge against an employer, a governmental official or society in general.

I want to destroy, get even, show the world.

But how?

I could purchase a gun through a catalogue, pick up a knife at the Boy Scout supply house or make my own torch with a rag, beer bottle and gasoline.

Why Be a Piker?

But why be a piker? A better way is being devastatingly demonstrated all around the nation today: Use dynamite, Dr. Alfred Nobel's terrible invention—the simple mixture of nitroglycerine, sodium nitrate and absorbent (usually sawdust) which has become the most popular nonmilitary explosive in the world.

True, I can't get it just anywhere. In some cities such as New York a dynamite buyer must be a member of a recognized construction firm or corporation needing explosives for normal business. And in some states such as New Jersey, where individuals are allowed to buy, permission is given only upon thorough investigation, including fingerprint identification.

A Cinch Elsewhere

But elsewhere, which is most everywhere, getting dynamite is a cinch.

Take New Hampshire as an illustration. There is a retail explosives store in almost every medium-sized town here. But there are no federal, state or seldom any city laws concerned with dynamite sales. The only regulatory agencies concerned with New Hampshire explosives are the explosive stores themselves. And their only regulation is that buyers must be, or look, over 21.

So remember now—I'm an irrational madman.

I drive up here from New York City and swing off Highway 93 into the Main Street of Concord, state capital. And just a few blocks from the downtown district is a big barn of a building, hard by the pavement, which is labeled the "New Hampshire Explosives and Machinery Co." I stop and enter.

"Yes sir, what can I do for you?"

"I'd like to buy some dynamite."

"Yes sir, how much?"

"Three sticks."

A Friendly Fellow

The store clerk is a friendly fellow dressed in blue coveralls. He puts a sales pad on the counter and asks for my name and address. I give him my real name and a fictitious address. He asks if I have any identification. I answer that I only have a New Jersey driver's license. He says it will do fine.

"May I ask what the dynamite is for?"

"Blowing up tree stumps."

"Have you handled it before, sir?"

"No. My neighbor has, though."

The store clerk apologizes for "being so nosy." But, he explains, "You must have read about those idiots in New York City

---

Waterloo Daily Courier, April 1, 1970. Reprinted by Permission of Newspaper Enterprise Association (or NEA).

blowing up buildings. Ever since that stuff started we've had to tighten up on our sales procedure."

I say I understand. But I add that I don't think the people using dynamite in New York are idiots. I say they probably feel they have good reason.

"Well," the clerk answers. "I still call them idiots."

"Suit yourself."

"They ought to outlaw the idiots, not dynamite."

"Maybe."

"That'll be $1.80, sir, 60 cents a stick."

Returns With Dynamite

The clerk disappears. Down into the basement of his shop, where the explosives are stored. A minute later he comes back up, with the dynamite. Three sticks. Eight inches by an inch and a half, wrapped in white waxy paper, identified in stencil as "Giant Gelatin, 40 per cent." He puts them back in a sack.

"Thank you, sir."

And I leave.

I have it now, in my hand. Power. Importance. Enough to kill fascist pigs. Enough to blow up a small building. Enough to get my picture in the papers.

If I really were a madman, that is.

Goes to Police Station

But I'm just a reporter. And the dynamite scares me. So I take it, quickly and directly, to the Concord police station, where I tell a cop what I've done. I say I think it's ridiculous that I'm able to buy dynamite so easy. He agrees. We both shake our heads and shrug our shoulders.

As I start to go, the cop adds: "You want to know something else for your story? Something funny? This state outlawed firecrackers a long time ago."

Questions

1. In what sense is this an argumentative article?
2. Which approach did the writer use in presenting his case—the formal or the informal narrative technique? Why?
3. Cite three instances of researched material in the first eight paragraphs of the article.
4. Discuss the writer's use of dialogue and humor.
5. Would you characterize the prose style as being moderately, or strongly, informal? What is your evidence?
6. How convincing is this argumentative article? How were you affected by it?

Suggested Writing Assignments

1. Write an argumentative article on a topic of your own choosing. Sample issues which ordinarily would not require library research include:

   The Case for (Against) Double Dating
   Why I Tip (Do Not Tip)

Smoking Should (Not) Be Permitted in the Classroom
Children Should (Not) Be Given Allowances
The Case for (Against) Large Classes

Sample topics which ordinarily would require library research include:

The Case for (Against) the Vietnam War
The Voting (Drinking, Driving) Age Should (Not) Be Lowered
Why I Favor (Do Not Favor) Euthanasia
The Case for (Against) the Use of Violence
Abortion Should (Not) Be Legalized

Review the text discussion and specimen pieces before you begin. Then prewrite your thoughts on your topic, making sure that you have considered *both sides of the question*. Remember that supporting evidence may consist of arguments, facts and figures, statements from authorities, and personal experiences.

Since mapping out strategy presents quite a challenge to the novice writer, you may want to study the common patterns summarized below. Having clearly established your stand on the issue in the introduction, you may set forth:

(A) Your first supporting argument
Your second supporting argument
Your third supporting argument, etc.

(B) Your answer to the first objection to your position
Your answer to the second objection to your position
Your answer to the third objection to your position, etc.

(C) Your first supporting argument
Your refutation of the objection to this argument
Your second supporting argument
Your refutation of the objection to this argument, etc.

(D) The problem
Then your solution to the problem

(E) The first objection which you would grant the opposition
The second objection which you would grant the opposition
The third objection which you would grant, etc.
Then the strong point in defense of your case

(F) An extended narration of a personal experience as support for your position on the issue

2. Compare and contrast any two of the pieces in the text on the basis of topic, audience, tone, language, evidence, and strategy.

3. Write a paper in which you argue against the point of view expressed in one of the text selections. Be sure to clearly indicate the author's position on the issue before you begin your refutation of his arguments.

4. Analyze an argumentative article taken from a magazine or newspaper which is not included in the text. Determine the writer's stand on the issue, the effectiveness of the lead paragraph and closing, the kinds of evidence presented, the strategy, and other points of interest.

12

Advertising Prose

At first glance words may not seem to be significant in advertising because attractively printed ads are often a consequence of the skillful combination of photographs, color, and white space. Cigarette advertisements are not impressive because of what they say, but because of how they look. The healthy people who smoke so beautifully are the message.

Even though this is true, words still play a significant part. Every product has a name and the name is important. Products also have their own catchy alliterative phrases, the slogans, that go right along with them. And there is the text itself. Most ads have a text and whether it conveys information or is just attractive language, the text itself may be the message.

There are two general types of ad messages: the hard and soft sell. The hard-sell variety makes a direct, unmistakable appeal. Such phrases as "a close-out sale," "a special introductory offer," or "enjoy 52 weeks of vacation a year for $21.00 a week," leave no doubt about the intention.

Other advertisements have a more subtle appeal: they only suggest (or even imply) that one should buy. They may simply display a picture and then move gently to the point. For example, one ad introduces a new culotte-type garment by saying, "Fall creeps up on you. The sky is a different color, and you need a sweater after dark. Greet the new season with gladness. Have a wool culotte jumper ready. . . ." Such prose does not so much shake you to attention as it takes you by the arm and leads you to the product.

Then there are advertisements that do not seem to sell anything, except perhaps goodwill. A major chemical firm, for one example, takes full-page ads in national journals to tell us that it has a company program to teach illiterate workers how to read. Another firm runs expensive ads to urge us to prevent air and water pollution. Still another asks that we donate to the private college of our choice. While such goodwill ads do not directly sell the company's product, they do keep its name before the public and in a favorable light, so that, in the long run, they are also designed to increase sales.

Whatever the nature of the advertisement, its language should be suitable for the audience and for the product itself. For example, if you were trying to sell an expensive automobile in a national news weekly, then the language would be different from the racy slang you might employ in an effort to sell amplifiers in a pop-music magazine.

When *Playboy* advertises itself in *The Saturday Review of Literature* there are no pictures of girls—only words: a closely packed, erudite text fashioned to appeal to well-educated readers. And a shirt ad speaks to its young male readers in their own language when it says, "Rats. It's that time of year again. Surf's down, school's in, and the painful sound of books being cracked is heard throughout the land. But look at the bright side. There are parties to go to, and games to be won, and what better way to dress. . . ."

In the main, advertisements feature a relatively informal and even conversational prose. The sentences are short, often without verbs or subjects, and contractions and slang are frequent. For example, a car ad explains, "Sure we're called Midget . . . But . . . we are anything but," and an ad for men's clothing reads, "Spring clothes do something for a man. Any man."

The language of advertisements seems so relaxed, so casual that it looks easy to write, but that is only an illusion. Such writing is done by high-salaried, hard working experts who know their business. Their seemingly casual phrases are not any easier to compose than Hemingway's deceptively simple sentences. Try it.

What-is-a truck?

A truck is an iceberg. You see a little of it on the highway but its greatest part —what it *does*—is invisible. Next time you see one, look beyond the words on the back and side. Look to the service it's performing.

    A truck is food. And clothes. And furniture, machinery, chemicals—three-quarters of all freight shipped in America. Need we ask what would happen if trucks weren't operating?

    A truck is your neighbor. If you think of trucks only as over-the-highway haulers, maybe you've forgotten how many others come knocking at your door. To collect trash. To bring milk. To move furniture. To paint your house. To deliver oil. To fix sink, television, telephone.

    A truck is a taxpayer. And a generous one. Trucks account for 16% of all vehicles; pay more than 33% of total vehicle taxes. Specifics? A large truck pays up to $3,500 and even more a year in road taxes. That's a lot of generous.

    A truck is a worker. Despite restrictions on sizes and weights, the trucking industry has matched our economy's growth and concomitant need for increased freight transportation. Those restrictions, by the way, are based on standards that date back to World War II.

    A truck is a servant. And we don't forget it. Our right to advance in technology and efficiency is based on the need for those advances. Our responsibility to give better service is based on our economy's need for better service. And that's what we're driving for.

American Trucking Associations, Inc., 1616 P St., N.W., Washington, D.C. 20036

After a few years, it starts to look beautiful.

"Ugly, isn't it?"
"No class."
"Looks like an afterthought."
"Good for laughs."
"Stubby buggy."
"El Pig-O."

New York Magazine said: "And then there is the VW, which retains its value better than anything else. A 1956 VW is worth more today than any American sedan built the same year, with the possible exception of a Cadillac."

Around 27 miles to the gallon. Pints of oil instead of quarts. No radiator.
Rear engine traction.
Low insurance.
$1,799* is the price.
Beautiful, isn't it?

Cadillac for 1968 introduces its all-new 472 V-8 engine—designed to give you full-range performance, plus the capacity to efficiently operate power steering, power brakes and Cadillac's many other convenience features. The 472 V-8 represents the fourth major development in V-8 engine design since Cadillac introduced America's first production V-8. It's almost like having two engines: One to give you amazingly quiet acceleration and road performance, the other to power all the luxuries that make Cadillac motoring so pleasurable. Drive it and see.

Elegance in action...with the greatest "inside story" in fine car history

Franklin D. Roosevelt [signature]

"If I were starting life over again, I am inclined to think that I would go into the advertising business in preference to almost any other. This is because advertising has come to cover the whole range of human needs and also because it combines real imagination with a deep study of human psychology. Because it brings to the greatest number of people actual knowledge concerning useful things, it is essentially a form of education...It has risen with ever-growing rapidity to the dignity of an art. It is constantly paving new paths...The general raising of the standards of modern civilization among all groups of people during the past half century would have been impossible without the spreading of the knowledge of higher standards by means of advertising."

Isn't it strange to find people in this country today who, in the name of everything Franklin D. Roosevelt stood for, criticize advertising and seek to restrict it? Well-meaning people who say that it is unfair competition for a big company to spend more on advertising than a small company. Ignoring the fact that it is advertising that helps small companies grow big . . . companies like Polaroid, Xerox, Sony and dozens more who have taken on the giants in the marketplace and won their niche.

These people think we should restrict the amount of advertising a company can do—just to be fair. But, of course, big companies spend more on research and development than little companies, too. And that's even more unfair because it helps develop new products the little companies don't have. So, perhaps, we should restrict research and development.

It's too bad somebody didn't think of this 40 years ago. Then we'd all still have iceboxes. And you wouldn't have to worry about getting all that frozen food home from the supermarket before it thaws. In your 1966 Model "T."

Magazine Publishers Association
An association of 365 leading U.S. magazines

"Control yourself, Gladys, or I'll stop using this stuff."

Watch your step, when you use any of these three masculine scents from the Kings Men line-up:

KINGS MEN—when it takes more than good looks.
THISTLE & PLAID—when you're on the prowl.
IMPERIAL GOLD—when caution's to the wind.

KINGS MEN®
Fine grooming aids from $1.25

High School French is designed to get you through exams.
Berlitz French is designed to get you through France.

At Berlitz, we don't think there's much point in knowing the pluperfect tense of the verb "to be," if you don't know how to find out whether that's your train leaving the station.

So we don't teach you anything about pluperfect tenses, or any of the other tiresome things you need for high school examinations.

Instead, we teach you what you need for vacations.

Conversation.

And we do it differently from high schools.

To keep you interested, we entertain you. In other words, our instructors don't so much *teach* you, as perform for you.

For instance, instead of just telling you the word for window, a Berlitz instructor stands up, raises an imaginary window and says *"la fenêtre."*

And the word sticks in your mind.

By the end of the first lesson, he's already demonstrating how to put these simple words into simple sentences.

"La fenêtre est ouverte."

Why, by the end of our ten-week course, you're speaking more French than most high school students can come out with after three years.

How much does our acting-cum-teaching method cost?

Call the nearest Berlitz® school and you can take a ten-week course in French, German, Italian or Spanish for as little as $140.

If you want to learn more, we have courses that cost more. A twenty-week course, a super-concentrated four-week course, and individual instruction.

Which should you take?

How long is it before you go on vacation?

Berlitz®
Practical language lessons

A funny thing happened on the way to a better banana.

When you already grow the best bananas in the world and try to make them even better, some pretty funny things can happen.

Like that...er, well...thing you see below.

And that's just one of some 800 triangular-shaped, flat-topped, red-skinned, orange-pulped, apple-flavored bananas we've been working with over the past seven years.

Now we're not claiming to be any Luther Burbank of the banana world. But as far as we know, we're practically the only people around who are doing any work to improve the banana.

And it's paying off.

Our bananas today are a far cry from the bananas they were five years ago.

They're meatier. They're plumper. And they've never been sweeter.

The peels are tighter and sleeker.

They have much nicer bloom. Nicer sheen. And a generally all-around better appearance.

Now. If we could only get a banana to juice like an orange. And keep like a coconut. But still taste like a banana.

Well, you can't knock a guy for trying.

Chiquita® Brand Bananas.

Chiquita is a registered trademark of United Fruit Company

Questions

What-Is-a Truck?

1. What is the overall message of this ad?
2. Show how some of the topic sentences employ metaphor.
3. Are the sentence fragments appropriate?
4. To what extent does the ad convey information?
5. Are the statistics used in the fourth paragraph effective?

Volkswagen and Cadillac

1. How do the Cadillac and VW ads differ in the selling points which are stressed?
2. Why does the VW ad mention a Cadillac? Is it likely that a Cadillac ad would mention a VW?
3. How do the Cadillac and VW ads differ in their treatment of the price of the product.
4. Contrast the levels of the language used in the two ads and show how each is appropriate. Illustrate your points.

Franklin D. Roosevelt

1. What is the point of this advertisement?
2. In what way does the quotation from Roosevelt provide an effective opening?
3. Identify the parts of the ad. Since space costs money, do you think the ad writer was justified in using a fourth of the page for Roosevelt's signature?
4. How convincing are the arguments which are set forth?
5. Explain the satire in the closing paragraphs.

Kings Men

1. Are the parts of this advertisement presented in an effective order?
2. What audience did the ad writer have in mind?

3. Identify the stylistic level of the language.
4. Which has the greater appeal—the picture or the prose?

Berlitz

1. Explain the effective use of parallel structure in the heading of the advertisement.
2. What is the argument which is set forth in the first four paragraphs?
3. What concrete example is used to illustrate the teaching technique used by the Berlitz instructors? Is it convincing?
4. Is the picture needed in this ad? Explain.

Chiquita Banana

1. What is the main point of this ad?
2. Is the heading a play on words? Is it effective?
3. Discuss the appeal of the opening and closing paragraphs.
4. What techniques does the writer use to create a conversational tone?
5. What does the picture contribute to the effectiveness of the ad?

Suggested Writing Assignments

1. Write up an original advertisement designed to sell a product or service now on the market. Study the techniques discussed in the text, such as the use of colloquial expressions, fragments, humor, and argument. If your ad requires an illustration, provide one of your own or collaborate with a classmate.
2. Contrast any two of the advertisements given in the text on the basis of subject, style, language, audience, and other pertinent factors.
3. Analyze some advertisements which are not included in the text. Your discussion might deal with an effective versus an ineffective ad, judged on the basis of personal appeal, humor, language, and so on.
4. Ad writers are frequently criticized for writing "bad English" and "lowering linguistic standards." Write a paper in which you agree or disagree with this charge. Illustrate your arguments with specific examples from ads in the text, from magazines, and newspapers.

13

The Personal Essay

The personal essay, which abounds in our magazines and yet rarely appears in newspapers, is not written to inform us about current events. Rather, it is relatively timeless prose, fashioned to entertain, intrigue, inform, or even inspire.

And the word "personal" in the title of these articles is a key to their character. They may be confessions or intimate accounts of especially significant experiences: religious, educational, or domestic. Typical personal essays might be the story of a widow who tells us how she freed herself of crushing grief, a minister who suffered a severe loss of faith, a soldier who experienced cowardice in his first battle, or a teacher whose faith in education was restored in a black ghetto school.

Personal essays, as you can see, will necessarily reveal the writer's own view of life, his own values. Frankly and purposely subjective, personal essays are the opposite of objective writing.

If an author is successful, he will convince his audience of the attractiveness and the importance of his inner world. A mother, for example, might tell us how she watched her courageous little son die in peace or a man who lost his fortune might describe the anguish of such a fall and yet show how the loss brought him closer to his family. If such pieces are well constructed and avoid sentimentality, then we are quite ready to become involved in the author's intimate account.

Most personal essays are of three kinds: anecdotal, reflective, or lyrical. The anecdotal, probably the most prevalent, tends to be concrete because it is usually a narration of one's experience. A famous author, for instance, might relive an especially happy childhood Christmas or an airplane pilot might describe a near miss in the air.

Reflective personal essays, as the name suggests, are apt to be abstract accounts of one's philosophy; hence the order of the parts will be what is logical and rhetorically effective. For example, an agnostic scientist might write an essay on how he came to think there was a God. In such a piece, there are going to be logical steps that move the reader in the direction of the conclusion. Or, another reflective essay might tell us how a celebrity laments his loss of privacy. In this case, he will have to make clear what he means by privacy and show why its loss is so important. Or lastly, a racing driver might explain why the danger of his vocation is actually attractive. In this last instance, the writer will not necessarily dwell on the narration of any particular race; rather he will tell us, in a somewhat philosophical way, why the danger is exhilarating and challenging.

In lyrical personal essays the order of the piece may be suggested by the emotion one wishes to convey. The form might be that of a winding line of development, leading from one mood to another. For example, the mood might change, in such an essay, from the somber colors of a serious illness, to the brighter hues of convalescence and recovery. Or, one's heightened response to a lovely summer day might increase in intensity up to the time of an especially brilliant sunset. In another lyrical personal essay, however, the author might explain how his maturity brought an increasing awareness of a dishonest and hypocritical world. Such a consistently somber piece might explain the essential disillusionment of maturity.

The style of a personal essay, relatively free, allows for more individuality than one finds in other popular prose. In this kind of article you can try out your own peculiarities of word choice and arrangement. If you prefer slang, you can use it in a personal essay, or if you want to flout the ordinary conventions of grammar or syntax, you can do it here.

Since emotions play such an important role in the personal essay, authors must call on metaphor and image to suggest the feelings they wish to convey. For this reason, if no other, the personal essay may be the most literary and the most difficult of all forms of popular prose.

Night of the Wolf Race

DAVID SNELL

At sundown on the cold Friday of the wolf race, Lonnie Cupples, who had acquired the nickname Red before he went bald, shut down the filling station, blew on his pepper-freckled hands and cast a glance at the sky. Waving me to his car, he said: "We are going to hear some hound dog music tonight!"

Red is an old friend. On my latest visit to the town of Minden in north Louisiana, where I was born, I had dropped in to see him and been caught up in his plans for the night. He was going out with some friends to set some hounds in pursuit of wolves—not to catch them, but to hear the old cry of the chase in a world now tuned to other sounds.

Life Magazine, February 14, 1969. © 1969 Time Inc. Reprinted by permission.

Mrs. Cupples served supper. Two others from the hunting party—John Evans and Boots Kirkley, the bulldozer operator who owns the hound pack—joined us at her table. When we sat down and grace had been said, she brought in platters of wild duck, cornbread dressing, string beans flavored with country ham, cloud-light yeast rolls, pickled spiced peaches and *true* buttermilk with flecks of gold in it . . . temptation stacked upon temptation until, mercifully, she reprieved us with blueberry cobbler and scalding coffee.

Under a high half-moon we arrived at Euel Mathes' house in the woods where Boots keeps the dogs, near Lake Bistineau eight miles to the south. Several more of the hunt party were already there, among them Red's father, Slim Cupples, who at 85 is approaching his prime years of hound listening. Standing by the pickup truck, Boots and Euel were deciding which and how many of the pack to take along. Beyond them in the trees I could see the dogs prancing about, big long-legged Walker hounds that now and then floated up to the top of the pen like pale ghosts. One of the Walkers pointed at the moon and called "yoo-yoo-yoo-yoo-yoo-yoo-yooooooo . . . ," the falsetto trailing off as do the strains of distant bugles. It was a song learned eons ego when hounds were wolfkind—so sweet, so clean, so hauntingly lovely on the crisp air that for some moments all talk fell silent. Boots was the first to speak. "All right," he said quietly, "let's load 'em."

With Boots leading out in the pickup and three cars trailing, we reached the night's "casting spot." It was at the fork of a dirt lane alongside a stretch of pasture land with a treeline beyond. To our left were the deep piney woods. Here the hounds would be set loose and here, hours or maybe days later, they would straggle back.

Somewhere out there would be the wolves —some of them the native species known as red wolves, of which in Louisiana maybe 200 survive; or coyotes more likely, nomadic newcomers from the Texas brush country; or mongrelized wolf-coyotes or wolf-dog and coy-dog crosses which resemble the great timber grays—but "wolves" one and all, by agreement of man and dog, to be chased but hopefully to escape to race again.

Boots let three "strike" dogs go—Buck, Cindy and Bad-Eye—gentling them over the tailgate. In an instant they were into the woods. If these scout dogs could pick up a scent and trail it until they jumped a wolf, Boots would then release the five runners.

The men stood around, their cigarettes glowing in the dark, their ears cocked for the sound of the dogs. It was time for the tall tales. Slim Cupples started it off, teasing with his toe at the jewels of frost forming on the weeds.

"You see that ring around the moon?" he said. "They say if you count the stars inside of it, that's how many days it'll be 'til it rains."

Then another voice: "Well, that moon's been shot at so much I don't know if h'it's going to shine or not. I hear tell they's a plan to pasture a milk cow up there."

And: "A milk cow! Now who was that feller in Minden when the tornado blew through in '33? You remember—he looked up and seen a ole cow come a-sailing over the courthouse, jist a-swishing her tail and a-chewing her cud as contented as could be."

And that, in turn, led to recollections of great wolf races:

"Oh, we *had* some runs back then. Why, I've saw the nights we had *fifty* dogs out all at onest. . . ."

". . . and the time up near Plain Dealing the wolf run right inside the house and the old woman come out and says, 'Hey, you hunter men, they's one of your dogs done crawl under my bed and I wisht you'd come and git him!' So we tooken a bed slat and poked and poked 'til the wolf lit out. . . ."

". . . it was too cold to stay and too pretty to leave, so we built a big campfire and when the dogs come by they was all caked over with ice. . . ."

". . . and the ole sow wolf used to live on Red River had pups, and she took and run ever' one of my dogs clean back into the trunk of the car. . . ."

". . . and I had about give up when I seen the pack tearing out across the tank farm, and they was running low and whistling. . . ."

". . . now which bitch do you mean—the one that clumb trees or the one that mated with that Winn Parish dog that's got the glass eye. . . ?"

Suddenly the strike dogs told us they had hit. Boots quickly turned out the runners—Jake, Dude, Slim, Pup and Fat Boy—to join them. Here at last was the music of the chase, the anthem of hounds in full cry which we had come to hear. Sometimes, when the air is still, the cry will go on for nights and days on end, over hills and across valleys but never out of earshot, until the dogs overtake or fall in exhaustion. On this night, though, a wind was rising. Within minutes the race had passed beyond a ridge and all we could hear was the stirring of the pines.

To pick up the cry we drove a mile or so back down the lane. When the lead car turned onto the blacktop John Evans caught a glimpse of something streaking across at the far reach of the headlights, a shadow almost, moving so fast he couldn't make it out. Then five or six hounds spilled onto the road where, bewildered by the brightness, they broke pace and scattered.

At any moment they might pick up the trail and follow it out onto the main highway just beyond the rise, and you could hear the cars and trucks thundering along at 70 mph. Like a cat Boots sprang for his flashlight, intending to get to the highway and try to slow the traffic. But the dogs turned back to the woods and this race was finished.

It was then that I understood. These men who were born to the soil, these men with loving memories of a virgin earth, could read the portent of their own filling station, of their own bulldozer, of the traffic on the Interstate, of the B-52s from the nearby air base. They know how the land is growing up, and they know the night will come when they will listen to the last race fading on the wind.

Questions

1. According to the text, most personal essays are of three kinds—anecdotal, reflective, and lyrical. In which of these categories would you place "Night of the Wolf Race"?
2. This piece consists of three general parts: getting ready for the wolf hunt, exchanging tall tales while waiting for a strike, and the chase itself. Do you believe that the middle section could have been omitted?
3. Why does the writer use Southern dialect in his quotations? Is dialect easy to reproduce in written form? Base your answer on some specific examples.
4. What techniques does the writer use to create the sense of excitement which can be felt on reading this essay?
5. How was the author able to create such a powerful closing for this piece in a brief paragraph? In answering this question, you may want to examine the last three lines in regard to style and idea.

A Shade of Difference

PAT ALFORD

It could be just an ordinary day. Nothing unusual would have to happen. The sun would rise in the east as always. I would get up and get dressed for class in the same clothes that I always wear. I could even comb my hair the same—everything could stay the same. I could keep my height, my nose, my mouth, the color of my hair and eyes.

Most important, though, I could keep the inward me—the same intelligence and the same outlook on life. Nothing would have to be exchanged. Nothing but a small trade of black skin for white skin. Then a whole new world would be open to me.

It would be different. It would happen the moment I stepped outside my room and started for class. No one would stare—trying to satisfy their curiosity about me as a member of a race of people with whom they had little or no contact.

I could even sit down without having a group of people, who don't realize that they are making me uneasy and even more aware of being different, stare intently at my every move. I could walk to class without meeting half smiles plastered on faces that seem to say, "I sympathize . . ." Faces that can't understand why I don't want their pity and, so, end up saying nothing at all.

I wouldn't have to look down to avoid those smiles and wonder how many were really genuine or merely a means of doing a good deed for the day by smiling at a little black girl. My classes would be different, too. No longer would I be sought out as a member of a depressed race of people to answer questions on racial issues. I wouldn't be called upon by an instructor who wanted to satisfy his curiosity about my views and intelligence.

No longer would I have to endure the frustration of being treated kindly, simply because any ill actions or feelings toward me would naturally be looked upon as race prejudice. I could save the embarrassment of students who beg "forgiveness of their ignorance" in asking what country I'm from. I would not have to endure flustered white male students who want to be nice but who don't ask black girls out because that might jeopardize their chances for dates with white girls who may not approve.

Perhaps most important, I would not have to spend hours of confusion wondering what it's all about. My skin color would no longer be a problem and I, like most Iowa State students, could forget that minorities even exist. It wouldn't be my problem. I, too, could smile when I saw a black student or I could stare in curiosity. Then maybe I'd have done enough. Maybe I'd have declared myself free of prejudices because I had shown pity.

I might even take time out to make a black student feel at home by showing him I wasn't prejudiced—never was, because some of my friends back home are black. That would be good. Then he'd know for sure I had nothing against his people. But if I neglected to speak to that same student when I was with my white friends, he'd understand that I personally had nothing against black people, but some of my friends did—that's all.

And the things I could do—anything—and nobody would ever notice. I would be

---

Ethos (Iowa State University), April, 1967. Reprinted by permission of Pat Alford.

accepted everywhere. If I chose I could even pledge a sorority without having an article appear in the Daily declaring that Iowa State is becoming more and more liberal in accepting minorities. Sorority girls who look upon me now as a threat to their comfortable and wholesome worlds of sisterhood would see me merely as another pledge. My dislike for too much attention would no longer be a problem.

I could follow everyone else. I could go to football games and basketball games and cheer on the spectacular plays of black athletes. And then I could go home and never ever think about them again, because after all, they are only jocks, and all jocks, especially black jocks, are all alike.

I could go to church on Sundays and listen to sermons on Civil rights—sermons that apply to other people who are prejudiced. I might even sign up to visit a black section of a large city to see how black people live. It is, after all, the current thing to be broad-minded and to get involved in racial projects.

I could feel comfortable in knowing that I had participated in a discussion on race, read John Howard Griffin's *Black Like Me*, or given an old sweater to the poor blacks in Mississippi. I could feel good, because I wouldn't have to know that the one thing freeing me of my prejudices, honest communication attempting to break the wall by seeing the black student as just another student—a real, live person—was so simple that I missed it altogether. I, too, could afford to neglect to see all these simple things, little things—the stares, the half smiles—that play on the minds of a select few of my fellow classmates and dorm-mates.

I could go on in a little world without ever stopping to wonder if something that I had done in the course of my day had affected those students who have the same hopes, the same fears, pains, desires, and joys that I would have. It would be so unimportant in my new world.

I would have no need to stop and consider what would or would not be accepted of me because of my skin color. I might even become lax in improving myself simply because I would never have to worry about being three times better than a white competitor for a job, or even for acceptance into friendship.

I would no longer feel a surge of pride when I read a black history book and marveled at the progress of my ancestors who had risen above the horror, the violence, the fear of being black, to fight for equality and acceptance in a world that had constantly deprived them of these things.

I would not have to feel twice as proud of parents who had, in spite of being black in the South, provided college educations for all of their children. It would not be the same. It would have required nothing but opportunity—and that would always have been there.

I could live a completely different life—a life free of the pressures of being a black on American soil. Then I would be free to forget those problems of race that overbear the typical problems of the average American white student. I would not have to force myself to accept these problems in a society that chooses not to accept me.

It would be different. But it can never be. I am black and I know that self-delusion, no matter how small, is a price no one can afford. But am I glad I was born black? That is a question that I am left to deal with only by myself.

Questions

1. Explain why the following lines, taken from the second paragraph, may be regarded as the central idea in the essay. "Nothing would have to be exchanged. Nothing but a small trade of black skin for white skin. Then a whole now world would be open to me."

2. In the text discussion, the terms "intimate account," "one's own values," and "subjective" are used to describe the personal essay. Show how these characteristics can be applied to "A Shade of Difference."

3. Note the repetition of the subject and verb "I could" and "I would" in the topic sentences (I wouldn't have to look down, I could follow everyone else, I could go to church). What effect is created by repeating these words? Is there any connection between these key phrases and the great number of short paragraphs in the article?

4. Indicate the supporting details which you found particularly effective.

5. Does the writer intend the following line to be taken satirically? "It is, after all, the current thing to be broad-minded and to get involved in racial projects."

6. Analyze the closing paragraph. Do you think the writer is glad that she was born black?

Confessions of a Kite Hustler

BARRY FARRELL

I thought my display looked terrific spread out there on the grass, with everything sorted into pyramids and piles and a raven-black fighter swooping overhead. I'd even burned a few sticks of Glory of India incense, just to set the tone for my show. All the same, the carny people kept telling me that I should have made a sign.

RARE IMPORTED HAND-MADE
FIGHTER KITES FROM INDIA
SPECIAL $2 & $3 SPECIAL
HERE TODAY NOW

Something like that might have brought on a buyers' stampede, and I suppose I would have put a sign up had I been selling kites for the sake of selling kites. But what I intended selling was my own performance (my professional debut, in fact) and a signboard would have been as vulgar and distracting as a toe-shoe ad on stage at the Royal Ballet. Those who saw the kite and fell under its abiding spell would have to be trusted to have sense and eyesight keen enough to follow the kitestring earthward to me and my diffident display.

The Rutland State Fair in Vermont seemed about my speed, a country fair with a midway and show, drawing about 15,000 visitors a day. Before setting up, I cased the grounds thoroughly, checking out the trees, the wires, the flow of the crowd. There was a tempting glade between the Maple Sugar House and the 4-H barn, but I figured the traffic in that zone would be a shade too apple-cheeked for my exotic wares. The Midway was less inviting still—against a

---

Life Magazine, September 19, 1969. © 1969 Time Inc. Reprinted by permission.

skyline of Rock-o-Planes, Tempests and Scramblers, a kite would look as frail as a city sparrow. At last I discovered the perfect spot, an island of grass between the race track and a gurgling Plexiglas tank where Skipper the Porpoise was swimming. Speed, the sea, the liquid sense of movement: this was where I'd find my people.

I was 200 feet high and holding when the gates were opened and the first day's crowd came pushing in. The wind was a warming westerly, steady and soft, just right for an India fighter. A thumb-slur across the line was enough to bring me around for a dive, and I came swooning down past the treetops, past Skipper's tank and the Navy recruiters' bus, down until I was spinning a foot or less above the choppy river of approaching sunburned faces. Maiming hands reached up to snare me, but I was already vaulting away. With the raven safe in the altitudes, I tidied my stores of tails and reels and string, lighting another joss stick for good measure. The crowd, I knew, was transfixed—too stupefied to stop.

As I waited for my first disciple-customer to emerge from the timid masses, it struck me that for pure mental attitude, I was probably the best-trained pitchman at the fair. So maybe I didn't have a spiel, maybe I didn't have a sign. Wht did that matter when my kites were like sons to me? I hadn't spent five years under the string for nothing. I had bought kites, built kites, flown kites in every weather, gathered in the breeze of the Atlantic, the Pacific, the Nile, the Seine. Could the Barca-Lounger man say as much?

My weakness was in letting the birds mean too much to me. A simple fly at sunset wound up a recital, a lesson in aerodynamics, a consultation with a silent oracle. Selling a few kites might serve as a cure, I thought. I would reduce all these spiritualized complexities to the healthiest American equation: $2 for the little ones, $3 for the big.

The wind turned fickle as the day grew warm and sticky, but a loudspeaker voice was summoning the crowd to Skipper's tank —the moment I'd been waiting for. Circus-style hot-doggery overcame me as the porpoise-fanciers assembled, and soon I was daring a corkscrew descent into the patchwork wind, circling close over the tank, risking everything. I could feel the weight of canny Vermont reckoning tied like a tail to my kite. Somewhere deep inside me, I sensed a sale coming on.

Skipper's silly stunts were handsomely applauded—as mine might have been given the porpoise's fancy signboard and MC. In an excess of resentment, I sent the raven into a series of slips and glides, a wicked parody of the splashing flippered thing in the tank.

"How much?"

With a folklorically correct economy of words, a crag-faced Vermonter was asking the price of a bird. He stood near the display of tails, squinting up at the sky like an outdoorsman in a cigarette ad. I needed only a second to collect myself—"Two for the little ones, three for the big."

Like many an amateur kite inspector, the Vermonter had trouble believing that the kite was in control. But the raven was on a maneuver of *haiku*-like perfection. I drove and climbed, turned and spun, calling my shots in advance. When at last I looked back with a forgiving smile, ready to do business, the Vermonter had wandered away.

It wasn't until King Kovaz and the Auto Daredevils took to the track that my act finally got itself together. The screaming cars were skidding through dirt-track slaloms that sent brown Sahara dust clouds billowing up across my grassy island, silting my tails, reels and birds, whirling the cloud up into the air. Every head turned to follow the rising pall—and there in the center, like a lunatic seagull, flew the raven. Suddenly, customers were jostling around my display. A kite? Of course. Two kites and a tail?

I sold $69 worth of kites at the fair, which meant 21 Vermont apprentices and $69 worth of crowd acceptance for my act. My gratitude made it impossible to push very hard for sales, and by way of compensation for the business I was doing in birds, I found myself apologizing for the price of my string.

Since my costs were the same as my prices, my profits were strictly emotional. Apart from the plain joy of flying, the fact of being part of a fair seemed to open conduits running 20 years back and more, to times when fairs stood like alps on my calendar. My heroes then were a clique of Filipino Yo-Yo merchants who worked the playground at my school, doing Dog-Bite-Me and Walka-Da-Dog. Their medium was different from mine, of course, but their message was clearly the same: trouble will come to you only when you're not holding onto the string.

Questions

1. Explain the significance of the word "confessions" in the title of this personal essay.
2. Although the author sold $69 worth of kites, he does not discuss any of his actual sales. Then what does he talk about in the essay?
3. The writer provides a number of vivid images. Discuss two examples which you believe are effective.
4. Indicate the two competing acts at the fair which the kite hustler used to his own advantage.
5. What is the meaning of the final statement "trouble will come to you only when you're not holding onto the string."

His Record Was Perfect Until He Won a Fight

PARKE CUMMINGS

Every time a professional prizefighter retires undefeated I get a feeling of kinship. When it came to fisticuffs, I, too, had an enviable record for consistency. Of numerous fights I engaged in I lost them all—every single one.

My first fight took place when I was 6 or 7. We lived in a Boston suburb, in what you might call fair-to-middling circumstances. My father made a modest income, and the family, both sides of it, was strictly middle class—no escutcheons, no blue blood, no pretensions to such.

On the way to school I had to walk through a rather tough neighborhood, and one day I got waylaid by one of its denizens. The boy—I remember he had red hair and a lot of freckles—called me a number of names I did not understand and declared that I was a stuck-up snoot who thought I

Reprinted by permission from *Sports Illustrated*, March 27, 1967. Copyright 1967 Time Inc. (Note: This article was published on regional advertising pages, so it appeared at different times in different parts of the country.)

was better than he was just because my father wore a white collar and worked in Boston.

He followed this up by asking me if I wanted to fight, and I was rash enough to say yes. The battle was a short duration. Even though he was a year or so my junior, my opponent outclassed me in all departments, landing a battery of rights and lefts to all parts of my physiognomy. In short order, I retired screaming in terror, with a black eye and a bloody nose. My only satisfaction was that I was able to escape before he floored me, a record I was able to maintain through most of my career.

One familiar with American mores might point out that this fight followed a typical social pattern—the immigrant's son usually licks the kid whose family has things just a little bit easier. The hungry fighter wins—and I suppose I *did* eat a little bit better, most of the time, than Red.

Our social critic might be right in general —I think he is—but he would have been wrong in my particular case. A year or so later I joined an Outing Class conducted by an ex-college athlete who coached our group of boys in such sports as football, baseball and track. And for one Saturday morning—unfortunately—boxing.

The opponent selected for me was a lad who lived in a mansion the size of the average French chateau. His mother was a Mayflower descendant, his father had 100 times as much money as my father if he had a dime.

On the class theory I have mentioned, it followed that if Red had licked me I should be able to annihilate this spoonfed aristocrat, didn't it? It did not. We squared off, and instantly I felt that I was being battered by a human-sized centipede. I never even got to launch a blow before our coach mercifully stepped in and broke up the "contest."

As the years passed, my home-town record of quick one-sided losses continued, and in time I was sent away to prep school. For reasons which should be obvious by now, I tried to avoid fights, but you never know. One day, engaged in some perfectly good-natured roughhousing with a friend, I accidentally knocked a pipe out of his mouth. Instantly he hauled off and landed a straight left between my eyes, causing me to stagger and reel back about six or eight feet. I started to retaliate, but then I reflected that, since I had broken his pipe, he had a stronger moral position than I had and I let the blow pass. However, the incident led me to the thought that it might be a good idea to take some boxing lessons.

The school's professional instructor was a wiry little Scotsman named Andy Kendall, who stood only a mite over 5 feet and could not have weighed more than 110 after a seven-course dinner. Because of this and because my father was willing to supply the requisite funds, I signed up for six or eight lessons and in so doing probably set up an alltime record for noncontact in the history of fisticuffs. I was by then a gangling youngster, and I had about a 50-pound weight advantage and around a foot in height and reach over Andy. He could, of course, have floored me instantly if he chose, but he was canny, like most of his breed, and knew which side his bread was buttered on. His lessons were on a day-to-day basis, and to discourage a fledgling pupil by busting him one on the proboscis could dry up his source of income at the very start. Andy therefore made it a practice never to hit a beginning pupil—or *any* pupil—unless he was dead sure the latter was capable of absorbing the punishment.

He started me off with the left jab, which meant that he had me launching a series of jabs at his jaw, all of which he dodged with such ridiculous ease that the punches might just as well have been started from Stockholm or the interior of Tibet. Since Andy made no attempt at counterpunching I faced no danger of getting hurt, but he was constantly urging me to jab faster. The result was that I wound up each session untouched but totally exhausted.

The worst of it was that Andy was always breathing encouragement. "That's a good jab," he kept telling me as he dodged and sidestepped effortlessly. "Very good indeed, lad—getting better all the time." It may very well be that I developed the most unique jab in the history of fisticuffs. But it had yet to find a target when I had completed my final lesson.

The lessons over, I went around the campus a little cockier perhaps than before. At last a boy who had been making a practice of needling me made an unusually insulting remark. Secure in my new skill, I launched my left jab—my $50 left jab—at him. It missed.

And then an extraordinary thing happened. As I saw him start to retaliate, some instinct made me pinion his arms. I then put a foot behind his heel, pushed with all my might and flung him to the ground. There was a brief struggle, and I had him on his back.

I then got a strong grip on his left arm and started twisting. "You take back what you said?" I demanded, twisting harder.

He cussed a little, then gave an agonized yell of pain. "All right," he said. "I take it back."

My perfect record was smashed to smithereens! Maybe, I thought as I pondered the wreckage, I should have been a wrestler all along.

Questions

1. What general point holds the article together?
2. Why are the accounts of his fights presented in this order?
3. Identify what you think are the two funniest scenes in the essay?
4. Find an example of the author's use of metaphor.
5. How does this essay reveal the author's own values? In your discussion provide evidence to show that this piece qualifies as an example of the personal essay.

The Simple Joys of Life

MINNIE M. BAUER

Now, in my senior years, as I sit and watch the world go by with its hectic craving for pleasure, fun, money, power, prestige and gratification of self, I wish someone would write about the simple joys of life. I have in mind the things that everyone can obtain —provided he does so before the infirmities of old age overtake him.

As I become less and less able to get around, I think of the joys of walking down a country road or sauntering along a running stream, observing nature at its best. Or

The Reader's Digest, September, 1968. Reprinted with permission of the author and publisher from the September 1968 *Reader's Digest.* Copyright 1968 by The Reader's Digest Assn., Inc.

the satisfaction of just doing one's daily tasks well, of taking time to fashion something for the pure joy of it.

As my hearing gradually leaves me, I think of the joys of a loved one's voice, the laughter of children at play, music, a bird's song, the distant church bell. Or the roll of thunder and the swish of the wind as it brings the rain. Sometimes just the near-silence of the softly falling snow provides a measure of quiet joy.

As my eyesight dims, I think of the joys of reading, be it a letter, or a book, or some subject for deep thought. How wonderful it is to see the evening sky bright with stars and full moon, to catch the glow of the rising sun at dawn, or linger with gorgeous sunsets at day's end. To see my neighbor's well-planned flower garden with its riot of color and bloom, or to look across my valley to the hills beyond and the well-plowed land that later will become a waving sea of golden wheat.

As my diet, for health's sake, becomes more meager, I think of the joys of plain food, well prepared—fresh eggs and country ham before the day's labor, a congenial lunch with neighbor or friend, the solid meat-and-vegetable meal at the close of day with the family gathered round. And the great abundance of food our land provides.

I have experienced countless simple joys such as these. Now, in old age, I live contentedly in the memory of them. And count the further joy of much leisure, a time to rest and pray. I have, finally, the greatest joy of all, a fervent, trusting faith in an all-wise Creator, a God of love, truth and justice, who always watches over us.

Questions

1. Is this essay primarily anecdotal, lyrical, or reflective? Explain.
2. Is the language and the style appropriate for the subject?
3. Identify the use of parallel structure to emphasize topic sentences.
4. What is common to all the "simple joys" that the author mentions?
5. What does the author's advanced age add to the effectiveness of the article?

Up on the Upholstered Frontier

HORACE SUTTON

I have spent a great many autumns feeling deep sorrow for fishermen who pass the fall weeks at fishing lodges enduring such rigors of the outdoors as no man has known since Gary Cooper stood off the attacking tribes at Khyber Pass. My remorse has been somewhat tempered, however, ever since I walked down the dock at the Lac Ouimet Club at Ste. Jovite the other day, got in a Norseman seaplane, and flew off to the Lake of the

---

Saturday Review, October 3, 1953. Copyright 1953 The Saturday Review Associates, Inc. Reprinted by permission.

Wolves in the Canadian northwoods. This roughing-it-at-a-lodge-in-the-woods may turn out to be a bigger fraud than the Teapot Dome.

The secluded location of our encampment, which is known as O'Connell's Lodge, has not kept Signor O'Connell from installing a bar with indirect lighting. Sleeping bags, I suspect, are a slow item at Messrs. Abercrombie and Fitch, for Mr. O'Connell's fishermen lay their leathery heads each twilight on Beauty Rest mattresses mounted on Slumber King bedsprings. Quiet, junior! Dad has had a tough day at the lake.

It seems to me I have been looking for many years at photographs purporting to show Indian guides cooking up a mess of biscuits by the open fire. Nowhere do I remember the likes of Mr. O'Connell's light pine dining room with appended outdoor terrace decorated all around with that border of bright geraniums. You can tell this is a fishing lodge because there is a stuffed moose and a stuffed fish on the wall.

We are sixty miles from the nearest permanent metropolis, a place named Maniwaki, which is Indian talk for Mary's Land. Indian words are bandied about up here like French in a Fifth Avenue salon. *Metchinomegus*, a man is liable to say, especially if he is an Algonquin. It means big trout. And there is *congway*, which is "jealous wife," and *hanwatan*, meaning "the wind has let down, now it is quiet." There is not much to the north of us except 114 miles of gravel road leading to Val d'Or, where the citizens mine gold, copper, and zinc.

We are back in the back woods all right, but any man who says he is going up to the Lake of the Wolves to do some fishing is leaving himself open for a very smart crack, especially if there's a congway in his house.

There are fifteen cottages at our outpost, every room with running water, most of them with bath, and all caressed by radio and recorded music piped in from the main building. In all there are 158 beds with rates running from $9.50 a day per person, four in a room, bunk-bed style, to $22 a day in Mountaintop Cottage. Mountaintop is just a simple little old log cabin with six picture windows giving out on Lac des Loups, where the giant fish repose. The logs are peeled and chinked with plastic tar, frontier style. Other backwoods touches are screened porches, stall showers, chrome plumbing, and draperies that run on trolleys.

During the summer many fishermen bring their families, and there are some family cottages which will hold four to six at $12.50 a head. Children play on the swings and slides, and mothers can slave over a hot tennis court while dad is out with the rod and reel. Pilgrimages are made to the garbage dump at dumping time, which is twice a day, to watch the bears pick through the leftovers.

This family business is all very well until the end of August, but when the last Lilliputian has been packed off in the direction of home and school, the serious fishing is on. From now on until the end of October, when the season closes, every fisherman is out on the Lake of the Wolves at the crack of dawn. Fishermen and skiers are worlds apart, they tell you up here, for when the skier is home from the hills he is ready for an evening of singing purple songs. A fisherman, however, is mainly ready for the sack. He is even too tired to be a loup. The lodge has organized corn roasts, weiner roasts, and barn dances, but when the serious season is on they are fabulous duds.

When the fishermen are concentrating on fish they hire a guide every day at $8 the day plus $2.50 for what the guide eats on the day he is guiding. With a guide in the boat it is a rare occasion in the province of Quebec that a man will come in fishless. However, Mr. George O'Connell, who is sixteen and who is the owner's son, has told me of a profitable venture he used to have, which was paddling around in a boat at day's end selling previously deceased fish to fishless fishermen.

There are thirty guides at O'Connell's,

Algonquins or half-castes, but the most famous of all is an ample Algonquin named Nona Monatch. The first time I met him he was sitting in a boat with two sports from Philadelphia who were fishing with their chauffeur. A man should not fish without his chauffeur at a fishing lodge that is worthy of the name. Nona has been guiding for fourteen years, and he likes it better than his old work, which was driving a dog team. In the winter he cooks for a paper company. "Last year nobody died," he told me with some surprise. Between the end of the fishing season and the beginning of the cooking season he takes parties moose hunting. He is an expert player of the birchbark horn, an instrument which makes a bull moose think he is being serenaded by a cow moose. Nona doesn't use music on the fish, however, and when he is guiding two men in his boat he rarely comes in without ten fish. Nona goes fishing 200 days a year.

Once when we were in the fish house where the catch is brought we saw some fellows sporting an enormous twenty-three-pound pike, and rumors were coming from the lake that another party had two others over twenty pounds. We asked about this oversized pike and a man in a smelly shirt and a battered cap said, "Caught it on a six-pound leader. Fuzzy's fish was so big it went right through the net."

I went out in one of O'Connell's three cruisers one day and worked the better part of the Lake of the Wolves. A French Canadian name of Al-bare was our guide and he put bait on the hook that I would have been proud to display as a catch. Why Nona Monatch is responsible for 2,000 fish a year and why some other people don't get any, I do not know. I do know that there was not a sign of a fighting pike. There wasn't even a sign of young George O'Connell bearing a limp pike, which at this point I would have cheerfully purchased. Chin up and don't lose heart, I have been advised. O'Connell's has fifteen other lakes in which to drop a hook, five of them for the especial purpose of catching none but the speckled trout.

If there is anyone who would like to top my record during the serious season, Lake of the Wolves can be reached by car by following Route 11 out of Montreal to Mont Laurier, and then taking Route 58 over seventy-two miles of gravel highway to the lodge. Three buses come up each day and three come down from Val d'Or. Wheeler Airlines has charter flights from Montreal airport landing on O'Connell's own mile-long, paved air strip, four miles from the lodge. Or Wheeler will take you by land or seaplane from Ste. Jovite, which is in the Laurentians. A hired Cessna with room for three passengers costs $88 for the excursion, and you can make it from either Montreal or Ste. Jovite in just over an hour.

The only thing is, don't come back with some story about roughing it with the boys at a fishing lodge in the Canadian northwoods. The next time some *Field-and-Stream* type tells me that, I shall wait until he is finished and then I shall say, "Hanwatan, brother, hanwatan." The wind has let down, now it is quiet.

Questions

1. Indicate the background details which are developed in the first two paragraphs.
2. What evidence does the writer give to support his view that the frontier is "upholstered"?
3. Which of the many humorous touches did you find particularly amusing?

4. Find the concrete details which the writer uses in describing Nona Monatch.

5. Explain the tie-back technique employed in the closing.

Suggested Writing Assignments

1. Search your experiences for a subject on which you could write a personal essay. Good topics include the anguish of growing up, the overcoming of personal handicaps, learning lessons in life through the school of hard knocks, and undergoing turning points which changed your outlook or values. Having found a promising topic, prewrite your thoughts on it by listing every idea which comes to mind. The more you put down in the prewriting phrase, the more apt you are to discover the approach and detail which will enable you to write freely and honestly in the style of the personal essay.

2. Using any three of the essays in the text, write a paper in which you analyze the techniques which were employed to give the reader an insight into the writer's inner world or set of values. In each essay you will want to examine topic, thesis approach, detail, language, and other facets which account for the emotional impact of the writing.

3. Examine a personal essay of your own choosing which is not in the text. Base your analysis of the essay on those aspects which chiefly account for its appeal—the writer's honesty, his insight into human nature, his appeal to the emotions, or his use of the language. Depending on your selection, you could write an effective paper on one or on several of these points.

14

Business, Professional, and Trade Writing

There is a whole world of professional, business and trade writing which the general public does not know much about because it is done for a limited and special audience. In fact there are few popular magazines compared to the professional, business and trade journals. There are, for example, a dozen or so leading popular magazines, but there are hundreds of less well-known publications with names such as *Engineer, Grocer Management, The English Journal, The Professional Photographer, Model Airplane News, The Pharmacist Journal, Today's Secretary, Sociology and Social Research, Baptist Leader, Illinois Master Plumber*, and *The Independent Banker*.

The authors of business and professional pieces are specialists in their particular field: lawyers, musicians, bakers, stamp collectors, doctors, or whatever. They write for other specialists and write about their own narrow interest. Several items from the table of contents of a music journal will illustrate the kinds of articles one finds in such a magazine: "New Role for the Composer," "Rossini and His World," "Mahler and Salvation," "Trends in Soviet Music," "Beethoven's Apt. in Vienna," "Historic Meeting with Copeland and Khachaturian." As one can see, such a journal focuses narrowly on music and its readers must necessarily share an interest in that field.

Some professional, business, and trade journals are written in a rather formal style. The doctor writing to other medical men does not translate his points into less technical terms, nor does the specialist in music bother to see that every one knows his terms. And their articles show other signs of a formal style: objectivity of tone, conventional grammar, and the sentences and paragraphs tend to be longer than those in popular prose.

To be sure, one can occasionally find in these journals articles which are suitable in subject, language, and style for the general reader, but they are indistinguishable from more popular writing. Such articles have none of the marks of the more restricted pieces.

Even though most professional, business, and trade writing is different from popular prose, it is, nevertheless, like popular prose in regard to motive, form, and variety. For example, the motive of the specialist author is exactly the same as that of the writer of more popular prose: he wants to inform and persuade.

In form, too, all specialist pieces, no matter how restricted the audience, usually have a solid and familiar structure: introduction, body, and closing. Even in variety, business and professional writing reflects the same forms we saw in popular prose. One finds, for example, interviews, editorials, how-to pieces, and the personal essay, to mention only a few.

As you look into this section, then, remember that the subjects are rather specialized, but remember also that you have special interests too and that you can find them reflected in the array of professional, business, and trade journals. What appears here is only a small sample from the field.

Runaways, Hippies, and Marihuana

JOSHUA KAUFMAN, JAMES R. ALLEN, M.D.
AND LOUIS JOLYON WEST, M.D.

In the summer of 1967 Haight-Ashbury seemed to offer youth a solution to the ills of modern society. Runaways, who used the district as a refuge from society or home, did not exhibit the delinquent characteristics observed by earlier authors. The complex and cohesive role of drugs, especially marihuana, was unprecedented. The authors feel that further attention should be directed not to the question "Why don't they stop using drugs?" but to "Can we offer them viable alternatives to drugs?"

The summer of 1967 was San Francisco's "summer of love." The newspapers predicted that 100,000 young people would flock to the bay area to join in it. Thirty thousand actually came, inundating the city. As part of a major reseach program in adolescence sponsored by the Oklahoma Medical Research Foundation, a large apartment in the Haight-Ashbury district was converted into a combination home, office, laboratory, commune, and "crashpad"—a place where transients, including runaway teen-agers, could spend the night. From this base, a research team of two psychiatrists, three college undergraduates, and three graduate students observed the life and times of the hippies.

Hippies

The mass media popularized the term "hippie" and created the Haight-Ashbury myth through extravagant reports about the district's psychedelic drug-using inhabitants, described as colorful "flower children," who espoused a style of life and a world view based on sharing, tolerance, love, and freedom for each individual "to do his own thing."

American Journal of Psychiatry, November (126:717-720), 1969. Copyright 1969. American Psychiatric Association. Reprinted by permission.

Most of these denizens of Golden Gate Park and nearby were either amused or disgusted by the hippie label. Asked if he were a hippie, one answered, "Hippie, what's that? . . . I'm just a human being." And when a prominent reporter asked a Haight-Ashbury "town meeting" what they preferred being called, one bearded spokesman declared, "People!"

Davis(4) suggests that the hippies represent a bona fide social movement, noting that they "are expressing, albeit elliptically, what is best about a seemingly ever-broader segment of American youth: its openness to new experiences, puncturing of cant, rejection of bureaucratic regimentation, aversion to violence, and identification with the exploited and disadvantaged."

Berger(2) has suggested that they are merely reviving elements of bohemias of the past: fraternity, salvation through the innocence of the child, living for the moment, mind expansion, and freedom of self-expression (provided that it does not harm anyone else). But the availability of synthetic psychedelic drugs and their role as a cohesive factor in Haight-Ashbury that summer had no real parallel in earlier bohemias.

West and Allen(12) call the hippies the Green Rebellion, distinguishing them from other rebellious youth such as the New Left and Black Power groups. They see the movement's goals as "beauty, freedom, creativity, individuality, self-expression, mutual respect, and the ascendance of spiritual over material values." They also differentiate true hippies from the many similar-looking drug-using pseudo-hippies, plastic hippies, teeny boppers, and runaways, who have become pharmacologically with them but are not philosophically of them. West and Allen warn that self-intoxication with powerful drugs, which is presently both a sacrament (LSD) and a unifying force (marihuana), will inevitably drain the Green Rebellion's energies and destroy it.

Runaways

In the summer of 1967 the Haight-Ashbury myth seemed to offer possible solutions to the problems of youth: an assurance of acceptability, a romantic new identity, and an escape from the hypocrisies of elders. It proffered magical solutions to some of the pressing problems of our time: violence, the dehumanization resulting from technological progress, and urban man's increasing alienation from and defilement of nature. The flow of runaways into Haight-Ashbury, together with the increasingly important role of drug use in the pattern of adolescent rebellion, quickly became an important focus of the research team's attention, and one of the authors (J. K.), was assigned full time to the study of the runaway and his problems, including marihuana.

A syndrome of prolonged absence from home, referred to and accepted by the individual as running away, has frequently been defined as a manifestation of juvenile delinquency. Foster(5), describing 100 runaways who had been referred to a juvenile court, noted a predominance of what he termed "typically delinquent" behavior. Reimer(10) reported three types of runaway: truants; children taking refuge from unbearable environmental situations; and runaways proper, showing "characterological abnormalities" manifested by antagonism, surly defiance, impulsiveness, unprovoked assaultive behavior, and periodic docility.

Following Cohen's(3) suggestion that differing delinquent acts have differing meanings for the individual, Robins and O'Neal (11), in their 30-year follow-up of children who were seen in a child guidance clinic, found that adults who were once runaways had a more frequent diagnosis of sociopathic personality than the rest of the group. Nye and Short(9) found that running away was characteristic of a population drawn from a juvenile correctional institution but rare in a high school population. . . .

For these youngsters, running away can

be formulated as a result of the interaction of socioeconomic history with personal history. Today's youth are, to use Keniston's (6) term, "post-modern," and the post-modern style is characterized by the conviction that in a world of rapid change adult (parental) models and values are increasingly irrelevant. Keniston(7) also suggests that the myth behind our society—society's goals and ideals—has become tarnished and negative. Post-modern youth are disillusioned with it and alienated from the society that spawned it.

Many of today's runaways, rather than being candidates for reform school, are reminiscent of the wandering bands of youth described long ago by Makarenko(8). Since the Children's Crusade, if not before, there have been times when large numbers of youngsters, almost in epidemics, have run away to seek fortune, romance, a dream. Many of the children who flocked to Haight-Ashbury were pilgrims, inspired by a myth that was largely a creation of the mass media; they were seeking a utopia where the problems of adolescence would not bother them.

The mind-expanding psychedelic drugs (LSD in particular) were often endowed by these romantics with religious properties. Some even waited until they finally arrived in Haight-Ashbury before partaking of the LSD sacrament, "saving" themselves for it like a virgin for her husband. But marihuana was their friend and companion, the medium through which camaraderie was found all along the road. The frustrations and hardships of that road were eased by the drug's beneficent euphoria, and interpersonal antagonisms among the travelers went up in its aromatic smoke.

Not all runaways were seekers of the dream. Some might be just as cogently termed "pushaways" as "runaways." One boy was a "caboose" child, pawned off repeatedly by his parents onto older brothers. Some came from broken homes. In some cases the parents had competed for the child's loyalties until he took flight.

Many runaways received either covert or overt parental sanction to leave, expressed as scorn, indifference, or obvious envy; here the parents used the child to act out vicariously their own immature desires for adventure and escape. For such adolescents the fashionable 1967 public myth of the flower children had a double appeal. Without the myth some of them might have stayed home, but other maneuvers would then probably have been sought for resolution of the conflicts within the family setting. Marihuana was already becoming available nationwide; some stay-at-homes were planting it in their backyards. . . .

The Role of Marihuana

Marihuana was almost always the first illegal drug used by runaways. Many had been introduced to it before leaving home or while on the road. In Haight-Ashbury it was so universally employed that it was considered a staple of life like bread and jam. But as Becker(1) notes, "turning on" is not as simple as just smoking; one must learn the technique: how to inhale and retain the smoke and how to recognize, enjoy, explore, and control the perceptual and affective changes that occur, hopefully maintaining the "high" without excessive intoxication. Acquiring these skills gave many runaways a sense of achievement, a talking point, and a password.

The horrible reactions to marihuana predicted by various authorities were virtually never seen. The runaways generally took this to mean that all the widely advertised dangers of drugs were establishment lies. This further alienated them from the social structure and made them more willing to experiment with all sorts of chemicals.

Meanwhile, the circumstances of the runaway made it unlikely that he would note the degree to which marihuana might interfere with his intellectual functioning. More chronic reactions (apathy, depression, loss of motivation) were seldom attributed to smoking pot. Instead, diminished aggressiveness was considered a desirable effect of drug use; the undesirable corollary effects (such as diminished energy) were minimized or interpreted as results of other factors.

The role of marihuana among the runaways is complex. To begin with, it offers the excitement of the forbidden, the companionship and acceptance of other explorers, and the promise of pleasure. Some users define the role of pot as a social experience, an escape, or a way to rebel, but most insist that the pharmacological effects are a significant source of gratification. Certainly marihuana and other drug use largely structures the Haight-Ashbury dweller's time. Most days are spent in getting money for staples (including marihuana and other drugs), taking drugs, and talking about sources, brands, prices, risks, legalities, and trips—both good and bad.

Observations to date suggest that most of the summer pilgrims—runaways and others—will eventually rejoin "straight" society, whether or not they return to their parents. But such returns are dependent on many factors, including psychopathology, affective state, cognitive dissonance, relationships with others (both in the psychedelic community and in the "straight" community), and the pressures of reality. Of those who do go home some, having had a bad experience, may not try drugs again. Others are now exploring meditation and other nonchemical "turn-ons."

Some Possible Lessons

However, a significant number of ex-runaways are continuing to use marihuana and are introducing it to others at home. Some of the psychosocial factors that are presently drawing millions of youngsters into marihuana smoking have been described, but further study is clearly required. For those youngsters who are graduates of Haight-Ashbury and for their friends (whom they are probably indoctrinating), the important question that faces mental health personnel may not be "Why don't they stop using drugs?" but "Can we as individuals and as a society offer them viable alternatives to drugs?"

It is difficult to compete with the fascination of the cabal, with its private slang, secret symbols, shared experiences, exhilarating cameraderie, and special mystical, presumably transcendental zeitgeist. The psychedelic posters and the acid-rock musical groups convey a host of messages and serve to expand or recreate the psychedelic experience. Such a song is "White Rabbit," by the Jefferson Airplane. There are many others referring to marihuana and other drugs.

One song that was of particular importance in the summer of 1967 was "She's Leaving Home," by the Beatles. Most of the runaways felt that it illustrated their inability to communicate their goals and values to their parents. The song's message seems clear: the youngster who runs away, whether his trip be geographical, pharmacological, or both, can best be understood in terms of the interaction of significant intrapsychic maturational variables, current sociocultural factors, and the all-important relationship of the child to his parents.

REFERENCES

1. Becker, H.: *The Outsiders*. New York: The Free Press (Macmillan Co.), 1963.
2. Berger, B. M.: "Hippie Morality—More Old Than New," *Trans-action* 5(2):19-27, 1967.
3. Cohen, A. K.: *Delinquent Boys*. New York: The Free Press (Macmillan Co.), 1955.
4. Davis, F.: "Why All of Us May Be Hippies Someday," *Trans-action* 5(2):10-19, 1967.
5. Foster, R. M.: "Intrapsychic and Environmental Factors in Running Away from Home," *American Journal of Orthopsychiatry* 32:486-491, 1962.
6. Keniston, K.: *The Uncommitted*. New York: Harcourt, Brace & World, 1965.

7. Keniston, K.: "Youth, Challenge, and Violence," *American Scholar* 37:227-246, 1968.
8. Makarenko, A. S.: *The Road to Life*. London: Central Books, 1967.
9. Nye, F. I., and Short, J.: "Scaling Delinquent Behavior," *American Sociological Review* 22:326-333, 1967.
10. Reimer, M. D.: "Runaway Children," *American Journal of Orthopsychiatry* 10: 522-526, 1940.
11. Robins, L. N., and O'Neal, P.: "The Adult Prognosis for Runaway Children," *American Journal of Orthopsychiatry* 29:752-761, 1959.
12. West, L. J., and Allen, J. R.: "Three Rebellions: Red, Black, and Green," in Masserman, J. F., ed.: *The Dynamics of Dissent*, vol. 13 of *Science and Psychoanalysis*. New York: Grune & Stratton, 1968.

Questions

1. Show how this piece, taken from *The American Journal of Psychiatry*, resembles popular prose in form, motive, developmental detail, and language.
2. How does it differ from popular prose?
3. Most of the technical language used by the authors can be translated without too much difficulty into simple English. Try your hand at simplifying the following statement: "Observations to date suggest that most of the summer pilgrims will eventually rejoin 'straight' society. But such returns are dependent on many factors, including psychopathology, affective state, cognitive dissonance, relationships with others, and the pressures of reality."
4. Was it the writers' intention to advance a specific thesis, or to report their findings? Explain.
5. Indicate two ideas in this write-up which gave you some new insight into the subject.

A First Step to Professional Identity

M. R. LOHMAN, P.E.

For years, many engineers have been concerned about the lack of identity in the engineering profession. Recently, concern has been expressed by many engineers because the public was apparently unable to distinguish between engineers and scientists.

Professional Engineer, August, 1969. Reprinted by permission. The author is Dean of the College of Engineering, Oklahoma State University.

Currently, this same concern is being expressed over lack of public discernment between engineers and technicians.

To overcome these problems of identity and image, there have been numerous attempts to define engineering. Probably the most common definition is the one used by the Engineers' Council for Professional Development which is as follows: "Engineering is the profession in which a knowledge of the mathematical and natural sciences gained by study, experience, and practice is applied with judgment to develop ways to utilize, economically, the materials and forces of nature for the benefit of mankind."

We have attempted to identify engineers by using this or a similar definition. However, as the definition lacks both precision and quantification, it has been found difficult to apply in specific cases. Consequently, there is little agreement on who is an engineer or on the number of engineers in the country. Estimates, depending on the definition used, vary from half a million to a million persons.

Lacking a precise definition of an engineer, the engineering organizations have varying criteria for membership; the councils, such as ECPD and Engineers Joint Council, have difficulty in determining the "bona fide" engineering organizations qualified to become members. Even the laws governing the registration of engineers have different requirements for registration in the various states, and laws with similar requirements may be differently interpreted by the various state boards of registration.

Possibly, the engineers' efforts to find an identity and a recognizable public image would be aided if we attempted to define an engineer rather than engineering, to define a professional rather than the profession. If one could find an acceptable and precise definition of an engineer, then the definition of engineering might be in terms of what is required to be an engineer. Further, the profession would thus become a collective of professionals who might be more easily identifiable.

If we accept the premise that a demonstration or certification of the mastery of a body of knowledge is the mark of a professional, we can examine how other occupations determine their professionals. . . .

Membership Gives Definition?

One might . . . look for a definition of an engineer in the membership criteria for various engineering organizations. Presumably, an engineering organization is composed of engineers. The criteria for "full" membership in the founder and other technical societies are of three general types. One type, such as for senior member in the Institute of Electrical and Electronics Engineers, requires that the engineer shall have engaged in ". . . the active practice of his profession for at least ten years and [that he] shall have attained distinction as measured by performance over a period of at least five of these years. . . ."

Other organizations, such as the American Institute of Aeronautics and Astronautics, state their membership requirements in terms of experience with an educational equivalent. "Persons who have acquired a professional standing in the practice of the arts, sciences, or technology of aeronautics, astronautics, or hydronautics. . . . They shall have eight (8) years of professional experience. . . . Engineering or science degrees from educational institutions of acceptable standing shall be considered equivalent to professional practice for an equivalent number of years. . . ." The third type of criteria for technical society membership states an educational qualification and then an experience equivalent.

Regardless of how the membership criteria are stated—without reference to education, experience with an educational equivalent, or education with an experience equivalent —it is clear that the official statements of membership requirements emphasize experience as the key factor in determining who is qualified to become a "full" member in an engineering society. . . .

Mastery Shown by Experience

The distinguishing characteristic between engineers and other professionals is that engineers measure their mastery of a body of knowledge by experience, while the other professionals require graduation from prescribed curricula. One can call himself an engineer if he performs engineering work, yet, as noted previously, engineering is imprecisely defined. As a consequence, the public is confused and cannot identify engineers, and engineering organizations have great difficulty in establishing and interpreting their qualifications for membership.

It appears impossible to precisely define engineering experience or, for that matter, any professional activities. Therefore, this seems to be an inadequate method of defining the engineer. Other occupations have avoided this difficulty by defining the qualified person by formal education. Taking one's blood pressure, taking a sample of blood, analyzing the sample, setting broken limbs, and many other activities may be performed by a physician or by another trained person. However, the mere performance of an activity does not make one a physician. Similarly, one may be well versed in the law and may, in some cases, plead his case before an appropriate judicial body, but the performance of these activities does not entitle one to call himself a lawyer. However, if one applies knowledge of mathematics and natural sciences to utilize the materials and forces of nature, he may call himself an engineer, be registered as an engineer, and be a full member of an engineering organization.

Possibly the time has come, or will soon come, when the title "engineer" should be reserved for only those who graduate from an ECPD accredited first professional degree program in engineering or the equivalent. Those having other educational backgrounds or experience may perform technical activities, but the mere performance of an activity will not qualify one as an engineer. When the title "engineer" is reserved for the graduate of prescribed curricula, some of the public's confusion may be alleviated and the problem of identity partially solved. While titles may be defined by the profession, they must be accepted by the public, and the degree requirement should further this acceptance. Obviously, experience or other additional qualifications may also be required, as in some of the other licensed professions, to insure proficiency and protection of the public.

Limit Full Membership

A further and equally important step would be to limit full membership in bona fide engineering societies to only those having the ECPD or equivalent accredited degree, and to limit the councils of engineering organizations and the directory of engineering organizations to bona fide engineering societies—that is, engineering societies whose full members are engineering graduates. Again, there may be additional criteria, but the basic and mandatory criterion would be the engineering degree.

If these two steps could be taken by the overwhelming majority of those who now possess an engineering degree and are part of the present ill-defined engineering profession, then possibly industry would limit its engineering titles to those who are registered, who are full members of an engineering organization, or who have the engineering degree. Thus, in time, the problem of title, image, and identity might be solved.

Questions

1. Define the problem which is discussed in the opening paragraphs.
2. In your opinion, would the editors of *Readers' Digest* be interested in reprinting this article?
3. What conclusion does the writer draw from his examination of the membership criteria required by various engineering organizations?
4. What positive solution to the problem is offered?

The Poet in the Classroom

ROBERT RUSSELL

Recently while on a lecture tour of some eastern colleges, Stanley Kunitz, Pulitzer Prize winning poet, stopped at Franklin and Marshall College in Lancaster, Pennsylvania. As an instructor in the English Department, I naturally looked forward to his visit. Since I was then teaching a course in the analysis of poems, I mimeographed Mr. Kunitz's "Green Ways" and passed it out to the class before his visit, saying that, if we were lucky, Mr. Kunitz might attend our meeting.

All good poetry is difficult to read and understand, but not all difficult poetry is good. A large part of the students felt that all "modern poetry" was merely difficult. Still, spurred by the prospect of meeting the poet himself, they outdid themselves in struggling with the lines. Mr. Kunitz agreed to join us for that hour, and the students were eager, loaded with questions.

I introduced the poet. "Mr. Kunitz," asked one of the students, "what did you mean when you said

The trellis of the crystal
In the rose-green moon?"

"Excuse me," he replied politely, "but I didn't come to explain the poem. I came to listen and perhaps to join in *your* discussion."

They lapsed into silent disappointment. Sensing this, he went on, "You see, it isn't *my* poem now. It's published. It belongs as much to you as to me."

Encouraged, the students began offering their interpretations of the lines. When we were talking freely, Mr. Kunitz interrupted. "Maybe it would help," he said, "if you thought of 'crystal' as being a kind of building block in the mineral universe. 'Trellis' is an accurate image of the architecture of a crystal."

This was the key, and as we talked the shape and power of the poem gradually revealed themselves. It is a cry of pain and exaltation—pain at being trapped in the great cycle of life and death, and exaltation

---

College English, May, 1967. Reprinted with the permission of the National Council of Teachers of English and Robert Russell. Poetry from *Selected Poems 1928-1958* by Stanley Kunitz, by permission of Atlantic-Little, Brown and Company.

in the joyful knowledge that, even in his own disintegration, the poet gives birth through love to new life and art.

> Let me proclaim it—human be my lot!—
> How from my pit of green horse-bones
> I turn, in a wilderness of sweat,
> To the moon-breasted sibylline,
> And lift this garland, Danger, from her throat
> To blaze it in the foundries of the night.

When the hour had raced by, even the most conservative felt that there was at least one great modern poem, and that was "Green Ways" by Stanley Kunitz. Although the poet himself had helped us, he had done so not as the omniscient author, but as an acutely sensitive reader.

This hour had been so stimulating that I later thought that I ought to offer a seminar in the poetry of Stanley Kunitz with visits from the poet himself. It was only three hours by train from his New York home to Lancaster, so it might be arranged.

It was, in fact, arranged. The money was put up by the Shell Assists Program, I was shaken free from some of my regular teaching, and the seminar was scheduled. Eight students signed up—an ideal number.

We met in a quiet, booklined room furnished with a long table, ten chairs, ash trays, a hot plate, a jar of instant coffee, and a stack of cups. We gathered around the table with our copies of Kunitz's *Selected Poems*, published by Little, Brown and Company, the volume which won the Pulitzer Prize for poetry in 1959. This was our reading for the semester—116 pages. We would read and re-read every poem, every line of every poem, and every word of every line until we understood.

The collection opens with "The Science of the Night," 46 lines dramatizing a lover's agony when he realizes that, even in the act of love, he cannot really possess his mistress. Even in his rhythmic ecstasy, no man can bridge the gulf which eternally isolates his identity from hers.

> And even should I track you to your birth
> Through all the cities of your mortal trial,
> As in my jealous thought I try to do,
> You would escape me—from the brink of earth
> Take off to where the lawless auroras run,
> You with your wild and metaphysic heart.
> My touch is on you, who are light-years gone.
> We are not souls but systems, and we move
> In clouds of our unknowing like great nebulae.
> Our very motives swirl and have their start
> With father lion and with mother crab.

This longing for "my own lost rib,"—this is the knowledge or "science" of the "night," which is also his dark ignorance of his beloved. The intensity of the longing and the certainty of failure sent the class reeling from the room leaving half-empty coffee cups beside the ash trays.

In "Hermetic Poem" Mr. Kunitz writes, "Who enters by my door / Is drowned, burned, stung, and starred." They had begun to enter.

I had scheduled the poet's first visit for the beginning of our second month. He arrived on a chilly Sunday evening early in March. Nervous about the morrow, he asked what the students were like as people, how they had been responding, and which poems they were likely to want to talk about.

It is hard enough for a man to put on paper the secret struggles of his heart and mind, but, once done, he can turn with relief to the privacy of his study. Mr. Kunitz, however, was being asked to face not a few casual readers, but a group which had done its utmost to pry into every heartbeat of every line. It was as if a mature and passionate lover were asked to meet a group of youngsters who had been studying his letters to his mistress.

I knew that they had understood, but did not know how they would act in the presence of the poet. After all, they knew me quite well, and I had not the poet's stake in the poems. I tried to quiet his concern and hoped for the best.

The next morning Mr. Kunitz huddled tensely in my usual chair at the head of the table, and the students filed in. They were dressed in white shirts, ties and jackets—a bad sign. They didn't expect to relax either. I did my best to capture the warmth, ease, and good-humored seriousness of our regular meetings, but it was no good. They were too embarrassed. Mr. Kunitz was nervous. I was disappointed in my own inability to bring them together.

"Well," he said after the class, "that ordeal's over."

"It will be better next time," I hoped.

His next visit was as fruitful as the first had been all but fruitless. Everyone was more relaxed. "Mr. Kunitz, we had quite an argument about 'Prophecy on Lethe' on page 61," I began. "There were two camps. If I can summarize their positions, maybe you would talk a little about the poem." I explained the arguments with help from the others and then gave Mr. Kunitz the floor.

"I must confess," he responded, "that I find those interpretations interesting, particularly since I had never thought of them before. That poem is a long way from me now. I'm glad I don't remember what I had in mind."

"Why are you glad, sir?"

"Because I want you to keep on asking questions, which are so much more important than any answers I might give you."

"But don't you have the right answers?"

"There aren't any. My intentions, even if I could remember them, are irrelevant; and my afterthoughts are not necessarily to be trusted. What matters—I say this hopefully —is the poem itself, in the give-and-take of each new encounter, as it struggles to come alive in your consciousness. The mistake is in supposing that the poem began as an idea, which was then transposed into verse. If that were true, we might as well publish the original idea and dispense with the poem that paraphrases it. Usually the poet doesn't really have what could be defined as an explicit intention. The poem demands to be written and gives no peace until it's done. Our subliminal drives are more likely to provide the motives for an action than any rationalization we can offer. Writing a poem is a very complex action, and I don't think I understand my subconscious any better than you do yours."

"Then you can't help us with this particular poem?"

"Not much . . . except to say that I suppose it's some kind of revelation, or epiphany, that I had at the time: an unusually deep awareness, sudden and fleeting, not a chronic condition. There are poems that don't seem to want to come up to the surface where they can be talked about."

"Actually," confessed one of the students, "I was really horrified by the last line, 'Your jelly-mouth and, crushed, your polyp eyes.' I think that's revolting!"

"I think it's beautiful," Mr. Kunitz laughed.

The time sped by. The class officially broke up at noon, but adjourned to a small dining room where the college had provided lunch for us, and our talk ran on for two hours.

When the last student had left to catch his next class, Mr. Kunitz said, "It went much better, don't you think?"

"Much better," I said. "They're more relaxed; but they're still too embarrassed to let you see how your poems have gripped them. But anyway, they'd have to be poets themselves to express that."

His last visit was scheduled for the meeting after we were supposed to have finished his book. He was to come on a Monday, but by Friday we still had four poems to go. I suggested that they simply work through those over the weekend by themselves.

"We need another class," they insisted.

I invited them to come to my house on Sunday evening.

Mr. Kunitz arrived on Sunday afternoon. I explained our plans for the evening. Other members of the English Department had offered hospitality so that he needn't sit through an extra session.

"I'd like to stay, if you don't mind, but I won't say anything. I just want to listen."

At 7:30 the students arrived, exchanged friendly greetings with Mr. Kunitz, and settled down on the livingroom floor with their books. They were sufficiently at ease in his presence now. Their voices soon rose in anger and excitement, turning the living room into the arena of our classroom. As usual, I was moderator, steersman, and, when our ship threatened to founder on a hopeless controversy, I interrupted, stated both sides, gave my opinion, and tried to move the group on. Sometimes this worked, but sometimes it didn't, for any or all of them were as ready to argue with me as with one another. Tempers flared, sometimes shedding light and sometimes only heat.

We were soon locked in a struggle over the identity of the "him" in the first stanza of "The Way Down."

Time swings her burning hands
I saw him going down
Into those mythic lands
Bearing his selfhood's gold,
A last heroic speck
Of matter in his mind
That ecstasy could not crack
Nor metaphysics grind.
I saw him going down
Veridical with bane
Where pastes of phosphor shine
To a cabin underground
Where his hermit father lives
Escaping pound by pound
From his breast-buckled gyves;
In his hermit father's coat,
The coat without a seam,
That the race, in its usury, bought
For the agonist to redeem,
By dying in it, one
Degree a day till the whole
Circle's run.

"I think the 'him' is Apollo," said one. "The burning hands are the hands of the sun by which we measure time, and Apollo is the god of the sun."

"It couldn't be Apollo. It must be Christ; the 'agonist' is certainly Christ, and he 'redeems.' Apollo doesn't redeem anything."

"But how do you know that the agonist and the 'him' are the same?" asked another.

Then one of them turned to the poet. "We're making an awful mess of your poem. Won't you help us out."

"I shouldn't call it a mess," he replied. "All your speculations are sensitive, which leads me to think they must be at least partly true. I can't expect you to know that I began to write the poem after making the steep descent down to the Grotto of Neptune in Tivoli, not far from Rome. The actual physical setting is of no consequence, for 'the way down' of the poem is into a mythic underground, older than self or history. Down there the protagonist confronts the mystery of his roots, endures his fate, and is restored to life."

"It's surprising that a modern poet should be so involved with the past. Shouldn't he cut himself off from the past so that he can be truly modern?"

"You might as well expect a tree to blossom and bear fruit after it has been hacked off at the base. Of course a poet has to be of his time—timely—before he can hope to achieve timelessness; but language itself continually reminds him that there can be no actual separation between past and present. Every word he conjures up comes dragging the chains of its history behind it."

After a pause, he continued, "Fertile ground is a place of many deaths. The past dies into poetry. In the end it is all imagination. Any tailor can stitch a coat; the miracle is to sew it without a seam."

We stopped at 11:00 and I turned to Kunitz. "I hope this wasn't an ordeal too."

"It was just as fascinating as it was difficult," he confessed. "The joke is on the poet who fancies he has written a poem. He finds instead that it is as many poems as it has readers."

Toward the close of our class the following morning, one of the students said, "Mr. Kunitz, may I ask you a personal question?" Everyone laughed.

"Shoot!"

"If you had your life to live over, would you live it differently? We can guess that things haven't always been easy for you. Would you change anything?"

"I guess I was stuck with myself," he said, "and did what I could with it. I made plenty of mistakes, but at least they were my own. I don't have much hope of changing the world, but I can try to change myself. I am changed by the poems I write. And I want to keep on living my life—and changing it."

"Would you say that your life has been happy?"

He hesitated. "I've had my joys. But that's a different story. Swift said that happiness is the art of being well-deceived. Only the young care about it passionately, perhaps because they are so miserable most of the time. Despite the philosophers, I should say that happiness is an over-valued condition."

Standing by the waiting train in the full sweetness of a hot May afternoon, we shook hands.

"This has been an experience that none of us will forget," I said lamely.

"It's I who must thank all of you," he replied.

He was gone, and I returned to what seemed an empty college. It was over. But not really. The essays that soon appeared on my desk proved that it was only beginning. All bore postscripts saying, in one way or another, that this seminar had changed their lives. One of the students, certain that he could not have said all that he meant in his paper, paid me a visit that no teacher would ever forget.

"I feel," he said, "as though I have been walking through the world in a stupor for 21 years. I'm just beginning to wake up to what I am—to what a man is, and to what his world is. I know I can't understand or predict all the consequences, but I do know that this has been one of the major experiences of my life."

The primary reason for our success was a simple one—the careful study of great art produces great impact, and our work had convinced us that Mr. Kunitz is a great poet. His poems are intensely personal, unflinchingly honest. He exemplifies the doctrine that only the most profoundly private experience is worth the artist's struggle to express. This alone is universal. While having this strong appeal, his poems also convey a sense of the vastness of the stage on which the individual has his instant of drama and the hugeness of the cycle of birth and death in which he is caught.

. . . What the deep heart means,
Its message of the big, round, childish hand,
Its wonder, its simple lonely cry,
The bloodied envelope addressed to you,
Is history, that wide and mortal pang.

. . . It wasn't only the "content" of the poems that was responsible for their impact. It was the content in motion, the movement preserved in static structure, for Mr. Kunitz is a consummate craftsman. As we worked together, the students came to realize this. They continually had that great, slow pleasure that comes from discovering a poem which at first seemed utterly confusing. After long serious work, the thoughts, the shape of the thoughts and the electricity that played back and forth among them, gradually became clear till at the end they had the sense of possessing the poem or of being possessed by it.

All this is only to say that we succeeded because Mr. Kunitz is a great poet and that we worked hard on his poems. There was another reason—a non-literary one, but nevertheless important. It was that Mr. Kunitz was more to the students than a signature. He was actually a person, and he proved it by coming down the hall, walking into our classroom and sitting down. Above all, he proved it by listening to what we had to say, by being surprised, pleased, uncertain, and by laughing. All this said to them in language that could not be misunderstood, "I am he."

The poems stepped from the page into the eyes, the voice and the substance of a man. The tumult and beauty over which we had struggled had become flesh. What other proof of truth remained to be given? And so the students walked from the seminar still shaking from the impact of the realization that literature was life and that they were actors in the same drama. . . .

Our colleges and universities have traditionally been defenders of the truths of the past. They sit in the present facing backward with broad-bottomed ease, and they say to the young, "Let us teach you about the mighty dead." And the young listen, if at all, with only one ear, for they are alive here and now. It might be well if some of our institutions recognized that not all the mighty are always among the dead—not all the giants have been slain. When a college invites a poet for any length of time, it asks that he disguise himself as a lecturer on his famous predecessors. Surely we can find some rooms in our halls of learning that are high enough for the artist to enter on the strength of his own stature and to stand up in—as himself.

Questions

1. Explain the *who, what, where, when,* and *why* behind the author's decision "to offer a seminar in the poetry of Stanley Kunitz with visits from the poet himself."
2. Which of the dialogues between the poet and the students did you find most interesting?
3. Show how the writer used narration as a means of organizing his material.
4. What changes, if any, would be required in this piece to make it suitable for publication in a popular magazine?
5. What did you learn about poetry and poets from this article? What do you believe teachers of literature could learn?

Is There a Nurse-Clinician Job in Your Future?

DONNA M. LEDNEY, R.N.

The nurse-clinician role is relatively new and exciting. The use of nurse clinicians has expanded in recent years, and indications are that it will expand even more in the future.

What is a nurse clinician? What education and other qualifications are needed to become one? What are the duties and responsibilities? What are the problems and rewards?

To find the answers to those and other questions, I visited hospitals on both the East and West Coasts where nurse clinicians have become an established part of the health-care team. In my interviews with clinicians as well as with administrators and educators, I found that (1) nurse clinicians are enthusiastic about their work and generally agree that the satisfactions of the job far outweigh the frustrations; (2) administrators say they could use many more clinicians; (3) educators predict a big increase in the number.

One thing I didn't find was a universally accepted definition of the nurse clinician's role. The American Nurses' Association has not taken an official position on the standards and functions of a nurse clinician, and the qualifications needed. Thus every hospital—and usually every nurse who accepts a nurse-clinician position—develops the role according to the needs of the hospital and the knowledge and skills of the nurse.

A review of the literature and of job descriptions from hospitals reveals that, for practical purposes, a nurse clinician can be defined in general terms only, as follows:

She is a registered nurse who is knowledgeable in general nursing theory and practice, and skilled in the clinical specialty in which she works. She is capable of functioning independently, analytical in her thinking, and able to suggest practical solutions to patient-care problems. She is also able to lead, teach, and work successfully with others.

This may sound like the description of a good supervisory nurse in any of many hospital departments. Indeed it could be, except for this important difference in the work each does: The supervisory nurse is usually so burdened with administrative routine that she can give only a minimum of attention to the *details* of patient care. In contrast, the nurse clinician is not burdened with administrative chores except a few pertaining directly to patient-care planning.

Frances Reiter, R.N., M.A., dean of the Graduate School of Nursing, New York Medical College, was the first to use the term "nurse clinician." She says: "One criterion for a clinician is that she must spend no less than 51 per cent of her time in patient contact. This may involve tasks and activities done directly for the patient or in his behalf, but not managerial activities or teaching of persons not involved in patient care."

In short, the nurse clinician's role is one in which an experienced and clinically qualified R.N. who likes to give patient care can continue this function and still move ahead in her profession. She doesn't have to climb the administrative ladder to receive more salary and recognition. Her salary is usually

---

RN Magazine, August, 1969. © Copyright 1969 by Medical Economics, Inc. Reprinted with permission from RN Magazine, Vol. 32, No. 8, August, 1969.

on the same level as that of a supervisor, and sometimes higher. Too, most hospitals pay nurse clinicians more as they increase their professional skills and knowledge. For example, the Bird S. Coler Memorial Hospital and Home—a New York City municipal hospital—has a salary scale that ranges from $7,900 for beginning nurse clinicians to $15,000 for those with extensive clinical experience and a master's degree in nursing. . . .

What credentials must an R.N. have to become a nurse clinician? Educational requirements vary from a diploma to a higher degree. Most educators and administrators recommend a master's degree as the theoretical ideal. But in reality few nurses have master's degrees. Thus, many nursing directors are emphasizing experience and personal motivation as the prime qualifications. Several hospitals have established inservice training programs to help R.N.s interested in becoming nurse clinicians to increase their skills.

Several clinicians I interviewed told me they are working toward either a baccalaureate or a master's degree. Explained Molly Goodson, M.S., a psychiatric clinician at the University of California Medical Center in San Francisco: "With more education I'm more articulate and can communicate more easily with other professionals about the patients." On the other hand, Dean Reiter cautions: "A higher degree in itself doesn't produce a nurse clinician. The nurse herself must have the personal commitment that care of patients is the primary function of nursing."

Just what does a nurse clinician do?

In the clinical area the answer depends, of course, on the nurse's clinical specialty. Nurse clinicians are working today in nearly all areas of nursing: medicine, psychiatry, surgery, obstetrics, gynecology, pediatrics, dermatology, coronary care, intensive care, and rehabilitation. There are even nurse clinicians in the O.R. at the University of Iowa Hospital, Iowa City.

When a nurse clinician is added to the staff of a unit, there may be a change in the administrative set-up to help prevent role-overlapping. A common arrangement is to have the nurse clinician work under the supervision of an administrative assistant to the nursing director. The clinician is not responsible to the head nurse (or unit supervisor), but works cooperatively with her.

Job descriptions of the nurse clinician's role state that she is responsible for (1) providing leadership in giving patient care, (2) providing consultation as a patient-care expert, (3) serving as a role-model of the professional nurse practitioner, (4) promoting "collaborative interdisciplinary working relationships," and (5) serving as a "creative and innovative force" in nursing practice.[1]

. . . Unlike other nurses, the clinician often determines her own hours and the pace of her activities. Though she usually works a 40-hour week, she does not necessarily work a regular shift but may come to the hospital at the times her patients and their families need her. On one day, for example, she may arrive at 8 A.M., go home at noon, and return that evening. Like a doctor, she may be on call 24 hours a day.

How are nurse clinicians adjusting to their new role? What are some of the disadvantages as well as the rewards?

For one thing, the newness of the role has led to some confusion because nurse clinicians themselves as well as other nursing personnel have not understood clearly their functions and the limits of their work and authority. This has often led to unpleasant situations. Some nurse clinicians told me that when they first came to a hospital, they

---

[1] Quoted from Massachusetts General Hospital department of nursing, Oct. 18, 1967.

were greeted with distrust and hostility. The head nurse or supervisor saw them as a job threat, staff nurses resented them as just one more authority to deal with, and physicians sometimes resented them because of the close relationship they established with the patients.

The biggest disadvantage, said many, is their lack of authority. The nurse clinician is in a staff rather than an administrative position, so she must rely on others to accept her ideas in order to get things done. "The clinician's power rests solely in her clinical expertise," explains Cynthia R. Kinsella, R.N., nursing service director at Mount Sinai Hospital, New York City. "Above all, she cannot be authoritarian."

"My philosophy," says Barbara Giordano, R.N., a nurse clinician at the same hospital, "involves showing and telling. I demonstrate the practicality of any care plan I suggest, and explain its principles and how they may be modified."

Says Mrs. Edwards, of Barnes Hospital: "One must have no illusions about making radical changes. One must function with whatever personnel and resources that are at hand. It is very important not to become discouraged, to understand that your advice may not be accepted immediately." A leading nursing educator and administrator, Marjorie M. Ramphal, R.N., Ph.D., responds to those statements thus: "It's rather a pity for the poor patient, though, that the most expert nurse is compelled to persuade others to accept her clinical judgment!"

Though it isn't easy, dedicated nurse clinicians find ways to solve these and other problems. Cathee Huber, M.N., a psychiatric clinician on the medical-surgical floors at University Hospital, University of Washington, Seattle, found that sharing an office with a supervisor "helped tremendously to promote a good working relationship." Miss Goodson, at the University of California Medical Center, won acceptance by working for several months as a staff nurse on her unit before starting as a nurse clinician. "It gave me time to learn about the unit and staff," she explains, "and gave the staff a chance to accept me."

Do the rewards and satisfactions outweigh the disadvantages? The nurse clinicians I spoke to agree that they do. For example, several R.N.'s at Massachusetts General Hospital who had made the transition from head nurse to nurse clinician point out that they now have freedom from routine, freedom to use their nursing knowledge and skills to their fullest potential. As head nurses, they would draw up patient-care plans but would not have time to follow through on them. Now they do. Even more important, says Barbara Noonan, R.N., "I can now become involved in a caretaking relationship at a deep rather than superficial level."

Over-all, the future of this new role for nurses looks bright. Nurse clinicians are in demand nearly everywhere, and their number is steadily increasing.

Questions

1. For what audience is this piece intended?
2. Much of the material is structured around questions posed by the writer, such as "What is a nurse clinician?" Find other examples of key questions.
3. Illustrate the effective use of direct quotation.
4. In discussing the disadvantages of being a nurse clinician, should

the writer have included the rather strong criticism made by Marjorie M. Ramphal, R.N., Ph.D?

5. State the writer's chief purpose as specifically as you can in one or two sentences.

New Trends in Fund Raising

A warning was sounded during the fund raising forum at NCWA's last Western Convention in Los Angeles that in some cases the consumer is no longer getting a dollar's worth of merchandise for a dollar spent. The business, many felt, could revert from fund raising to asking for charity. To explore this trend in further detail, we asked one of the country's foremost experts, George T. Edwards, Edwards Distributing Co., Richmond, Va., for his observations. Here are some eye-openers for every wholesaler in the fund raising field:

Q: *Mr. Edwards, you have been in candy wholesaling for several decades and you have dealt in fund raising merchandise for many years. What are some of the new trends in fund raising you have noted during the last year or so?*

A: The dollar items seem to be coming into their own strongly. As a matter of fact, we lost an account for the first time this year to a dollar item.

Although the dollar item is gaining in popularity, it brings into the market its own special problems. One manufacturer, for example, has for years had a dollar box fund raiser, which started out as a pound box. Then they cut the box to about 12 ounces. Now they have it cut to 8¼ ounces, but are still running it for a dollar. They offer the fund raising group a commission of 44 percent. Their business has been good, but we have had a number of complaints.

Q: *You mean to say that the final purchaser is not receiving full value for his dollar?*

A: That's right. The consumer is getting a reduced weight. We may get by with this for a year or two, but if that trend continues, we could revert to charity. We would not be selling merchandise, but just asking for a donation. We went through a similar phase some 25 or 30 years ago, and it proved detrimental then. It forced everybody to work on such a small margin of profit that no one could stay in business.

Q: *What do you think brought about this trend to the higher priced package?*

A: It's tied in with the overall increase in cost of living. Inflation has put such a heavy demand on the fund raising organizations that they have to go shopping for packages that carry a good profit for them. Where a group needed $1000 for a project some years ago, they now need $1500.

Q: *Do you carry dollar items now?*

A: No, we don't have them now, but we will put in a complete line of dollar items next year. We will have to if we want to stay in business. We have not suffered as far as volume is concerned. But we should have shown an increase this year in accordance with the rising economy of the country, and this we did not do. We held our own.

National Candy Wholesaler, June, 1969. Reprinted by permission.

Q: *What kind of fund raising merchandise do you mostly handle?*
A: The big item with us is the 10¢ bar. We are doing well with it, since we work with a lot of youth groups that can handle the 10¢ item. Of course, most of them have been cut in size too. One manufacturer cut his bar as much as 50 percent, others cut 25 percent. One bar is down to 1⅞ of an ounce. As far as I know, there is only one 2-ounce dime bar left on the market.

Q: *Obviously, you are not happy with the reduced sizes of the bars. Have you noted any changes in the quality of merchandise?*
A: No. I don't think there has been any change in quality. But the thought of an 8½ ounce coconut bar for a dollar is ridiculous, especially if you remember that six months ago you could sell a 2 ounce coconut bar for a dime. I realize that the manufacturer is making the changes to help fund raisers make a bigger profit, but I want to sound the warning that, even while the trend exists toward the dollar package, the consumer is not getting what he pays for. Sooner or later this will have its detrimental effect on all of us.

Q: *Do you push seasonal merchandise in your fund raising campaigns?*
A: Yes. And as a matter of fact, we have been very successful in this. Last year, we filled Nu-Pak Christmas canes with a Just Born line of candies, and we could hardly fill all the requests. This year, we added a Bunny Bank, which was larger than the cane, and therefore not a 50¢ item. So we filled one batch of the banks with jelly beans and it weighed about four ounces per bank. The second bank we filled with Marlons, and it would hold about six-and-a-quarter ounces. The jelly bean pack we sold for 30¢ to be resold at 50¢ and the Marlon pack we sold for 36¢ to be resold at 60¢. Surprisingly enough, the packages sold equally well.

Q: *What type of organization will sell your seasonal merchandise?*
A: For the Easter and Christmas items, we had a PBX Club, telephone operators. They were our biggest account on the canes. For Halloween, we have scout troops mostly. We handle bagged items for Halloween, and we have done well with them. We will get started on Halloween in September, and start packing canes in the early fall.

Q: *How do you see the future for the fund raiser?*
A: I see a good future. The business is going to be bigger and bigger because of the growing demands. Fund raising is here to stay. If wholesalers are not getting the business, it is only because they are not going after it enough.

Q: *When you say the demands are growing do you mean there are more outlets today?*
A: No. The increasing demands are brought about by the economic situation. Take churches, for example. If they are going to buy choir robes, I would say they have to pay 25 to 40 percent more today than two or three years ago. Consequently, they need to raise more money.

Q: *Do you see a danger in this trend?*
A: We are beginning to get a little more cautious, because the demand for more money is causing some groups to over-emphasize their possibilities. They know what they need and they are going after it, but they do not always reach their goal. That could cause the wholesaler to get stuck with a lot of merchandise. . . .

Q: *Do you ever turn down groups or individuals who wish to arrange a fund raising deal with you?*
A: Yes. Not a day passes that we don't turn down anywhere from $100 to maybe sometimes $500 worth of business right on the phone. We get all the details on the potential customer before we even quote prices. We want to know what type of an organization they are, how big they are, what their qualifications are. If they don't look good to us, we turn them down. We would long be out of business if we took on every fund raiser who asks us for a deal.

Questions

1. Into which category of writing does this piece fall—professional, or business and trade?
2. Do you believe that the questions asked by the interviewer were worked out in advance or devised on the spot? Explain by making specific references.
3. What are some of the "new trends" in fund raising which are established in the interview?
4. Would you agree that, in planning this piece for the *National Candy Wholesaler,* the author had a good insight into his audience?
5. Characterize the level of the language used in the interview and cite two examples which reveal the jargon of the candy wholesaler.

Power Powder

DOLORES DAVIS MILLER, ED., *The Dairyman*

A mustard-colored, coarse powder that packs a hormonal wallop is being fed to increasing numbers of dairy cows. The powder is thyroprotein, a controversial substance that is both praised and damned.

Despite growing acceptance, thyroprotein isn't winning popularity contests—yet. Evidence shows it's coming up in the polls.

Lack of knowledge and past mis-use of the product has given it a smudged reputation.

Take southern California. Approximately 15 years ago, milk producers in the big Southern Metropolitan milkshed, which encompasses Los Angeles and several surrounding counties, discovered thyroprotein. Unfortunately, they didn't at the same time discover how to utilize it for optimum results. In many cases, because a little bit boosted production, a lot was used. Pure thyroprotein was fed in various quantities to all cows; it was unevenly mixed with grain rations which meant the amount cows got depended on the luck of the draw; insufficient concentrates were given to replace the extra energy expended producing more milk.

Dairymen burned out cows so fast they couldn't keep enough body weight on the wretched animals for them to bring decent cull cow prices. It was a painfully costly experience. Yet today, in the same milkshed, dairymen are successfully and profitably feeding thyroprotein.

To find out why it's working now, we talked with 10 of the approximately 60 dairymen presently feeding thyroprotein in southern California. They all championed its use.

Before we look into their stories let's find out more about thyroprotein: what it is, how it works.

Thyroprotein is thyroactive iodinated casein. In simple terms it is a synthetic thyroid gland hormone. It was invented two decades ago at the University of Missouri by Drs. C. W. Turner and E. P. Reinike. It

---

The Dairyman, August, 1969. Reprinted by permission.

contains thyroxine. Thyroxine stimulates body growth, reproduction effectiveness and boosts milk production. . . .

To understand how thyroprotein works, one must know a bit about the thyroid gland. The thyroid gland located in the cow's neck and wrapped around the windpipe, is an endocrine gland, meaning it secretes hormones directly into the blood stream. These thyroid hormones are important to growth, reproduction and milk production. The reproduction and growth influences are connected with the pituitary and hypothalamus glands in the brain. The thyroid activity heats up the body by causing the body cells to utilize or consume energy.

For example, it is known that hyperactive blood circulation boosts milk production. Dr. Turner says that used properly, thyroprotein speeds up the heartbeat, which increases the blood flow through the cow's udder, increasing milk production. In a 24-hour period, from 15,000 to 20,000 pounds of blood must flow through the udder to produce 50 pounds of milk. Production of 75 pounds of mik would require a blood flow of 22,500 to 30,000 pounds in the same period of time. . . .

The best way to feed thyroprotein, or protamone as it is better known to most dairymen, appears to be to give it to cows when the lactation decline begins after peak production. This usually occurs from 30 to 60 days after calving, and the drop frequently is both sudden and severe.

This is the program commonly followed in southern California. Thyroprotein is added to a cow's feed when production drops below 50-60 pounds of butterfat per month. The 10 pound variance depends on what the dairyman wants to achieve, other feeding practices, the herd's mean average. . . .

It is apparent that good management practices are necessary for successful utilization of thyroprotein.

"Some people never can feed properly because they're just not paying attention to what's happening in the barn," says Mary Atsma Storm, one of the few women dairymen in the area, and by all estimates one of the best.

She instituted the use of thyroprotein 2½ years ago at her 185-cow dairy in Cypress. With exceptionally good records, which she keeps herself, a clear picture of each cow's status is available.

The cows are tested once a month, and those that are in early lactation and have dropped to a combination of 110 pounds of daily milk and monthly fat production (i.e. 55 pounds milk per day and 55 pounds fat per month) are marked as "possible protomones." A judgment factor is added in the decision of which cows to put on thyroprotein.

"Cows in poor physical condition, I don't put on protamone—unless they're destined to be cull cows in which case it might be worth trying as a way of saving the cow." . . .

Bob Hills, a young dairyman of Arlington, had an interesting experience. Just over a year ago he bought a run-down dairy and began a tedious rebuilding job.

Ten cows were "on their way to beef, dropping fast and hardly worth saving."

"Just to see what they would do," Hills started them on protamone. He saved eight. They became good cows, he said.

Perhaps the most dramatic effect, however, concerned an old cow that looked even worse because of a broken hip. She had been a good cow, however, so instead of beefing her, he started feeding her protamone. She not only carried through that lactation with acceptable production, but "got in calf again right away and has just wound up another lactation—drying up at 60 pounds." . . .

These dairymen rate thyroprotein high, but some dairymen are leery of feeding it. Maybe they've heard of problems, or had unsuccessful experiences themselves in the feeding of thyroprotein.

In our investigation it appears that most of the problems are caused by incautious or improper use of the product.

We have learned, for example, that it must be fed regularly. Adequate feed must be provided to allow maximum utilization by the cow. If weight loss is excessive, added feed is necessary or present feed should be tested to see if it is lacking in essential nutrients. Cases of over or under feeding of the thyroprotein are also known. . . .

We discovered that not all cows will react the same. Some will even be nonreactors —presumably because of preexisting endocrine conditions or optimum or overactive thyroid activity. One dairyman noted that when he first began feeding thyroprotein, while some of the cows reacted immediately, a good many did not until a month later when these laggards responded on par with the first ones. It just took them longer.

This may be the case with the way dairymen are adapting to using thyroprotein. Because it is still a controversial subject, because past mistakes and present misunderstandings are hard to overcome, some dairymen are just taking longer to get around to it.

Questions

1. To what extent is this piece informative and persuasive? In your answer, consider the intended audience.
2. In what sense are the sixth and seventh paragraphs transitional?
3. Would a man in the dairy business be more impressed with direct quotations from those who have used thyroprotein, or with the data presented in an impersonal manner?
4. Identify the stylistic level of the language in this article and provide two examples of the jargon used by dairymen.
5. In the closing paragraphs the writer acknowledges the fact that although many people use and recommend thyroprotein, "some dairymen are leery of it." What explanation does he give?

Suggested Writing Assignments

1. Write a paper in which you analyze an article taken from a professional or business journal in your major field, such as law, home economics, or education. As an alternative, you could analyze the contents of one issue of a journal in regard to the various kinds of articles which it contains. In both analyses you will want to touch on form, types of articles, language, and audience.

From the text discussion and specimen pieces it should be obvious that trade, business and professional magazines are published in all of the major fields. Consult your library for lists of published periodicals arranged by subject.

2. Analyze an article taken from a technical journal which represents your hobby, such as stamp collecting, motorcycles, or fishing. Or you may want to analyze the contents of a single issue of the magazine to show how the editor meets the needs of his specialist readers. Consult the library for titles of periodicals.

3. Compare and contrast two different journals published in the same field, such as art, medicine, or engineering. Note the subject matter, slant, and intended audience appeal as evidenced in the articles which appear in the two magazines.

4. Study your library's copy of the *Writers' Market,* a guide for free-lance writers to the requirements of writing for journals and trade magazines.

Then write a paper on any of the categories which you find interesting, such as Animal Magazines, Juvenile and Young People's Magazines, or Quarterly, Literary, and "Little" Magazines. Note that each magazine listed contains a statement of its editorial needs in regard to topics, slant, length, style, audience, and photos, as well as the amount paid for articles and other material.

15

On-The-Job Writing

Many college students have serious misconceptions about the importance of writing in the professions, business, and trade. They sometimes think that on-the-job writing is really quite different from scholastic composition. They believe that the writing one does in school is somehow artificial and academic compared to what they will do when they finally "go to work."

This conception is erroneous. The truth is that successful on-the-job prose has exactly the same characteristics as the writing one might do for a college class. Naturally, the student writer's audience is different from the adult audience, but a business and professional person encounters the same obligation to inform and persuade that the student does.

A second misconception which students have about business and professional writing is that a businessman does not really do much writing.

Again the facts are different. The amount and variety of on-the-job writing is immense. Consider the quantity of written communication that is necessary to keep any large corporation operating. Those who run giant corporations must be informed: their credit departments must communicate constantly, their production departments must have clear lines of communication, their distribution apparatus functions only if it has a delicate system of intercommunication, and their maintenance departments cannot be effective unless they have reliable information.

This great volume of over-the-desk writing is made up of letters, reports, memorandums, directives, proposals, and policy statements. And these illustrations are only a sample of the kinds of writing one may do on the job. The business and professional man must write constantly.

Another misconception that students have about on-the-job prose is that the quality of the writing is not really important.

Again, this notion is mistaken. A businessman's ability to write can be significant for his success. Imagine yourself high enough in the firm so that you have to rely on employees to keep you informed. Would you prefer to advance those who cannot get the facts straight? When you think about it, you will see how much your own success in a professional or business life might rely on your ability to communicate on paper.

Still another wrong idea which young people sometimes have about business and professional writing is the notion that a businessman does not do his own writing—that he can hire a clever secretary who will do it for him.

It is true that executive secretaries handle routine communications, but in all other instances the businessman, the professional man, or the man in trade must do the composition himself. Since he is the one who has to make decisions, he is also the one who must be able to inform and persuade.

A final misconception about professional and business writing is that it is a cliché-ridden world of business jargon and technical terms.

Of course, business and professional writing, like any other, has its hackneyed expressions. And it also has its own technical terms, whether they be from medicine or engineering. But this is not at all to say that business and professional writing is especially marked by jargon or by excessive technicality. The business and professional writer is as free as any other to be creatively clear and powerfully persuasive. He cannot, in his prose, stumble along or hide behind technical terms.

If you hold to any of these common misconceptions about on-the-job writing —that it is incidental, unimportant, or inferior—the examples which follow may make you see this kind of prose in a new light.

Business Letter

```
                              Rightway Farm Equipment
                              1818 Clear Street
                              San Francisco, California

                              October 29, 1968

Mr. John T. White, President
Farm Credit Bureau
105 South Avenue
Chicago, Illinois

Dear Mr. White:

Thank you for sending us the information on the new
Machine Parts Credit Book published by your firm.  In
attempting to analyze the code key which you use to
rate various businesses, we find that you're
```

attempting to give a lot more information than the other reporting agencies that we use rather extensively.

Since the great majority of our customers fall outside the industries which you list, we cannot consider at this time switching our reporting services.

But we would like to ask one question. In your code key 3 you identify a customer as being "slow but good." Number 4 indicates "slow, unsatisfactory." We would like to know how a slow pay customer could be considered a good one. Perhaps you are attempting to indicate the difference between two types of slow-pay customers; one that is a little bit slow and one that is slower than a little bit.

It has to be acknowledged that a slow-pay customer is borrowing money, interest free, to his own advantage and to the deterrent of the supplier and to his advantage over his competitors. It is the writer's opinion that the entire credit fraternity including its very valuable reporting services should continue its never ceasing battle of attempting to collect from all customers on a prompt basis. I have always felt that to report a customer slow but good was advertising defeat in convincing the customer of the propriety of terms of sale.

Anything that you would care to add to assist the writer's thinking on the subject will be deeply appreciated.

Yours very truly,

A. P. Andrews
Credit Manager

Questions

1. What is the occasion of this business letter?
2. Is the touch of humor in the third paragraph appropriate?

3. State in your own words the writer's argument against distinguishing between slow-paying customers.
4. Does the writer present his view in a dogmatic manner or does he hold open the possibility that he could be wrong?
5. Characterize the level of the language and produce two examples of the word choice peculiar to credit correspondence.

Inter-Company Directive

```
KENT AUTOMOTIVE ACCESSORIES
              COMPANY

DATE:     11/11/69

TO:       All Sales Managers - Eastern Division

FROM:     R. D. Ryan

SUBJECT:  SEAT CUSHION SALES - OCTOBER
```

One of the areas that needs our best attention is the sale of seat cushions. Washington is the only sales area in the Eastern Division which showed an improvement over a year ago on this line of merchandise. We need some specific follow-up by your salesmen. This line represents a high contribution item. Sales here bring in dollars fast. We really believe that these items get lost because your salesmen are under a great deal of pressure from all of the other products and programs we have to sell.

Why don't you review your figures and try to pinpoint exactly where the losses are. If you have some problems as to why the business has declined, let's get down to the specifics by accounts and items and work with Jack Jacobs to get this business on track and moving forward again. Jack brings to Kent some real experience in seat cushion sales, and he deserves our best help. Please review and come in with an analysis on this line, giving a copy direct to Jack so we can make plans to regain this business.

RDR:apz

cc. Jack L. Jacobs

Questions

1. In what sense is this piece a "directive"?
2. Can the pattern of problem-solution be applied to this communication?
3. Show that the writer is critical, but diplomatic, in handling the problem.
4. Illustrate the informal, conversational tone of this directive.
5. Explain the abbreviations which appear at the end of the correspondence.

Business Letter

```
                              Midwest National Bank
                              Kansas City, Missouri
                              October 9, 1969
```

Mr. B. E. Marcus, Corporate Banking Manager
Tri-City Trust Company
111 North Lake Street
Chicago, Illinois

Dear Mr. Marcus:

I was pleased to visit with you again by phone and I am sure you realize how much importance we attach to obtaining the Tri-City Trust Company account. As indicated in my conversation with you, we are willing to handle the account on a no-charge basis. We are convinced that it can and will be a profitable account for us and that our service rendered to you will be completely satisfactory.

I regret that it will be necessary for me to alter my comments somewhat regarding the amount of credit which we can extend to you. Since our legal limit is $120,000, I feel that it might be quite difficult for us to obtain an over-line commitment in the amount of $280,000. In fact, my investigation bears this out. We will, however, commit a line of $200,000 since we do have a commitment in the amount of $80,000 from one of our correspondents.

I sincerely hope that this change will not prevent us from being favored with your banking business. I feel certain that if conditions required a larger line that it would be possible for us to obtain it for you. It will, however, be necessary for us to stay with the $200,000 commitment.

Yours truly,

Phillip A. Henry
President

                                    Midwest National Bank
                                    Kansas City, Missouri
                                    November 8, 1969

Cashier
Mutual Bank & Trust
Independence, Missouri

Dear Sir: Re: Tina Jones, Acct. 34-456-7

Our mutual customer, Mrs. Tina Jones of the New House Hotel, Kansas City, Mo., has approached me several times regarding her account or accounts in your bank. This woman is an elderly widow who is thoroughly confused about her business transactions. She has a son who apparently resides in your area which accounts for the fact that she was a resident in your locality for a few weeks.

Mrs. Jones maintains a checking account in our bank. She has a difficult time in handling her account and is constantly coming in for reassurances and explanations. Her account is quite nominal and her social security is almost all she has to live on. We have, however, had information that there is a time certificate or checking account or possibly savings account in your bank. In fact, one of our officers verified this by phone some months ago. But since this lady is confused, forgetful, and suspicious, we need a letter from your bank detailing any accounts or assets you are holding for her. I feel certain that this will ease her mind and at the same time give us the information needed to advise her regarding future financial plans.

There is no conservatorship or trust involved in this matter. Mrs. Jones is simply a long-time customer of our bank and appears to rely on us in connection with these matters. She is at times quite irrational and our work with her is nothing more than an attempt to help rid her mind of these worries and frustrations.

We would sincerely appreciate having the information requested above and any information you might have regarding the manner in which her accounts are being handled in your bank.

Very truly yours,

Phillip A. Henry
President

Questions

1. State the purpose of each of the two letters.
2. How do these letters illustrate the skills and wide insight required of a successful banker?
3. The letter to the Tri-City Trust Company is "firm but friendly." Explain.
4. Discuss the level of the language in the letters. Are there examples of business-ese?
5. How do these on-the-job communications illustrate the elements of form, detail, and audience which we discussed in regard to popular and professional writing?

Memorandum

KRAMER ENGINEERING COMPANY

TO: CN - Shop Foreman

FROM: HL

Just had a phone call from Bob Weston of Weston Company. He says three of the last shipment of 100 gears we sent them split the long way through when they were put in the gear box assembly. They discontinued use. Please pick up a carton of them from their plant, have the lab analyze, run usual shop tests. Needless to say--speed!

KRAMER ENGINEERING COMPANY

TO: HL

FROM: CN

Metallurgy tests indicate poor steel. Called Weston who said their steel was not certified. (They had an awful time tracing source of that shipment--buy from 5 Chicago suppliers.) Our heat treat o.k. They have requested certification from all suppliers on future shipments. They will receive first certified shipment next Monday--will shape gears next week and we are to heat treat following week. They are junking last bunch. Glad it wasn't our fault--Bob's a tiger when he's mad!

```
                              Specialties Candy Co.
                              12/1/69
```

ATTENTION: B. G. Siebert

BOXED CHOCOLATES FUTURE ORDERS -- TED WILBER,
ROUTE 172

Wilber originally submitted orders for the large accounts in Jacksonville, Florida, for approximately 1500 cases back in early November.

Then, last week he came in wanting to defer shipment on these orders for two weeks.

In checking into the matter, I am pretty sure this was a matter of Wilber's submitting orders without any concrete understanding with the customers; and, as a consequence, we produced some 1500 cases of boxed chocolates.

After we would not let Wilber extend the shipping date, the orders were reduced to a total of 50 cases.

We are not going to do business in this manner and I suggest we get Kelly in the act and let's get Wilber straightened out on his future order tactics.

```
                              D. L. Riggs
```

Questions

1. Briefly explain the problems which occasioned the correspondence from Kramer Engineering and Specialties Candy.
2. What are some of the characteristics of memo writing as evidenced in the Kramer Engineering exchange?
3. Although the Kramer memos represent practical, across-the-desk communication, both CN and HL reveal traits of a lively, colorful style. Illustrate.
4. In the Specialties Candy memo, the point is made clearly and constructively. But show how vagueness on the part of the writer could have resulted in bad feelings on all sides.

Business Letter

```
                                    Fredericks and Kelso
                                    Counsellors at Law
                                    914 East Park Street
                                    Canfield, Pennsylvania
                                    March 13, 1968

The Barlow Packing Company
P.O. Box 140
Chancely, Kansas

            Re:  Midtown Fruit Co., Inc.
            vs:  The Barlow Packing Company

Gentlemen:

We have been retained by Midtown Fruit Co., Inc., to
resolve your indebtedness of $225.50 to our client.

Although our client's matters were temporarily
transferred to a receiver appointed by the United
States District Court, District of New Jersey, a
creditors' settlement was effectuated with the Court's
approval, and your account receivable due and
owing to our client is now being handled by this
firm for collection.

From the facts presented to us, there can be no doubt
as to your legal liability to pay the amount stated
above.

Kindly contact us within ten days of the date of this
letter as to your intentions to pay this amount, as
I am sure all concerned would like to terminate this
matter on an amicable basis.

                                    Very truly yours,

                                    FREDERICKS AND KELSO


                                    Norman S. Fredericks
```

```
                            The Barlow Packing Company
                            P. O. Box 140
                            Chancely, Kansas
                            March 18, 1968
```

Mr. Norman S. Fredericks
Attorney at Law
914 East Park Street
Canfield, Pennsylvania

                Re: Midtown Fruit Co., Inc.

Dear Mr. Fredericks:

This is to acknowledge your letter of March 13 in reference to an alleged amount of $225.50 due Midtown by Barlow. At the request of our Legal Department, I have looked into the situation and have discovered that the charge occurred over delay in delivery of product shipped back in April, 1966. The delay was due to transfer company breakdown; therefore, this can in no way be considered the fault of the supplier.

We have communication from our brokers on this matter to the effect that Mr. Irving Taylor of the Fast Freight Service, Newark, New Jersey, agreed to reimburse Midtown. This was confirmed by letter from Mr. Joseph Rosen of our Shipping Department to Mr. Ralph Barnes of Midtown by letter December 12, 1967. Copies of same sent your office March 16, 1968. Trust this disposes of the matter.

                        Very truly yours,

                        C. M. Thompson
                        Credit Manager

Questions

1. Explain the occasion for the exchange of letters between the law firm and Barlow Packing.

2. Find three examples of legal terminology in the first letter.
3. Identify the attempt at good will in the first letter.
4. What is the intended effect of the heading in the first letter—Re: Midtown Trust Co., Inc., vs. The Barlow Packing Company?
5. In your opinion, was the letter by the credit manager of Barlow Packing written in such a way that it "disposes of the matter"?

Progress Report

THE RATH PACKING COMPANY

To our stockholders:

For the first time in five years we have completed a profitable fiscal year. The level of profitability was far from satisfactory, but the turn-around program begun three years ago continued to progress and this, we think, is encouraging.

Net income for the year ended September 27, 1969 was $101,811, or $0.10 per share, including an extraordinary credit of $46,600, or $0.04 per share, arising from utilization of our federal income tax net operating loss carry-overs. This compares with a net loss of $694,208, or $0.70 per share in fiscal 1968. Net sales increased to $265,317,412 in 1969 from $236,031,707 in 1968. While tonnage shipped was approximately 5 per cent greater than the previous year, most of the increase in dollar sales was brought about by the substantially higher price levels on both raw materials and product prices which prevailed during the year.

As reflected in the balance sheet, our financial condition continued to improve. Working capital increased almost $1,700,000 principally because capital expenditures were substantially below the depreciation charged against earnings and because we were not required to make all the contributions under

---

Reprinted by permission of The Rath Packing Company.

our retirement and pension plans with respect to the 1968 plan year which otherwise would have been payable in the 1969 fiscal year. The finance company loan was $2,500,000 lower at year end than at the corresponding date a year ago. Working capital was more than double what it was two years ago and the ratio of current assets to current liabilities increased to 1.49 to 1 compared with 1.33 to 1 last year and 1.16 to 1 at the end of 1967. In short, our financial condition today is much improved from the precarious condition of two years ago.

Further significant improvements in production efficiency were accomplished during the year, but unfortunately most of these savings were used to meet the constantly increasing cost of doing business brought on by the highly inflationary trend of the economy. Our fixed expenses, which had been drastically reduced during each of the preceding two years, rose appreciably during the past year because of inflation and despite stringent measures to hold them in control.

The short-term borrowing arrangement with the finance company continued to work well. Notwithstanding upward adjustments in interest rates, our total interest cost for the year was $333,000 lower than the preceding year. We feel that the finance company is satisfied with the progress we are making and will continue to provide us with our short-term financing requirements.

Three new directors joined our Board during the year. James C. Hillier and Charles F. Swisher were elected at the Annual Meeting in January to replace two retiring directors, and Robert H. Borchers was elected in July to fill a vacancy. Dr. Hillier is Head of the Department of Animal Sciences at Oklahoma State University, Mr. Swisher is a practicing attorney and General Counsel for the Company, and Mr. Borchers is a retired Executive Vice President of Armour and Company. We are extremely pleased with these strong additions to our able Board of Directors.

Shortly after the close of the fiscal year we made extensive changes in our sales and marketing organization. Milton E. Gary, former Vice President of Sales, was elected Senior Vice President of Sales and Marketing. Frank E. Walsh, former Vice President of Marketing, resigned from the Company. Burton G. Adkins, James L. Van Hemert, and Kenneth C. Wallace were named Sales Vice Presidents, and Herbert E. Williams was named Vice President of Marketing. Other extensive executive changes in this area were also made.

This new organization is designed to provide closer co-ordination between all of our sales and marketing activities as well as more effective direction of and communication with our field sales organization. We feel that this reorganization will give real impetus to our total marketing effort, the area which holds the greatest promise for substantial improvement in the year ahead.

With the progress which has already been made and the momentum and enthusiasm which that progress has generated, we feel that 1970 could be the year in which this Company is returned to a respectable level of profitability. Industry conditions, of course, will play a vital but unpredictable role as they always do in the meat packing business, but given a reasonably favorable industry climate, we expect 1970 to be a very significant year in Rath's turn-around program.

I again express my deep appreciation for the loyalty and support of our many fine stockholders, employees, customers, and suppliers.

Harry G. Slife
President

December 10, 1969

Questions

1. What topics are discussed in this progress report?
2. Explain the meaning of the phrase "turn-around program" and show how it is a key idea in the organization of the report.
3. Are there any instances of the technical language peculiar to this industry?
4. Is the language more, or less, formal than that which appears in most popular prose? Use examples.
5. Do you believe that the "stockholders, employees, customers and suppliers" mentioned in the last line would be favorably impressed by the content and style of this report?

Letter of Recommendation

```
                              WESTERN CAN COMPANY

                              Zenith Products
                              1500 E. Maple
                              Dearborn, Michigan

                              March 24, 1970
```

TO WHOM IT MAY CONCERN:

Mary Jeanne (Scott) Robinson has been in our employ since March 7, 1969 and intends to terminate May 19, 1970. Her position with us was that of an Industrial Relations Clerk. I have read her resume and can say that her responsibilities were as stated.

When Mary Jeanne was employed by us, there was no personnel department as such at our plant. Since her employment, the department has expanded into many previously unhandled areas. The growth of the department to its present capacities is due in great part to her cooperativeness and ability to handle the addition of each new responsibility. She has been able to modify the methods used as necessary to increase the work load she carries.

For the three month period stated on her resume, she was responsible for the hiring of production personnel. This function was discontinued in January with the employment of a new supervisor who believed a modification in hiring methods was necessary to allow the department supervisors to hire their own employees rather than to have the Industrial Relations department do the hiring for them. This in no way reflects on the quality of her performance as the hiring agent during that period.

I would highly recommend her to any employer. She is a capable and efficient employee.

                                          Ralph A. Knight
                                          Plant Manager

                                          A C E Drafting Service
                                          583 Johnson Court
                                          Kirksville, Missouri

                                          January 10, 1970

Mr. John Smith, Personnel Director
Cyanite Corporation
521 Jewell Drive
Austin, Texas

Dear Mr. Smith:

In answer to your request for information regarding Mr. Justin Bowers, who has applied to your firm for employment, I hereby verify the fact that he was employed by Ace Drafting Service from August 7 to October 5, 1969, as a drafting trainee.

Your query regarding work habits and general aptitude must be answered in the affirmative; Mr. Bowers' abilities are remarkable and all of the drafting which he completed (under supervision, of course, due to his trainee status) was of the finest quality.

Unfortunately, the final qualification which you questioned, regarding personal habits and initiative, was our reason for releasing him at the end of the sixty day trial period. His absentee record shows that he was off the job one to two days each week, in most instances without reporting that he would be gone. He was three hours late on two other occasions and he seemed to be lacking in drive and enthusiasm.

It is unfortunate that a young man with his capabilities lacks incentive, but we find we cannot recommend him for the opening you mentioned. If, however, you could establish a firm working week which he would observe, and if you were able to get to the root of the personal difficulties which seem to bother him, he could become a valued employee. Our contract drafting service, since it is based on extremely high production, had neither the time nor the inclination to develop his talents.

                        Cordially,

                        Everett Akers
                        Chief Draftsman

Questions

1. Sum up the chief point made in each of the four paragraphs in the letter written in behalf of Mary Robinson.
2. In your opinion, is this letter of recommendation well written?
3. Comment on the organization of the letter concerning Justin Bowers.
4. Did the writer generalize in regard to Bowers' problem, or did he spell it out?
5. Do you believe that the Bowers' letter is unfair and subjective, or fair and objective?

Committee Report

UNIVERSITY OF NORTHERN IOWA

FACULTY SENATE MINUTES
December 22, 1969

The Faculty Senate met in Seerley 102, 3:00 p.m., December 22, 1969, Keefe presiding.

Present: Chang, Crawford, Gelb, Holmes, Schurrer, Blanford, Finegan, Lott, Ryan, Smith, Keefe, Knutson, Rhum, Thompson, Whitnah.
Alternates: Nielsen for Albrecht, McCollum for TePaske, Wilson for Poppy.

1. Extension Advisory Committee.

   Keefe recommended that Rhum be appointed to the Committee. Holmes moved this appointment. Motion was seconded and carried.

2. Evaluation of Department Heads.

   Vice-President Lang requested postponement of discussion of problems relative to the evaluation of Department Heads until he had received reports from committees studying the matter. The Senate consented, after some discussion, to this postponement.

3. Non-discrimination policy statement.

   The Senate had at hand the memorandum from the Office of the President dated November 17, 1969, recommending amendments to the University Non-Discrimination Policy Statement: that _sex_ be added to those things on the basis of which the University would not discriminate.

   Smith moved that the Senate recommend adoption of the changes suggested. Motion was seconded.

Smith moved to add to the last sentence of the preamble: <u>and nothing in this policy statement shall be construed as contrary to the principle of the University's commitment to work actively to provide opportunities for disadvantaged individuals</u>.

This amendment was voted and carried.

Motion to recommend the adoption of the recommended changes was voted and carried.

4. Thompson moved adoption of the following memorial resolution:

    As we refresh our memory of Brock Fagan, the scholar, teacher, and man, let us dispense with the customary laudatory adjectives and attend to what he stood for and meant to three generations of students, colleagues, and community friends.

    By his colleagues who knew him best, he will be remembered for his high academic standards; his interest in students who, as he said, "meant business"; and his unrelenting ironical approach to students with ability who refused to use it. His most loyal supporters were those students who, having once smarted under his demand for excellence, had themselves become older and wiser, and as teachers learned to admire him. He was respected for the right reasons, never loved for the wrong ones. As late as 1960 the most often inquired-about teachers in the department by former students were Brock Fagan and Hazel Strayer.

    By his most knowledgeable English colleagues he will be remembered for his intelligent, inductive approach to the English language and linguistics which made him an early defender of descriptive grammar as opposed to prescriptive grammar. Until about 1946-48 when younger men with special knowledge of the English language were brought into the department, Brock

Fagan was, by dint of self-education, years ahead of his colleagues in this discipline.

He will be remembered for his philosophical habit of mind which often illuminated both sides of a controversy, his humor and salty wit, and especially for his subtle, gentle irony, the indelible mark of the civilized man. Were he alive among us today at forty years of age, he would understand the country's campus dissidents: he was an early faculty pioneer in the controversy himself as he urged the use of the democratic process in all campus affairs. Indeed, in a very real sense he lived too soon. As he grew older it was the newer, younger staff members who understood him best, and accepted him as a modern fellow spirit in academic life. He was withal an unusual combination of the classical eighteenth-century man of reason, order, and restraint; and of the twentieth-century inductive investigator who accepts a democratic morality as his first article of faith.

Requiescat.

H. W. Reninger

Motion was seconded and carried.

Meeting adjourned, 4:15 p.m.

Respectfully submitted,

Merrill F. Fink
Secretary pro tem

These minutes shall stand approved as published unless corrections or protests are filed with the Secretary of the Senate within two weeks of this date, Monday, December 22, 1969.

Questions

1. Explain the purpose of recording and distributing senate minutes and show how they afford us an example of on-the-job prose.
2. What technique does the writer use to structure the main topics?
3. Examine the language in this report. Can the use of formal terms be justified? Provide specific examples.
4. According to the text, "The business and professional writer is as free as any other to be creatively clear and powerfully persuasive." Show how this statement can be applied to the memorial resolution in item 4.

Memorandum

```
                    HISTORY DEPARTMENT

                    BRANCHTOWN UNIVERSITY


TO:    Dean Forsythe, Dean Baker, Dr. McHale, and all
       members of the History Department.

FROM:  Dr. William Van Horton

SUBJECT: The present probation system in the History
         Department.


       I should like to register my opinion of the
present system of probation in the History Department.
I think the method now employed, which requires that
all new teachers be subjected for a period of three
years to class inspection visits by tenured colleagues
and to written evaluations by their students, is wrong
for several reasons.

       In the first place, the system makes no
distinctions between experienced teachers and scholars
on the one hand, and raw recruits on the other.
Everyone, regardless of his experience, is subjected
to the same three years of examination. I submit that
for an experienced teacher this is at best an
```

impertinence and at worst an indignity. The present method does not keep good men away because of their fear of being inspected and scrutinized so much as it does because they conclude that a school that employs such a method is likely to impugn their professional status and deny their independence. To subject an experienced scholar to this method is to deny the validity of his experience and to question whatever recommendations were written in his behalf.

In the second place, the present method is out of step with every large university I know of. With no such rigorous method they seem to attract and keep good scholars. It takes no genius to realize that this department, as now constituted, consists of a tiny elite of senior members and an enormous proletariat of relatively inexperienced teachers, with little in between. Why, I ask, does this department find it difficult to get, and keep, good men? There are perhaps several reasons, and the probation system may be one of them.

In the third place, the present method fosters quiescence in the new men and makes of those who have tenure not colleagues but judges. If anyone denies that a gulf exists between the tenured members and the new arrivals, regardless of their abilities or experience, he does not know this department. No fraternity in this country, no matter how exclusive or excluding, would dare employ such a method.

In the fourth place, there is an absurdity in the assumption that it takes three years to know whether anyone is acceptable or not. One way of removing the dubious necessity for the present method would be to hire with care and intelligence. Another would be to judge the inexperienced with discretion and tolerance, and to respect the majority decision of a fair number of judges at the end of the first or second year.

In the fifth place, there are several facets not now covered by the present method. One of these is a man's ability to function on committees. Freshman

Congressmen may not be given chairmanships or positions on key committees, but they are not excluded from every committee, as they are in this department, for three years. If that were the case, some Congressmen would be out of office before they had served on a single committee. Another objection to the present practice of keeping a new man cooling his heels in the antechambers of the great for three years is that it is a waste of talent and ability. Who knows? Some of the recent arrivals may have something valuable to contribute.

In the sixth place, now that this school is at least nominally a university it might begin to let a man's scholarship as well as his pedagogical prowess enter into the equation that determines whether he is indeed in a state of grace or whether he is to be cast into outer darkness.

In the seventh place, one should be judged only by men of tried experience who are committed to, and skilled in, the subject being examined. I see no satisfactory way of separating technique from matter.

In the eighth place, I suggest a greater tolerance for different techniques; there are different roads to salvation, and the choice of road should not be dictated by any dogma dear to the examiner.

In conclusion, I suggest that those who enter the department with substantial experience be completely exempt from the present method of scrutiny, and that those with little or no experience be judged in the first year and put into one of three categories: those who pass without qualification and who are then free from further examination; those who pass, but with reservations; and those who fail. The judges' reservations, in the case of the second category, could then be given to some senior member of the department particularly interested in that course and the probationer coached on ways to overcome his shortcomings. By the end of the second year the university should know whether the probationer is hopeful or hopeless.

Questions

1. Explain how this memo is an example of on-the-job writing.
2. Before one can write persuasively, he must clarify his stand on the issue. How well does Dr. Van Horton handle this point?
3. Discuss the organization of this piece and the strategy used in presenting the arguments.
4. In your opinion, is the tone and language of the memo appropriate for the subject and intended audience?
5. How convincing is this argument? Do you think it might help bring about some changes in the tenure program at Branchtown University?

Suggested Writing Assignments

1. Analyze three or four of the selections in the text in an effort to pin down the chief characteristics of over-the-desk communications. Attempt to identify and illustrate the features which these pieces have in common.
2. Assume that you are the recipient of one of the text letters, directives, or memos, and write an appropriate answer. In trying your hand at business writing, remember to imitate the layout, tone, and style which would be required.
3. Request some samples of on-the-job writing from local businesses, professions, and trades. Such material could be obtained from teachers, administrators, doctors, psychiatrists, lawyers, and businessmen in the area—with the names of the persons involved changed. Then analyze the correspondence on the basis of purpose, tone, word choice, audience, and other elements representative of business writing.
4. Compose a good and a bad example of on-the-job writing on the same topic. In the first instance, illustrate the positive elements which are found in effective business correspondence. Then write the same letter, progress report, or memo in which you do everything wrong.

16

School and College Writing

There is an abundance of student writing, both in class and out. College students are often asked to write expository or analytic essays, term papers, lab reports, and essay tests. And if they go on to professional school, they are asked to do even more writing.

But beyond such obvious and mandatory outlets for the student author, there are extracurricular opportunities for campus writing. Schools and colleges have student newspapers, yearbooks, and magazines. In addition, those who are active in student government must write up their resolutions, political speeches, or handbills. In fact, with the new black and white political activism on our campuses, schools reflect many of the same political currents that run through the whole society. And lastly, students write letters to prospective employers, to their girl or boyfriends, and to their parents. In short, a campus mirrors society as far as writing is concerned, and it both requires and invites student authors to try to inform and persuade.

Even so, young writers are often confused about an obvious point: they sometimes forget that the quality of writing their teachers ask for is exactly the same as the quality of any good writing. If you write a personal letter, it will be more impressive if you are mindful of the fundamental principles of organizing your thoughts and feelings. While composition standards are obviously relevant to a letter of application, they are also relevant to a love letter. And the same is true of a lab report, an essay examination, or a research paper. They are all written compositions and should have the same sort of clarity, precision, and organization that is described in earlier sections of this book.

And most important, the quality of your writing directly affects your success. High school and college classes now encourage discussion and it can be an important part of your performance, but you must remember that discussion is necessarily ephemeral. Teachers can mull over and carefully evaluate your written essays, whereas an oral discussion literally vanishes into thin air. It is no wonder, then, that teachers must rely heavily on the more permanent written record. For this reason alone it can count more than other facets of your contribution.

One of the places where your power to compose is important is in devising answers to essay questions. It is true that objective tests are in vogue and educators claim they can test anything with multiple choice questions, but many of your teachers still rely on essay answers and these require that you compose an impromptu essay.

Take, for one example, this open-ended question:

"The primary cause of America's Civil War was a deep division in the nation over slavery. Discuss."

Faced with a question like this, a student would do well to fall back on the phase of composition we call "prewriting." Having first collected his thoughts on the question by writing down on a scratch sheet what comes to mind, he could then structure his material around, say, other causes of the war, pro and con evidence on slavery as a major issue, with a closing paragraph which affirms his belief that slavery was indeed the "primary cause" of the Civil War.

Whatever course one pursues, he must come up with a good "little" composition: an introduction, development of the thesis, and an appropriate closing.

In addition to the common essay exam, there is another standard college exercise, the research paper. An important distinction to make about research writing is that it can be broadly of two kinds: the formal and the informal, the strictly academic or a more popular form. And when we make this distinction between formal and informal research, we do not imply that one is necessarily any better than another, anymore than we would say that formal dress is superior to informal dress.

Some of the characteristics of formal research are that the information is chiefly derived from books, the data is collected on note cards, all sources are footnoted in the text, either at the bottom of the page or at the end of the article, and a list of all of the sources, a bibliography, is placed at the end of the essay. Other marks of the formal research essay are that it will usually contain technical terminology, conventional grammatical construction, and follow a formal style in the choice of words and their arrangement.

As you know from your study of the popular prose selections in this book, informal research is usually done for a less specialized and a less academic audience; hence the topics are general in nature. The length also tends to be shorter than formal exercises. In informal research, moreover, there is no listing of periodicals at the end of the exercise, and references to authors and books are included within the text itself.

As a student, you will certainly be called upon to write both impromptu essays and the more carefully planned and researched compositions. If you have been working through this book, you should now have some insight into the essential qualities of popular prose, professional and business prose, on-the-job, and student writing. You should see that any good writing displays certain basic principles of form and content which are the same no matter what the occasion.

Student Article

A Freshman Speaks: College May Be Hazardous to Your Health

JENNY MATTHEWS

A friend of mine once speculated, "Wouldn't it be wonderful if we could get 15 units of credit (a normal quarter's work) for taking off by ourselves with just cameras, writing paper and back packs so we could spend the quarter traveling around and learning about life?"

"In other words," I retorted, "give us 15 units of credit for no work?"

"But how are we ever going to learn about living," she went on, "if studying leaves no time for it? How is a student supposed to grow up and find out about the world outside when he's always cooped up *inside* behind a desk and a bunch of books?"

Growing up and discovering the world outside? That rarely took place for me in a classroom. Few of my professors seemed to be concerned with it.

When I try to think back on the most significant educational experiences of my freshman year at Stanford, I come to the conclusion that hardly any of them occurred in a classroom or behind a desk. This realization is nothing new, I guess. Students have been complaining for years about the irrelevance of much of their formal education.

But when courses, exams and papers start to conflict with a student's desire for other types of learning—discussing problems with friends, following current events, becoming involved in politics, doing free reading and spending time in idle speculation—a hard choice must be made.

Do I help my roommate work out the problems that are getting her terribly depressed or do I spend the next three hours plowing through Thucydides' account of the Peloponnesian Wars?

Should I read Alan Watts and Erich Fromm's *The Art of Loving* tonight or should I put up with St. Augustine's pratings for tomorrow's class discussion?

For the serious student there would be no question about what to do. "You are at this hallowed institution to get an education," the old maxim declares, "and if you don't take advantage of the opportunities, you are wasting your time."

"I am here to get a college education," I would try to convince my sleepy head as I stayed up the entire night before an exam.

A college education . . . books, studying, papers, studying, exams, studying . . . Caution: It may be hazardous to your health.

The lounge of my dormitory at 3 a.m. looked like a battleground in the wake of a terrible slaughter. All around there were bodies trying to "crash" on the floor to gain a few minutes of blissful relief.

Other bodies were trying to keep themselves upright in chairs while they forced more and more material into their unwilling minds. Still others were sleepily hunting and pecking on typewriters in order to add to the reams of written papers mass-produced at the end of each quarter.

"What kind of garbage are you writing?" someone asked a dazed typist.

"Worm-infested," was the response.

Reprinted from *Pace* Magazine (a Division of Pace Programs, Inc.), November, 1969, by permission.

"You mean, 'word-infested,'" a dozing body commented from the couch.

"My professor is a sadistic slave driver," the typist continued.

I thought of a discussion I had recently had with a professor. "I'm just a poor, overworked instructor who's trying to do his best for his students," he had said. Pointing tragically to a gigantic stack of blue books and written work, "Do you see all those papers? Well, I have to read them all by tomorrow morning."

So here we students were, killing ourselves to produce papers and write decent exams so professors could subsequently kill themselves reading them all.

A friend of mine once told me that at her university a "Suicide-Prevention Service" is set up during every finals' week.

I, therefore, ask the age-old question, "Is this 'education'?"

It gets you a degree. Surviving through one set of exams gives you a little computer sheet with a row of capital letters which, in the proper combination, "entitles" you to go through similar agony next quarter.

It may even open your eyes to the wonders of coffee and NoDoz (or something stronger).

Yet a college degree is a prerequisite for membership in the "community of scholars." And the concept of such a community, in which everyone is obsessed with his own academic pursuits, used to fascinate me. When I first got to Stanford, was I impressed with all the PhDs and graduate students and full-fledged professors walking around! My feet were treading on hallowed ground!

I was overwhelmed.

But upperclassmen chided me for such "freshman" opinions, warning, "Just wait until you meet a few immature and socially misfit PhDs. Just because a person has a long string of degrees after his name doesn't mean he's learned how to live.

"A person can use academics as a way of escaping from life, you know."

"What kind of blasphemy is this?" I wondered at first, but as my educational career progressed and as classes got more and more meaningless, I began to believe it.

I was saddened when another Stanford student told me about the consistent suicide rate among college students. Studying is grueling, escape is often longed for but I never imagined that a student could be driven to destroy himself.

"Oh, students rarely kill themselves because of academic pressures," the student explained. "They usually come to the conclusion that life is just a lonely, meaningless existence. They look for a purpose, and when they find none they see no reason to go on."

Life, purpose . . . living and its problems . . . in which academic course is a student taught how to live?

It's been said that the younger generation is too preoccupied with such concerns. It's a function of our affluence or something. Maybe we are a new breed.

Maybe a freshman year free of requirements, free of the pressure of grades, free for independent exploration and independent thinking would give a student more time to confront the new world he is thrust into.

Sometimes I used to get the impression that it didn't really matter if I was satisfied with what I was learning as long as the instructor was. Often in the middle of a class discussion in which students were graded for their participation, I would listen to competitive students spout out illogical and often worthless statements and I'd want to scream.

Why should I have to *impress* someone with what I've learned? What I learn is for *my* benefit, isn't it? Why should I care if you're impressed?

And since I sincerely believe that students are hungry for the knowledge that is relevant to their lives, I think they're entitled to sufficient time at the beginning of their college careers—perhaps most of their freshman year—to sniff around for this knowledge without the pressure of fulfilling antediluvian course schedules and without having constantly to ask the question, "Tonight . . . should I learn what I want . . . or learn what I'm going to be tested on tomorrow?"

The student should be entitled, furthermore, to pursue knowledge without the fear of making mistakes. One of the major faults in our entire educational system is that it doesn't allow for mistakes. "We learn through our mistakes," our teachers tell us in an attempt to comfort us for points deducted and grades lowered for incorrect work. Yet the points are still deducted. Trial and error may be a legitimate technique for the researcher who has had enough experience with knowledge to realize that that's the way most of it has evolved. But when the student errs, the student suffers.

I am not dissatisfied with the overall scope of my learning at Stanford. My greatest educational experiences, of course, were the ungraded ones—those that helped me to cope with the new life I was leading, since I was female, suddenly 18, and 2,000 miles away from home. And they included. . . .

. . . Joining seminars and discussions in my dormitory (which helped me not only to feel that I was a participating member in my own generation but that I was also not alone in the confusing struggle for maturity and identity).

. . . Working for the *Stanford Daily* (which helped me stay tuned to what was happening both inside and outside Stanford's "Eucalyptus Curtain"—heartily recommended for the diligent graduate student who hasn't yet had the time to find out who won last November's Presidential election).

. . . Working for $1.65 an hour clearing tables in the student union (a must, if you think that tuition money grows on trees or that the workers of the world are happy with their lot in life).

. . . Spending time "blowing my mind" in the main library and amid the shelves of paperback books in the bookstore (all around there are rows and rows of books that are crying out to be read. You're surrounded, engulfed, by knowledge and it's all free, just waiting for you to find out about it).

. . . Lying under a palm tree and wondering why a blue sky and a yellow kite are just made for each other . . .

I once asked a senior friend, who was studying at his desk one Friday night, to join an encounter group that a number of the people in my dorm were organizing. He looked at me somewhat regretfully and said, "I've never let myself take the time to do that kind of thing. I've always allowed studying to take precedence over every thing . . . And I guess I've never really had the chance to get to know people."

He sure has missed something . . .

And after a number of spring student demonstrations at Stanford, a conservative student was once asked, "What were you doing while the radicals were busy demonstrating?"

He replied, "I was busy studying."

Yet there are students (and some professors) who believe that political activism, demonstrating and even getting arrested are educational experiences that greatly enhance personal development.

Of course the demonstrators' grades suffered. And because of my job, my coffeehouse discussions and my Free U. classes, my course work often suffered. But I would probably look back on my freshman year as a rather insignificant expanse of time had I missed these experiences because I was "busy studying."

Questions

1. State the writer's thesis in your own words and indicate the line of thought which is given as support.
2. Illustrate the use of effective quotation, humor, and slang.
3. Identify two of the major arguments which the student gives in making his case.
4. Provide one objection to the writer's case against the traditional system of teaching which he might have acknowledged and answered in this paper.
5. Does the writer present a wholly negative view of the college learning experience or does he include positive elements as well? Base your answer on concrete examples.

The Campus Newspaper

A Handful of Dust

GARY BRITSON

T. S. Eliot wrote "I will show you fear in a handful of dust." These words are particularly relevant at the end of a decade in which human beings have been reduced to dust—by war, by bigotry, but most of all by neglect.

But this editorial is not going to be about Vietnam or Alabama or Biafra. It is about Roberta Albert.

There is a girl by the name of Roberta Albert who is a patient at University Hospitals. She has been a patient there for eight months.

To be more specific, she has been a kidney patient there for eight months. She has suffered kidney failure. Years ago, back in the old days when we were not civilized, she would have died quickly. But things are different now. There is a machine, a complicated machine with a complicated name, and this machine is keeping Roberta Albert from dying.

But machines, even in this civilized, sophisticated, with-it world, seldom constitute eternal panaceas. Soon the machine will no longer be able to help Roberta Albert. She needs a kidney transplant.

Someone did some research once and came up with the estimate that our physical beings are worth about $2 in terms of household materials—soap and stuff like that. After you eliminate all the blood, veins and arteries and all the other goodies and get down to that unattractive organ called a kidney, you find that a kidney—in terms of hard cash—is probably worth about as much as a newspaper.

But dig this. If Roberta Albert is going to stay alive, someone is going to have to come up with $20,000 for the operation. $20,000. That's not a misprint.

Go home for the holidays. Eat, drink, laugh, listen to music. Listen to the deejays tell you to be full of Christmas cheer. Listen

---

The Daily Iowan (University of Iowa), December 20, 1969. Reprinted by permission.

to the songs that say this is the age of Aquarius, the age of harmony, understanding, sympathy and trust. Go to church and be thankful.

For this is the season of cheer and merriment, buying Christmas presents and buying funny cards and receiving expensive presents. But unless the twenty grand materializes, Christmas, Thanksgiving and all the other vacations and all the other days of their lives will be ruined for the family of an unknown Iowa girl whose ten-cent kidneys suddenly decided to quit.

I realize that you don't have $20,000. But I also realize that you pay a lot of taxes—whether or not you like them. But, after everyone in this civilization gets done paying taxes, there's a hell of a lot of money in somebody's hands.

Whose?

I don't know his name but I do know what he'll be doing on December 25. Or rather, I know what he will not be doing on Christmas Day. He will not be dying in a hospital. He will not be in desperate need of twenty thousand dollars.

There was a picture in the paper this week of a Christmas tree. It is a famous Christmas tree and it stands big and green and beautiful in front of a beautiful house on Pennsylvania Avenue in Washington, D.C. I haven't checked the statistics, but it is reasonable to assume that after they pay for the lights on this famous tree, after they pay for the electric bill to light the lights for several weeks, after they pay the gardeners to take care of the tree, after they feed the tree, after they pay someone to decorate the tree, after all of these things are done for this magnificent symbol of Christmas and beauty and the Christmas spirit of love and humanity and brotherhood, after all of these things are done, a lot of money will have been spent. Maybe even $20,000.

Do you see what Eliot was getting at? "I will show you fear in a handful of dust." He followed that with another: "I think we are in rat's alley."

Questions

1. Indicate the writer's purpose, the who, what, where, when, and why information, and the chief supporting ideas.
2. Is there any evidence in this piece to indicate that it was composed by a student writer for the school paper?
3. What use does the writer make of the fact that ". . . our physical beings are worth about $2 in terms of household materials. . . ."?
4. What is the technique used to tie together the opening and closing lines?
5. How convincing was the writer?

Campus Letter to the Editor

Experienced Vet Backs Moratorium

Just two weeks after I had arrived in Vietnam in May of 1966, I was informed that one of my best friends—a college "egghead," but a rotten soldier—was killed after almost completing a field "orientation." Just five days prior to that, he was bidding goodbye to his parents and his fiancee. How would you like to have been the deliverer of the telegram that read, "It is our duty and regret to inform you. . ."? Can you imagine how his folks felt?

Shortly afterward, my sergeant landed in Walter Reed Hospital with a piece of shrapnel in his brain. He wound up a "vegetable" and I wound up with a tent full of holes. Claymore mines are very effective "air-conditioning" but hell at discriminating.

Purple "Shaft" Reward

Then another friend of mine decided to peek around a tree to get a look at a sniper we had cornered—the sniper got a peek first. My lucky friend is now able to raise his disfigured arm to the height of his deformed shoulder. I found this fact out when I caught up with my buddy in a hospital in Japan. Oh, yes! I was lucky—but three close-calls is all you get in the Nam. Nothing heroic—just did my damn job and was rewarded with the Purple "Shaft" and the doctor's observation that he didn't think they'd have to amputate my leg.

After six or seven weeks, when I was allowed a wheelchair, I reported every afternoon to the whirlpool bath. There I met a guy with half of a face. He told me (it is hard to understand someone with just half a mouth) that he, too, had been "lucky". He and three other Marines were hit with Napalm (remember that only we have Napalm.) Two men died instantly, and the third was apparently asphyxiated—napalm literally sucks the air out of your lungs. The young Marine I had talked to explained how he had just been splattered with a little of this jellied gasoline. He tried to wipe it off. He got enough off to save his life, but he also wiped off half of his face and has a worthless, "skin-and-bone" right hand. He took pride in showing me how well be could write, already, with his left hand.

Some Return In Coffins

There were many more young men I befriended while in the hospital. Some with amputated limbs, napalm burns, incurable diseases (some will never see home unless a cure is found), and many others with mental and physical disorders. Many come back in coffins draped with the U.S. flag. Some of the coffins have bodies in them, some contain plastic or rubberized bags with indescribable contents, and some contain only sand.

As disgusting, offensive, and appalling as these experiences and observations may seem to you, I hope that you take them constructively by giving ear to an alternative—"Peace, Dignity, and Courtesy." The Moratorium on the Vietnam War, Wednesday, Oct. 15, promises to be such a humane experience. For your support, others may live without fear, degradation or shame.

MICHAEL J. KNIEVEL

Northern Iowan (University of Northern Iowa), October 10, 1969. Reprinted by permission.

Questions

1. In this letter, the writer's purpose is to win reader support for the Moratorium on the Vietnam War. Does he employ good strategy in holding his thesis until the last paragraph? Explain.
2. Briefly illustrate the use of narration as a unifying device in this piece.
3. Provide two examples of the effective use of slang.
4. A common error in student writing is the lack of specific supporting detail. Is this writer weak, or strong, in the use of concrete detail?
5. In your opinion, did the writer build a strong enough case for the moratorium to win over or strongly influence those readers who were opposed to it?

Campus Newspaper Article

Barriers Tumble If You Are Willing To Learn

ROBERT P. HOGAN

At the age of 17 Grace Wong had a strong interest, in fact a love, for science. She also decided, at that tender age, that she wanted "something more practical than pure science."

So Grace looked to the western hemisphere for her University studies and, in the summer of 1967, arrived in a strange country to enroll in the College of Home Economics at Iowa State University.

Miss Wong had prepared herself well for the western ways. How? Like any teenager would, of course.

"I read all the teenage magazines I could get my hands on," she frankly reports. "They are very helpful."

Today the affable and articulate young lady is a 20-year-old senior in dietetics with extra emphasis in biochemistry and organic chemistry to better prepare her for graduate work.

She hasn't been back home since enrolling in the university. Home is Hong Kong, perhaps 9,000 miles from the campus here, a trip that is too costly for her slim budget. She has permitted herself few idle moments, partly to offset any homesickness and partly to satisfy her insatiable desire to experience and witness as much of the American life as possible while on a student visa.

Lives 'American'

By design she has lived in a University residence hall, spent one academic quarter living-in in a sorority house, and is now a second-year member of an American family, the Robert McCarleys of Ames.

Her first Iowa summer was with a classmate, Ann Ryerson, a daughter of the R. A. Ryersons of Council Bluffs. While there she fulfilled one of the dreams of all teenagers when Mr. Ryerson taught her to drive the

---

News of Iowa State (Iowa State University), January-February, 1970. Reprinted by permission.

family auto. Last summer the ISU coed traveled in California then worked for two months at the convention facility operated at Green Lake, Wis., by the American Baptist Assembly.

The budding dietician is establishing a fine academic record. She will receive her degree in November, two quarters ahead of schedule. And one contributing reason for her accelerated program is that she tested out of several courses, enough to give her 21 credits while exempting her from taking the course work. A second-year student in the Honors Program which is offered to students with high ability and achievement, her cumulative grade point is 3.65, not far from a perfect 4.00.

Perhaps the highlight in her active University career came last year when she was a member of the Iowa State Singers. "It was a tremendous experience and I really hated to give it up. It was my hardest decision. I just felt that with my other work I couldn't give enough energy, time and devotion to it."

With Keynotes

She still continues as a member of the Cardinal Keynotes which, like the Singers, is under the direction of W. Douglas Pritchard.

Miss Wong has many other interests. She is president of Omicron Nu, home economics honorary, and is a member of another professional honorary Phi Epsilon Omicron, the Food and Nutrition Club, Cosmopolitan Club, and the American Home Economics Association. As one of nearly 150 Chinese students on campus, she is active in the Chinese Students Association.

Grace believes that "students here are more liberal and open" than their counterparts in China "but then maybe that is because I am comparing college students with the high school students in Hong Kong." She is certain about another fact: "I study two or three times as hard as I did in Hong Kong, not that it is necessarily harder but it seems to take more time. There are more quizzes in college but they tend to keep me from getting behind."

Willing to Learn

This practical 20-year-old coed has adapted easily to the college scene.

"I have not found it hard to become accustomed to the American ways," she reports. "If you are willing to learn, that is all it takes. I have not had to try very hard to become adjusted."

She fields political questions gingerly, especially on issues like the Viet Nam war. She threads her way delicately in responding to inquiries on such subjects. For instance, queried on her feelings on the recent moratoriums, she responded: "I try to learn from observing such things. I am not sure of my own standing, so I learn a lot by watching."

If she maintains that pace she may become a politician as well as a dietician.

Questions

1. Is this piece designed to appeal to a college audience?
2. Would you call this an interview or a personality sketch? If you are in doubt, look again at the sections on these forms of popular prose.
3. Does the writer give us any real insight into Miss Wong's character or do we stay outside the personality?
4. The last two paragraphs contain such expressions as "fields political questions," "threads her way," and "maintains that pace." Are they metaphorical and are they appropriate to the piece?

5. Judging from this sample of his work, do you believe this student writer has a future as a professional journalist? Provide some specific evidence in your answer.

Underground Press

Law (and Order But Justice?) In America

TERRY CANNON

If you didn't know anything about how the law works in America, if all you did was read the papers, you would know that American courts and American law are the enemies of the people. If you're too poor to pay the rent, who puts you out on the street? The law. If workers go out on a wildcat strike, who lays an injunction down on them? The law. When people rebel against tyranny, what does the President call for? Law—law and order.

Law is the tool that politicians and businessmen use to keep down the people they oppress.

Did you ever hear of a cop busting in the head of a supermarket owner because he charged too much for food? Was Lyndon Johnson ever arrested for the murder of Vietnamese? No. Law is the billyclub of the oppressor. He isn't about to use it on himself.

Let's take "a typical case of American blind justice," as Arlo Guthrie says. A man gets arrested. The heavy odds are he's a working man, a poor man, or black or brown. The gyp artists, price fixers, money lenders, war profiteers, capitalists—they don't get arrested. So first of all the defendant comes from certain classes of society.

To get out of jail you have to pay money. We got rid of the poll tax a few years ago; you don't have to pay to vote. But you still have to pay to get out of jail. Freedom under the legal system is a commodity you have to buy—if you got enough money. If you can't bribe your way out you stay in until you come to trial. Most felony cases do not come to trial for a year or more from the time of arrest. This time does not count toward your sentence! If you get 5 in the pen, that means 6½ in jail, counting the time you spent waiting trial.

So you make it to trial. You have to buy a lawyer. A lawyer gets paid per case: the more cases he has the more money he makes.

A lawyer, like any other businessman, makes money on a high turnover. He gets $100 just for filing a piece of paper that takes him an hour to write. A three-week trial cuts him out from handling a lot of flat-fee deals that are pure profit. The economic system pressures him to avoid trials. He doesn't want you to go to trial—he'll lose money.

Trials cost the city, county, state, or country big money to put on. The government and the judges don't want trials. If you can't afford a lawyer, you are assigned a Public Defender. Since there are so many people who can't afford lawyers, the Public Defender is loaded down with cases. He gets

---

Abas, July 22, 1969. Copyright © 1969 by *Abas* Magazine.

paid a salary so the more cases he gets the more work, but no more money. He wants to get cases out of the way fast. He doesn't want a trial.

NOBODY IN THE LEGAL SYSTEM WANTS A TRIAL BY JURY—EXCEPT THE DEFENDANT.

Trial by jury—the right given us in the Bill of Rights—is the exception, not the rule. Only a tiny fraction of legal cases ever come before a jury. Trial by jury is a shuck promise—the name of the legal game is "How'd you like to cop a plea?"

"Copping a plea" runs like this. The District Attorney meets with the lawyer and offers to drop 4 of the 5 charges against you if you will agree to plead guilty to the fifth charge. The reason you had five charges against you in the first place is that the cop who busted you knows that a deal will be made so he adds on a lot of extra charges to make sure that you are found guilty of one of them.

The lawyer, the District Attorney and the judge gang up on the defendant. They put it simply: cop a plea and the judge will go light. Insist on a trial by jury and you'll get the maximum. Some judges will tell a defendant point blank: plead guilty and you get 6 months; go for a jury trial and you get a year. Few defendants have the resources or the knowledge of the law to withstand the pressure.

(They say that ignorance of the law is no excuse—but who the hell keeps us ignorant of the law? Who writes legal verdicts in hocus-pocus language full of Whereases and Parties of the First Part? Who sets up the legal system in terms of back-room and countryclub deals where the average person can't even get in the door? Not us, brothers and sisters, not us.)

If you make it past this part—and most don't—you get a trial by jury. The "law" says that a man has a right to a jury of his peers, which means people like himself. Jury members don't get paid (maybe they get $5 a day). Working people can't afford to serve on juries; they can't take a pay cut down to $5 a day for two or three weeks. Black and Third World people are excluded from juries by District Attorneys because they have a tendency to go easy on people like them, knowing the reasons why their brothers and sisters are forced to commit crimes. Juries are also selected from the voting rolls of the county. Non-whites tend not to register to vote because they know that voting doesn't mean anything. Young people are also kicked off juries for the same reasons.

That leaves the middle class and the rich, who fill most juries. They are the classes of order and they sit in judgment on the classes of rebellion.

You face a jury of people who share none of your experiences, know nothing of your motivations, and who are threatened by the desires and angers of your people. When you plead your case you are not allowed to use motivation to defend yourself.

Were you poor, hungry, sick and tired? Were you unemployed? Did you have to break the law just to survive? Were you mad, or too proud? American class justice does not recognize these as defenses. All we want to know, buster, says the court, is did you rip off that liquor store, or get drunk, or call a rally without a permit?

After the jury finds you guilty, the judge lays down the sentence on you. The judge owes his job to the people who run the state; he serves the rulers. In California several months ago, a congressman called a meeting of Superior Court judges. He laid it on the line. He told them that if he caught any of them giving light sentences to student demonstrators, they would face "well-financed opposition" to their re-election as judges.

The election of judges is a farce anyway. A retiring judge usually agrees to resign in the middle of his term. The State Governor appoints his successor—from a lower court. This gives the Governor another spot to fill and makes sure that the lower court judges kiss up to him in order to get higher court appointments. Once appointed, a judge runs in election unopposed (unless he goes against the wishes of the ruling class and they put up a "well-financed" campaign against him).

People take trial by jury, freedom from illegal search and seizure and free speech for granted. The Constitution as written says nothing about the rights of the people. The original Constitution is an aristocratic, racist document. The first ten amendments, the Bill of Rights, were only added to the Constitution after the left-wing of the revolutionary aristocracy under Thomas Jefferson forced its acceptance.

In practice, the aristocratic, racist intention of the Constitution is carried over in the application of our so-called legal rights. The Bill of Rights has never set well with those who profit from the business of racism, war-making, and industry.

Last year a group of Congressmen confronted a member of the Justice Department, demanding to know why Stokely Carmichael hadn't been busted. The Justice Department man was a little embarrassed.

"He hasn't committed any crimes we can get him on," he said.

"What about all that stuff he says?" said a Congressman.

"He's protected by the First Amendment," said the Justice Department man.

"Well, then what are we going to do about that goddam First Amendment?" the Congressman shouted.

Questions

1. Indicate the thesis of this student-written article and briefly illustrate the chronological nature of the supporting material.
2. Provide two or three specific examples of the research which went into the writing of this piece.
3. Cite three examples of the colloquial, straight-from-the-shoulder style of the writer.
4. Has this young writer learned to save some good material for his closing?
5. Identify what you believe to be some of the strengths and weaknesses of this article.

Essay Questions and Answers

MID-TERM EXAM -- THE AMERICAN NOVEL

DIRECTIONS: Provide brief but specific answers to the following questions. Read each question carefully and remember to proofread. This is a fifty-minute test.

1) Define the proletarian novel. (5 points)
   The proletarian novel tells the story of the working man or the poor man from his point of view.

It shows the evil practices of the rich and disparages capitalism while putting the common man in a good light.

2) <u>Define the naturalistic novel.</u> (5 points)
In the naturalistic novel, the author treats his subject matter like a scientist would and shows that people are acted <u>upon</u> by forces outside their control. No free will is shown by the characters. This type of novel tends to depict the simple form of man and shows many of his baser inclinations.

3) <u>List four general characteristics of existentialism.</u> (8 points)
   1. Existence comes before essence.
   2. Life in this universe is absurd.
   3. Man is alienated from God, nature, himself, and others; "God is dead" theory of Nietzsche.
   4. Reason is impotent to deal with the depths of man; there are too many "dark places" in man that cannot be handled by reason alone.

4) <u>Explain the major conflict in the novel, "Miss Ravenel's Conversion."</u> (12 points)
It would seem to be that of a moral issue which we have dealt with in all these novels. De Forest seems more interested in discussing the Civil War in moral tones. He wants to show what this kind of thing does to man in his relationship to other men.

5) <u>One theme that is present in all of the realistic novels we have read this semester is the contrast between two ways of life -- forthright simplicity and subtle sophistication. Show how this contrast is used in "Miss Ravenel's Conversion" and "Huckleberry Finn."</u> (20 points)
The major proponents of simplicity in <u>Miss Ravenel's Conversion</u> are Lillie Ravenel and Captain Colburne. Lillie is honest and direct in her feelings -- she loves her father, the South, and

---

Printed with permission of Mary Jo Girsch.

Colonel Carter with a childlike devotion that borders on adoration. She never tries to hide this love and is in fact openly proud of it. Colburne is naively patriotic: in his poem "A National Hymn" he calls upon God to save the stars and stripes and "let truth and justice reign." He, like Lillie, expresses his feelings in an open and simple manner.

In contrast to these two characters are Colonel Carter and Mrs. Larue. They are both experienced in the ways of the world and sophisticated in their love affair. They secretly rendezvous in a private room behind Carter's offices and thus deceive his wife. They cover their amours with an outward show of decorum and Carter can walk from Larue's arms to his wife's with no sign of guilt.

Simplicity meets sophistication abruptly when Lillie discovers the affair. Although she is badly shaken by Carter's unfaithfulness, she faces the situation head-on and is matured by the tragedy. She can even cry for him when he dies -- because she is sorry she quarreled with him. Colburne meets sophistication from a different quarter -- that of battlefield experience. By the end of the book and the Civil War he is a mature man, serious about fulfilling his responsibilities (he gets his reports done, malaria notwithstanding), and he is not as naive as the man who once wrote patriotic poetry. In Lillie and Colburne, then, William de Forest shows how two honest, simple people can confront sophistication and mature in the process.

With <u>Huckleberry Finn</u>, we see simplicity in the character of Huck and sophistication in the rest of society. Huck is always quick to see the good in people -- he instinctively and readily has compassion for Jim Turner, the Wilks girls, and even a gang of robbers. Although he artfully lies to others, he is always true to himself and never disguises his opinions in his own mind.

In contrast to this simple boyish honesty, we see society as an almost perpetual mob scene -- a twisted kind of sophistication in which people are blind to the feelings of their fellow man. Through the Boggs-Sherburn duel and the Grangerford-Shepherdson feud we see how cruel man can be to man and yet have no qualms of conscience about his behavior.

Huck is disgusted by this inhumanity and is constantly leaving civilization and land for the peacefulness of the raft and river. As he confronts society's sophistication and its subtle cruelty, his honest simplicity is defeated, he is disillusioned, and in the end he returns to the land. Mark Twain seems to be saying here that it is futile for a simple individual to fight society -- sophistication is a group effort and will be the ultimate victor.

Questions

1. Bearing in mind the time limitation involved, how many points would you give the student writer on the first three questions? Discuss each question separately.
2. Is the "major conflict" clearly identified and explained in the fourth question? How many points would you give the student on this one?
3. Indicate the key terms in question five which the writer must perceive before he can provide a specific answer.
4. Block out the student's answer to question five and show how the question and the answer constitute a "little essay."
5. How would you rate the student's grasp of the material and his overall writing ability?

Term Paper Assignment

HUMANITIES I

Each student is required to submit a term paper on a subject related to the course. The term paper counts for 20 percent of your course grade. The student may choose any topic which falls within the chronological scope of the course. The subject must receive approval from the instructor no later than October 12. On October 5, the student is to turn in a 3x5 index card with the following information:
1. general topic (EXAMPLE: The Ninety-Five Theses);
2. specific question to be considered in the paper

(EXAMPLE: What was Martin Luther's purpose in posting Ninety-Five Theses?); 3. brief bibliography (EXAMPLE: Dillenberger, John. <u>Martin Luther.</u> 1961).

    The paper is not to exceed 1,500 words and must be written according to scholarly specifications. You may find Campbell's <u>Form and Style in Thesis Writing</u> and the <u>MLA Style Sheet</u> helpful. Since the conventions of bibliographical citation vary, it is important to be consistent in the method which you employ.

A Student Term Paper: Formal Research

```
STONEHENGE, AN UNFOLDING MYSTERY

              by

        Mary Jo Girsch



     Humanities I, Section 27

        Professor Wilkins

         January 4, 1969
```

The following paper is printed with permission of Mary Jo Girsch.

STONEHENGE, AN UNFOLDING MYSTERY

"Stonehenge is unique. There is nothing like it anywhere else, and from the earliest times it has aroused the awe and curiosity of its visitors."[1] This megalithic monument of grouped standing stones is located two miles west of Amesbury on Salisbury Plain in Wiltshire, England.

Its main features are: a low, circular outer bank with a ditch outside; the Avenue and heel stone within the bank; fifty-six Aubrey holes; four station stones; the Y and Z holes; the sarsen circle of thirty sarsen uprights capped by lintels; the bluestone circle of fifty-nine stones; a horseshoe of five sarsen trilithons (uprights with lintels); a horseshoe of nineteen bluestone monoliths, or single standing stones; the altar stone and slaughter stone. The floor plan of Stonehenge is not clear to the naked eye today because of several fallen stones and the human damage caused by builders, farmers, and souvenir hunters. The photograph on the facing page will give the reader an idea of how Stonehenge appears now.

The exact date that this monument was built is difficult to determine because no recorded writings of its builders have ever been found. Therefore other devices have been employed, notably the radioactive carbon method and the study of objects and bone fragments found in the ditch and Aubrey holes. Even

---

[1] R. J. C. Atkinson, <u>Stonehenge and Avebury -</u> guidebook (London: Her Majesty's Stationery Office, 1959), p. 13.

A Student Term Paper   283

The trilithons and sarsen circle, July 1963, from the north. (<u>Stonehenge Decoded,</u> G. S. Hawkins, Doubleday and Co., 1965.) British Crown Copyright. Reprinted by permission of the Ministry of Public Buildings and Works, London.

in using the same methods, the conclusions of some men vary by one hundred years or more. For example, R. J. C. Atkinson lists an inclusive date for the building of Stonehenge as 1800 - 1400 B.C.[2] Gerald S. Hawkins, however, gives this as 1900 - 1600 B.C.[3] Considering the vast time span involved here, a discrepancy of one hundred years is not too significant. Since Professor Hawkins' research is the most recent, I will use his figures.

Stonehenge I was begun around 1900 B.C. by the late Stone Age people of England. In one hundred and fifty years they completed the ditch, two banks, three standing stones, and the fifty-six Aubrey holes. About 1750 B.C. the Beaker people -- first of the Bronze Age groups -- arrived at Stonehenge to begin Period II. In one hundred years they added to the monument the Avenue and bluestone circles. The third building period was composed of three divisions, the first one beginning in 1650 B.C. with the Wessex people. During Period IIIa the trilithons, sarsen circle, and slaughter stone were erected. During Period IIIb, around 1625 B.C., a bluestone oval was built and then suddenly dismantled; the Y and Z holes were also dug and the altar stone added. In the final session, Period IIIc, the horseshoe of bluestones was reconstructed and with it a circle of of undressed bluestones.

This, then, was Stonehenge in its finished state.

---

[2] Ibid., p. 18.
[3] Gerald S. Hawkins, _Stonehenge Decoded_ (New York: Doubleday and Company, Inc., 1965), p. 39.

But to understand the significance of the monument it is necessary to look deeper into its construction. The smaller stones -- the bluestones -- came from two hundred and forty miles northeast of Stonehenge.

The stones were moved from the Prescelly Mountains to the sea by means of sledges, and then were transferred to rafts for the journey to Stonehenge.[4] Boats were used next on the River Avon, which runs 1¼ miles southeast of Stonehenge; from there the bluestones were hauled along the Avenue to the building site. Once erected there, the height of these stones varied from six to eight feet and they were tapered gradually from ground to top.[5]

The other stones -- the sarsens -- are quite large (the heaviest ones weigh fifty tons), and are the remains of a cap of Tertiary sandstone that once covered Salisbury Plain.[6]

Since there are no large rivers in the Wiltshire area, the sarsens had to be hauled overland for twenty miles. Sledges were used that ran on a track of rollers laid in front of them. For a stone weighing

---

[4] Lt.-Colonel B. S. Browne, in a June, 1963, article in *Antiquity Magazine*, advanced the idea that early Stonehengers never lacked manpower or timber because tribes could easily be gathered to carry on the sacred task of the building.

[5] R. J. C. Atkinson, "Stonehenge," *Encyclopaedia Britannica*, 1966, XXI, 440.

[6] Glyn Daniel, *The Megalith Builders of Western Europe* (Baltimore: Penguin Books, Inc., 1962), p. 18.

twenty-five tons, fifty men were needed to handle the rollers and to help guide the stone over level ground; two hundred and fifty were used on the steepest slope.[7]

Once the stones were at the monument site, builders used planks and rollers to haul them to the placement holes, then raised the huge slabs by levers resting on piled logs and pulled them upright with leather ropes. The holes were then filled with boulders for support. When lintels were raised to the top of the upright stones, the builders used a platform of stacked lengths of timber that gradually heightened around the uprights and brought the lintels even with the upright tops. Their average length is eighteen feet, with four feet buried beneath the ground.[8]

The stones were perhaps roughly shaped at their source, then polished by a stone-bashing process when they reached Stonehenge. All of the sarsens show some signs of dressing, most noticeably the curved lintels and the "peg and socket" method that held the trilithons together.[9]

Once the construction of Stonehenge has been discussed, the next question usually is "Why was it built?" To provide an answer, many legends were begun, some of which are still with us today. For

---

[7] R. J. C. Atkinson, What Is Stonehenge? - guidebook (London: Her Majesty's Stationery Office, 1962), p. 17.

[8] Atkinson, "Stonehenge," p. 440.

[9] Grahame Clark, F. S. A., Prehistoric England (New York: Charles Scribner's Sons, 1941), p. 113.

example, it is widely accepted that prehistoric man observed that the rulers of day and night entered and left this world at special places; it is only natural, then, that they would mark those points. Inigo Jones, the celebrated architect of the seventeenth century, was ". . . clearly of the opinion it [Stonehenge] was originally a temple."[10] Some people felt the monument was used as an agricultural calendar while others believed it was used for a memorial to dead warriors. One legend tells of the wizard Merlin magically transporting the huge stones from Ireland to Salisbury Plain; however, this belief died a rather early death.[11]

A very popular idea believed to some extent today is that Stonehenge was built by the Druids. Proponents of this theory say that Druids were interested in heavenly, secret things; that the open construction of the monument shows their metaphysical interests; and that they were noted for circular temples. Opponents claim that the Druids had no mathematical knowledge, and no monuments comparable to Stonehenge have ever been found in places where they are known to have lived. The clinching statement for disproving the Druid theory is the fact that this sect existed in Britain after 250 B.C. -- Stonehenge had already been built for more than a thousand years and may have been partly in ruins by that time.[12]

Another proposed idea is that Stonehenge was built as and used for an astronomical observatory.

---

[10] Ibid., p. 115.

[11] Hawkins, *Stonehenge Decoded*, pp. 5-6.

[12] Atkinson, *Stonehenge and Avebury*, p. 28.

In recent years, enough proof has been offered --
most successfully by Professor Gerald S. Hawkins, a
noted astronomer -- to substantiate this claim and
to provide startling additions to it. First, it is
well-known and widely accepted that the Avenue axis
does point to the heel stone, which directly marks
the spot on the northeast horizon where the sun rises
on midsummer day, the longest day of the year. Thus
Stonehenge is oriented to the midsummer sunrise,
but ". . . if the builders of Stonehenge had wished
simply to mark the sunrise they needed no more than
two stones. Yet hundreds of tons of volcanic rock
were carved and placed in position."[13]

Professor Hawkins wondered about this and other
puzzling facts about the monument that seemed to be
trying to tell him something. For instance, why
are the trilithon archways narrow to the point of
almost forcing the viewer to look only one way?
Why was the viewing line of archways important? For
the answers to these and other questions, Hawkins
turned to astronomy.

A plotting machine first transformed various key
positions of stones, archways, mounds, and holes into
X,Y coordinates on punched cards; then this information was fed into a computer. The results were
astounding: Stonehenge I and II were found to have
eleven key positions pairing with each other to point
sixteen times to ten of the twelve extreme positions

---

[13] Gerald S. Hawkins, "The Secret of Stonehenge,"
Harper's Magazine, June, 1964, p. 96.

of the sun or moon. Complementing Stonehenge I were the eight alignments found in the five great trilithons of Stonehenge III. They combined with the heel stone axis, erected first, to point to eight extremes of the sun and moon. . . .

In all, ten sun correlations had been found that were within one degree of accuracy to the actual positions; the fourteen moon correlations were accurate to 1.5 degrees.[14] The significance of these findings is that *all* twenty-four alignments are between key positions which paired with others to point to a sun or moon rise or set. This gives strong evidence that they were deliberate, basic, and important in the construction of Stonehenge.

A further proof that the monument was built as an observatory is that ". . . the lines of the Solstice [extreme of sun or moon] sunrise and moonset or sunset and moonrise are at an angle of 90°. This feature occurs on the earth's surface only at the latitude on which Stonehenge is situated."[15]

Then, two years after the above findings, Professor Hawkins added three previously omitted stone hole positions for computer analysis and again obtained astonishing results: they yielded eight

---

[14] Hawkins, "The Secret of Stonehenge," p. 141.
[15] R. S. Newall, F. S. A., *Stonehenge* - guidebook (London: Her Majesty's Stationery Office, 1959), p. 16.

correlations with the half-way points -- the equinoxes -- of the sun and moon. Now there were fourteen key positions in Stonehenge I placed to combine in pairs to produce twenty-four alignments. The grand total comes to thirty-two correlations with sun/moon positions from only twenty-two earthly positions.[16] There was some speculation that the monument might be keyed to other heavenly bodies, but no evidence was found to support this claim.

Was this plan of Stonehenge merely a coincidence? Bernouilli's theory of probability states that there is less than one chance in ten million that Stonehenge I and III would have the same alignments: the chance that its precise alignments was only luck on the part of the ancient builders is negligible.[17]

Yet there is one more discovery that adds to this already surprising feat of architecture -- it concerns the fifty-six Aubrey holes, named after archaeologist John Aubrey. They form a circle 284 feet 6 inches in diameter around Stonehenge and have such a careful and even arrangement (the greatest error in spacing is only one foot 9 inches) that it only seems reasonable to assume that they were used for some purpose.[18] Their filling is not uniform: it includes wood ash, flint flakes, and bones of human cremation; however, no stones were placed in them.

---

[16] Hawkins, *Stonehenge Decoded*, p. 140.
[17] *Ibid.*, p. 136.
[18] Newall, p. 9.

But these holes are aligned to the various stones or archways which mark an extreme sun or moon position, and hole 56 lines up with the heel stone. The Stonehenge builders, Hawkins believes, were in a way more advanced than our modern astronomers, for they saw what has gone virtually undetected for years: eclipses of the moon occur in cycles of approximately 19, 19, and 18 years -- a total of 56 years.[19] The Aubrey holes could have been a reliable eclipse predictor.

An arrangement like this would have allowed priests or tribal leaders to summon people to Salisbury Plain to witness a spectacle -- the death and resurrection of their gods -- that would have terrified them. If those in charge knew when an eclipse would occur, they could appear to have the power of predicting the "disaster" and could then say the prayers that let the moon or sun out of the blackness. This would give them great "power" and the people would respect them.[20]

The actual operation of this primitive computer is really quite simple. "If one stone were moved around the circle one position, or Aubrey hole, each year, all the extremes of the seasonal moon, and eclipses of the sun and moon at the solstices and equinoxes, could have been foreseen. If six stones, spaced 9, 9, 10, 9, 9, 10 Aubrey holes apart, were used, each of them moved one hole counterclockwise

---

[19] Hawkins, *Stonehenge Decoded*, p. 140.
[20] Archaeology: "The Eighth Wonder," *Time Magazine*, 86:20 (November 12, 1965), 98.

each year, an astonishing power of prediction could have been achieved."[21] The following diagram illustrates the operation of this eclipse predictor.

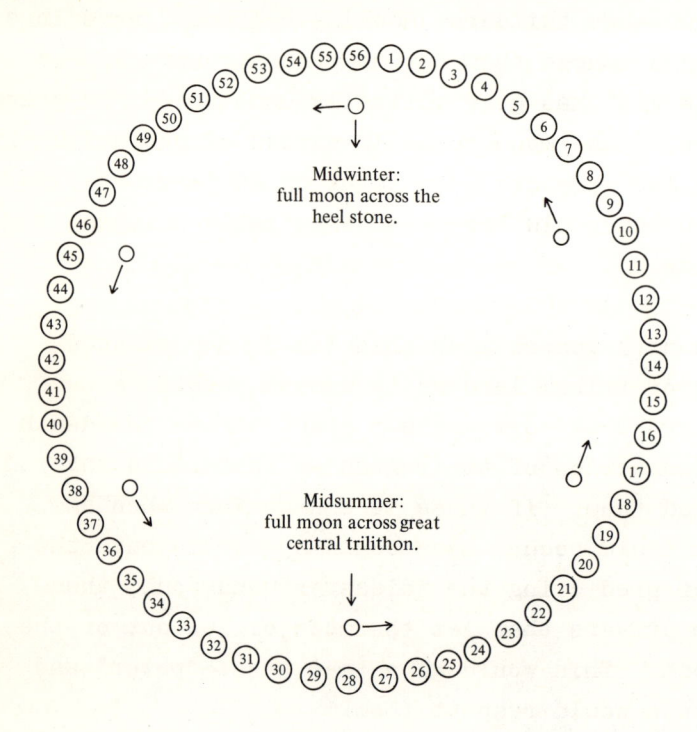

(Diagram: circle of 56 numbered holes. Arrows indicate: Midwinter: full moon across the heel stone. Midsummer: full moon across great central trilithon.)

For example, ". . . a black or white stone at hole 56 occurs at intervals of 9, 9, 10, 9, 9, 10 years. This predicts the heel-stone moon events. A white stone is at hole 51 at intervals of 18, 19, 19 years, predicting the conditions of the high moon at +29°. A white stone is at hole 5 at intervals of 19, 19, 18 years, predicting the events associated with the low moon, at +19°.[22]

(Illustration from Gerald S. Hawkins' Stonehenge Decoded, p. 142. By permission of Gerald S. Hawkins.)

[21] Hawkins, Stonehenge Decoded, p. 141.
[22] Ibid., pp. 142-143.

If it were thus possible to predict the years and danger months of eclipses with the Aubrey holes, would the Stonehenge builders also have provided a way to foretell the days of the eclipses? One good possibility lies in the thirty Y holes and the twenty-nine Z holes. They were about the last things built at Stonehenge and could have been used as day markers -- a finishing touch of the monument-computer.[23] As for the exact hour of an eclipse, this could have been learned by watching the changing interval between sunset and moonrise. Since the moon must be just opposite the sun to be eclipsed, the danger times would have occurred when the moon rose just before the sun set. The ancient Stonehengers could have been forewarned of this by observing the shorter intervals between the sunset and moonrise as an eclipse neared. This would have been a very accurate method in the hands of a careful observer.

In summary, then, the great stones on Salisbury Plain seem almost certainly to have been deliberately and skillfully oriented to the sun and moon. The monument was erected with such precision and aligned so many times to the basic positions of these heavenly bodies that it must have been built by highly intelligent workers. It must have ". . . required of its creators an absolutely extraordinary blending of theoretical, planning abilities and practical building skills."[24] But some people still think of all the prehistoric Englishmen as Neanderthal-like

---

[23] _Ibid._, p. 146.
[24] _Ibid._, p. 115.

creatures more animal than human, and this concept dies hard. As an example of this, a colleague of Professor Hawkins once asked a British government official, " 'What do you think of Professor Hawkins' findings at Stonehenge?' He replied, 'I've heard about those findings but I don't believe them. You see, the ancient Britons couldn't have been as clever as all that.' "[25]

And yet Stonehenge *was* built -- and the recent discoveries about its purpose seem to prove quite conclusively that those ancient people succeeded in building a remarkably ingenious computing machine. This should make twentieth-century man with all his elaborate scientific machines stop and think of the type of people who went before him. It is almost like finding intelligent life on another planet -- and every bit as exciting in the discovery.

---

[25] *Ibid.*, p. 166.

Bibliography

Archaeology: "The Eighth Wonder," <u>Time Magazine</u>, 86:20 (November 12, 1965), 98.

Atkinson, R. J. C. "Stonehenge," <u>Encyclopaedia Britannica</u>, 1966, XXI, 439-440.

-------. <u>Stonehenge and Avebury</u> - guidebook. London: Her Majesty's Stationery Office, 1959.

-------. <u>What Is Stonehenge?</u> - guidebook. London: Her Majesty's Stationery Office, 1962.

Browne, Lt.-Colonel B. S., F. S. A. "Neolithic Engineering," <u>Antiquity Magazine</u>, XXXVII (June, 1963), 140-144.

Clark, Grahame, F. S. A. <u>Prehistoric England</u>. New York: Charles Scribner's Sons, 1941.

Daniel, Glyn. <u>The Megalith Builders of Western Europe</u>. Baltimore: Penquin Books, Inc., 1962.

Hawkins, Gerald S. "The Secret of Stonehenge," <u>Harper's Magazine</u>, June, 1964, pp. 96-99.

-------. <u>Stonehenge Decoded</u>. New York: Doubleday and Company, Inc., 1965.

Newall, R. S., F. S. A. <u>Stonehenge</u> - guidebook. London: Her Majesty's Stationery Office, 1959.

Owen, A. L. <u>The Famous Druids</u>. London: Oxford University Press, 1962.

Questions

1. The opening section of the paper sets forth a description of Stonehenge and details on its construction. Block out the remaining parts.
2. Did the student writer employ good strategy in using a problem-solution approach to the material? Explain by making references to the paper.
3. To what extent is this writing informative-persuasive?
4. Provide three examples of the similarities between this term paper and popular prose. What are some of the differences?
5. Examine the writer's technique in building and documenting this paper: What is the frequency of direct quotation and paraphrase? Is the material skillfully tied together or does it have the effect of "cut and paste"? Is the level of the language appropriate? Was the writer consistent in setting up the footnotes and bibliography? Are the visual aids effective?
6. Write a teacher's comment for this paper together with the grade you would give it.

Suggested Writing Assignments

1. Analyze the writing in an issue of your school paper or yearbook on the basis of topic, type, language, and audience appeal. You might wish to restrict your examination to news stories, columns, or letters to the editor.
2. Compose a letter (real or imaginary) to your parents, friend, or sweetheart. Then analyze it in regard to the basic principles of informative-persuasive prose as described in this text. Your analysis could be serious or humorous, depending on the material.
3. Collect examples of essay-type questions from your instructors and classmates which represent one or several of the various disciplines—history, literature, physical education, art, and science. In your analysis, consider these factors: Are the questions specific or general? Do they contain key terms? Are response patterns such as contrast, cause-and-effect, comparison, and problem-solving indicated? Do they carry warnings in regard to exactness and the use of examples? On the basis of your collection, you might want to set up guidelines for students in answering essay questions.
4. Of the many available books on how to write research papers (several were mentioned in the term paper assignment), examine one or two and then write a paper in which you discuss some of the

major considerations in composing formal research. Note the various bibliographic techniques which are acceptable, the use of resource cards, quoted and paraphrased material, as well as some of the pitfalls involved in writing such a paper.

17

Prevising the Theme for Common Problems

This reference section contains a brief discussion of some of the common problems which occur in the formative stage of a composition. Errors are classified under the headings of *thesis, background, topic sentences, detail,* and *closing*.

You may wish to read through the entire chapter or refer to parts of it when necessary. The important thing is to watch for and solve these problems in the prewriting phase of your theme.

At the end of the chapter a checklist of Errors for Prevision has been included, which you may find helpful.

Thesis

1. Vague or Missing A composition consists of a thesis which is stated, developed, and brought to a close. If your paper is not guided by a clearly stated or implied thesis it is not a composition at all, but a series of miscellaneous paragraphs.

Consider the following theme introduction.

An Evaluation of the Variety Show

I sat through two performances of the College Variety Show last Friday and I responded in a number of ways. I asked several of my friends who attended the opening night but, unfortunately, they did not have much to say. There was no doubt, however, that there were different points of view in regard to the ability of the local talent. Bill

Jacobson, the student director, is certainly to be congratulated for the fine job he did in working out the stage sets for the six acts.

What is the writer's purpose? Was the variety show good, bad, or indifferent? If there were several points of view, what was his view? Or does the writer intend to explain why he believes that the director did a good job?

Compare this vague statement of thesis with the one which follows.

An Evaluation of the Variety Show

I sat through two performances of the College Variety Show which opened last Friday and I must say that the presentation was a bust. The singing groups rendered off key versions of dated songs, the comics provided unfunny humor, and the instrumentalists showed little technique and imagination on the guitar and piano. I am sure that everybody tried, but the six acts were uniformly bad.

In this version the thesis is unmistakable: the writer will develop the view that the singing groups, comics, and instrumentalists did not, in his opinion, give a good performance.

The chief reason beginning writers try to compose a theme when they have not worked out a clear purpose is that they have not grasped the actual connection between a thesis and a theme. A thesis is a belief or judgment which, when given form and content, *becomes a theme.* Thus, if you attended the variety show and found it mediocre except for the guitar player, that judgment will constitute your paper. The same thing is true if you wished to write a column on the best way to catch bass with a fly rod, an argumentative article on why you are opposed to a volunteer army, or a personal essay on the beauty of your river retreat. In each instance you are making and supporting a judgment designed to inform and persuade the reader. The term "judgment" is, by the way, a particularly good synonym for thesis because it indicates that unless you have judged a thing as being good, bad, wrong, right, amusing, surprising, confusing, questionable, helpful, dangerous, inspirational, tragic, educational, wasteful, pleasant, unpleasant, innovative, backward, or challenging, you are not ready to write.

The prewriter rarely attempts to launch a theme on an unclear thesis. As one who has learned to take great care in selecting his approach to a topic, he is not likely to write on the first vague notion that floats by.

2. Unrestricted Thesis Even when the writer forms a clear statement of thesis he may discover that it is too broad to be effectively covered in a short paper. The error of unrestricted thesis is, in fact, the most common failing in freshman writing.

Let us suppose that you spent two weeks last summer camping in the desert and that you have selected for your thesis this formulation, *I thoroughly enjoyed the experience of camping in the New Mexico desert.* Note that this statement obliges you to discuss the entire episode: your arrival, setting up the tents, cooking out, exploring the canyon, rock hunting, taking pictures, finding the snake, and so on.

At this point you object: "Why can't I write on all of these things? They were all interesting." Yes, they were interesting, but you cannot make all seven points interesting for your reader in a short paper. At best you can provide a comment or two about the canyon, another brief observation about the kinds of rocks you found, and a brief reference to the snake. You must then rush on to the remaining topics so that you can give a brief account of them. A moment's thought will tell you that you cannot compose interesting, in-depth details on a topic if you are obliged to cover seven different points. As the following graph reveals, the wise writer knows that every topic contains a number of facets and that he must *restrict his thesis to one facet of the topic and form a judgment on that.*

Camping in the New Mexico Desert

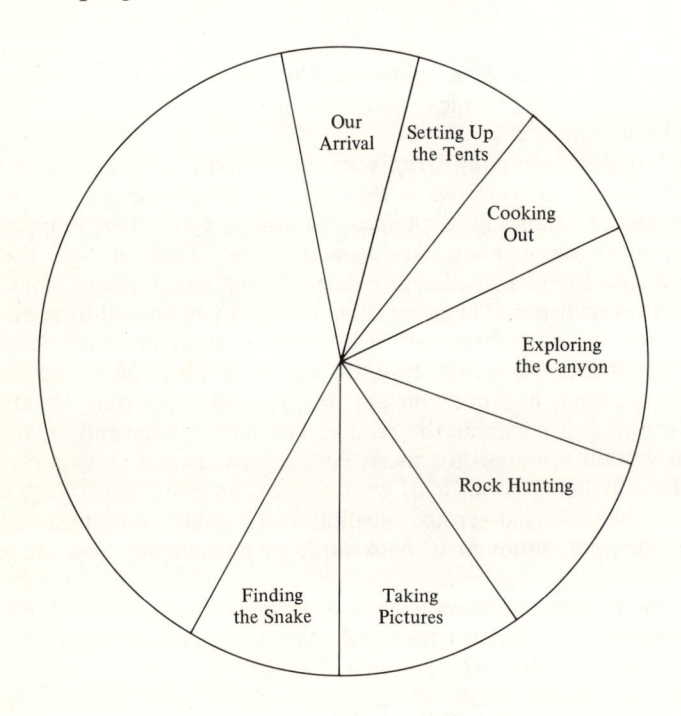

The snake episode would make a good thesis in itself, or perhaps you might want to use it as a climax in your account of exploring the canyon. Or you might wish to limit to the highlights involved in taking pictures of desert sunsets. One thing is certain: you cannot please your reader with a superficial account of the hundred and one things you did on your camping trip. You must employ your taste, not merely your memory, and determine which episodes tell the best.

And, by the way, in restricting your thesis you need not throw out all of the rest of your material. Much of it can be worked into your theme in one place or another in subordinated form. For example, your introduction might read:

> The two weeks I spent camping out with my family in the desert near Taos, New Mexico, were memorable not because we arrived in a rain storm and discovered that we had no knowledge of how to set up a tent, nor even because we explored a 500 foot canyon, gathered rare rocks and arrowheads, and met up with a three foot rattler. No, the one thing that made the trip unforgettable for me was the desert sunsets. They were breathtaking—absolutely beautiful. I know that I cannot match in words the color pictures that I took, but I am going to try.

Unrestricted thesis is fairly easy to identify in the prewriting stage, especially when you enlist the aid of your instructor. If you have worked out a list of your thoughts on a topic and uncovered some tentative approaches, the two of you can discuss the material and find those facets which make the best focus for your theme.

3. Lack of Specific Purpose All too often the inexperienced writer restricts his thesis to one facet of his topic but fails to formulate a specific purpose. This problem is so deceptive that we must discuss it in some detail.

Again, suppose that your topic is the college variety show and that you have restricted it to one facet—the guitar player. You then frame this thesis, *Of the various acts in the College Variety Show, I have decided to discuss "Sam the Guitar Man," as he was billed*. Note that although this statement is restricted to a single facet of the topic, it does not contain a *judgment* in regard to that facet. To say that you will "discuss" a thing is not to judge it. Did you like Sam's playing or did you like Sam's singing and not his playing? Was Sam's act the best or the worst? Were all of Sam's songs good or was it just the last one titled, "Take An Old Cold Tater And Wait"?

You could write a theme on any one of the foregoing points because they are all theses. That is, they are all judgments. But you cannot go anywhere with an "I will discuss" purpose.

It should now be clear that restricting the topic to a single facet is, then, only the first step in thesis formulation. The second step is to make a specific judgment on that facet.

Now observe a second kind of thesis which lacks specific purpose—the "I've always been interested in" and "I enjoyed most of all" statements, of which there are endless variations. Consider the theses, *I enjoyed the guitar player's act most of all*, and, *I was really interested in the desert rock-hunting expeditions*. The judgments in these formulations are so general that they do not provide a specific point of departure. Why, specifically, did you enjoy the guitar player, and what, specifically, interested you in the rock hunting venture? The answers to these questions would make very specific theses, but of course you cannot use what you have not thought out. And this brings us once again to prewriting.

The writer who begins by listing all of his thoughts on a topic will not be tempted to write on a thesis which lacks a specific purpose. But the student who selects a thesis in haste before he has had a chance to go to the bottom of his subject is almost certain to make such a mistake.

4. Wrong Focus Since half of the prewriting phase consists of discovering the most interesting facet of a topic, the error of wrong focus is hardly a new consideration.

Teachers of composition are constantly writing comments such as these on themes.

> "Wrong focus—you ought to have written on how you reacted when you saw the tornado lift your neighbor's house, not on the clean-up involved in the aftermath of the storm."

> "You failed to focus on your best material—your satirical view that smoking can be best understood by regarding it as a hobby. You ought to have made this original insight your thesis and explored it at length."

> "Wrong focus. Your visit to Mexico City lasted four weeks and must have involved you in a number of new and exciting activities. Yet you chose to discuss your illness during the last two days of your trip. Did you think through this topic before you wrote?"

Think through, indeed! No, that is the very thing which the student did not do. He wrote on the first idea that occurred to him—his upset stomach. Consider the many interesting possibilities which were closed off for this writer because he did not re-create his experience in a prewritten list of thoughts: the señoritas—their dress and flirtatious manner; the strolling musicians—their songs, instruments, and graciousness; the street beggars—the old woman in rags and the gypsy children with the blind dog.

Of course, you can miss your best material even when you prewrite. But there is this difference between writing and prewriting a theme. In the former instance there is little chance for progress. On each assignment the student selects the first workable idea which occurs to him and writes it up.

But continued prewriting can result in real gains for the beginner. He comes to see that any topic contains a number of theses, that these can most easily be determined by taking an inventory of his ideas, and that a good writer is simply one who refuses to write a theme until he has first worked out his most interesting focus.

5. Trite Thesis There are a dozen ways to define trite writing—dull, boring, hackneyed, uninteresting, stereotyped—but they all boil down to the same thing: a theme which offers the reader so little that is fresh and perceptive that it is not worth reading.

Although no one can make an infallible prediction about the quality of a theme simply by looking at the thesis, the following ideas are so worn, so obvious, and so generally tired that it would require a skillful writer and a very apt selection of focus to make them interesting.

People complain about the rain but they don't think about the poor farmer whose crops depend upon it.
Why do so many students conform?
It is becoming more and more difficult to study in the library.
Something should be done to improve the system of registration in this school.

These statements express sentiments which we have all heard over and over again. It is as though they were turned out by a computer.

On reading the word "trite" penciled on their themes, many students throw up their hands and moan, "What does he want?" Others complain that trite writing was their problem in high school and they see no way of solving it. Actually, there are a number of solutions:

1) Instead of writing a theme on a ready-made thesis, begin by listing your thoughts on the topic, whether it is farmers, conformity, registration day, or what have you. If you cannot discover a fresh approach on one topic, try another one. Note that some theses are so trite that no one would bother to prewrite his ideas on them.

2) In selecting theme ideas, be guided by the good compositions which you read every week in magazines and newspapers. Look at the topics in your scrapbook of clippings. Professionals get their material published largely because of their ability to hit on new concepts and novel approaches.

3) File away fresh ideas in your journal for a rainy day. The thought you recorded last week as to why many people talk about, but fail to follow, a daily five-minute exercise schedule might make a far more interesting theme than one about campus parking problems or the food in the Commons.

4) Learn to distinguish between theses which are acceptable and those which are excellent. Why are you writing if not to *please* the reader—to enlighten him, amuse him, convince him, or challenge him—and you cannot do this with a routine or merely acceptable thesis. Remember that a good writer refuses to budge until he has prewritten his way to a good idea, one which he has dug out, thought through, and tested as being sure to please.

The sad thing about the student whose material is marked trite is that he often completes the course in composition convinced that he has no imagination and nothing to say. It is true that some people have more natural ability in writing than others do, just as some of us are better mathematicians, but no student should pronounce judgment on himself until he has tried prewriting—and not as applied to one or two themes but to many themes. As in all disciplines, there is no royal road to success, but prewriting is one path every young writer should explore.

Background

1. Failure To Create Interest The inexperienced writer usually succeeds in communicating his purpose, but in doing so he bores or at any rate fails to arouse the reader who, if he has a choice, lays the piece aside and engages in some more profitable activity. He knows that the writer who is unable to hold his interest in a paragraph or two is not likely to take him very far. As always, the best way to learn a thing is to study the efforts of those who have mastered it. In analyzing the professionally written introductions which follow, we will attempt to find some of the chief features of effective openings.

The novice should certainly be aware of common leads. These are standard introductions which build suspense, employ anecdote, pose a problem, or deal with a little-known or frequently misunderstood fact. The example below shows how suspense can be used to create reader interest.

Race Against Death

The car, shaped like a great teardrop, crouched on Utah's Bonneville salt flats. Its front wheels rested astride a painted black line that led, arrow-straight, across the shimmering surface for a measured 11 miles. This was August 1, 1960, and some 500 persons were admiring with awe the "City of Salt Lake." They knew that in minutes a man's life would be gambled in an effort to break what was then the land speed record of 394 miles an hour.

Floyd Miller, Reader's Digest, October, 1963

Of course, the excellence of a given introduction seldom revolves around a single device. Thus, in addition to the element of suspense, the writer of "Race Against Death" also employed effective figurative language and smoothly worked in most of the five w's of the journalist.

The use of anecdote is a favorite way of opening a piece. As illustrated by the sample which follows, the reader's attention can be caught by an amusing incident.

Women Have No Sense of Humor

When I was six I said to a little girl who lived next door, "I bet I can stand two inches away from you and you can't touch me."

"How?" she asked.

"By standing behind a door." I laughed so hard that marbles rolled out of my pants' pockets.

The little girl looked at me as though I were a frog. "What's so funny about that? Nobody could touch you if you were silly enough to stand behind a door."

In all the years since, I still haven't been able to figure out a woman's sense of humor.

Robert T. Allen,
Macleans, June, 1951

Since life is full of unsettled questions, it is logical that many writers begin by posing a problem. The lead paragraphs provided below reveal the range of problems, from the serious to the lighthearted.

Stupid Highway Signs Can Kill

Every hour of every day on almost every road and street in the country, stupid signs are confusing motorists and leading them dangerously astray. When road signs don't make sense, the driver always hesitates—and a hesitating driver is a hazard.

Leon D. Adams, *Popular Science Monthly*, May, 1965

A Line O'Type Or Two

I am convinced that one of the most troublesome frustrations facing Americans is the difficulty of getting ice cubes out of those wretched aluminum trays that are imbedded in refrigerators. And mind you I am not one to complain about trivialities.

Chicago Tribune,
November 13, 1967

Since no one wants to be misinformed or ignorant of the facts, the opening which promises to set us straight has much appeal.

Facts and Non-Facts About Eye Care

Do you believe that reading in dim light will ruin your eyes? That television can harm a child's eyesight? That cheap sunglasses injure the eye? That excessive reading causes nearsightedness? That you would not need glasses today if you had worn them as a child? That parents need not worry about a child's cross eyes because he'll soon outgrow them? That eyestrain can cause headaches and make you ill?

All these statements have this in common: They are untrue.

J. K. Lagemann, *Reader's Digest*, April, 1962

Despite the fact that these standard leads are easy to use, the beginning writer usually fails to employ them because he does not consider his opening paragraph until the last minute, and then he puts down whatever pops into his head. The experienced writer knows better. In prewriting his material, he keeps an eye peeled for good opening lines.

Tone and authority also play a part in creating reader interest. Tone is the attitude or personal voice of the writer which grows out of the subject matter and sets the stage for the entire composition. Depending on the topic and the occasion, the tone of a piece can be provocative, whimsical, pensive, satiric, enthusiastic, critical, or profound.

For example, the tone of good-natured amusement in the introduction below wins us over because it signals a carefully fashioned piece of writing, one in which a single attitude will be maintained throughout.

So Sorry!

British manners have the polish of old wood. Ask a British secretary if you may speak to Mr. Jones, and she says, "Oh, I'm *so* sorry! He's gone for the day"—as if she'd like to kill herself because she can't deliver him. Or phone for a cab on a rainy night, and the lady says, "Oh, I'm *afraid* there isn't one available right now," her voice trilling with heartbreak.

John Crosby, *New York Herald Tribune*, November 4, 1963

For contrast, compare the deeply critical tone of the following lead.

Girl Dropouts

When you hear the word "dropout," you probably picture a delinquent teenage boy hanging around a poolroom. Yet each year approximately half the one million young Americans who quit high school before graduating are girls. In some areas the proportion is as high as two-thirds. These hundreds of thousands of young girls make up the most forlorn and forgotten segment of our society.

H. J. Pollack, *Parade*, October 3, 1965

Now read a third example of an introductory paragraph in which the tone conveys a sense of quiet dignity.

Man Belongs to Man

> Three kinds of progress are significant: progress in knowledge and technology; progress in the socialization of man; progress in spirituality. The last is the most important.
>
> Albert Schweitzer

From this brief analysis it should be clear that tone is created through prewriting. As the spirit of the whole composition, tone emerges naturally as the writer works with his material: it cannot be glued on to an introduction in the final stages of the paper.

Authority, a second feature of strongly written leads, may be defined as "the ring of writer confidence." Nothing commands the reader's attention as much as the belief that the writer knows what he is doing.

For example, in reading through the following paragraph, most of us would agree that the author has researched and thought through the material and will have something to say.

Why Women Act That Way

> Why are women so clumsy at pitching a ball and running? Lay it to bone structure. The reason most women can't pitch an efficient overhand may be connected with the "carrying angle" of their arms. The average woman's arms are more bent at the elbow than a man's. This may help to cause the stiff downward motion in ball-throwing that men find so hilarious.
>
> Judith Churchhill,
> *McCall's*, August, 1955

When a writer fails to open in a confident manner, we say that his material "lacks authority." The following introduction is an example of this shortcoming.

My New Job

> Cutting meat is my new job. My old job was welding in a sheet metal factory. In this paper I will explain why I think I like my new job better than the old one.

Unless the reader were a captive audience, he would not read beyond the first paragraph of the foregoing composition.

Professionals write leads which convey a sense of confidence not because they have some special gift but because, as prewriters, they have already been where the reader is going. This is why their openings carry the command: Follow me, reader. You will find this worthwhile because I've worked it out and tested it.

2. Missing Who, What, Where, When, and Why Information   Beginning writers often fail to provide the preliminary facts which are needed to clarify their purpose statement.

Note the missing details in the following introduction.

The Barrios of Colombia

Many people believe that Colombia has adequate living conditions, but my visit to the slums proved otherwise.

But why did the writer go to Colombia? How long did he stay there? When did he go? With whom? And where is Colombia? Unanswered questions of this kind alienate the reader at the outset, and for good reason: no one wants to waste his time reading a piece which begins in darkness.

Compare the rewrite below in which the missing background facts have been supplied.

The Barrios of Colombia

Many people believe that Colombia has adequate living conditions, but my visit to the slums proved otherwise. Last summer, seven other students and myself visited this South American country as part of a Language Exchange Tour sponsored by the Spanish Department of our college. We were appalled at the poverty, disease, and ignorance which we found in the slum areas in all the major cities of this country.

Topic Sentences

1. Unclear and Irrelevant   Since topic sentences mark the divisions of our thought, we cannot expect the reader to follow us when these key sentences are vague or when they introduce irrelevant material. Many student writers do not appreciate the importance of topic sentences because they have not grasped the concept of the "organic wholeness" of a theme. They have not learned that written thought is constructed on a topic framework, that all of the discussion in the body of a composition is clearly tied to the topic sentences which in turn must relate to the central purpose of the paper, and that what may appear to be a casually composed series of paragraphs is at bottom a carefully contrived line of thought which moves the reader forward from one idea to the next.

Study the graph which follows.

```
┌─────────────────────────────────────────────┐
│              Thesis                         │
└─────────────────────────────────────────────┘
                  ↑
              Topic Sentence
┌─────────────────────────────────────────────┐
│  ─────────────────────────────────────────  │
│  ─────────────────────────────────────────  │
│  ─────────────────────────────────────────  │
│  ────────────Supporting Details──────────   │
│  ─────────────────────────────────────────  │
│  ─────────────────────────────────────────  │
│  ─────────────────────────────────────────  │
└─────────────────────────────────────────────┘
```

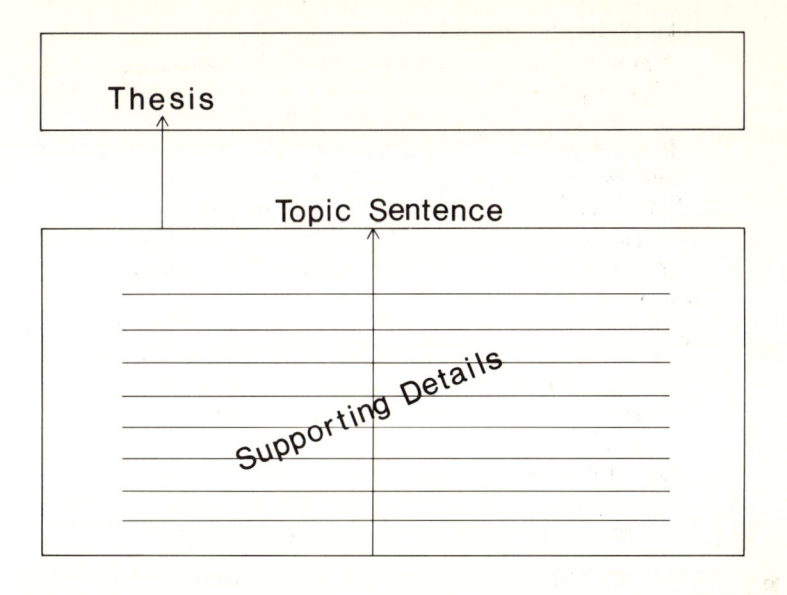

To illustrate that topic sentences are indeed the pegs on which a writer hangs his thoughts, we have only to block out a finished prose selection. As an example, we can use an excerpt from Thurber's *University Days,* in which the author's purpose is to describe in a humorous manner some of the courses which he found especially troublesome. Observe that it is solely by means of the topic sentences summarized below that Thurber is able to identify for the reader each of the courses in question.

> I passed all the other courses that I took at my university, but I could never pass botany.
>
> Another course that I didn't like, but somehow managed to pass, was economics.
>
> If I went through anguish in botany and economics—for different reasons—gymnasium work was even worse.
>
> Ohio State was a land grant university and therefore two years of military drill was compulsory. . . . As a soldier I was never any good at all.

It should not be supposed that setting up a line of clear and relevant topic sentences is peculiar to Thurber. All writers must provide signposts if they wish to be understood.

As a second example we will note the technique employed by Philip Wylie in his article, "Science Has Spoiled My Supper" (*Atlantic Monthly*, 1954). Having announced his thesis, that food which has been scientifically prepared is tasteless, and having caught our interest by certain references to the fact that his wife still cooks from an old-fashioned garden, Wylie supports his view with a series of very plainly marked references to the foods which science has spoiled.

Take cheese, for instance.
  A grocer used to be very fussy about his cheese.
  What happened? Science—or what is called science—stepped in. The old-fashioned cheeses didn't ship well enough.
  It is not possible to make the very best cheese in vast quantities at a low average cost.
  Imitations also came into the cheese business.
Perhaps you don't like cheese—so the fact that decent cheese is hardly ever served in America any more or used in cooking, doesn't matter to you. Well, take bread.
  Most bakers are interested mainly in how a loaf of bread looks.
  Yesterday, at the home of my mother-in-law, I ate with country-churned butter and home-canned wild strawberry jam several slices of actual bread, the same thing we used to have at home every day.
For years I couldn't figure out what had happened to vegetables.
  Our vegetables . . . come to us through a long chain of command.
  Homes and restaurants do what they can with this stuff—which my mother-in-law would have discarded on the spot.

Since Wylie knows that the reader will not be convinced by his argument unless the topics and sub topics which support it are identified, he takes great pains to mark them—"Take *cheese*, for instance," "Well, take *bread*," "For years I couldn't figure out what happened to *vegetables*."

The inexperienced writer proceeds in an opposite manner. He plunges on in great haste, with scarcely a side glance at the clarity and relevance of his topic headings, only to discover at the end of his journey that he has left his puzzled reader far behind.

Two terms are commonly used in relation to topic sentences—*coherence* and *unity*. When a composition contains topic sentences which connect the parts in a clear and logical manner, the piece is said to be coherent. And when the topics introduce only relevant ideas, those which have a direct bearing on the writer's purpose, the paper is said to have unity.

Many student writers have been trained to check their material for relevance and unity in the final stages of the writing, and so they should. One can oftentimes repair at the last minute a vaguely stated topic sentence or a point which is only remotely related to the thesis. But if the writer has clarified and established as relevant his ideas in the prewriting stage, he will usually not be obliged to make such changes in the final copy of his paper, some of which can be frustrating and time-consuming.

Detail

1. *Missing Examples, Explanations, Facts, and Arguments* Beginning writers who apply themselves soon acquire a sense of form. That is, they learn to shape their compositions into the logical pattern of beginning, middle, and end. But the element which at once sets the novice apart from the professional is his failure to provide full and satisfying detail. Typically, the beginner

establishes a thesis, but unconvincing background details; topic sentences, but few lines of effective discussion; a concluding idea, but little elaborative detail. The result is that he turns in compositions which consist chiefly of skeletal framework. The parts are there but they are not filled out or supported.

Details are important because they constitute the actual content of a piece of writing. Take out the details and you have nothing left but an outline, the bare bones of a review, a column, or a news story.

Since the use of detail in the opening and closing paragraphs is discussed under other headings, our interest here is restricted to the manner in which topic sentences are developed. Four kinds of details are used to expand topics—illustration, explanation, fact, and argument. Remembering that categories invariably overlap, we will begin by noting the various kinds of illustrative detal.

The first consists of providing a number of examples to illustrate your topic. In reading the following paragraph from J. H. Pollack's, "Ten Keys to Being a Good Conversationalist" (*Reader's Digest*, September, 1959), observe that the author clarifies his topic by citing five examples of trite expressions.

> *Shun Trite Expressions.* Don't let yourself be described as "a person of few words who uses them over and over again!" Some women use the word "wonderful" in nearly every sentence. Other trite talkers keep repeating: "Absolutely," "You can say that again," "It's out of this world!" "Understand what I mean?" Avoid such rubber-stamp phrases. And don't quote yourself. Few of us are so witty as Bernard Shaw, who could wisecrack, "I often quote myself; it adds spice to my conversation!"

Illustration often takes the form of a single sustained example or anecdote. In developing a supporting unit of thought in her article, "Say It Now!" (*Christian Herald*, October, 1965), Margaret B. Johnstone uses an extended example with very good effect. Note that the topic sentence opens the selection.

> For by *not* saying perhaps some simple word of commendation, such as "You're doing very well," or "I'm proud of you," we may suppress some unguessed strength, talent, or contribution that we might have brought to life.
>
> Industrialist-writer Sherman Rogers told of the day he was made foreman of a logging camp in Idaho. Almost at once he considered firing a glum, spiteful worker named Tony. But the camp's owner appeared and said, "Whatever you do, I suggest that you don't bother Tony. He's cantankerous and a holy terror sometimes, but I've never had a better sander. Not a man or a horse has been lost on this hill."
>
> That morning Rogers walked over to Tony and said, "Good morning, I'm the new foreman. The boss told me what a good man you are." Then he told Tony what the owner had said.
>
> "Why didn't he tell me that before?" Tony cried, the tears running down his cheeks. "Thank you, thank you." He pumped Rogers' hand. Then, grabbing his shovel, he seemed to fly at his sanding job.
>
> That night the teamsters' washup topic was Tony. "He's thrown enough sand today to cover a dozen hills. What hit him? Why, he's smiled and joked all day."

> Only Rogers knew, and he had the satisfaction of seeing the sequel—12 years later—when he found Tony working as the superintendent of railroad construction in one of the biggest logging camps in the West. Said Tony, "That one minute you talked to me back in Idaho changed my whole life!"

The foregoing samples should show us that illustrations are vital to good writing. Remove the concrete examples of trite expressions in the first piece, and you have an empty paragraph. Remove the extended example in the second selection and you have nothing left at all.

A second kind of detail involves explanation. As indicated in the material below taken from Bill Surface's article, "Why Football Is Getting Dirtier Than Ever" (*Argosy*, October, 1968), explanatory detail is commonly used in prose for the simple reason that an explanation is often the only way to clarify key statements. In this instance, the writer finds it necessary to explain why the knee is vulnerable in professional football.

> It is readily apparent why the knee was not meant to be abused by football players and, furthermore, why many so-called aggressive players do so. Many marginal players realize that they can avoid being released and many starting defensemen know that they can demand an extra 10,000 or so a year if they help win by stopping first-rate players fairly early in the game. They are also aware that shoulders and hips, besides being heavily padded, are held together by strong sockets resembling automobile ball bearings; that ankles encased in elastic gauze and adhesive tape are often difficult to injure except when players inadvertently twist or break them themselves, and that players' faces are protected by masks and that there are penalties for anyone seen grabbing them.
>
> But the almost unprotectable knee resembles a hinge. It connects and stabilizes the kneecap and thigh bone with thread-like bands of ligaments no more than an eighth of an inch thick, and gristle-like cartilages that serve as shock absorbers. Unfortunately, ligaments can be shredded and even ripped loose from attachments to the bone, and cartilages can be easily torn by merely bending a knee sideways; by getting blocked or tackled from the rear or side; by being tackled around the shoulders or neck while another defenseman is grabbing a player's ankles, or by casually falling across a leg extending from a pileup.

Like all skilled writers, Surface enriches his material with a number of related details, such as the monetary reward given for taking out first-rate players and the relative difficulty of injuring other parts of the body, but it is his explanation of the "unprotectable knee" which is chiefly emphasized and retained by the reader.

A third category of detail is fact—the statistics, testimony, and other data which are necessary to convince us of the truth or plausibility of a topic statement.

In his write-up, "Safety Devices Which Kill" (*This Week Magazine*, March 16, 1969), Raymond Scheussler contends that highway direction signs, light poles, and safety barriers which are intended to promote safety can cause death.

An interesting thesis, but not without the facts and figures which the writer supplies to back up the argument. Thus, a government committee inspection revealed that "a typical modern highway had about 30 major fixed roadside objects per mile." Of the thousands of Americans who will die in one-car smashups in 1969, "12,000 to 14,000 of these deaths will occur when the car crashes against a solid projection of some sort." A 1¼ mile long stretch of road outside Washington "has been the scene of 78 accidents, 60 of them off the road. A U.S. Government committee found that light poles, guard rails and massive sign supports were the worst hazards to motorists."

The author provides statistical detail of this nature throughout his article because he knows that it is only by bombarding the reader with such evidence that he can hope to convince him of the seriousness of the problem.

Factual detail is often used to develop an informal thesis. For example, Lester Sullivan in an article titled "Crying Slay and Havoc!" (*This Week Magazine*, November 12, 1967), offers some amusing historical proofs in support of the view that students have not changed much over the centuries.

> Nor is there anything "modern" in the withering opinions modern students entertain of the faculty. Students of medieval Bologna, according to Dr. Fowler, "would fine their professors for coming late to a lecture or wandering from the point."
>
> The art of writing home for money was as esteemed then as it is today. The father of a medieval Italian student complains, "A student's first song is a demand for money and there never will be a letter which does not ask for cash." Many of the boys had ecclesiastical patrons, and one of the most practical documents of the Middle Ages—shades of those where-the-girls-are guides for today's undergrads!—outlined 22 different methods of extracting cash from an archdeacon.

A final kind of detail is the argument, which can be defined as a logical reason given in support of a proposition. For instance, if you advance the view in a topic statement that you are opposed to the practice of giving children money for making good grades, you must provide reasons, such as those which follow, for your belief.

> 1) Children should be encouraged to study for knowledge, not for money.
>
> 2) Giving money for grades will engender a materialistic attitude in a child.
>
> 3) The other children in the family who do not get good grades will be made to feel inferior.

The giving of reasons is such a common form of detail that its importance is often overlooked by the student writer. Note that taking a position on any of the following issues would require supporting arguments: euthanasia, capital punishment, a volunteer army, civil rights, and the voting age.

It might be necessary to remind you at this point that the four kinds of detail which have been discussed—example, explanation, fact, and argument—are not pure forms. Thus, in a piece of writing, a given detail could be regarded as being an example or a fact, or perhaps an explanation or an argument. Fortunately, hard and fast distinctions are unimportant here. What *is* important is that the writer must never fail to provide convincing detail of one kind or another for his topics.

In an attempt to focus the student writer's attention on the importance of content, teachers often say that supporting paragraphs are little themes in themselves, in which a topic sentence is stated, developed, and brought to a close. The selection below will afford us an example of one of these "miniature themes" and at the same time illustrate the use of dialogue, a very effective form of detail. In this sample taken from a student essay by Vick Riba, "A Friend Is Not a Jury" (*Seventeen Magazine*, 1967), the writer argues that people should be permitted to select their own friends.

> These days friendships are much more demanding; other people try to attach many strings to it. . . . Just last week a young man and I went for a walk in my neighborhood in the course of which we met a girl I know. That night she telephoned me:
> "Where did you get that beautiful boy?"
> "John's Bargain Store," I answered. "Three for a dollar."
> "He looks like a living doll, but if I were you, I'd let him go." I visualized the time in camp when I'd caught a fish but had to throw it back.
> "You mean he's too small to eat?"
> "No," replied the girl. And then, very seriously: "But I don't think he's for you."
> "Why?" Had I failed to notice something important? A third eye perhaps?
> The receiver screeched, and although I pulled it from my ear quickly, I still heard: "He lisps. And he wears white socks."
> And so he does, so he does. But am I expected to abandon a pleasant friendship because of non-sibilant *s*'s and a bad taste in haberdashery? It's so illogical. Neither condition is catching, after all.

The above piece functions as a link in the overall theme and as a little composition in itself: the topic sentence serves as "thesis," the detailed dialogue constitutes the "body," and the conclusion drawn in the final lines makes up the "closing."

Despite the fact that the novice writer has grasped the four kinds of detail which are used to expand topic sentences and can appreciate the fact that supporting paragraphs in a composition often form little themes in themselves, he still finds critical comments such as these in the margin of his papers:

> "Provide details. Name and discuss the books which were your 'first teachers.'"
> "A *full explanation* is needed to show how you finally learned to take effective notes. You stopped short."
> "You say that 'your job at the summer camp taught you many valuable lessons.' *What* camp and *what* valuable lessons? Don't cheat your reader of the most interesting examples."

"This paper is full of unanswered questions—why did you decide to work your way through college, in what way was delivering mail disagreeable, how much did you make at the drugstore, what did your father say in his letter that convinced you to accept his help, and how do you feel now about taking money from your parents?"

"This statement is an unsupported generalization. Los Angeles may be the greatest city in the nation for young people, but you must back up your contention with some concrete evidence."

Is there any further advice which can be given to the student whose themes are marked down in this manner? The truth is that anyone can solve the problem of incomplete development *if he will prewrite his compositions*. In almost every instance the quickly planned theme results in a bare outline with few or no elaborative details, whereas the prewritten list contains a multitude of particulars.

For example, if you composed a quick outline on the issue of cluttered versus uncluttered desks, you would produce a plan something like this:

Contrary to what many people believe, a cluttered desk is not always proof of a cluttered mind.
1) Those who work at cluttered desks often get more done than those whose desks are neat and tidy.
2) What looks like a cluttered desk often consists of organized stacks of papers and books.
3) A desk top is where things get done; it is not an ornament.

Now where are the *details* which will make your topics clear, interesting, and convincing? You say that those who work at cluttered desks often accomplish more than those who keep their desks orderly. Perhaps, but without concrete examples based on the work habits of students, professors, and businessmen, you can hardly convince the reader. Or do you propose to think up these examples and write the rough draft at the same time?

Your second point is a perceptive one—that what often appears to be a clutter is actually organized stacks of work—but it will fall flat without supporting detail. To persuade the reader, you must provide, on the basis of your own experiences, actual illustrations to show what these "organized stacks" may contain and how they are handled by an efficient worker in the course of a day.

Your last topic sounds convincing—that a desk top should be a work bench and not an ornament—but you cannot expect to sell the reader with this bare statement. Why, specifically, should a desk be defined as a place where things get done? And what's wrong with neatness? Cannot a desk be neat and still a place where the work gets done? If you do not answer these charges, you reader will answer them against you and refute your argument as he goes.

Even if you began with a fuller outline, it would not include the details found in a prewritten list of your ideas. For instance, how will you open your case in defense of cluttered desks? Ordinarily an outline does not include background material, but in working from an inventory of ideas you would be sure to find a good opener—perhaps a humorous anecdote concerning a Professor Jones, whose desk was so cluttered that students claimed no one had seen the color of the paint since 1925. You might also get in the rumor about the safety inspector who tried to condemn the building on the grounds that Jones's desk was a fire hazard. Using this little story as your lead, you could launch your thesis:

> There is no denying the condition of Professor Jones's desk. It had at least four layers of student papers, catalogues, books, and other paraphernalia. But it is also true that Jones never failed to get his assignments and tests out right on schedule. In fact, old Jonesy got more work done on his cluttered desk than ten other instructors could turn out in a week!

Thanks to the particulars which you turned up through prewriting, this paper would contain more interesting detail in the opening paragraph than most students manage to get into an entire theme.

Nothing has been said concerning the other kinds of detail, such as the use of narration, contrast, and character sketch in developing a topic sentence and the method of asking yourself questions about your key ideas as a way of finding the necessary particulars; but you will encounter all of these devices and a dozen more by reading the informative-persuasive pieces published in magazines and newspapers. The chief thing is to grasp the importance of detail—the fact that as readers we remember, not the entire line of thought in an article or a column, but rather the memorable details which highlight the piece—the valuable insights, the touches of humor, the curious facts, and the bits of sound advice.

If you read the prose pieces around you with the eye of a craftsman, it should not take you long to learn that details make the composition, and details come from prewriting.

Closing

1. Lacks Punch and Sense of Completeness Since weak closings constitute a serious roadblock for the novice, we must carefully examine the various elements which are related to this problem.

Simply defined, the closing section of a composition rounds out and adds a note of finality to what has gone before. This can be achieved by summarizing the chief points, by drawing a conclusion, or by restating the thesis or a key phrase in the introduction. As a matter of fact, end paragraphs often contain a combination of these elements.

An article in a trade journal by Rex R. Gogerty, "Soybean Growing Pains" (*The Furrow*, May, June, 1969), will afford us an example of a summary closing. The author's thesis is that "scientists have been taking a closer look at the critical stages of soybean growth. By studying these various stages, they're able to suggest ways to ease the crop through troubled times." After analyzing at length the problems which attend each stage, the writer neatly sums them up in a closing paragraph.

> In short then, calendarized planting, pre-harvest planning, careful seed selection, and especially combine operator care help put more beans in the bin. With less dependence on luck and more on management, every stage of soybean growth can be less critical.

The "tie back" technique, in which the writer restates his thesis or restates a key phrase taken from the lead paragraph, is a very effective means of closing. As an example, let us suppose that you have written this opening for a theme called, "All About Perch."

> I'm a perch fisherman myself. People have been saying for years that perch are a kid's fish, but don't you believe it. Perch, variously called sunfish, blue gill, and bream, have more fight per ounce than trout or bass and beat them all in taste. In short, they're good catchin' and good fryin'—*if* you know how.

Let us further suppose that you have written the body of the paper, in which you give the reader tips on how to catch and cook perch, and are now ready to close. A tie-back to the line about being a perch fisherman might be just the touch you need to give unity to your paper.

> So if you knock on my door any evening from May through September and I'm not at home, you're pretty sure to find me under a tree at the nearest lake or creek. That's the way with us perch fishermen.

The most common method of closing is to draw a conclusion in the form of a suggestion, prediction, warning, reminder, or preference. Any idea will serve as a closing as long as it follows logically from the line of thought which you have set up.

For example, C. Terry Cline Jr. in his article "Canine Basic Training" (*Catholic Miss*, April, 1969), provides the reader with a step by step method of training a dog and then closes with an idea which the reader can apply to the entire training program.

> And don't lose your love for your dog if training him is difficult. When the going is slow, remind yourself that his relatives are serving man all over the world in many ways. . . . Just remember, your dog is like other dogs—he loves you, or at least wants to. He'd like to please you. With training, he will want to serve you. Go slowly. Enjoy one another.

Concluding ideas often appear in the form of quotations and anecdotes. In an article entitled "Dare to Make Mistakes" (*Guideposts*, December, 1965), Beth Day develops the point that many people do not live fully because they are afraid to make mistakes. She uses a passage from Emerson to cap her argument.

> To admit mistakes takes a sense of humor, and this wisdom, too frequently, does not come until late in life. But, in the words of Emerson: "Finish each day and be done with it. You have done what you could. Some blunders and absurdities no doubt crept in; forget them as soon as you can. Tomorrow is a new day; begin it well and serenely, and with too high a spirit to be cumbered with your old nonsense."

In "How to Handle Your Parents" (*This Week*, March 23, 1969), C. W. Shedd gives teenagers a set of rules on how to avoid parental conflict, such as doing something nice for their parents at least once a week and learning to say "I'm sorry." The concluding idea is carried by a humorous anecdote.

> "But—twelve rules or twelve *hundred* rules—it's no use!" you say. "My folks are simply impossible!"
> So?
> So, I'm sorry.
> But then there was this one boy who wrote: "I was thinking all these horrible thoughts about my parents when suddenly it hit me—if they're all that bad, how come I'm so wonderful?"

As a glance at popular prose will reveal, there are unlimited ways of closing. It would certainly be a mistake to count the techniques we have listed and assume that they exhaust the possibilities. One article writer set forth the do's and don'ts of safe highway driving and closed with a short reader's quiz on the material. Another writer worked up an interesting feature on turtles to show that they are a "gourmet's dream," and ended the piece very appropriately with a recipe for Terrapin Newburg. An ad writer wound up his pitch on used Volkswagens with a slogan—"Look for this sticker and you won't get stuck."

To turn now to problems which young writers face in composing closings, we will observe that most of the difficulties can be attributed to some shortcoming in the prewriting process.

For example, students who have not grasped the organic wholeness of a theme which comes through prewriting customarily omit the closing and leave their readers hanging at the end of the last paragraph. These writers must learn that the theses which they state and support must also be brought to a suitable close. The solution to their problem consists of trying out in the prewriting stage of a theme the various closings which we have described, as well as noting the great variety of end paragraphs in magazine and newspaper selections.

It is true that in some instances the last paragraph in the body of a paper adds the necessary concluding note to the development, but in most cases the writer must provide a final ground for his discussion, a deliberate resolution of the thesis in the form of a closing paragraph.

A second error involves gimmick closings—the hackneyed "It was all a dream" and "I was only fooling" devices which are supposed to titilate the reader. But the reader cannot be put off by last minute dodges, and the writer who uses them is only deceiving himself. The same verdict must be made of last gasp attempts at melodrama—*The known cases of shoplifting in our country cry out for action—action—action is needed—now!* Far from shoring up a weak presentation, closings which strain for effect can result in the complete collapse of a piece of writing.

Perhaps the chief reason novice writers are tempted by gimmicks is their belief that the closing constitutes a "do or die" situation in which the reader is either won over or lost. It is true that concluding paragraphs are important, but if you have not earned your reader's respect by the time you get to the end of your paper, it is doubtful that a final all-out effort will succeed. One often hears that the closing represents the writer's "last contact" with the reader, but it must be remembered that the end paragraph is only one part of an entire line of thought, and usually a subordinate part at that. Clearly, the best closing is an honest closing—and this can be found only by taking thought in the prewriting stage of the composition.

Perhaps the most common failing is the lame conclusion, which covers a multitude of sins: an obvious, unimaginative conclusion, a far-fetched or irrelevant concluding idea, or a simple-minded restatement of the writer's thesis.

As to how to avoid weak closings, we need not labor at this point the importance of the exploratory stage of composition. Compare two writers. One has prewritten his thoughts on a topic. With a wealth of ideas before him, he has a choice of closing thoughts. The other writer has composed a meager outline. Far from having a choice of closings, he must hunt to find supporting detail for his topics. Typically he will not even consider the closing until he writes his rough draft, at which time he will wonder why forming a good closing is always such a difficult task.

Professionals say that until you have worked out a strong closing, you are not ready to write. This familiar advice shows us that prewriting is not a new concept, because when do you "work out" a closing if not in the prewriting stage?

The beginning writer must learn from professionals to scan his material early in the writing process for good closing lines. By having his wits about him, he can usually spot an appealing detail and save it for his closing. This is what the staff writer did who composed the news item, "69, He Refuses to Act His Age" (*Des Moines Register*, May 11, 1969). After catching our eye with a good lead about Herman Thoden, a U.S. speed walking champion from 1931-34 who at 69 still walks five miles to work every day and takes fifty-mile hikes on the weekend, the author follows through with an abundance of details on Thoden's life. We learn that he became a speed walker in World War I "as a 106-pound private carrying an 80-pound pack," that his other hobbies include hunting and rope skipping, that in helping to train the heavyweight boxing champion Jack Dempsey, he had him jump rope "until his tongue was hanging out," and that he credits his own health and vigor to "55 years of walking almost everywhere." One might think that the writer had used up his most interesting notes, but such is not the case. He wisely saved the best detail to clinch his closing paragraphs:

> He [Thoden] is often kidded about his stamina and endurance. One such incident occurred during one of his annual deer hunting trips to Upper Michigan.
>
> "One year," he chuckles, "my companions couldn't find a bullet hole in the deer I shot. They claimed I walked it to death."

Use the following checklist of errors as a guide in prewriting your themes. Although the errors summarized below are by no means exhaustive, they do account for many of the chief failings in freshman writing. And remember that this list is compiled for use in the *planning* stage of your composition—for *pre*vision, not for *re*vision.

In using the checklist, if you are in doubt as to the meaning of an entry, go back and re-read the discussion given to it.

Checklist of Errors for Prevision

1) Thesis
   Vague or missing
   Unrestricted
   Lacks Specific Purpose
   Wrong Focus
   Trite
2) Background
   Failure To Create Reader Interest
   Missing Who, What, Where, When and Why Information
3) Topic Sentences
   Unclear and Irrelevant
4) Detail
   Missing Examples, Explanations and Proof
5) Closing
   Lacks Punch and Sense of Completeness

18

Revising the Theme

Good writers know that it is not enough to previse their material through the initial list of thoughts, the outline, and the rough draft. It is also necessary to revise the last copy for final changes before it is submitted to the instructor.

The extent of this revision or "second look" depends, of course, on the nature of the assignment and the skill of the writer. Long papers usually require more revision than short ones, and the greater the experience of the writer, the fewer changes he is required to make. But for all authors, hindsight remains an essential part of composition. It is, after all, the final touches which make a good work excellent, and this is true of all endeavors.

It might be useful to note that professionals revise their material in two ways: they judge the entire composition for overall effect, and they read for specific problems in mechanics and diction. In overall revision, the writer asks, "How well do the ideas add up in this paper?" If he discovers that the general effect is marred by a bad transition or a skimpy closing, he makes the necessary changes. In checking the mechanics, the writer is apt to consult his dictionary for a doubtful spelling or the reference section of his handbook for the rules on *who* and *whom*.

As to the actual steps involved in revising a paper, there are only a few, but they are all important. The first is: never attempt to revise your paper immediately after you have completed the final copy. Instead, put the paper aside and let it "cool" for a few days. This lapse of time will give you the distance you need to play the role of the objective critic. It will enable you to distinguish between *what you intended to write* and *what you in fact wrote*. There is, by the way, a moral here for procrastinators: if you begin a written assignment late, you usually have time to revise it only once. But if you begin the paper early, you can revise it at your leisure.

A second rule, and one which many beginning writers are unacquainted with, is to proofread for one error or one category of error at a time. This means that every paper must be proofread, not once, but several times. Teachers often hear this defense of a badly revised theme: "Well, I read the paper through once and proofed it." But what can be accomplished in a single reading in which the writer attempts to judge all the elements in his paper? Can he identify bad grammar, unclear topics, inadequate development, slang expressions, poor content, and errors in punctuation at a glance? A better plan is to allow for separate readings. For example, you might want to test first for overall effectiveness. Are the key sentences clear? Do the parts of the paper hang together? Then read through for errors in grammar and diction. Some writers make it a habit to proofread once for their own particular weaknesses, such as literary flourishes or the overuse of the comma. The checklist provided at the end of our discussion will give you some help in working out your own method of proofreading.

By all means learn to proof your material by reading it aloud. Errors such as wordiness, wrong diction, and awkward construction are more readily heard than seen. The oral reading of your theme is not a foolproof device, but it will enable you to catch many mistakes which would otherwise go undetected.

Whenever possible, type your theme rather than write it out. Aside from looking more professional, typed copy is easier to proofread: matters pertaining to diction, punctuation, and spelling are highlighted by the increased legibility, and weaknesses in the general effect are more easily perceived.

Some beginning writers find errors by proofing but fail to correct them. A response commonly heard is, "Yes, I knew that was the wrong word for the context when I turned the paper in." It is true that finding the right word or phrase does not always come easily, but the good writer perseveres. He never settles for second best.

It is a strange thing that some student writers labor over subtleties but ignore obvious errors in their themes, such as inverted letters, omitted articles, and lack of end punctuation. Perhaps they believe that these "typos" constitute excusable errors. But it is a discourtesy to burden the reader with mistakes of any kind, particularly those which would take only a moment to correct.

The same thing can be said concerning neatness and correct manuscript form. It is difficult for the reader to overlook illegible writing, numerous crossed out passages, and a missing title.

How much time should you spend in revising your material? As much as is needed to give it the smoothness and polish of a well-wrought finished product. Although you need not follow to the letter Margery Allingham's suggestion, her often-quoted advice reveals that revision is more of an art than you may have supposed: "I write every paragraph four times: once to get my meaning down, once to put in everything I left out, once to take out everything that seems unnecessary, and once to make the whole thing sound as though I had just written it."

The checklist which follows may prove useful as a guide in the revising of your themes.

Checklist of Errors for Revision

1) Revising for Overall Effect
   Is the thesis clear?
   Do the topic sentences guide the reader from one idea to the next?
   Are the main points fully developed?
   Is the closing effective?
   Do the parts combine to convey a total message?
2) Revising for Mechanics and Diction
   Grammar
   Punctuation
   Word Choice
   Spelling
   Careless Errors
   Neatness and Correct Manuscript Form
   Your Own Weaknesses

Glossary

      This reference section provides a list of entries on grammar, punctuation, rhetorical terms, and usage.

    The following labels will be employed:

    Informal describes the everyday language found in magazines and newspapers.

    Colloquial refers to familiar and idiomatic expressions used in conversation.

    Formal means the scholarly language characteristic of literary, scientific, and other specialist publications.

    Nonstandard pertains to expressions in uneducated speech which are not acceptable in popular, business, and professional writing.

    Since usage is constantly affected by technological and social changes, the labels applied here are intended as guidelines, not as definitive judgments. If you are in doubt concerning the use of a word in a given context, consult your dictionary. You might also refer to the section on language in Chapter 1. When authorities differ (as they often will), you must determine for yourself the appropriateness of a word on the basis of your subject and intended audience.

abbreviations   Abbreviations of government agencies (*FBI, CIA*) and biographical terms (*ibid, pp.*) are found in all levels of writing, but abbreviations such as *Xmas, e.g.* and *St.* are inappropriate unless the style is very informal.

affect, effect   These words are often confused. *Affect* is a verb meaning "to influence." *Effect* is a noun meaning "result."

    He was *affected* by what she said.

    The *effect* of her speech was unmistakable.

  NOTE: *Effect* can also be used as a verb to mean "bring about."

    A settlement was at last *effected*.

agreement Subjects and verbs should agree in number.
>   *One* of the boys *is* here.
>   *Were* there many *objections*?

> Pronouns should agree with their antecedents.
>   *Each* of the girls must do *her* own work.
>   If a *person* has something to say, *he* should say it.

all the farther, faster Colloquial for "as far as" and "as fast as."

anecdote A short narrative, often humorous, used for illustrative purposes, particularly as a means of opening or closing an article.

alliteration Using words which repeat the same initial sound. This technique is employed to create special effects, such as euphony, emphasis, or humor.
>   Even the weariest river
>   Winds somewhere safe to sea.
>
>   Peter Piper picked a peck of pickled peppers.
>
>   He went from rags to riches in three short years.
>
>   Williamstown Wallops Whiteside—15 to 1.

alot An unacceptable variant spelling of "a lot."

alright "All right" is still the preferred spelling.

altho A shortened form of "although," used in highly informal prose.

and etc. The "and" is redundant, since "etc." means "and so forth."

apostrophe Used to indicate omitted letters (*I've, the class of '49*), the plural of letters and numbers (*Your 5's look like Z's*), and the possessive case of nouns and pronouns (*man's hat, teachers' cars, somebody's book*).

awful, awfully Colloquial and overworked—*an awful painting, awfully bad coffee.* Substitute a specific modifier or omit—*an unimaginative painting, bad coffee.*

as Colloquial when used to mean "because" or "since."
>   *ineffective:* *As* I was tired, I left early.
>   *revised:* *Since* I was tired, I left early.
>
>   *ineffective:* I could not look up the author's name *as* I had lost my book.
>   *revised:* I could not look up the author's name *because* I had lost my book.

being as Nonstandard for "since" or "because."
>   *ineffective:* *Being as* I have been elected, I will do my best.
>   *revised:* *Since* I have been elected, I will do my best.

capital letters Used to identify direct quotations, proper nouns, geographical areas, and the main words in a title.
>   The man said, "We will go with you."
>   His favorite saying is, "Nothing succeeds like success."
>   He did not know that Aristotle developed the Aristotelian method.

>We are traveling south, but we are not yet in the South.
>In the chapter titled "Popular Prose," the author makes a number of references to *Time* and *The Saturday Review*.
>The title of my last paper was "How Not to Fish for Bass."

case The function of a pronoun determines whether the subjective, objective, or possessive case will be used.

>Give the paper to Bob and *me*. (object of the preposition)
>It is *we* who must establish the new freedoms. (renames the subject "it")
>I didn't mind *your* saying that. (modifies the gerund "saying")

The pronouns "who" and "whom" present a special problem. Use "who," the subjective case, as subject and linked complement.

>*Who* called yesterday?
>It was *who* on the phone?

Use "whom," the objective case, as object of a preposition or verb.

>For *whom* do you work?
>*Whom* did he invite?

In popular prose, "who" is sometimes used for "whom" when it opens the sentence.

>*Who* are you looking for?
>*Who* did they elect?

choppy sentences A string of short sentences which suffer from lack of variety.

>*ineffective:* This is an interesting book. The subject concerns wild monkeys. It was written in 1925.

Correct by condensing to the main ideas in each sentence.

>*revised:* This interesting book about wild monkeys was written in 1925.

clipped words It is important to distinguish between shortened forms which have found general acceptance in the language (*plane, lab, gym*) and those which are considered colloquial (*prof, Phys. Ed., gent*).

colon Used chiefly to introduce a series, a quotation, and a re-statement or explanation of an idea.

>Please send me the following items: two reams of paper, three pens, and two small notebooks.
>Jones gave the press this statement: "I am not interested in the office of mayor and I never have been."
>This poem is a fraud: it lacks idea, structure, and image.

coordination, subordination An element is said to be coordinated when it is given a rank or emphasis equal to another idea.

>I was tired. I went to bed early.
>Jack will be here soon. He is an old friend of mine.

When an element is given a lesser rank or emphasis in relation to another idea, it is said to be subordinated.

>Since I was tired, I went to bed early.
>Jack, an old friend of mine, will be here soon.

colloquial expressions Familiar and idiomatic expressions used in conversation. Magazine and newspaper writers frequently employ colloquialisms as a means of achieving color and tempo:

> Where do we go from here?
> Shape up or ship out.
> That's the way it is, baby.
> The American tax payer has had it but good!

comma Used mainly to mark independent clauses, elements in a series, contrasted elements, and interrupting elements:

> I read the play written by your friend, and I must say that I enjoyed it.
> He collects proverbs, short poems, and anecdotes.
> Study the first chapter, not the second one.
> I do not, by the way, owe you two dollars.

A comma is also employed to prevent misreading.

> Surprisingly, enough money was collected for the project.

Overuse of the comma can be distracting.

> *ineffective:* If, by any chance, you talk to my old coach, please say, that I learned a great deal from him, last year.
> *revised:* If by any chance you talk to my old coach, please say that I learned a great deal from him last year.

comma splice (comma fault) A comma should not be used by itself to join two sentences.

> I spoke to John, he ignored me completely.

Correct spliced sentences by using a period; a comma plus *and*, *but*, *or*, *nor*; a semicolon; or a semicolon plus *however*, *consequently*, *therefore*, etc.

> I spoke to John. He ignored me completely.
> I spoke to John, but he ignored me completely.
> I spoke to John; he ignored me completely.
> I spoke to John; however, he ignored me completely.

Exceptions: A comma can be used by itself to connect short sentences in a series. The comma is often omitted in short compounds connected by *and* and *but*.

> I tried, I failed, I quit.
> I knew Bob and I knew his brother.

contractions As a general rule, contractions should be avoided unless one is trying for the breezy, conversational tone found in highly informal prose.

> If this isn't a good buy on a new stove, we've never seen one.
> I said to myself—Let's see. Should you or shouldn't you? I decided that I shouldn't.

could of, must of, should of Nonstandard for *could have, must have, should have.*

cute An overworked colloquialism. Use specific modifiers such as *pleasing, attractive, beautiful, pretty.*

dangling modifier A modifier which does not refer logically to some other word in the sentence.

> While climbing the hill, a tree was hit by lightning.

Revise dangling modifiers by adding the word needed to make the meaning clear.

> While *I* was climbing the hill, a tree was hit by lightning.
> While climbing the hill, *I* saw lightning hit a tree.

dash Used chiefly for emphasis and to mark an interrupted thought.

> She lacks one thing—brains.
> He graduated—and I know you will have trouble believing it—in four years.
> He was—well, indiscreet.

ellipsis marks Used to indicate omitted words in a quoted passage.

> Jones said, "I believe that people in this state, and indeed throughout the whole country, need to think more and argue less."
>
> Jones said, "I believe that people . . . need to think more and argue less."

enthuse Colloquial for "enthusiastic."

etc. A shortened form of *et cetera*, (and so forth) used in informal writing.

fallacy An illogical statement. Common errors in logic include these fallacies:

a) faulty (hasty) generalization in which the writer fails to provide supporting evidence
b) false analogy, a strained or illogical comparison
c) non sequitur, the attempt to discredit a person's viewpoint by criticizing his personal habits, beliefs, or appearance
d) name-calling, the use of labels (*revolutionist, atheist, hippie*) rather than logical arguments
e) either-or reasoning which excludes valid alternatives (Love America or leave it)
f) the all-instead-of-some error which overstates the point (All freshmen are immature).

fine writing The inappropriate use of ornate and literary language.

> *ineffective:* I went to see my advisor, *albeit* I had been told that he was ill.
> *revised:* I went to see my advisor, *although* I had been told that he was ill.
>
> *ineffective:* As I *rounded* the corner—*lo*, who should appear but my *mentor*, Mr. Williams.
> *revised:* As I *turned* the corner, who should appear but my *teacher*, Mr. Williams.
>
> *ineffective:* I never did trust Bill, and one day I caught him trying to steal my *lexicon*.
> *revised:* I never did trust Bill, and one day I caught him trying to steal my *dictionary*.

fused sentences   Main clauses which are run together without any punctuation.

> *incorrect:*   I have already met your brother he's my roommate.
> *revised:*   I have already met your brother. He's my roommate.

good, well   Two modifiers often confused. "Good" is an adjective; "well" is an adverb.

> Thomas is a good writer, but he does not spell very well.

hyperbole   The use of exaggeration for special effect.

> I would give a million dollars to see him again.
> Now on Sale—The World's Best Hamburgers
> She wouldn't say good morning if her life depended on it!

hyphen   Used to join compound nouns, fractions, numbers from twenty-one to ninety-nine, affixes, and compound modifiers.

> Is it possible that the *Lieutenant-Governor* is an *ex-pug*?
> This is the *twenty-fourth* cafe on the list.
> Is *three-fifths* more than *four-fifths*?
> Here is a *do-it-yourself* kit.

> NOTE: Do not hyphenate words spelled as solids or as separate forms.

> *incorrect:*   I studied for two hours; *never-the-less*, I failed the test.
> *revised:*   I studied for two hours; *nevertheless*, I failed the test.
> *incorrect:*   I contributed to the fund, *even-though* I questioned the purpose of it.
> *revised:*   I contributed to the fund, *even though* I questioned the purpose of it.

idioms   Figurative expressions which are established in the language.

> I finally got the hang of it.
> We struck a bargain.
> Many a man has loved her.
> She looked daggers at me.

induction, deduction   Induction is the process of reasoning which goes from the particular instances to the general truth or proposition. Deduction goes from the general proposition to the particulars which support it.

Prewriting a topic is an example of induction: the writer often begins by listing the particulars, which lead him to a proposition or thesis. The finished theme illustrates deduction: the writer presents his thesis, then the particulars which illustrate or support it.

image   A vivid picture drawn by the writer. Composition students are often urged to *show* the reader through images, rather than *talk about* their subject. Compare these versions:

> *vague:*   Joe was homely but still charming. Everybody liked him.
> *revised:*   Joe had beady eyes, a pug nose, freckles, and stringy red hair. But when he smiled—which was most of the time—all was forgiven. There was enough warmth and love of life in that broad grin to charm the devil himself.

imply, infer Two words which are often confused. Generally, *imply* means to *suggest*, and *infer* means to *conclude*.

- a) Are you *implying* [suggesting] that because it is late, we should leave?
- b) No, I did not mean for you to *infer* [conclude] that. I don't want to leave yet.
- a) All right, but the tone of your voice conveyed that *implication* [suggestion].
- b) I'm sorry, but you drew a wrong *inference* [conclusion].

irony A term used to describe a tongue-in-cheek statement in which the writer means the opposite of what he says.

Oh yes, the food at this school is delightful. Students are happy to stand in line for hours waiting to be served. Sometimes there are fights over who gets the leftovers.

I have never taken a better test. Just think, there were only *250* questions and a *whole hour* to complete them in. And the questions were so *easy*. I am sure that everyone in the class will get an A—at least!

is when, is where Do not use *when* and *where* clauses to complete a definition.

ineffective: A fused construction is when (is where) you run two sentences together without any punctuation.

revised: A fused construction is an error in which two sentences are run together without any punctuation.

it's, its Do not confuse *it's*, a contraction meaning *it is*, and *its*, a pronoun which shows possession.

I know that it's [it is] too late to register.
Do not look into its eyes.

italics Used for emphasis and to mark titles, names, foreign words, and words out of context.

I must repeat that the young writer should *not* attempt a full-length article on the first assignment.

I sketched the *Mona Lisa*, finished Graham Greene's *The Heart of the Matter*, and saw the picture *The Dolphin* all in one night.

The Spanish word for *everybody* is *todo el mundo*, which means literally *all the world*.

NOTE: See *quotation marks*, which are often used interchangeably with italics.

kind of, sort of Overused colloquial expressions for *rather* and *somewhat*.

loose, lose Two words which are frequently confused. *Loose* is an adjective, *lose* is a verb.

If the bolts on that carburetor are *loose*, we could *lose* this race.

lot of, lots of Overused informal expressions for *many, much, a great deal, a great number*.

metaphor A comparison of two basically dissimilar things which are shown to be alike in some striking way.

> My dad's a bear in the morning.
> In his eyes, the girl was an angel.
> He can't dance. He's an ox.
> The people are the backbone of the nation.
> Do you call this steak? I call it shoe leather.

A simile is a metaphor in which the words *like* or *as* are included.

> My dad is like a bear in the morning.
> He dances like an ox.
> This steak is as tough as shoe leather.

misplaced parts Words and word groups which are in the wrong position in the sentence.

> *ineffective:* You don't even need *sometimes* an introduction.
> *revised:* *Sometimes* you don't even need an introduction.

> *ineffective:* The man made a kite for the little boy *with a long tail*.
> *revised:* The man made a kite *with a long tail* for the little boy.

> *ineffective:* I could never remember whether the Greeks or the Romans came first *in my history class*.
> *revised:* *In my history class* I could never remember whether the Greeks or the Romans came first.

nonstandard Expressions used by uneducated persons, such as *I ain't did nothing, them there, it don't matter.*

nice An overused colloquial expression. Substitute *pleasant, charming, interesting, friendly*.

omitted words (∧) Do not omit words needed for clarity.

> *ineffective:* This paper is as good, if not better than, that one.
> *revised:* This paper is as good *as*, if not better than, that one.

> *ineffective:* I feel the rules should be changed.
> *revised:* I feel *that* the rules should be changed.

> *ineffective:* Do co-eds like mathematics better than boys?
> *revised:* Do co-eds like mathematics better than boys *do*?

parallel structure The balancing of similar grammatical elements for rhetorical effect.

> *One for the money*
> *Two for the show*
> *What you did* was a noble thing, but *why you did it* is quite another matter.
> *We live, we die, we are re-born.*

Note the effect of faulty parallel structure in which the elements are not balanced.

> *ineffective:* They taught us *to do our own work, to respect our parents, and we should ask for help* if we needed it.

revised: They taught us *to do our own work, to respect our parents,* and *to ask for help* if we needed it.

ineffective: Wright is a student *with energy* and *who has enthusiasm.*

revised: Wright is a student *with energy* and *enthusiasm.*

paraphrase Putting another person's idea into your own words.

original version: Schopenhauer said, "It would generally serve writers in good stead if they would see that, whilst a man should, if possible, think like a great genius, he should talk the same language as everyone else. Authors should use common words to say uncommon things. But they do just the opposite. We find them trying to wrap up trivial ideas in grand words, and to clothe their very ordinary thoughts in the most extraordinary phrases, the most far-fetched, unnatural and out-of-the-way expressions."

paraphrased version: Schopenhauer said that writers should think deeply and write simply. But they often reverse the process. Instead of expressing profound thoughts in plain words, they set forth trivial ideas in fancy language.

Students often suppose that because the wording is changed in a paraphrased version, the source of the material need not be indicated. This is incorrect. All borrowed ideas must be acknowledged, whether the original is quoted or paraphrased.

past, passed Two words which are frequently confused. *Past* is a preposition or an adverb. *Passed* is a verb.

A car passed us.
It sped past.

personification The rhetorical device of treating an inanimate object or an abstract idea as though it were human.

Father Time is slow but sure.
The eyes of Texas are upon you.
Fate stepped in.
Blizzard Swoops Down on Midwest
Whispering summer breezes caressed her hair.

principal, principle Distinguish carefully between these two words.

Principle is a noun meaning "fundamental idea." *Principal* is a noun and an adjective meaning "chief," "official," or "sum of money."

These two ideas are based on the very same principle.
The principal thing to remember is that he is the boss.
How much interest do I pay on the principal?
The principal of the school was out of town.

pun A humorous play on words which conveys a double meaning.

Strip Tease Artist to Plead Own Case in Court
Wants to Reveal Bare Facts

Suspect Foul Play in Disappearance of Governor's Parakeet

Dog Puts Bite on Tax Collector

quotation marks Used to identify direct quotations, minor titles, and words used in a special sense.

"I like you very much," he said.
According to Maugham, "Simplicity is not such an obvious merit as lucidity."
I just read an article in a recent issue of *Field and Stream* called, "How to Save Our National Parks."
His "expensive" car turned out to be a 1957 Chevy.
What does the word "parse" mean in grammar?
I have noticed that the "in" thing doesn't stay in very long.

As a general rule, periods and commas are placed inside the quotation marks; semicolons go outside.

"Yes," he said, "but I do not have a dollar."
The word "thesis," by the way, ends with an "is."
His last words were, "See you later"; but he never did.

Exclamation points and question marks are placed inside the quotation marks when they are part of the quotation. When they apply to the whole sentence, they go outside.

"Billy, get away from that stove!" she shouted.
You don't even know the meaning of the word "study"!
"Can you tell me where Pine Street is?" she asked.
How do you spell "nincompoop"?

real An overused colloquial expression—*real tired, real hard test, real intelligent.*
For variety, use *very, unusually, rather,* or some other modifier.

reference Pronouns should refer clearly to their antecedents.

vague: I enjoyed the two years I spent at that school. *They* were very friendly.
revised: I enjoyed the two years I spent at that school. The students were very friendly.
vague: Bob liked the steak and the salad. *It* was rather small, however.
revised: Bob liked the steak and the salad. *The steak* was rather small, however.
vague: The language in his novel is technical, the plot is complex, and the theme is obscure. *This* should be considered before you check out the book.
revised: The language in his novel is technical, the plot is complex, and the theme is obscure. *These problems* should be considered before you check out the book.

repetition An effective device when used deliberately for effect.

Plans? Why plans are everything! Life itself is, or should be, a plan.
Of the people, by the people, for the people.
Do you know what freedom is? Well I will tell you what freedom is. Freedom is living without your foot on my neck.

Note that unnecessary repetition is distracting.

ineffective: When I asked him for a *job*, he said that there was a *job* available last week, but someone had already applied for that *job*.
revised: When I asked him for a *job*, he said that there was a *position* available last week, but someone had already applied for *it*.

run-on sentence   A series of main clauses in which *and* and *so* are used excessively as connectors.

> *ineffective:*   I did not believe that the printer would accept our offer, so I wrote him a long letter and he said the price was all right, so I sent him the money.
>
> *revised:*   Since I did not believe that the printer would accept our offer, I wrote him a long letter. When he said the price was all right, I sent him the money.

satire   A popular rhetorical technique in which the faults and shortcomings of a subject are treated humorously. Satire, which often takes the form of ridicule, mockery, or burlesque, may be gentle or biting, depending on the aim of the writer.

> Being a farmer is quite the life. Just think, a farmer can set his own hours, daylight to dark, and the overtime pay is great. And there is no one around to tell him he is doing something wrong—he gets to learn from his own mistakes. Being around livestock is rewarding too—a good swift kick from a cow helps toughen a man so that he can meet life's problems. And there is always the drought. With the crops all dried up, there's lots of time for praying.
>
> Well, I've just seen my first hockey game. Talk about throwing lions to the Christians! The gate is opened and twelve big bruisers carrying clubs are put into the arena. Two of these men are stationed in front of lopsided baskets and the other ten then try to beat them up.
>
> These two basket-watchers are bundled up in padding, ostensibly for protection, but actually this is so the spectators can't see the blood run out.
>
> The basket-watchers have the stout hearts of Christians. Every two minutes ten fresh men are set in to give them another drubbing, but they go right on defending themselves. I never did see one carried out in the basket.
>
> "Law and Order on the Ice Rink,"
> Kathryn Love, *Des Moines Daily Register,* December 1, 1968

semicolon   A mark of punctuation which has the following chief uses:

a)   To connect main clauses which are closely related in meaning.

> My job is to lead; your job is to follow.
> As a writer, he is superb; as a teacher, he is a total flop.

b)   To connect main clauses separated by transitional expressions such as *consequently, nevertheless, however, therefore.*

> I like him; nevertheless, he is not the right man for the job.
> Mrs. Taylor resigned; consequently, the committee is short one member.

c)   To connect main clauses which contain internal punctuation.

> Mary arrived last night, I was told; and on her arrival at the base hospital, she found her uncle still alive.

NOTE: A comma is also acceptable in these constructions.

> Mary arrived last night, I was told, and on her arrival at the base hospital, she found her uncle still alive.

d)   To connect compound elements in a series.

> We invited Tom Clift, the president; Mary Jacobs, the vice-president; and Frieda Klein, their mutual friend.

He shook hands with the students, teachers, and administrators; smiled at the local dignitaries and their wives; and exchanged pleasantries with the governors, senators, and other political representatives who turned out for the occasion.

Do not misuse the semicolon by treating it as the equivalent of a comma or colon.

incorrect: Because I like her and her brother very much; I invited them to dinner.

revised: Because I like her and her brother very much, I invited them to dinner.

incorrect: Please send me the following articles; three reels, two casting rods, and one minnow bucket.

revised: Please send me the following articles: three reels, two casting rods, and one minnow bucket.

sentence fragment An incomplete sentence.

fragment: He should read some of the great novelists. *Such as Thomas Hardy and Jane Austen.*

revised: He should read some of the great novelists, such as Thomas Hardy and Jane Austen.

fragment: We cannot understand why she chose Smith. *When even his best friends admitted that he was not qualified for the job.*

revised: We cannot understand why she chose Smith. Even his best friends admitted that he was not qualified for the job.

fragment: I want to do a number of things before I die. *Go to college, race cars, search for lost gold mines, and maybe sail around the world.*

revised: I want to do a number of things before I die—go to college, race cars, search for lost gold mines, and maybe sail around the world.

Sentence fragments are often used for emphasis and to create the intimate tone of conversation.

Why did we vote this man into office? *Because we had no choice.*

Guess what? White's Paints cost you less now. *Same high quality paint at a greatly reduced price. Check it out. OK?*

shift Avoid unnecessary shifts in person and tense.

ineffective: A *man* should live each day fully because *you* do not know what tomorrow will bring.

revised: A *man* should live each day fully because *he* does not know what tomorrow will bring.

ineffective: We *huddled* there in the darkness. No one *spoke*. Then the captain *shouts* and we *rush* toward the unseen enemy.

revised: We *huddled* there in the darkness. No one *spoke*. Then the captain *shouted* and we *rushed* toward the unseen enemy.

simile See **metaphor**

so A frequently overused connective in informal prose.

> *ineffective:* *So* then I re-read the first chapter. I was still confused *so* I asked Bob for help.
>
> *revised:* Then I re-read the first chapter. Since I was still confused, I asked Bob for help.

spelling The best advice has not changed over the years: 1) when in doubt as to the correct spelling of a word, use a dictionary, and 2) keep a record of misspelled words for periodic review. Listing misspelled words is a valuable device for several reasons. For one thing, it will enable you to avoid repeating the same mistakes. For example, if you record and quiz yourself on the words *dormitory* (not *dormatory*) and *argument* (not *arguement*), it is not likely that you will miss them again. Listing words will also help you to pinpoint your specific problems, such as those analyzed below.

1) addition of letter
   athlete (not *athalete*)
   disastrous (not *disasterous*)
   tragedy (not *tradgedy*)
2) omission of letters
   quantity (not *quanity*)
   probably (not *probly*)
   candidate (not *canidate*)
3) transposition of letters
   receive (not *recieve*)
   performance (not *preformance*)
   gamble (not *gambel*)
4) confusion of *a, e, i, o* letters
   appearance (not *appearence*)
   maintenance (not *maintanance*)
   optimistic (not *optomistic*)
   actor (not *acter*)

NOTE: A very common error consists of combining words which are spelled separately.

> in fact (not *infact*)
> at least (not *atleast*)
> ever since (not *eversince*)

split infinitive The awkward separation of the parts of an infinitive.

> *ineffective:* I wanted *to* only *borrow* five dollars.
>
> *revised:* I only wanted *to borrow* five dollars.
>
> *ineffective:* I will try *to* not *say* anything foolish.
>
> *revised:* I will try not *to say* anything foolish.

Split infinitives which are not awkward are, of course, acceptable.

> One of the students tried *to* completely *re-write* the theme which was due Friday.

suppose to Nonstandard for "supposed to."

> *incorrect:* We were suppose to read the play.
>
> *revised:* We were supposed to read the play.

there's   A contracted form of "there is" used in highly informal prose.

> There's one thing you should know.

But do not use "there's" with a plural subject.

> *incorrect:*   There's a few things you should know.
> *revised:*   There are a few things you should know.
> *incorrect:*   There's three basic rules of etiquette.
> *revised:*   There are three basic rules of etiquette.

tho   A shortened form of "although," used in highly informal prose.

titles   Generally, titles should be short and to the point.

> *ineffective:*   Why I Am Opposed to the Present System of Giving Final Examinations
> *revised:*   The Case Against Final Examinations
>
> *ineffective:*   Three Constant Specters in My Life As a Writer
> *revised:*   My Writing Problems

NOTE: Imaginative titles can be effective when they reflect the purpose and tone of a composition. For example, in giving a humorous account of his successful battle against alcoholism, one author used the title, "Coming Through the Rye." Another writer presented arguments against euthanasia, titling his paper, "There Is No Good Death."

transitional expressions   Words and phrases which identify and connect the main points in a composition. The list which follows contains some of the more common transitional markers.

> first (in the first place)
> second (in the second place)
> finally
> on the other hand
> then too (moreover, in addition)
> but (nevertheless, however)
> for example (for instance)
> in conclusion (to sum up)

trite expressions   Overused, worn-out phrases.

> busy as a bee
> pretty as a picture
> thin as a rail
> rode off into the sunset
> got what was coming to him
> handsome as a Greek god
> like a ton of bricks

use to   Nonstandard for "used to."

> *incorrect:*   We use to go there often.
> *revised:*   We used to go there often.

verb The most common error in regard to verbs pertains to the use of the wrong principal part. As a general guideline, use the past participle of the verb with the auxillaries *have*, *has*, and *had*.

> *incorrect:* He has *drank* all the milk.
> *revised:* He has *drunk* all the milk.
>
> *incorrect:* You must have *went* there often.
> *revised:* You must have *gone* there often.
>
> *incorrect:* We had already *saw* it three times.
> *revised:* We had already *seen* it three times.

wordiness Omit words which are unnecessary or repetitious.

> *ineffective:* Here is a notebook *in which* to put it in.
> *revised:* Here is a notebook to put it in.
>
> *ineffective:* In today's *modern* society, we must be prepared for sudden changes.
> *revised:* In today's society, we must be prepared for sudden changes.
>
> *ineffective:* As to his *or her* chances for advancement, I believe that he *or she* will have many opportunities.
> *revised:* As to his chances for advancement, I believe that he will have many opportunities.
>
> *ineffective:* It has *long been one of my strongest* beliefs that the new law should *and will* be passed.
> *revised:* It is my belief that the new law should be passed.

wrong word for the context Select words which are logical and appropriate for the context in which they are used.

> *ineffective:* It is impossible to teach an *unwanting* student.
> *revised:* It is impossible to teach an *unmotivated* student.
>
> *ineffective:* I have always enjoyed working with friendly, *lethargic* people.
> *revised:* I have always enjoyed working with friendly, *easy-going* people.
>
> *ineffective:* As I turned the key in the lock and slowly entered, I must admit that my first impression *sank clear to the ground*.
> *revised:* As I turned the key in the lock and slowly entered, I must admit that my first impression *was one of complete surprise*.